THE NAMA STAP

by

David Richardson

© 2021 David Richardson. All rights reserved.

This a work of fiction based on historical facts, people and place. Any references to historical events, real people, or real places are used in a fictitious context. Other names, characters, places, and events are products of the author's imagination, and any resemblance to actual events or places or persons, living or dead, is entirely coincidental.

Book Cover Photo by Margaret Courtney-Clark. Nama women performing the Nama Stap, Maltahöhe, Namibia, 2015. ©

Published by the Zangvil Lane. ZangvilLane@icloud.com

Author's Note

One of the benefits of living in the utilitarian, almost grim, post-WWII condominium on the Upper West Side of Manhattan was the 24-hour concierge service. It was 2006, and my career at the time involved frequent and extensive international travel. Mail, packages, and laundry were dispatched and collected, the apartment was serviced, and an email or call would ensure that you had fresh milk and other minimal supplies in the fridge, saving the chore of having to go out so soon after getting back to JFK.

"We have something for you", the concierge said, as he handed me the accumulated mail when I stopped at the front desk. "But first I need to check it with you – security asked." He returned from the storeroom at the back with a large, square, carboard box that had clearly been opened and re-sealed. A heavy "Inspected by US Mail and Customs" label had been stuck across the sender's address, so that didn't help me identify it. But the stamps were from South Africa, where I still had family, so that was reassuring. It was surprisingly heavy. "I'll send it up with your laundry", the concierge said.

Showered and restored with a sip of Bushmills, I sliced open the carton. Polystyrene beads secured a bubble-wrapped bronze head – a sculpture made by my aunt in South Africa. I recognized her handwriting on the envelope lying on the top:

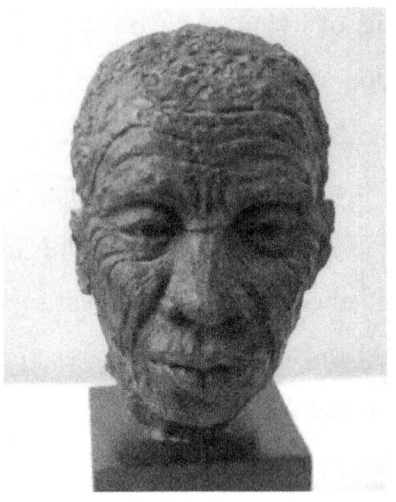

This is Doeseb. It's not his real name – but it was the nickname your uncle Jack used to scare you and your cousins when you were little. He would say that if you did not laugh and smile enough you would become like Doeseb! Not very clever... He was a Damara, one of those men Larry used to find on the railways.

I am sending this to you as I've stopped working. I have arthritis in both hands now and can't mould clay. I'm giving up the studio and getting rid of old pieces. This one is yours – you may not remember, but you did the tight curls on his head with a loop...

The "Larry" my aunt referred to in the letter was her late husband, who had been a doctor working for the South African Railways in Windhoek, then South West Africa. By 2006 it was independent Namibia. As a child I'd lived in South West, as it was known, and had spent hours playing with cousins and friends in their house and garden. I did remember watching her create heads in clay on a simple wire frame, and the quiet, dignified men and women who would sit for her in the courtyard behind the kitchen.

These were desperate people from around the country who had walked, travelled by rail in goods wagons, and ridden in the backs of open trucks to get to Windhoek to find work. They were "natives", "tribesmen", "country people" – Bantus, Ovambos, Hereros, Nama, Damara, Tswana, sometimes "Bushmen", in short – non-whites or blacks from distant tribal areas who required "passes" or permits to work in apartheid-riven South Africa, which at the time controlled South West as its fifth province. Without the requisite documents, many would eventually wind up destitute at the railway yards at the northern entrance to the town. Some were ill or injured, and my uncle would bring them back to his private clinic after work. Revived with food, treatment and care, some would sit for my aunt as she honed her skill as a sculptress.

Doeseb sat on the desk in my living room watching my frenetic comings and goings. Slowly I began to sense his presence as a rebuke. Or perhaps, it was the beginning of middle-aged self-assessment. A long-dormant interest in Namibia and my childhood there began to surface.

Sometime after, with this "receptor" awakened, I was browsing my way back home via Barnes and Noble on Broadway when I came across a small paperback: "The Kaiser's Holocaust – Germany's Forgotten Genocide" by David Olusoga and Casper

W. Erichsen. Nowhere in the title or the front-cover blurb does it mention South West Africa or Namibia. But the picture on the cover was eerily, unpleasantly, familiar – emaciated blacks and mounted white soldiers in field dress that I recognized from statues and pictures seen in my youth – Herero prisoners and German Schutztruppe.

I had grown up with white characterizations of the Herero, once a mighty tribe in South West, as "haughty" or "depressed" because of their defeat by the Germans in 1905. Vague, mysterious rumours explained that their demeanour and diminished numbers were not from losses in the war but because they had decided to commit national suicide following their defeat in battle, that Herero women could limit conception, or later, when I assume I was old enough to be told such things, that they even practiced infanticide. The Nama, who suffered a similar fate, were rarely mentioned. Nor was the fact that the Germans had a deliberate policy of extermination, and had established concentration camps and worked people to death in the service of their economic expansion – precursors of the Nazi Holocaust almost forty years later. Herero numbers were reduced by eighty percent, the Nama by more than fifty, through direct conflict, executions, deliberate starvation, illness, and being worked to death. Other native peoples, particularly the Damara and the San, were also persecuted. Many of the German settlers and troops couldn't distinguish between them, and did not care. German losses and heroism were and are amply memorialised in large plaques and bombastic statues. I knew too that the relationship of my extended family with the local German community was "complicated", but I never knew why.

As I read more, and the Namibian struggle for independence came into focus, the brutality, desperation, and utter depravity of the South African campaign to maintain white rule stood like a bookend to the German chapter of a hundred years of colonialism. Much of the South African clandestine war in South West came to light during the hearings of the Truth and Reconciliation Commission established in 1995 by the newly-elected Nelson Mandela. If this quasi-legal process wasn't documented, recorded and videoed, one would regard the testimony from victims and perpetrators as fiction. But it is not, and where appropriate I have quoted from it to emphasize the horror and absurdity. Some of the escapades of the apartheid security apparatus run amok are so bizarre that you could dismiss them as isolated instances of evil. But these were initiated, approved, and funded at the highest levels of a white government, as part of a deliberate strategy to ensure white hegemony for as long as possible. Similarly, a British study of German practices in the territory until their defeat during the First World War – referred to as the "Blue Book" and published in 1918 – while certainly problematic in its motivation, is illustrative and is quoted from where appropriate.

That is the gestation of this story. It is historical fiction, based on major events and referencing a few of the major characters. Most, however, is invention, an attempt to tell the story of the one hundred odd years when white people dominated this vast, largely arid, and utterly romantic country through individual lives as I imagined them. It is important, too, to emphasize that the Herero-Nama genocides were preceded by years of colonial brutality and discrimination, and did not stop with the end of the war. Police action against them, expropriation of land and cattle, and forced labour continued until the South African invasion in 1915. The South African regime, put in place under a United Nations mandate after the First World War, was also racist and exploitive. Nothing was done to redress the dispossession and suffering of the Herero and Nama. Apartheid applied by the Afrikaner Nationalist Party in 1948 echoed the racist ideologies of the German settlement and administration fifty years earlier, and that of the Nazis some ten years before.

Where material is quoted, I have used the original format as far as possible. Where not, or if the material is historical background, I have used this sans-serif font – **Verdana**, 11 point, one-and-a-half line spacing. In cases where material is not a direct facsimile, I have edited and redacted the text to suit the plot, and indicated this appropriately.

I have used German spelling during the period of German control of the territory – "Windhuk", and Afrikaans or English – "Windhoek" following the establishment of the South African administration in 1915. I have also used common short forms for some place names such as "Swakop" instead of Swakopmund, etc; I have avoided any attempt at linguistic accuracy in trying to indicate the Khoekhoegowab "clicking" sounds, and generally resorted to an ! or an X where appropriate, so that the reader may know and hopefully have a sense of the true sound and perhaps the "music" of the word. I've used the term "Khoekoe" or "Nama" interchangeably to refer to the people and the language, as many local people do. Similarly, I have avoided trying to reflect Otjiherero grammar in translation, and refer to the people and their culture with the single English word "Herero", and their language as Otjiherero. The terms San and Bushmen are also used interchangeably, skirting the ongoing academic debates about what is and is not a pejorative description of these still brutally marginalised indigenous hunter-gatherers.

In general I have used italics for non-English words and where context permits explained these in the sentence or paragraph. There is a glossary at the end, but once I and my editor felt terms had been established I have used either the original or continued with the English words subject to the context and the rhythm of the sentence. I have attempted to be accurate, but for ease of reading of what is fiction, have chosen to simplify.

The seeds of this project were planted by my parents – my mother's social conscience and my father's love of storytelling. This book is for them.

Relationship Tree

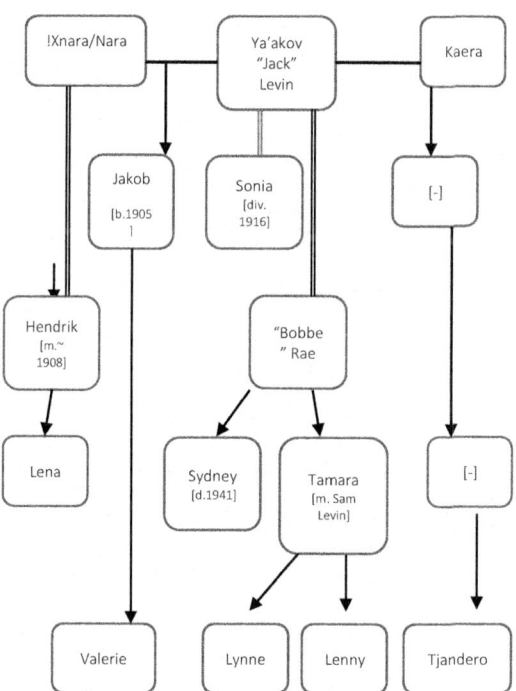

Early 1900s					Off Pelican Point, South Atlantic

Stench...

... wakes him. Teasing unease in his nostrils – harsher than the stale farts of the other passengers. Another breath and an acrid spear of putrefaction sears his sinuses, grabs his pharynx. Smothering and inescapable, it clings to his face and envelops his head even as he pulls up the blanket to evade it. Rot is like a malevolent presence in the gloom.

Oxen bellow in the hold below. Do his mules smell it too? Groans and coughs from the other passengers in the steerage cabin as they also try to cope. He reaches to feel for the wallet in the inside pocket of his folded coat under his head.

Reassured he rises, and stumbles out for fresh air despite the cold of the early hour. Fog with the foul tang distilled into each drop cloaks the ship. It clings to his hair, his coat, and the scarf he pulls across his face.

This wasn't like the foulness from the pulpous carcass of the goat that had drowned in the cesspit behind the *mikve*, the Jewish ritual bath in his home village. It had lain rotting there for weeks, the smell stalking the streets of the shtetl like a wolf. It had been too dangerous to get to until the ice and snow had melted, and the men could see where to lay planks and ladders. This putrefaction was of a place, beyond a single decomposing corpse. Stench like this can only come from deliberate slaughter.

"*Vot izsh det shmell*" he asks a Coloured crewman who pushes past him on the gangway.

"*Vis, kleinbaas*", answers the man, in Afrikaans. "*Wal vis*"[1].

+++

Walvis Bay lies behind a long spit of sand that sticks out into the South Atlantic like a narrow yellow finger. It is the visible part of an undersea range that runs from the African coast to Gough Island and the volcano of Tristan da Cunha, three thousand kilometres to the south west. This ridge funnels the cold Benguela current up against the hot deserts of southern Africa. The sudden contrast in temperature often causes thick banks of fog, which can last for hours and shroud miles into the hinterland.

The fog was too dense to approach the port, so the ship swung round and dropped anchor, the beat of the engine subsiding soon after the rattle of the anchor chain had stopped. A lull of a few breaths, then he heard the slower thud of breakers crashing against the shore to the east. He could see nothing through the fog, although the sky was brightening with the dawn. Alone on the clammy deck with, the awful smell and the sound of the breakers against an invisible coast, his youthful enthusiasm deserted him. For the first time since arriving at the bottom of Africa eighteen months earlier, he felt a sense of foreboding.

In the days it had taken to steam up the coast from Cape Town, the rise and fall of the South Atlantic swells had become familiar

---

[1] "Fish, little boss, whale fish"

and reassuring. As they made their way north along the yellow-white coast, the days had been clear, the night sky as bright and dramatic as Africa could present. There had been a flutter of excitement when someone pointed out the green smudge that was the mouth of the Orange River which led to the Kimberly diamond fields. During the journey from Southampton and the arrival in Cape Town, he'd been optimistic and curious about the country ahead, and the opportunities it might present. Now the stench of decay quashed his boyish optimism, and anxiety overcame his curiosity. His hand gripped the clammy rail as a particularly large swell lifted the ship.

+++

That swell had started out almost two weeks before and seven thousand kilometres to the south, in the vast expanse of water off Antarctica. There was nothing between the frozen continent and its ice fields and the southern tip of Africa to slow the reach of the giant concentration of energy moving north through the water. Countless such swells had preceded it and countless would follow in a relentless cadence – the pulse of the heart of the earth.

Dust from North Africa's deserts and decayed organic matter from the equatorial forests of central Africa and the Amazon flushed down the giant rivers had accumulated on the ocean floor over millions of years. This nutrient-rich sediment slowly fed into an ocean gyre in the South Atlantic. Just off Cape Point, the water temperature plummeted. An upwelling of bitterly cold water over two hundred kilometres wide surged upwards, pushed towards the surface as if by a giant pump. These pulses would move along the coast, driven by the south easterly trade winds. They could be followed by weeks of stratification and relative calm in the water mass, giving sunlight at the surface time to ignite photosynthesis. A bloom of trillions of hair-thin diatoms created oxygen and started a vast food chain, from molecular phytoplankton to the Right Whale. Huge shoals of anchovies, pilchards, and their predators were driven north by the flow of the icy Benguela, the ocean current that flowed along the edge of southern Africa almost to the River Congo on the equator. The Walvis Ridge funnelled all this life into a narrow strip along the coast to create one of the world's richest fisheries. British mariners, interested in the natural harbour formed in the lee of the sandy spit, named it Pelican Point, after the voracious birds feeding on the plentiful fish.

Shortly after the swell lifted the ship, the rising ocean floor compressed its energy and drove it up to become a wave a few metres high. As if sensing the end of the long journey, it seemed to pick up speed and, with height in the coastal wind, began to throw off white spume in a showy display of its suicidal finale. The grey-green flanks were speckled with ochre spume – the agitated sap of the kelp forest below. And then, with a continental thud, the wave died on the coast. As the surf receded, uprooted kelp, driftwood, broken shells, and the odd dead animal lay deposited on the beach of the world's oldest desert – the Namib.

+++

A band of women and girls emerged from a wide delta in the low ashen yellow dunes, intent on what they could find on the beach. They were slight, with tawny skin and crinkly black hair. They called themselves ǂAonin, which Europeans mispronounced as Topnaar – fewer than a thousand people eking out an existence in a string of tiny settlements around springs and riverbed wells up the dry course of the Kuiseb River behind Walvis Bay and around Lüderitz further south.

Inland, the women gathered *veldkos*, the meagre food that their intimate knowledge of the desert could provide. Where there was water, they kept small livestock and cultivated bedraggled plots. Along the sands of the river and the delta they jealously guarded and harvested the !Nara, a spikey leafless melon that could survive years of drought, sustaining itself with a deep tap root and the dew of the fog from the cold Atlantic. Here, along the coast, they gathered shellfish and the odd carcass, and collected flotsam and jetsam washed up on the beach. The men hunted in the canyons and on the uplands where they could find game, herded where they could find pasture, or lounged about waiting for work in Walvis Bay.

Their isolation in the desert diminished the need to differentiate themselves much. They were part of the Nama nation, who predominated in the southern part of the country as well as the northern Cape. For scores of years they had had more contact with white traders, hunters, and explorers along the coast than with the black peoples who lived further inland and to the north, or the San, or Bushmen – who were similar in colour, size and language, but almost completely nomadic. Skirmishes over hunting and grazing were common, and there were constantly shifting alliances as they sought allies to protect them from the more powerful peoples encroaching on their traditional hunting or grazing areas. The White people who traded with them, and even some of their upland Nama cousins, derided the Topnaar as "*Strandlopers*" – a derogatory Afrikaans term for beachcombers. And that is what the women were doing.

The long ochre stalk of a kelp tree rolled onto the beach as the surf of the large wave receded. A young girl ran ahead of the group of women and pulled the thick stalk up the slope of the beach. Oysters and mussels might be clinging to the holdfast of calcified sand under the gnarly tubular roots dislodged in the ocean churn. She knew the food would be fresh and the plant itself free of the sand fleas and flies that plagued the beach.

She squatted to tease apart the tube-like tendrils, and exposed a round grey and encrusted shell bigger than her hand. An abalone. Her aunt would be pleased. Pleasing her aunt was a key to her life.

Touching the shell would trigger the muscular foot to grip the stone. She slipped a short bone with a chisel edge under the lip and lifted the abalone loose. Half embedded in the calcified sand underneath was a shiny stone about the size of her toenail. She pried this loose too and standing up, held it up against the morning light beginning to burn through the fog. A pink, smoky translucence refracted the pale orb of the sun. This was different, she knew, and her prize, hers alone. She dropped it into the leather pouch she wore on a thong around her waist. She skipped along to join the others in their search and soft chatter and showed her aunt the abalone before dropping it in their family basket.

+++

Jacob was the first to enter the mess. He'd looked down into the hold to check on the mules that were crucial to his future. The warm smell of hay and animals, their urine and manure rising from below, was pleasant and reassuring compared to the reek of putrefaction. He'd also checked his cart, which was lashed to the deck. Nothing had been tampered with or stolen as far as he could see.

Clatter in the galley as breakfast was being prepared. Normally he looked forward to the hot porridge and dark treacle, but now his stomach heaved at the idea of food. Glumly he read and re-read the ship-builder's plate welded to the galley wall to take his mind off the depression settling on him.

SS Mandingo
Harland & Wolff
Belfast 1882

The ship had been at sea already for twenty years, he calculated, wondering where else it had sailed and traded.

+++

Late   March   1989

Daweb-Eshel – a farm west of Keetmanshoop

Steyn picked up the handset of the black Bakelite phone, and stiffened when he heard the young man's voice. "*More, meneer Lenny*", he said, immediately deferential to the man who owned the farm. Lenny hardly ever called him directly and there was a slight rasp of tension in his voice.

"The accountants need a new valuation of the farm. The political situation makes it necessary, you understand. I've asked an assessor to come out to the farm. Dougie de Waal will bring him. I hope next week is all right? Sorry it's such short notice...."

"It's ok, Lenny", Steyn said. "That's good. I'll be here."

He walked back out onto the stoep, clasping his mid-morning cup of coffee as he leaned forward against the wooden veranda rail. The Ridgeback sensed his unease, and clambered up to stand by his side. The absent-minded rubbing of the dog's ears reassured them both, another of the hundreds of little things that bonded them so closely. The old farmer's eyes wandered over the orchard, and then, as they always did, to the pile of rocks in the southwest corner where his son was buried. House, orchard and grave overlooked a broad plain that ran almost to the Fish River Canyon. It was already hazy with desert dust.

He tossed the coffee dregs out over the rail and walked back down the cool corridor toward the closed kitchen door. He was a big man, and the tread of his steps on the red concrete floor stilled the murmur of the women's voices inside. The last strains of some light *Boeremusiek* on the radio faded as he opened the door. His wife Frederika was seasoning meat at the kitchen table. Lena, the Nama maid who had been with them for maybe 30 years, was rinsing potatoes and carrots under the tap at the window. Neither of them looked at him. Not for the first time he realized that Lena was probably closer than he was with his wife. So much time together here in this kitchen, the shared sorrow of lost children overcoming the gaps of colour and apartheid.

He was about to speak when the familiar signature jingle of the SABC news interrupted: the lead item was about an explosion outside the headquarters of the Natal Command in Durban, attributed to ANC terrorists; also, President P.W. Botha was in "better health" following a stroke a few weeks earlier; and the UN Special Representative, Finnish diplomat Martti Ahtisaari, was due to arrive the following week, on April 1st 1989. UNTAG[2] personnel were beginning their deployment in South West Africa.

"That was Lenny Levin", Steyn said, when the bulletin ended. "He's sending Dougie de Waal, the manager, down here next week. He'll probably stay for two days, in the old house. He'll want to go hunting. He'll be bringing an assessor."

Neither of the women acknowledged him in any way. He watched

---

[2] UNTAG - United Nations Transition Assistance Group

the pink cotton of Lena's maid's uniform stretch across her back as she leaned forward across the sink. The brass tap squealed when she turned off the water. The fabric of their lives creaked. It didn't need saying. The farm was to be sold.

First the ox… then the kaffir

Jacob was his current English name, although he realised that it would become Jack. He was Ya'akov among the other eastern European immigrants he mingled with in the bustle of Cape Town. But he'd grown up as Yankele – the common Yiddish diminutive his mother and the family used for him at home. The German and English Jews in the city, who were his mentors and backers for this trip, had quietly suggested that "Jack" would be more agreeable to the people he would have to deal with. They had preceded his wave of immigration by years, and were far more attuned to the social and commercial nuances of the Cape Colony. Fitting into the wider Gentile or English society of Cape Town was more than a necessity; it was a goal to strive for. "Yankele" was fading, as was boyhood in the eighteen months since he'd left Lithuania.

Eventually the heat above the desert burnt off the fog and drew in a sea breeze to dissipate the foul smell. The ship upped anchor and came about to sail into Walvis Bay.

The passengers, all men, stood on the deck and watched the ashen desert coast emerge behind a line of white surf. There was none of the grandeur of the Cape. No mountains, no greenery. The town was a haphazard collection of low buildings and rusted warehouses sprawled along the beach. At one end a Union Jack flew from a tall pole, and beside it a steeple marked a church. Not a tree, not a shrub, and beyond everything, an empty expanse of flat sand and low dunes that stretched on forever.

As they rounded the breakwater the source of the smell became clear. Whale carcasses, low and black in the water, were tethered to two American-flagged whalers tied up at the jetty. Behind the jetty another dead whale, an Antarctic Blue, the largest animal he'd ever seen, was being winched up a slipway. Gangs of men with long blades and hooks were stripping and hacking large hunks of flesh off yet another carcass on the dock behind. Black smoke belched from fires where cauldrons were reducing the animal's blubber to oil.

"It's not only the whale carcasses that cause the smell", said a forwarding agent who was returning to the port. "That grey mound behind the cauldrons is guano – sea bird shit that they collect from the islands offshore. It's sold as fertilizer. It's so foul it burns your throat. Gore and shit – the smell of money."

Jack stared with morbid fascination at the scale of the butchering. His chest grew tight and his mouth dried as stress coursed through his body. It seemed right that the atavistic industriousness of so much slaughter was happening on the remote edge of the desert and the sea, away from people and civilization. But he was here, threatened by it, surrounded by it. Swarms of gulls, gannets and cormorants screeched overhead, driven mad by the scent and sight of so much food. Despite the plenty they squabbled constantly, stealing from each other in mid-flight or when they dipped into the offal-fouled waters below the ramp of the flensing yard.

There was no room to moor at the jetty, so they tied up to an iron buoy inside the breakwater. The crew rigged up a block and tackle above the hold and a lighter came out to begin unloading their cargo.

First out of the hold were the oxen, winched up by their horns. They bellowed in terror, their eyes bulging and their bodies twisting as they sought a solid surface. Thin-limbed black dockhands in the lighter grabbed their legs and, as soon as they were standing, pushed and clubbed the animals onto both sides of the open barge to maintain an even keel. Space became cramped as the vessel filled up with the lowing beasts. One of the stevedores stood up on the gunwale to grab a dangling animal's legs and guide them into the lighter.

Jack's eyes widened and his breathing tightened with foreboding. The ox twisted and kicked out, pitching the man into the grey-green water. There were shouts from both boats, and a rope was thrown from the lighter at the bobbing head of the man, who clearly could not swim. "Get the ox first, you dumb bastards", the captain yelled – paid as he was for goods delivered – "then get the kaffir". The crews of both vessels hesitated.

A dull dark form rose through the murky green water behind the thrashing man. The water seemed to rise with the bulk of its shape, and a stream of white bubbles trailed prettily from a triangular fin that surged forward and closed implacably. There was not even a gurgle as the shark took him.

April 1989   Daweb-Eshel

It took de Waal a full day to drive down to the farm from Windhoek. He'd stopped in Rehoboth, Mariental and Keetmanshoop to meet the local managers of the businesses he was responsible for. Each town had a large building-and-farm supply yard. Rehoboth and Keetmans were large enough to support thriving car and agricultural machinery dealerships as well. It was late by the time he reached the farm, and after an awkward supper with the Steyns, he went to the guest room he used in the old farmhouse built almost seventy years before by Jack Levin.

The Steyns had lived on and managed the farm for much of that time. De Waal knew enough of the intertwined histories of the families to feel troubled by what was happening to them. Frederika was a Malan, a family of *Dorsland trekboers* who had settled in the Grootfontein area of the north. Her grandfather, Teunis, had been partners with Jack when he established the original wagon-building and repair business in Otjiwarongo at the beginning of the century. That business was the foundation of the multi-million rand group de Waal now ran. *Ouman*[3] Jack and *Oom* (uncle) Teunis as they were known remained close, even after the partnership was dissolved when Teunis Malan wanted to pay off his farm loan. The farm was lost in the drought and crash

---

[3] Afrikaans for Old Man – often used as a term of endearment and respect

of 1929-31. The family became destitute, the old man too broken and frail to work, the son employed on the railway. When Frederika married Kobus Steyn, Jack offered the young couple the chance to return to farming, to manage Daweb-Eshel.

Their children had been born and raised here, and he understood that they had every reason to live as if the farm was theirs. Jack's visits tapered off as he grew frailer. His children and grandchildren were not farmers or even *Suidwesters* but Cape Town-based businessmen who, if they visited at all, did so on holiday.

When Jannie, the Steyns' son, was killed in Angola, it was Lenny, Jack's grandson, who agreed to their request that they bury him on the farm. "My grandfather would have agreed", he said, when de Waal raised the formalities and difficulties it created. But now that Lenny had decided to sell, the Steyns and their son's grave were an impediment.

The assessor, a local man familiar with every farm and farmer in the southern part of Suidwes, arrived early the next morning. He knew the Steyns well and spent a few moments by the grave praying with them.

The three men then set off in one of the farm bakkies[4] and spent six hours driving around the farm, checking the health of every ram and the odd ewe. There were hardly any wethers, castrated

---

[4] Afrikaans for a generally open pickup truck popular in southern Africa, especially among farmers

males, as the Karakul sheep were raised predominantly for their pelts, which came from the lambs. Occasionally the assessor stopped to talk to the Nama shepherds about the health of the sheep, the land, the water, predators and disease. He'd squat down to touch and even chew the *bloudak, knietjiesgras* and *litjiesgras* to assess the grazing. They stopped in a wide flat riverbed that ran down toward the farm gate and he walked to a thicket of untidy green bushes – the *daweb,* or wild tamarisk - that gave the farm its Nama name. He broke off a few of the spindly leaves and licked them. In the midday heat the leaves had turned a grey-green colour as the plant extruded the salt it took up from its deep tap root, revealing how brackish the water in the riverbed was.

"One of the best-run farms in the district", he said, after he'd been through the books of the past five years, "but there are a lot of properties up for sale now because of the political uncertainty."

At dawn the next day, Steyn and de Waal drove up to the plateau behind the farmhouse. Sparse outcrops and meagre veld sloped down towards a valley to the north through which game migrated. De Waal was after kudu, which grazed in the thick bush of the ravines that cleaved the plateau. Two of the farm "boys" who were good trackers sat with the dog in the open section of the bakkie. They stopped before the edge of the *kloof*, and the two white men took their rifles and quietly began their hunt. They were all experienced and did not need to be told to avoid breaking the skyline, or step on twigs. When the prevailing wind switched, they stopped and waited so their scent would not carry. The Ridgeback followed.

Squatting in the pool of shadow below a quiver tree just below the ridgeline, they searched the thickets in the ravine. A sudden bounce of a branch alerted one of the trackers. Carefully, he pointed it out to de Waal, who searched the bush through the telescopic sight on his Remington. A well-camouflaged kudu bull had used its curved horns to pull down younger leaves on the branches. Somehow, it sensed the moment it became prey, and swivelled its head to look at them, the white chevron between its eyes fixing their stares as de Waal squeezed the trigger. The magnificent animal dropped where it stood. The boys ran down, severed the arteries behind the ears, and sliced off the penis and testicles. Steyn brought the bakkie round the hill. They attached a steel cable to its hind legs and winched the carcass up the slope, its lovely spiral horns forlornly furrowing the earth in a gesture of departure.

Steyn, who prided himself on his eyesight and hardly ever used telescopic sights, missed a springbok in the open veld on the valley floor an hour later. Crestfallen, he borrowed de Waals' Remington and bagged another on the circuitous route they took back to the farmhouse.

They had been out for almost five hours and had hardly talked. But now, while the boys were dressing the kills in the barn behind the house, they sat on the stoep with a Windhoek lager and a bowl of biltong before lunch, and acknowledged the impending sale and change in their lives.

"So, when do you think they will sell?", Steyn asked.

"I don't know, Kobus", de Waal answered, deferential as their relationship had always been. "The young Mr. Levin is like many of the others, they are liquidating because no one knows what's going to be."

"Ja, I know his heart's not in this place, not like the old man, who loved it here", his eyes drifting over the veld and the desert valley below them. He gestured at the adjacent farmhouse where de Waal had spent the night. "He hasn't stayed there in three years, and I think his wife and the kids were last here at least five years ago."

"The thing is, Dougie", he said, using de Waal's first name, "old man Jack, Lenny's grandfather, promised me that I could retire here. Daweb-Eshel has been my life for more than forty years. Nothing was ever written. You know *Ouman* Levin didn't do that.

It was always his word and that was always good enough. He also told Sam, Lenny's father, but you know he died suddenly. When Jannie died, I asked Lenny, the young Levin, for his agreement to let me bury him here based on that. He agreed. My wife and I want to end our days here."

De Waal, himself the son of a farmer, looked out over the orchard, not really seeing it. He felt for Steyn, knowing his own father's love of the land even without the added anguish of a son's grave as roots in a place. But he was of a different generation, and understood farming was now about business, and not where one grew old. He felt awkward, compromised, but knew he had no choice. "I didn't know about this, but I'll speak to him."

After lunch, de Waal's Mercedes was loaded with ice chests containing the butchered kudu, and a box of biltong. Steyn walked out to the car with him. "Kobus, I'll see what I can do. But for young Mr Levin I think it's just a business, you know. I think you should prepare on that basis."

As he drove away, he looked through the rear-view mirror and saw Steyn's wife on the stoep looking after him. He knew she had tears in her eyes.

+++

Early 1900s   Walvis Bay Harbour

Other sharks, drawn by the whale carcasses, darted across the harbour and devoured the black body in a frenzy of churning water and writhing grey shapes. Silence like that which follows a thunderclap enveloped the dock, and work came to a stop.

The harbour master stopped the use of the lighter, and ordered a whaler to make room for them to berth and unload. When Jack's mules were lowered onto the dock, he rushed to get them stabled with fresh water and fodder to calm them. Now he sat beside them in the shade behind a warehouse where his cart and goods had been delivered, calming himself as the bellows of terror of the oxen slowly subsided to a regular lowing from the stockyard further back.

Clumps of reeds traced the banks of a lagoon running back from the docks. Strange gangly birds with dirty grey plumage stepped about the shallows, dipping curved necks to feed. Stench still assaulted him. Flies, mosquitoes, fleas buzzed and bit. Not a blade of grass or a tree. Bedraggled bushes trapped like rags in the wind. Miles of white sand, harsh on his eyes. He'd heard of whales, but had no idea of what was involved in reducing them to oil. He'd never even heard of sharks. The relentless lunge of the grey shape through the water was terrifying. Deep breaths slowed the pump of adrenalin.

He cast back for a memory to ward off the despair pressing on him. There had been a soar of excitement and enthusiasm at the first sight of Table Mountain from the deck of the Union Castle boat that had brought him and scores of others like him to Cape Town. They'd all been anxious but optimistic, and somehow, as individualistic and scrappy as many of them were, there was a sense that they were in this together. Here he was alone.

Cape Town was a hustle and bustle of trade and opportunity. Exotic goods being imported, bought and sold, and endless stories of adventure in the interior. Gold, diamonds, and ivory had brought people from all over the world. People were poor but food seemed plentiful – at least compared to Lithuania. And it was exotic, with colourful and delicious fruits and vegetables, a huge variety of fish and meat, flowers, spices and condiments. Buildings were impressive ,and at the top of Adderley Street a public park, The Gardens, laid out by the Dutch centuries before, was a cool, leafy glade where he loved to stroll on Sundays. Climbing the forested lower slopes of the dramatic mountains that cupped the bay, and walking along the beachfront were pleasures that helped him and the other single immigrants cope with their longing for their families and their struggles to build a life. The Cape of Good Hope was what its name promised – a port of entry to a brighter future. It was pure contrast to the grey skies and dull oppressive reality with no prospects from which he'd escaped. The two short *smousing*[5] expeditions he'd made into the countryside north of the city had confirmed that. Estates with neat rows of vines set around magnificent white Cape Dutch houses, fruit orchards, blue-grey mountains, and farmland with fat sheep and cattle. It was an abundance he had not imagined, and it was intoxicating. But now he confronted this violent, endless, sandy,

---

[5] Smous - South African term for an itinerant peddler – the archetypal Jewish trader now romanticized as the South African Jewish myth of origin.

reeking desert. He could always go back, he reassured himself.

Jack was almost eighteen. For all the poverty, discrimination, and anti-Semitism of life in the Lithuanian *shtetl* where he'd grown up, his youth had been relatively sheltered. It was the threat of conscription into the Tsar's army that had made emigration his destiny. There was no talk of a future in East Prussia or Lithuania. His father had become a Zionist, but the family's poverty and the flow of generally enthusiastic reports from the early emigrants to the *goldene medina* pointed to South Africa as the primary destination.

There had been skirmishes with marauding Lithuanian gangs and fights with drunks in the nearby market towns, but he'd never really been on his own. Binyamin, his older cousin, had protected him at the yeshiva and at school when the older boys had picked on him. Binyamin seemed to enjoy the fights, or at least boasting about them. It was part of being worldly. Jack wasn't sure. He hero-worshipped "Benny" and was relieved when the families decided that they would travel together to South Africa. Benny had been to Vilna and Königsberg, drank vodka, and hinted at a knowledge of girls. Benny was fascinated by America, but the families had pooled their resources to send their oldest boys to South Africa. The buzz in the community around their impending journey seemed to have swept Benny's preference aside, and for all of his bravado, they had comforted each other on the cart when they left the *shtetl* and their weeping families. They knew they were unlikely to ever come back. In the train on their way to Königsberg they cut off each other's *payot* (sidelocks), their first overt break with their past.

At the gangplank of the ship Benny announced that he would be continuing on his own to Hamburg, and from there to New York. He had made his plans in secret. Only after landing in Hull, in the brief privacy of the hostel room, did Jack discover that somewhere along their journey Benny had stolen most of the money their families had pooled for the journey to South Africa. He had written to tell his parents that Benny had gone to America, and reassure them that he would manage on his own. But he had yet to admit to them that he'd lost most of the savings they had given him. Jack still smarted at his gullibility. Over time, this had hardened to a scepticism which he learned it was polite to hide. But beneath this was the realization that in his naivety, he had failed his family's trust in him.

A gang of black labourers carrying bales on their heads passed him. His eyes were drawn to the pale pink-yellow soles of their bare feet as they walked past, tall and seemingly indifferent to the hot sand and sharp stones. The man in the water had pink hands too, with eyes huge and white in panic.

The pervasive and stark hierarchy separating whites from the other people was background reality he never thought to question. Like the difference between men and women, established and enforced by education, wealth, organization, and habit. A tinnitus of discrimination, exploitation, and racism – always there but never acknowledged. As a struggling immigrant encountering other prejudices, he had no sense of the privilege he enjoyed. If he paid attention at all, it was to the curious differences between the various groups and not to the inequality. And why should he notice it? He was white.

Calmer, he noticed the change in the colours of the desert in the mid-distance. The harsh white brightness was softening in a golden orange glow. A warm wind began to blow sand towards him, and he got up to walk round the warehouse to watch the sun set over the sea. But a commotion in the lagoon stopped him. The strange birds in the mud flat were marching in a tight formation, almost in step, into the breeze. Then they began an ungainly run on their long spindly legs, and lifted, their necks and legs stretched out as they spread their wings. They wheeled over the lagoon, and the setting sun lit up the soft pink of their plumage and their crimson legs.

A soft intake of breath at the wonder of this new place. Africa presented so much drama that he wanted to share. He owed his family a letter. It would still be winter in Lithuania by the time it arrived, but hopefully his description would carry the colour and sense of the place, and brighten their lives. It was best sent from here, where there were ships. He knew little about what to expect beyond this British outpost on the coast of Deutsche Suidwes Afrika.

"... Vat die meisie... (take the girl)"

The next morning, fog smothered the coast again. It was still cool, and a westerly wind off the sea slightly dissipated the stench. Jack woke with his more familiar sense of energy and set about preparations to move on from Walvis. He needed a guide and mule driver, and had been given a name and told where to go.

A track ran inland alongside the lagoon and then descended into a wide shallow space in the sand dunes, pockmarked with animal and human waste. A mile or so along, a haphazard sprawl of shacks along the edge of the wide riverbed was where the Topnaar and the Coloureds lived. He'd seen poor dwellings on his trips into the Cape countryside, but these were even more primitive. Uprights of whalebone and driftwood covered with mats of woven grass and reeds, rags and torn canvas, dried strands of kelp and seaweed, animal skins – it was poverty beyond anything he had ever seen. An adult would not be able to stand up in them. Flies everywhere. An elderly man sitting in a patch of shade watched him vacantly.

"I'm looking for Piet Witbooi"[6] Jack asked, in broken Afrikaans. The man pointed along the track – "*by die geraas*" - where the

---

[6] Witbooi – Afrikaans meaning "white boy", a common surname among the Khoi and Coloured people of the Cape, and the name of one of the most powerful Nama clans.

noise is.

+++

!Nara[7] was sorting her collection of trinkets on the sand between her outstretched legs. Her two infant cousins were playing in the shaded space between the shacks where they lived.

There were things from "here" – seashells and pebbles polished smooth by the sea, coloured rocks that had been washed down in the floods and found on the riverbed, a porcupine quill, the shell of a tiny tortoise and the translucent moulted skin of a snake. The abalone shell with its iridescent green, blue and pink mother-of-pearl interior was drying in the sun on top of the shack. Ants would eat out the remains of the animal that still clung to its surface.

Then there were things that came from "elsewhere" – bits of tin and brass and the neck of a glass bottle, a piece of rope unravelling at one end and the other stuck together with a black substance. These were from beyond her world – the world of Walvis where she had not yet been – the world of the ships and the white men she'd only seen at a distance.

She played with the pebble she had found under the abalone the day before. She tried to categorize it. It was almost clear, like the glass bottle neck, but came from the earth, not from the white man. She held it up – bright and almost brittle – and it caught the

---

[7] ! used to indicate a sibilant sound or dental click, like "Ts TS" or "tut tut tut", so Tsnara.

light, but with a smoky pink-grey interior. There was nothing in the desert and dunes here or up the Kuiseb where she had come from several summers before that looked like this.

She enjoyed this quiet period of the morning. The two infants were playing quietly out of the sun. She'd completed her chores of the morning – fetching gourds of water, sweeping out the floor of the shacks, and raking the *kraal*, the compound around their hut. There was enough food from their expedition to the coast the day before, and she could enjoy time on her own in the relative cool before the fog burnt off and the sun began to scorch. Then the shacks would bake, the flies and fleas would become active, and people would become irritable.

Her aunt had been pleased with the abalone. They were rare, and it was delicious. The family had eaten well. "Our *'sa'as'*[8]" her aunt called her. Approval from her mother's sister was reassuring. !Nara knew she was quicker and better than the other girls her age at finding *veldkos* and other things they could use. Providing for her aunt's family was for her own good. As an orphan, she knew her life here was by sufferance.

Shouting interrupted her reverie. Piet, her aunt's husband, was among the loudest. They were drunk, as her aunt had said they would be. Whenever a ship came into the port the men got hold of Cape brandy in exchange for goods or labour. She knew to avoid him and the other men when they were like this. They

---

[8] Nama word for female gatherer

became violent, brawling among themselves, beating the women and children, and sometimes smashing their meagre hovels in staggering rages. !Nara rapidly gathered up her little collection and dropped it into the leather pouch on a thong around her waist. Apart from a small animal skin apron, she was naked.

+++

White and overdressed in his dark serge suit, white shirt and a black waistcoat, he feels oddly confident as he walks further into the shantytown. In Lithuania and Cape Town the Jews were generally smaller than the goyim. Here he's taller and sturdier. His clothes, which even in Walvis mark him as a shabby immigrant Jew, set him apart from the ragged and semi-naked people he passes. He doesn't know or care if it's deference or resignation, but the absence of any sense of hostility or resentment, and their primitive living conditions, make him feel superior. A projection of power, an aura, protects him.

A gaggle of people, some of the men obviously drunk, are jeering and cackling outside one of the hovels. A man with a bottle in his hand is staggering about, shouting at a woman in front of him.

She shuffles left and right blocking him from the entrance to the hovel where a young girl and two infants cower. He hurls the bottle at her and grabs a branch from a pile of firewood. "*Vok af! Ek wil die meisie* - Fuck off, I want the girl", his voice rising in a roar of rage. The thrill of mounting violence hushes the crowd. He lunges at her, grabbing her stained shirt. She pulls away and the shirt comes off her brown shoulders. Full breasts swing free.

Jack's pulse races and blood rises to his face. Atavistic lust surges through him as he's riveted by the women's large breasts and her naked brown skin. Shame follows. He's rooted to the ground by fear and the shock of the violence.

She twists out of the shirt and motions at the girl to move away with the children. She faces the man. "*Vat my* - take me", she says, offering up one of her breasts. She half turns to the entrance of the shack and lifts the back flap of her animal-skin skirt. Her large brown buttocks transfix the man, the crowd, and Jack too.

The man lunges forward grabbing her by her short black hair and forces her to her knees. He raises the branch to club her.

A flicker above Jack's head barely registers as a shot rings out. It's not a gun but the crack of a whip, flipping back with menacing sibilance above the couple.

Silence envelopes them all. A red-faced man on a horse urges the animal forward with a shout and kick of his boots as he draws a long cattle whip back over his shoulder. He kicks out at the man, sending him to the ground. "You fucking drunk!"

His curse breaks the silence, and the crowd begins to jabber and move. The woman gets up and goes to the infants cowering with the girl. Piet tries to crawl to his feet, but the man kicks him down again from the saddle. "*Haal hom weg* - take him away", he shouts, motioning to men in the crowd.

Tall and dressed in khaki with a wide bush hat, he wheels the horse around to come up to Jack. "What's a Jew doing here, then?" And then, with hostility in the pale blue eyes – "You're not selling them brandy, are you? And it better not be guns either!"

"A mule driver I'm looking for. I need my cart in Swakopmund. In the town they said Piet I should look for."

"He'll be no good to you or to anyone." His accent marks him as English. "Damned brandy makes them all useless."

He pushes the horse towards a group of men and speaks to them in Afrikaans. "How many mules and carts you have?", he calls back.

"Four mules, one cart", Jack replies.

"You came in on the boat yesterday?", the man asks, when he comes back. "I have oxen from there too. We have to inspan and pair them before we set out. They also have to be fed up and well-watered. The same for your mules. That can take a day or two. That lot will help us", he said, pointing with the long-handled whip to the group of men he'd been speaking to. "You can join me on the trek to Swakop." He pulls away, and then turns the horse back. "Don't set out on your own. The Namib will kill you. You don't know the Namib, they do. I'll find you later in the town."

"Denk you", Jack says, struggling to moderate his Yiddish accent. "Vot is your name?"

"Cameron" he says as the horse moves away.

Intent on leaving too, Jack looks back towards the hovel. The woman has pulled on the tatters of her torn top, but her breasts are still exposed, and she is watching him. She says something to the girl and comes forward towards him. The girl bends to enter the shack.

"*Vat die meisie, baas* - take the girl, master", she says quietly. Jack flushes – at her nakedness and at the directness of her gaze. The few people still standing around are watching them. He feels they sense his discomfort. He hears what she's saying but it seems distant. He doesn't want to understand. "*Vat die meisie*", she repeats now, close up to him. "Take the girl. She's good at finding food. She'll help you."

The girl emerges from the hovel with a rolled-up bundle in her arms. An animal skin is draped over her slight shoulders. Small high breasts and wide frightened eyes. She comes forward to stand by the woman, who calls to the two toddlers. They come to the girl and clasp her hands in theirs to say goodbye.

He knows a decision had been made for him. But he has yet to grasp that the slight brown girl has become his responsibility.

+++

Her breath is short, a painful tightness in her stomach. They'd been waiting to eat before Piet stumbled into the *kraal*. But deeper than the hunger is fear. Her eyes are bulging and tight. She can't cry. If she does her aunt may slap her in front of this young white man. She hasn't quite realised that she is now his, but instinctively knows she must not be rejected.

She knows this terror already. It rose like bile when she and her mother left their home to come down the Kuiseb. There had been grief when her father died. She remembered the other men carrying him to their *kraal* after a fight with Bushmen in the desert. He'd been shot with a poison arrow and took a day to die. He moaned all the time, his suffering spreading despondency like sickness in the family. Her mother's and grandmother's constant wailing overwhelmed her, and she held her hands over her ears. For days after his burial, silence crept around the *kraal* as the adults who normally loved her and cared for her became distant like the stars.

She'd not understood the cataclysmic consequences of his death at the time. There had been sadness and less to eat after his death, but the grandparents held the little family together. They had given her love and care even as her mother remained withdrawn in grief. But in the early summer, with no one to hunt or take their few goats to fresh pasture, there was not enough food. They'd had to leave. She felt abandoned as they left her sobbing grandparents alone in the little *kraal* in the desert that she had known as home. Terror stalked them as they moved down the Kuiseb.

They'd trekked for days with very little water. During the day it got so hot they couldn't walk on the burning sand and rocks, and they sheltered under meagre bushes or in the shadows of the canyon walls. At night she heard jackals nearby, and occasionally the chilling mad cackle of hyena. They were attracted by the small kid goat her grandfather had given them. But !Nara knew she was small too, small enough to draw a hyena or leopard.

For the first few days her mother trudged ahead, urging her to stay close, searching for food and water in the *gorras*[9] and watching out for predators. When the kid tired, she carried it on her shoulders, and at night she would light a fire and surround them with thorn bushes. In the morning and evening she would share out a little of the *goa-garibeb*[10] or some dried goatmeat they had brought with them. Her mother became spiritless. Her silences grew longer, and she'd stare into nothingness. !Nara withdrew too – she knew her mother had no patience or energy for her. It was !Nara who searched for water holes or springs, which were mainly dry or too brackish to drink. By evening of the fourth day they had nothing left to eat or drink.

As evening began to creep up the canyon walls her mother trudged away from the riverbed up a sandy bank. !Nara watched her sprawl beside some boulders in a patch of !Nara melons, indifferent to where her daughter was. These patches were usually associated with families or clans, and they had hoped to find someone along the way. But it was too early in the year to harvest the spiny fruits, which were still small and extremely bitter. They

---

[9] Shallow wells animals dig in the sand in their search for water.
[10] Dried fruit paste of the nara melon which forms an important part of the diet of the Topnaar. The paste is sweet and very nutritious and keeps for up to a year.

knew not even to extract water from the pulp, as it caused severe burning in the mouth and stomach cramp. This stretch of the Kuiseb was so remote that no one appeared to check on the plants.

Hunger was like a stone in !Nara's belly and her lips were scaly, she was so parched. The goat's bleating was drawing predators closer. She had known her mother to be fierce – hurling stones at snarling dogs if they threatened the goats, and clubbing snakes if they slithered into the *kraal*. Now she didn't even bother to light a fire, and held onto her daughter's body to get her warmth. In the middle of the night a jackal crept into the thorny melon patch where !Nara had hobbled the goat to try and protect it. Her mother turned away and groaned when the terrified bleating woke them as the kid was carried off.

The next morning !Nara had to almost drag her to her feet to continue the trek down the widening gorge. Her constant protector, full of life and laughter and always intent on teaching her about the world, was abandoning her. She stumbled along behind the little girl, silent and apathetic.

A party of hunters found them and brought them to Gobabeb, a larger settlement in the Kuiseb. At first, they could not hold down any water or food. An old woman made them a bitter tea that stopped their retching, and they began to retain water and then some food. They were able to rest and recover for a few days, but her mother remained withdrawn. It was !Nara who decided it was time to continue their journey down the Kuiseb to Walvis Bay where her mother's sister lived.

Her aunt had cared for them when they got to the sprawl of shacks and hovels on the outskirts of Walvis. Piet resented them and the burden they imposed. He was incensed when they told him about the loss of the kid her grandfather had contributed. Her mother never really recovered. She would sweep out the *pondok* they used, and the *kraal*, cook pap and fetch water, but she would rarely join her sister and the other women in their search for *veldkos*, or go down to the beach to gather seafood. !Nara knew it was up to her to justify their place in the *kraal*. When her mother had died the previous winter !Nara had felt relief, despite her grief. Her aunt had come to count on her, and Piet was less hostile. Her life did not unravel.

But now it has. The riverbed becomes the lagoon, the shacks that had been home have disappeared behind the dunes, and Walvis appears by the coast. The stench grows stronger as the westerly breeze moves inland. She is hot and pale with anxiety. Her aunt had warned her recently not to be alone with men, especially Piet. Now she has sent her away with a man —- a white man – into the town which is mainly men. Since her father and grandfather disappeared from her life, all men have seemed to be a threat. Maybe because her body is changing. Maybe because that's how her aunt and the other women she's been around see them. Know them.

She follows the white man's dogged trudge, his head down and self-absorbed. He's struggling with her presence and with himself. He resents her just as Piet had. He is white and the town is white. She doesn't know what to anticipate.

Her bare feet make a soft sound a few steps behind him. He's irritated. What can he do about her? He was weak and stupid to allow this to happen. Now she's a responsibility. He doesn't need this. But he needs to piss.

He motions to her to wait where she is. She misinterprets him and squats down submissively. "No, just wait here", he says, confused, embarrassed at his nastiness. He walks away across the sand and faces away from her.

When he turns around, she's squatting on the other side of the path – doing the same. The intimacy of the moment makes him smile. Slightly thrills him too. He's never seen a girl urinate. When she comes back, he offers her some water from the canvas pouch he's carrying. They look at each other properly for the first time.

"My naam is Jack", he says pointing to himself. "Jeck", she repeats reflecting his heavy Yiddish accent. "!Nara", she offers, touching her chest. The sibilant glottal of her language stumps him. "Nara" he murmurs – an exhalation from deep inside him.

+++

April 1989   Keetmanshoop

Steyn's Mercedes sedan is like a siren going off as he searches for Lena's sister's house in the bleak grid of identical housing set aside for the Coloureds in the south east of the town. Hardly a bush anywhere to break the monotony of the sandy waste. Stumps of trees long chopped down for firewood, or stripped of their bark by the goats kept in the yards and lean-tos. Sun glints on shards of broken glass everywhere. Mangy dogs scent the stranger and bark, howl and growl. Dirty curtains twitch, and bedraggled children stare at the tall white man who gets out and locks the car carefully outside the two unfinished cinderblock rooms. Prolonged scurrying inside follows his knock on the door.

A woman, maybe in her late twenties, opens the door, an infant on her hip and a dirty housecoat barely pulled closed about her body. The smell of cheap wine registers before her fearful "*Ja, meneer?*". This must be the daughter, he realises. Lena had said that her sister's daughter was a drunk with children from several men. One of them he knew as a layabout and a thief. He notices holes in the corrugated tin roof as Lena's sister comes in from the lean-to kitchen at the back. Anxiety flickers in her eyes. He registers how she's aged.

"*Moenie worrie nie,* don't worry, Lena is well. I've not come about her." The ingrained discrimination of race and class make it awkward for all of them. He declines the kitchen chair they offer. Barefoot children stare at him from everywhere, it seems, even though there are only two rooms. Flies buzz incessantly, maddened by the baking heat under the tin roof. "*Die mense -* these people", he says to himself, with the gnawing distaste of the privileged white at how they live. He's used to it, resigned to it and would say that fundamentally, they choose to live this way.

"I need an address for Valerie, Nara's granddaughter. Lena says she lives in Windhoek and that someone here might know how to contact her."

An older girl in the brood is sent off to a neighbour. Halting small talk and a chipped mug of water until she returns with a postcard – snow-covered Bethlehem at Christmas. Valerie's address is neatly written alongside the "From:" Steyn copies it into a notebook and asks the older woman to come outside with him.

"I'm sorry about your son's death, Baas Steyn", she says. "It makes the heart sore." He nods and suddenly remembers that her son had been badly wounded in Angola, and asks after him. "His wife looks after him, but his pension is very small. Her brother helps them when he can. I can't." The family puzzle drops into place. Her brother had also served in the army, doing well and becoming one of the first Coloured senior NCOs. He'd also served with Jannie up on the border. "How is Willem?", he asks, recalling the man's name. "He's good. He has a job now with De Beers. He is down by Lüderitz most of the week." He presses some rand notes into her hand, their mutual *"dankie's"* as much for the help with Valerie's address and the money as for bringing the awkwardness to an end.

Steyn had been born into and lived with apartheid all his life. For him it was an obvious reality – the races were different. And the whites were superior. You only had to look at how they treated each other to see the natural order of Africa. The Basters – the mixed-race people around Rehoboth further to the north - were more sophisticated, but that was because they had white blood and had chosen to emulate the Boere – Steyn's people. But they too were ravaged by alcoholism.

The war, international pressure, black resistance, and white dissent were constants in their lives. The dominee, the minister in their local Dutch Reformed church, often talked about South Africa's race problems, but the conclusion was always that the Afrikaners were chosen by God to settle this land. The non-whites were unsophisticated children, and no good would come from educating or promoting them, as they would only fail and become frustrated.

But Steyn knew too that these were old ways of thinking. He'd read interviews with SWAPO leaders. He didn't like what they said, but they were not the uneducated or simple people he encountered in his daily life on the farm or in town. The world condemned apartheid, and maybe Boer history didn't justify everything that was being done.

And terrible things were being done, he knew. Koevoet – the police counter-insurgency unit – had a particularly gruesome reputation. It was spoken of in whispers, often with a perverted relish at their gruesome exploits against the kaffirs. "*Onchristelik* - un-Christian", he said to Frederika, without repeating the details he heard from other men.

They wondered sometimes with discomfort if Jannie had been involved in this and kept it from them. Jannie's death had reinforced the innate scepticism and dislike he had of the city types who were the politicians and security leaders – Boere or otherwise.

Frederika, who never spoke of politics, spat out one day that Jannie's death had been a waste. Frau Bruns, their German neighbour who always made her feel uncomfortable with her bluntness, had asked her one day as they talked in the hairdresser's "Why is it that it's mainly your boys getting killed up there?"

She brooded on this, and on the Sunday confronted the dominee publicly with the question. She bitterly rejected his attempts to reassure her otherwise. "I know Jannie wasn't sure why he was fighting", she said.

Suidwes as they knew it was coming to an end.

+++

26 April 1989
Dear Ms Valerie,
(he'd hesitated about the "Ms")
My name is Steyn. I'm the farm manager at Daweb-Eshel where your mother and grandmother lived. Lena Isaacs, who lives with us, says you used to come to the farm too.

I am writing to tell you that the farm is to be sold. Lena has found things that belonged to your mother and grandmother. There are some suitcases and a locked tin trunk that we don't think we should open. Also, we don't have a key for it. Lena thinks you might.

Can you come and collect these things? This is not urgent – it will take time for things to happen but perhaps when you have holidays or a long weekend?

You can write to me c/o P.O. Box 173, Keetmanshoop and let me know when you are coming. The farm telephone is Keetmans 131. We will collect you.

+++

Steyn pulls into the petrol station on the way back to the farm after posting the letter. His mind is on their future, and what his alternatives are if they cannot stay on the farm. He and Frederika are old and sad. New owners wouldn't want them. He had a pension, but it was Jannie's grave that mattered.

A tap on the far-side window startles him. A tall blond man with a red, acne-scarred face grins at him. "Bessie", as they all called him, seems weirder than Steyn remembered him. He's in his forties now. Pale blue eyes dance about above a sparse blonde moustache that barely hides a purplish welt. Still with the disconcerting tics and twitches that he'd developed as a teenager. Steyn had not seen him for years, although he had heard rumours of gruesome exploits in the security forces.

"Hoe gaan it, Meneer Steyn?" he asks as the window is wound down. "I'm fine, Bessie, thank you. What are you doing here?" The question has a subtext. Both know that Bessie has an evil

reputation in the town.

"*Staatsbesigheid* - state business", he says, with a smirk. Sunlight catches the sparse yellow moustache he'd grown to cover the purple welt above his lip. A few more inane exchanges, then – "maybe see you on the farm another time" – delivered with another twisted grin.

Opgemors, Steyn thinks - screwball, as he drives away.

Cameron...

...and his gang of men and boys took two days to assemble the spans of oxen for the trek. Tall, sandy-haired, and quick to colour, he was decisive about dropping lazy or unskilled handlers, and studied about switching and pairing the long-horned oxen into teams to pull the massive wagons. He sent an older man to help Jack get the mules hitched to the cart and broken in to pulling as a team. Once the animals had been whipped, pulled and goaded into semi-obedience, a youth came and led them on practice journeys on the track behind the warehouses.

The *transportryers* used long rhinoceros-hide cattle whips – *sjamboks* – that they cracked above and alongside the oxen rather than striking them directly. Some of the *sjamboks* were so long they used both arms to flick the thin snapping thong spliced onto the end above the lead oxen. The sharp cracks, whistles and shouts, and waving sticks were sufficient to terrorize most into obediently succumbing to the forward rhythm and unfamiliar weight of the wagons.

The girl spent the time sitting in the shade behind the warehouse, or riding in the cart once the mules got settled. Idleness gave her time to adjust to the sudden change – the town, the absence of women, being surrounded by men and being alone with the white man. Soon after they'd arrived at the warehouse he'd rummaged among his goods and given her a slip to wear. That had made her aware of her nakedness. She sensed too that he was embarrassed by her presence, blushing when people noticed her and asked him. Her stomach had become unsettled. He had brought her bread and smoked fish, but she was not used to the food or to the quantities. She was stressed. Here she could not just walk over a dune to shit as she was used to. Nor could she leave to forage for plants, which would ease the bloating she felt. He was the only constant in her life now, and she followed his movements all the time.

'Jeck' hadn't been unkind to her, but he was obviously young and inexperienced. From the way he followed the preparations and asked questions she sensed he was apprehensive. He struggled with the desert – squinting, deflating with the heat, not knowing where and how to sleep. He wore too many clothes– a dark black suit, he was constantly thirsty and sweated easily. Quietly, before dark of the first day, she showed him how to rake the sand to make sure there were no ants, beetles or scorpions, and make a depression in the sand for his hips before he lay down beside the cart.

"Baas Kemron", as the *transportryers* called him, was the opposite, and all deferred to him quite naturally. He was massive from her perspective, and wore khaki clothes and a broad-brimmed hat. Despite that, his face, neck, and forearms were burned pink, and his sandy hair was out of place amongst everyone else. But he was more at ease in the desert and the climate, and masterful with the animals, their handlers, and with the wagons. Jeck was shorter, with a thicket of wiry black hair, and clumsy by comparison. Cameron's light blue eyes seemed to look into the distance most of the time. Jeck had deep blue-grey eyes that seemed to focus on whatever was before him, or inward on himself. They were unsettling and almost magical against his swarthy skin.

On the day before they were to set out Cameron had them practice again, but headed back to the *kraal* before the real heat of the day set in. As they passed the lagoon, he had some of the men collect crusted salt from the dry pools on the banks. "Mix some salt into the feed to make the animals drink when you get back to the stable", he told Jack. "Feed them well and let them rest. We'll be setting out at nightfall to avoid the heat. Better load up on salt too – there's never enough up country."

In the dark, Cameron had him move out in front of the grunting oxen of the first massive Cape wagon. Their long horns glinted with moisture in the moonlight, and the white canvas covers swayed to and fro like ghostly ships. "Your *touleier*[11] knows the way, but don't get off the track or too far ahead. It's all sand and I don't want to start this trek pulling you out of it", he said.

Jack was exhilarated at being out in front. The line of white surf to his left and the moonlight on the silent, ethereal, low dunes to his right eliminated the need to navigate. Animals and men were happy to be on their way and out of the foul-smelling town. Cameron rode up and down, intent on keeping them in as tight a column as possible. At dawn, they stopped briefly to feed and

---

[11] Afrikaans - the span leader, usually a young boy – responsible for leading the first pair of oxen by a thong – the *leiriem* - attached to their horns.

water the animals, but then he urged them on again while the fog sheltered them from the heat.

When the fog lifted, a huge blue sky opened up above him. Massive African skies were no longer new to Jack, but the openness of the desert and the sea made his spirits soar like the odd gulls that swept in from the sea. The draw of adventure in this amazing continent thrilled him. Walvis was grimy and violent. It was rotting flesh and rusting iron, and hard men scrabbling between the desert and the malevolent ocean. But that was behind them now. Being in front they were spared the dust thrown up by the oxen and their wagons. The *touleier* walked beside them, hardly needing to use the whip to keep the mules moving. The calls, whistles, rattling of the chains, and lowing of the oxen behind them slowly synched in Jack's mind with the rhythm of their motion and the distant crash of the waves. The herd of cattle at the rear of the column moved in a brown cloud far behind them.

Soon after midday the Namib delivered its first lesson.

The wind changed. No longer off the sea and cooling, it shifted to the southeast off the desert. The dry air burned Jack's nostrils if he inhaled deeply. He'd been squinting to cope with the glare but now he could see little difference between the sand in the air and the desert that had been blown smooth. Swirling dust masked the sea and the sky, grit clogged eyes, nose and mouth. Ears, cheeks, hands were singed by blasts of sharp sand. The mules kept pulling to turn away from the wind, and the *touleier* yanked them forward, while Jack whipped them with increasing exasperation.

Sand began to obliterate the track they had been following and Cameron gave up the fight. The mules were unhitched but hobbled, left to survive as best they could.

Jack and the girl stacked the boxes and bundles on the windward side to stabilise the cart and shelter them from the lashing sand and wind. They huddled in the narrow space that remained. Their *touleier* went back to shelter with the others underneath the ox wagons. Sand was everywhere and relentless, matting their hair and caking their eyelids. He learned to breath only through his nose, as the sand invaded his mouth, dried out his cheeks, and made his teeth grind. They acknowledged each other and their shared misery by occasionally passing the water pouch, adjusting to make space for each other in the yellow gloom and then in the dark after night fell. There was no silence – the wind moaned or roared. Eventually exhaustion won out and they both fell asleep.

+++

She wakes with the lightened sky. Registers the soft fur of her kaross below her and the rough fabric of his blanket covering her. Gently she brushes the sand from her eyelids and eyelashes. Reassured by the softness and familiarity of her own fingers, reality slips in slowly – the desert, the storm, the cart, the man. There's warmth from his body behind her and she hears his soft breathing. The sourness she'd smelled before has gone.

She has not shared a sleeping space with a man since living in her grandparents' *!haru oms* more than two summers ago. Physical affection had come mainly from her mother and her grandmother. Memories of her father's touch had faded. Her grandfather would cuddle her, but he was old and so thin he felt brittle. As a baby she'd struggled against his embrace, he said. She only relaxed with the songs and poems he would murmur. He'd named her !Nara after the spiky melon – prickly outside, bitter to taste, but sweet when ripe. She missed the warmth and reassurance of his voice, his wrinkled fingers and the sharp smell of his tobacco, but sensed his fragility. She could not conjure up a memory of his proximity. Memories of her mother were warm and enveloping, but overshadowed now by the sadness and fear of her withdrawal, decline, and death. There had been a little sister too, but she had died before she could even crawl and Nara had no memories of her. Recent physical affection had come only from her aunt's children. Her aunt had become brusque after her mother's death, and when displeased would slap her.

Still half asleep and lulled by the warmth, she's languid and unthreatened by the man's body behind her. But she's curious. He's larger than Topnaar men, but small compared to Cameron, who is an intimidating giant. She tries to imagine him without the dark clothing. She'd seen his white shoulders when he'd removed his shirt. Almost grey, unnatural, unhealthy.

Girls her age in the shantytown had grown up sharing sleeping space with brothers and cousins. She'd played with boys until a few months ago, and was used to their shape, their voices, and the way their bodies moved. She was used to their nakedness and they to hers. But her friends seemed to have a deeper intimacy or familiarity with their brothers and fathers.

A few months before, the boys of her age started to separate, sent out to herd the goats or hunt and fish with the men. The larger families had a separate hut where they slept with older brothers and cousins. Now there was little time playing together, and the girls joined the women's *veldkos* and beachcombing expeditions, or stayed at home looking after the infants and the other domestic chores. Imperceptibly almost, as her breasts began to bud and soft hairs began to appear between her legs, "womanness" and "separateness" draped themselves around her.

Her fingers fluttered over her breasts, which only recently she realised she enjoyed. The glances of some of the older boys and younger men would linger on her, which she found flattering and confusing. She enjoyed the attention, especially as an orphan, but found it frightening too – something beyond her control. It also seemed to irritate her aunt and some of the other women, who'd begun to admonish her not to be alone with the boys and to avoid the men. They tracked her meanderings round the *kraal*s with what she sensed as hostility and suspicion.

Piet had started being kind, playful, and more physical towards her, which provoked sharp words from her aunt. She would be viciously scolded and sent off on chores. Piet would grin awkwardly and slink off. When he was drunk, which was often, her presence seemed to enflame him, and his anger at her aunt would erupt into rages and threats of violence. Later, her aunt would berate her, confusing her even more. Now, when he had become so violent and screamed that he "wanted the girl", her aunt had protected her. But she had also rejected her and sent her off with this boy-man sleeping beside her. So far, he had not been threatening.

Soon she and other girls her age would be *hokmeisies*[12]…

"It is always when the there is a new moon", her aunt had explained, "when the moon looks like the cut of the young maiden. A new moon is born from the cut. Like a child. Then the *taras*[13] will guide you to womanhood, like a tortoise emerging."

She had stood in a circle with the other village women, singing, clapping and stamping as the *taras* led the still shy but somehow discernibly more mature girls back into the village. The rite was a mystery, and somehow involved pain, vulnerability but also the potency that came from being a woman. She didn't feel ready for this passage from childhood, but she knew that when she came back after the ceremony, she would be eligible for marriage.

Jack stirred, sensed her presence, and they were both awake.

The wind eased in the afternoon as the cold Benguela restored atmospheric pressure over the ocean. Cameron said they would

---

[12] Afrikaans word meaning "hut maiden" referring to the mat-covered hut constructed at the back of the home or on the edge of a village where young girls are separated and undergo the socialization and initiation rituals of puberty. The re-entry of the initiates into their society is often celebrated with a ritual meal and dancing of the women alone.
[13] Nama word for older woman and mothers, a term of respect

continue the next morning. "Use the time to see to the animals. Wash the sand out of their eyes and clear the sand off the cart – you don't need the extra weight."

The girl was happy to fall into helping after being cooped up in the cart. They'd hardly attempted to communicate – just passing the water pouch or some nara nuts she'd brought with her. They finished the bread and dried fish he'd brought.

Jack walked down towards the beach as evening began to compose itself in a pale sky clear of dust. His eyes were drawn to the horizon by the contrast between the dark ocean and the sunset, and he was indifferent to the ashen sand about him. It was only when he turned around to check on the cart that he realised the sand wasn't ashen at all, but a creamy yellow. Away in the distance, behind the white wagons and oxen, the sand dunes were golden, reflecting the sun. Their flanks, now in shadow, were a deeper rose, and behind them the higher dunes were a soft mauve. The green fields and forests at home are more restful, he thought, but didn't ever put on a display like this.

As he meandered back in the gloom, he stumbled over a dark green hump on the wasteland. Strange leaves arranged untidily around a calloused core[14]. As he stood up, another hummock

---

[14] *Welwitschia mirabilis* (called *kharos* or *khurub* in Nama, *nyanka* in Damara, and *onyanga* in Herero) is endemic to the Namib desert, and survives from precipitation of the coastal fog on its leaves and (perhaps) a shallow root system, although there is almost zero rainfall in the area. Some plants are estimated to be over 1,000 years old.

further off moved – Cameron was sitting on a rock watching him. "There is no water, but these plants can survive here", he said as they walked back. "The land and these people will teach you to find water and food if you let them. Ignore them and you won't survive."

The caravan reassembled at dawn. Sand had obliterated the path, and progress was slow as the animals and wagon wheels struggled through it. Some oxen and cattle had also been semi-blinded by the sand, and Cameron pushed them towards the centre of the herd. He rode up to Jack as they crested the last low ridge before the broad green slash of the Swakop River, and pointed out where he wanted to him wait until they could cross as one group.

"The Germans will send someone to make sure none of the cattle have Rinderpest. It's obliterated the Herero herds. That's why there's a market for cattle here now. If we cross as a group, they may miss the semi-blind ones and not make any trouble."

Jack and the *touleier* fed and watered the mules and washed their eyes. The young boy then went to sit with the girl on some rocks, chatting in their strange click language as they shared some *biltong* and a sweet and sour orange-coloured *goa-garibeb*. Jack had tried it but found it sandy and full of pips. He watched them for a while, idly jealous of her obvious pleasure in talking to the boy. She smiled and giggled, and he enjoyed her prettiness as he watched them from afar. He toyed with the idea of sending her back with the *touleiers* when they'd been paid off. He picked up the boy's whip and wandered off some distance to try it out without spooking the mules. He needed to rid himself of his frustration and confusion.

The leather had been smeared with animal fat and was greasy to touch. It tapered off to a thin thong that had been carefully spliced into it. This produced the sharp crack when flicked. The leather itself was very flexible, unlike the *sjamboks* used for the oxen. Jack had used whips before when he went on trips with his uncle, and there was a pleasurable memory of power as he felt the weight at the end of the stick, and flipped it about on the sand. It took a few flicks before he remembered the flick of the wrist necessary to get the thong to crack in the air.

The boy had been watching and came across to coach him, teaching him to use his shoulder for greater reach and momentum. "Good for snakes", he said. He set a stick into the sand, stepped away, and with a deft flick whipped it out.

He handed the whip back to Jack, who practiced doggedly until he got the knack. As the caravan began to reassemble around them, he walked back to the wagon and was about to hand the whip back to the boy when on a whim he rummaged among his goods and found a penknife that he offered as an exchange.

Cameron rode up and dismounted as the caravan got underway slowly to move down off the dunes. "So, how old are you then, young Jack?" he asked, as he walked beside the cart. Jack hopped off, handing the reins to the girl sitting beside him. Initially confused she smiled, pleased at the implied trust and acknowledgement. She felt useful.

"Eighteen", Jack said, pleased to be able to talk. "For how long you been here?" he asked the Englishman. "In South West — about two years."

"And you come, vy?"

"I started on the Cape Town to Windhuk route – that takes two months. But the Boers control most of the business – they have good relations with the Nama and the Basters who live along the route, as they speak near as dammit the same language. I've been doing Walvis to Windhuk for about six months, as the Germans are bringing in more and more goods as their colony grows."

"From Swakopmund to Windhuk, how long?" Jack asked.

"Can take two weeks or more, depending on the loads, the wagons, the oxen. There are mountains, and it's dry and hot as hell in summer, bitter in winter. The Germans are building a railway, but I don't know if it can take your cart, or how far it goes. Also, the army and their horses have priority – they'd probably buy your mules if you want to sell."

"A railway? Not good for you?", Jack asked.

"Not immediately", Cameron said, appraising him. "The Germans don't have a jetty yet in Swakop, and heavy goods will have to come in from Walvis. The railway lines, the locomotives, the cars, sleepers – even the water we drink – comes in from Walvis. It's a much better harbour, and that will always be

British."

"Once you've sold your goods, what are you going to do?" Cameron asked.

"Try for business. I'm a tailor and shoemaker, but I want a trader to be. In Cape Town I have partners who want business here."

"You speak German?"

"Better than my English. Sorry ..."

As they trekked across the sandy expanse of the dry river towards Swakopmund two men rode out of the town to meet them.

+++

May 1989   Daweb-Eshel

Steyn waited until Lena had gone to her room in the servant's quarters to tell Frederika about meeting Bessie. Frederika reddened with anger. "He's evil, perverted. He should keep away from here. The Nama will kill him if they can, and he'd deserve it."

She got up and stabbed at the ornaments and mementos on the spotless shelves and tables in their living room. Steyn could see tears glistening in her eyes and her lips narrow. He braced himself for a tongue lashing he'd known was coming. Her resentment and anxiety about the imminent sale of the farm had been building for days, and she usually took her stress and frustrations out on him.

He knew the pattern – she would sit in the chair opposite his and skewer him with small angry eyes and a vicious tirade of complaints and insults which neither reason nor silence could counter. But she surprised him.

"What was he doing here?", she asked.

"'State business', he said. I don't know what that means or whether to believe him", Steyn replied.

She snorted disparagingly and came back to her chair. She seemed calmer.

"I know you wanted to help him", she said, "and the dominee said he needed a father figure. But that boy was broken before he got here. And how could he not be - with a drunk for a father. That family, the Bezuidenhouts, are rotten. The whole district knows that.

"You know, after Bessie molested Lena here, she told me that the Nama on the farm where his father worked said he'd raped his wife in front of the boy! They found Bessie hiding in the barn unable to talk. After the mother died, he would run away because his father beat him so badly! Then the father had a child with the maid!

"You let Bessie fill Jannie's head with all that military nonsense. But Bessie was no hero – he was in the army to escape prison for raping his half-sister! You know where they found him afterwards?", she challenged him. "By his mother's grave in the old cemetery. That's what he was missing - a mother, not another father to fight against. You men, you always think you know best!"

Steyn leaned back, looked at the ceiling, and stretched out his long frame. She was right. He had taught both boys to shoot. He had thought that Jannie, who was quiet and respectful, would counter Bessie's wildness. But Bessie had a cruel streak that could not be curbed. When they sat together on the stoep, the gangly youth couldn't keep his hands away from Steyn's .22 or the pellet gun he used to keep birds out of the orchard. He would spend hours by the dam shooting needlessly at the *kelkiewyn* (Namaqua sand grouse) that came there to drink. The shepherds complained that he'd maim their dogs.

After he molested Lena he was placed in an orphanage in Windhoek. It didn't take long for the staff and the other boys to find out that he had a coloured half-sister, and he was viciously bullied. He ran away and hitched down to his father's farm on the remote edges of the Kalahari east of Keetmanshoop. One night, when his father was too drunk to drive home, Bessie raped the girl.

Bessie ran away but the shepherds knew where to find him – they'd seen him as a boy hiding by his mother's grave in the old cemetery opposite Tseiblaagte, the Coloured and Nama township outside Keetmanshoop. They brought him back to the farm, where his father tied him to a rack used to dry the karakul pelts and sjamboked him so severely he had to be hospitalized. Bessie never took off his shirt in public again, and explained away the red welt under his eye and across his lip as combat injuries.

To avoid the community's shame of sex between whites and Coloureds, and of rape within the family, the dominee and the local police chief urged him to volunteer for the army. He started off in the general infantry, but his sniper skills and his obvious enjoyment of combat saw him transferred to the special units that fought in Rhodesia. *"Ek het die terrs in hoenderdraad gedraai"* - I turned the terrs[15] into chicken wire - he would boast, his small pale blue eyes dancing about madly, almost choking on the saliva in his mouth. He'd wound up in the Koevoet, where his local knowledge and lust for killing and torture were an asset.

From there he was eventually recruited as an agent for the CCB, the SA defence establishment's Civil Cooperation Bureau – a secret unit of ex-soldiers and policemen, mercenaries (often ex-Rhodesians), hired assassins, and criminals from around the world who were paid in cash for ruthless and increasingly bizarre operations around the globe. It was as the CCB's point man in South West Africa that he'd tapped on Steyn's car window earlier that day.

+++

Early 1900s   Swakopmund

"*Algemeine gutter* - general goods", Jack said to the uniformed German official. "Clothing, tools, knickknacks", he explained, as

---

[15] South African slang at the time for terrorists

the man rummaged in the back looking for banned guns and ammunition.

"*Geherik kultuur*" (real culture) came from Berlin and not from Kovno, his mother insisted, urging him to master German. Before the Czar's edict to conscript young Jewish men for 25 years, she'd had dreams he would go to university in Germany. For a while German had been taught in addition to Lithuanian at the village school, when they could afford the private teacher. Commercial life in the district where they lived had also brought Poles and Russians, and he could understand these languages too. But for Jack, German was the language to master. That is, until he reached London and then Cape Town.

He struggled with English and was embarrassed by his accent. Afrikaans was necessary but he felt no judgement when he spoke it badly. But the German and English Jews who were already well established in the city disparaged the "Peruvians" – the eastern European Jewish immigrants like himself who were flooding in. The anglophile professionals, merchants, and businessmen found almost everything about these *grieners* unpleasant and embarrassing – their looks, their clothing, their poverty, accents and manners (or lack thereof), their peddling and crime. They were almost as intolerant of their raucous and smelly immigrant brethren as were the increasingly hostile and anti-Semitic English who were at the top of the pile in Cape Town.

"You don't speak to the customers Yiddish", Mrs Katz, his first employer, told him when he started as a waiter in her kosher restaurant on the edge of District Six. "A clean shirt you verr everry day." She took him on because of his German, which appealed to her well-established customers like Mr Sonnenberg, who was now his main backer. But unlike her, Sonnenberg's English was perfect and almost accentless. He too forbad Jack from using Yiddish in the three-storey wholesale and chandlery business he ran on lower Buitengracht Street.

The trek column rode into Swakopmund as the heat of the day withdrew. It was neat, laid out symmetrically with wide streets. Nara wondered at the few two-storey buildings, and Jack had an immediate sense of an Eastern European or at least German-influenced town – if you ignored the expanse of desert sand between and beyond the buildings.

Cameron trotted up and pointed out a house where he said he would be staying and where Jack could also get a room. He peeled away to take the cattle to the fort on the eastern outskirts and outspan the wagons and oxen.

The landlady told him that the train to Windhoek was scheduled to leave in two days. After agreeing a price for a room and stabling, Jack went back to unhitch the mules. A maid in a colourful full-length dress and tall headdress followed him and spoke briefly to Nara who was sitting on the bench. "The girl will come with me", she said in German.

He blushed – he'd seen to himself, the mules and the wagon, and had not thought of the girl. "*Danke*", he replied, relieved of the embarrassing responsibility and need to explain. Nara's eyes were large and glistening, her lips taut, showing her confusion and fear of being abandoned. "Go with the lady", he said softly nodding his head trying to reassure her and cover up his own discomfort. He sensed she knew he'd forgotten about her. She gathered her few things and followed the tall black woman.

"*Ich vergessen*" – he said to the landlady, scrambling his German in embarrassment – "I'd forgotten, I have a young girl with me." "Yes, I've seen her", she said. "She'll be taken care of."

He had a warm bath as soon as he'd stabled the mules and secured the wagon. Nara stood naked on wooden slats in the yard behind the servant's shacks, swilling away the sand and grime of their journey with her hands from a bucket of cold water. He wolfed down the hot beef stew and potatoes served at the table in the hostel dining room. She squatted outside the kitchen with a tin plate of pap and boiled offal. Both fell asleep quickly, he in a bed with clean sheets, she on a floor of cow skins that she shared with the other kitchen staff.

He woke early relishing the softness of the bed and the warmth under the blankets. For the first time in weeks he was also on his own. He lay on his side savouring the relaxation, the feeling of being clean, and the privacy. Slowly he became aware of his erection, and stretched his legs to ease the tension in the small of his back. The rhythmic crash and rattle of the waves breaking and withdrawing on the beach reminded him where he was. Early light probed at the window, but the gap under the door to the corridor was still dark. Occasional snoring from the adjacent rooms.

Eyes closed, languid under a sheet and blanket, scenes of the days since his arrival rise and fade. Diaphragm tightens with terror as the shark emerges from the grey-green sea. He is powerless. Now, sweet sea air – the awful stench of Walvis is only a memory. Everything is vast. Huge blue skies, somehow bigger than those above Cape Town. Those above the *shtetl* were so often grey and overcast. His jaw relaxes and he savours breathing slowly and easily through his mouth and nostrils now clear of sand and dried knotty mucous. Amazed, intimidated and excited. He's overcome the harsh light, intense aridity, and intimidating endlessness of the desert. His tongue sweeps slowly across his lips – moisture and sweet saliva clear away lingering recollections of sand.

Sudden, his voyeur's shame as the woman's full brown breasts swung free. Her dark nipples and large haunches transfixed him. The drunk's raw lust that grabbed him too. Also, panic as the violence screeched. His groin contracts and he turns onto his back.

Surreptitiously he'd enjoyed the girl's slim body, the small high breasts, and her almost complete nakedness before he gave her the slip to wear to hide his embarrassment. Her smooth, yellow-brown skin, at first alien, is now attractive, healthy. Unlike his. Still so much a child, though – gangly and awkward. Vulnerable.

Leah, his sister was like this – suddenly taller than the boys of her age, and prone to moods and pensiveness. Nara seemed younger, and Leah had a fuller body, though he'd long stopped seeing her naked. Longing for home welled up. It was almost two years since he'd left his family. How had Leah changed? And his mother?

Secure in the privacy of his mind and of the room, he relived the moment of his sexual awakening.

On Friday afternoons while his father went to the public bathhouse, his mother would get all of the younger children bathed. When the children were dressed for Shabbat, she would shoo them out of the kitchen with dire warnings not to disturb her while she bathed. They had all learned to let her enjoy her time alone ...

He was not sure what drove him to barge into the kitchen on this summer day. Partly curiosity, and partly a sense that as the eldest, it was his right to be alone with her without his sibling's incessant vying for her attention – a competition which in his mind he always lost. There was also a delicious sense of illicitness, of probing a barrier.

She was bent over the tin half-bath using a small towel to soap herself, her large white breasts swinging free. She straightened up to face him, the deep pink nipples transfixing his gaze as they moved back against her body. Her skin was glistening from the water, and his mouth went dry as he took in her round belly and the dark patch where her legs came together.

Blood rushed to his face, but he couldn't drag his eyes away. He had seen her nurse his siblings but had never seen her like this. She was watching him. But not with the shock or disapproval he was expecting. It was an appraisal quite unlike the enveloping motherly love he was used to as a child. And then there was a play of amusement in her eyes and around her lips as she took her time in wiping away the suds, watching him as he watched her.

"What is it, Yankele?", her tone still of the loving reassurance he had grown up with. He mumbled as she wrapped a towel around herself, bringing the moment to an end.

A few tugs at his *schmekel* and he ejaculated into his shirt. The ball of pain at the root of his spine and the ache in his balls subsided.

+++

"Give your laundry to your girl", the landlady said.

Nara was at a pile of firewood in the kitchen yard. She straightened up when she saw him, and he thought he saw a brief smile or flicker of relief. He gave her his dirty laundry, tied up in the shirt. She'd been given a grey tunic to wear, and that gave him an idea.

"Do you think you or anyone could use the girl?", he asked the landlady when he went back inside. "Or do you know if there are her people here where she could find a place?" He was not sure what he even meant by the phrase "her people", but he knew she was different from the darker people he had seen so far around the boarding house.

"I'll ask my women", the landlady said. "They're Herero and Damara, the girl's a Topnaar. We'll see."

After booking a seat for himself and space for the mules and his cart at the railway station he wandered down the neat main street. This was Germany's main outpost on the shores of Africa and on the south Atlantic. The railway station and the more substantial buildings had large windows and were clones of buildings he'd seen in Lvov and Konigsberg. The neatness of the urban layout and the stores was reassuringly familiar. Here wide verandas, or "stoeps" as they were called in South Africa, surrounded all the buildings to provide shade. There was also a raised wooden sidewalk outside most of the buildings on the main street, but elsewhere it was sand, and more sand.

The stores were still shuttered, and he wandered down to the shore as a large ship pulled into view. He stood on the short wooden jetty watching as the ship swung round to drop anchor, sounding its horn as it did so. Gangs of near-naked black labourers were rolling handcarts of rocks and timber past him to extend the jetty. Two red-faced German men, who seemed bad-tempered to judge by their shouts, supervised the construction.

A young German in uniform clomped onto the jetty and joined Jack to watch other gangs of long-limbed black men push boats out into the surf and begin rowing out to the vessel. "They're from Liberia", the young man said, pointing at the boat crews, "the local natives, the Ovambos", he said, nodding at the men on the jetty, "don't know anything about the sea". Jack noticed the officer's shoulder strap and asked if he was meeting someone on the boat.

"*Bruns, Rolf, Leutnant mit der Kaiserschutztruppe*", he introduced himself formally. "I'm here to meet a company of new troops and conduct them to the garrison at Okahandja."

Jack introduced himself, and explained that he'd arrived a few days earlier in Walvis from Cape Town. Bruns was immediately curious. "Did any British soldiers arrive with you? Did they have horses or cannon?"

"No, why do you ask?", Jack said.

"We think that now the British have finished with the Boers they will want South West Africa. Walvis Bay is the only real port close to the settlement at the moment, so they have an advantage. Horses are important in the territory, and we can only really bring them in via the Cape or Walvis until this jetty is completed."

For Jack, the Boer War had meant a flood of Jewish refugees from the Rand who came back to Cape Town when the gold-driven economy there had collapsed. They competed with him, scrabbling for work and housing, and many would stop at nothing to make a shilling.

His German gave him an advantage, first with Mrs Katz in the restaurant and then with Sonnenberg. It was the clawing competition and the poverty it kept him in that had driven him to look for new opportunities in this new territory. Sonnenberg, who had been in the Cape for almost twenty years, and some of the other more established businesses he'd badgered for work or trading opportunities had done well supplying the British army during the Boer War. Jack had persuaded Sonnenberg to put together a small syndicate to explore new opportunities in Suidwes, and they had loaned Jack goods on consignment and some cash to get started. Had they thought of potential rivalry between the Germans and the British, he wandered? Did that mean opportunity?

They continued to chat as the passengers clambered awkwardly up onto the jetty from the heaving boats. Bruns said that he too would be taking the train the next day with his new recruits. Jack was surprised to see women among the passengers. "Some, not too many, of the settlers come as couples now because it gets so lonely out on the farms. Single women are rarer than horses", he sniggered. "If you have things for women you should do well – anything that comes from Cape Town is fashionable."

The passengers were happy to be on a stable surface at last, but the desert starkness clearly shocked them as they walked down the jetty to the shore. "There are no trees – just sand." They milled around in smart clothing, waiting for their baggage to arrive on the rowboats but put out that there was no one to welcome them. "We came here with the encouragement of the government", one woman complained. Bruns assembled his company into loose ranks and checked their names off against a list.

Most of the soldiers were Jack's age – happy too to be on land again, and horsing around to get rid of their pent-up energy. The few older men, most with big moustaches and often fleshy faces, were quieter, even grimmer. Passengers and troops had been burnt pink by the sun as they passed through the tropics. Jack's olive complexion responded well to the sun where it was exposed, and his face, neck and arms were tanned brown.

Jack followed as the troops marched into the town, where the stores had now opened. The traders were all keen to know what he'd brought with him. There was a need for anything, it seemed, but women's clothing, tools and foodstuffs were highest on their list. And Cape brandy. Prices were much higher than in Cape Town. Two of the traders offered to buy his entire stock then and there, but Jack realized that he could get higher prices further inland.

The curiosity about Walvis, Cape Town, and British intentions repeated itself often. The traders, farmers and clerks he encountered seemed to trust him because of his near perfect German, and did not regard him as British. "We were late to the African game", said a clerk in the post office where he'd gone to send a telegram to his backers. "This is a challenging place because of the heat and the strangeness of Africa – especially for women, but you can make a fortune here. There is so much undiscovered. The big problem is the natives – they steal, and they don't want to work. There will be a war with them, and we need many more Schutztruppe."

"We've not found any of the girl's people yet", the landlady said after the afternoon *schlafstunden* (siesta) when he emerged from his darkened room. "They will turn up – they come into town to trade and steal. You can leave her here – we can teach her to work, and there are hotels that could use her. She'll grow up to be pretty enough. Pay me for a week's lodging and food for her upkeep."

He hesitated. "I'd better tell her myself", he said. uncomfortable with her bluntness. "She's been told already", the woman said, opening up the shutters in the lounge and swishing back the curtains that had held the glare and heat at bay. The restful gloom was obliterated.

"It's probably for the best", he muttered to himself. "I can't provide for her, she's a child and a girl. It's too limiting and too awkward." He thought of going to see her, but chose to avoid the awkwardness. "Can be done tomorrow."

As soon as he walked into the bar, one of the merchants he'd met in the morning waved him across. "This is the young Jew I was telling you about", he said to the others at the table. "He's just arrived from Cape Town."

They deferred to an officer, who introduced himself stiffly as an aide to the Governor, von Leutwein. The others followed – a farmer from Otjiwarongo, a local merchant, and a government clerk. Jack tried to roll the strange place name round his tongue.

"Are British troops moving back to Cape Town?", the officer

asked, leaning forward across the table and referring to the close of the Boer campaign. "There seem to be more in town and more down by the docks", Jack acknowledged. "What about the navy?" Jack shook his head. He had little military type information or insight to share with them. "All the refugees from the Transvaal have made the situation in Cape Town much worse. There is no work, and British military purchases have pushed up prices of everything. The people I know in Cape Town", he said, referring mainly to his partners, "are sure the British will not stop until there is no threat to their control of the Reef. The Boers are too weak and have no one backing them."

"They have been very brave", the merchant said. "But they had no chance."

"Did you see troops in Walvis?" the clerk asked, sparking off an intense discussion about possible British designs on South West. "They are consolidating their hold on South Africa now and are busy with that", the officer said. "For the time being there is nothing drawing them here – no diamonds, no gold. That's why we have to intensify our conquest of the territory."

"For that we need to defeat the Herero", the clerk said.

"Yes", said the farmer. "The Herero are less willing to sell us land now, and are holding onto their cattle. They are getting more arrogant. Best we initiate a war with them and defeat them before they unite behind one of their chiefs."

"No, it's easier for us to deal with a single chief or a few, rather than many different squabbling tribes and clans", the officer said. "Their chiefs like the good life and are in debt to white traders. They will sell their land and their cattle. The big challenge is to keep them unaligned with the Nama. They are well armed and a serious force who know this territory. We are kaput here if they get together."

Talk of war and soldiering was not unfamiliar to Jack. After all, it was the Tzar's policy of conscripting young Jews like himself for 25 years that had driven him and others to leave. But that was much more remote than what he was sensing here. Even in Cape Town, the Boer War, still ongoing, was a series of British battles with the Boers in the Transvaal, the Orange Free State, Natal – just distant, romantic place names to Jack and his fellow immigrants. There had been an influx of refugees and soldiers, but few wounded. With all the scrabbling poverty of the recession the war had brought, he was not involved. British domination seemed assured, and with it a sense of stability and opportunity. This had helped him persuade Sonnenberg and the others to provide the capital he needed for his expedition.

The swirling conversation among the German settlers made him sense for the first time that violent conflict with the native population lurked on the outskirts. The natives too were so varied, and seemed in conflict with each other. In the few days since he'd arrived, he'd heard of Herero, Nama, Damara, Ovambo … and he sensed that the differences were significant and important, but way beyond him.

The brown-skinned people he lived and worked with in Cape Town were labourers and artisans, market traders and fishermen, making a living like the Jewish and other immigrants who lived among them. They had skills that the native people he'd encountered seemed to lack. He knew they were Malay or Coloured - "mixed-race", but he hadn't given the term much thought. Their origin as slaves was never mentioned. There were very few Blacks in Cape Town, and the few he did encounter seemed to be transient workers on the docks or on the railways. Cape Town's social hierarchy of Whites, Coloureds and a few Blacks seemed stable. He had no real sense of the makeup of the rest of the country. What strife there was seemed to be between the very dominant English and Boere farmers up north. But here in Suidwes things seemed far more unstable.

He was not uncurious. If anything, he was probably nosy and keen to engage with people and learn. But he preferred one-on-one conversations. Asking the crowd would show him as naïve.

The bar got louder as more people arrived and more beer was consumed. Jack leaned forward to try and engage the farmer, whom he sensed would have more direct experience of life in the interior, but the man's attention was suddenly focussed beyond him. With a wink and a nod, he motioned to Jack to look back. Two youngish women, quite fashionably dressed, were sitting at a table by themselves. One saw him turn and gave a brief, coquettish smile.

Probably *zoine* – prostitutes, from the way they're dressed and being alone in a bar. Jewesses, he recognised. He'd not known Jewish prostitutes in the shtetl, but Cape Town, and especially District Six where he'd lived, was full of them. Many of their stories were terrible. Tricked, raped and coerced while on their way through London, Southampton and Liverpool to a new life. He'd heard that it had even happened on the boat he was travelling on. The girl who'd smiled muttered to the other, who looked at him directly too – judging him as he was them.

"*Ven hat ir onkumen?*", a sharply-dressed man asked him as he waited at the bar a few minutes later. Jack was relieved to slip into Yiddish, and happy to meet a *landsman* who might be a natural ally. "Fischel", as he introduced himself, said he was a cattle and horse trader who had been in Suidwes for three months. "The army are desperate for horses. They needed to bring in more of the Schutztruppe if they are serious about establishing the colony. I have contacts as far away as Argentina scouting for animals", he said. "The Herero and Nama want horses too, but if you ask them to choose between a horse and some brandy, they would pick brandy."

After a few more exchanges about business, he offered to introduce the *yiddishe meidele* sitting at the back of the bar, revealing his real business as a pimp. Jack mumbled an escape, and waved at Cameron who was standing further down the bar. "Come on, they're tired of *goyishe shmek*", Fischel cajoled. "Don't stay a virgin too long", he called after Jack as he moved away – loud enough for the girls to hear.

A hint of empathy

About eighteen months before Bessie saw Steyn at the petrol station in Keetmanshoop, he had been summoned to meet one of his former commanders from the Angolan border war in an office in South Africa's sprawling defence complex south of Pretoria.

"I'm offering you a job outside the regular army", said Fourie, now dressed in an expensive dark suit. He was as curt and as intimidating as ever. "I'm the managing director and chairman of a number of defence-related companies. I still hold the rank of Brigadier General. This is bigger and more secret than you can imagine. It is also very well-funded. It will require a lot of travel – here as well as abroad. We will also want you to build up an organization in Suidwes, where things are becoming difficult. It's a big chance for you, you can make good money and it will get you away from all the kaffir killing, which even you must be tired of by now."

"*Dankie General*", Bessie mumbled, dropping into his habitual meekness when confronted by rank. He'd been searching for years for an exit from the stress and brutality of Koevoet, and for the recognition he felt he was due. A chance to join the clandestine units he knew were springing up in the defence establishment was thrilling, and the validation he craved.

"This stuff is really sensitive and critical", Fourie continued. "You can't talk about it to anyone. You will need to be vetted again by security, and that includes an interview with a psychologist. They're waiting for you now. Bezuidenhout, they've been through your file. So have I. We know more about you than you know about yourself. So, no boasting and no *kak*. You'd better cooperate if you want this chance."

Fourie didn't tell him that the psychologist was a woman. Middle-aged, with wire-framed glasses, she sat to one side watching him while the internal security investigator went through an endless rote of questions from a multi-sided form longer and more detailed than Bessie had ever completed before: political associations – he had attended a few Broederbond[16] meetings – not a member; ("Application rejected", a note from the Broederbond recorded); criminal associates – none (he'd been a partner in a brothel, the Durban vice squad had reported, and had been forced out by his partners because he'd abused the prostitutes); drug use – "occasional" dagga[17] and amphetamines (common among soldiers on the Border), had "tried" cocaine. "Any heroin?" "No, never", Bessie was relieved to be able to answer; family – mother – long deceased; father – no contact for more than fifteen years; close friends – ex-soldiers and policemen; girlfriends – "occasional" (prostitutes, various reports noted); foreign travel, debts, etc. He had to account for almost every year of his life and the major milestones in his military

---
[16] An Afrikaner secret society which was the real source of power in South Africa following the ascendency of the Nationalist Party in 1948. See Notes
[17] South African slang for cannabis

career. The security interview took more than an hour, during which time the woman sat silently, watching him and making odd notes in a soft brown manila school exercise book. Bessie feared her.

"Let's get a coffee", she said after the interrogator had left the room. They walked about a shaded garden talking of innocuous things like city versus farm life, recent holidays, boating on the lakes in the Transvaal and fishing in Suidwes. By the time they returned to the interview room she'd put him at ease, and told him to take one of the easy chairs. "Tell me about the time you lived with your mother in Lüderitz?", she asked.

"Those were the happiest days", he said softly, tears welling up. Emotion rose in a crimson tide up his chest, neck and face, and his forehead glistened pink. Bessie babbled and blabbered for almost ninety minutes. The more he talked, the less he held back. His need to lie, evade, and boast washed away in the surge of release at being really listened to for the first time in his life. Distaste and fear did not dart across her face as he was used to with other women. Her light grey eyes behind her glasses watched him with curiosity, engagement – he did not bore her. Her woman's voice, the roundness of her body, hinted at the empathy he craved. Patiently she worked him through the litany of abuse, resentments, frustrations and inadequacies to approach his experiences in Koevoet and assess his current state of mind. That was her brief.

She'd not worked with Fourie and his unnamed organization

before. Most of her experience had been in assessing the competence and suitability of Military Intelligence and National Intelligence Service (NIS) case officers. Fourie said he was looking for people who could lead similarly clandestine lives, but would carry out their mission in spite of what he called "a high level of ambivalence".

She met Fourie the next morning to present her assessment. He was sitting with two other men, one of whom introduced himself as Colonel Viljoen. The other man did not even bother. She knew the type - internal security. Fourie interrupted her after a few minutes. "We know he's a psychopath. Incapable of remorse. That's why we chose him. The question is can he function on his own here and abroad, and will he be stable enough to rely on despite his drug habit?"

"Removing him from the stress of border combat could help reduce the drug consumption. He's an individual who craves a father figure and the approval of superiors. You asked me to explore his capacity to handle 'ambivalence' – I assumed ethical dilemmas. As a psychopath he will not care as long as he feels he has the approval of his superiors. Missions that boost his self-image with the promise of reward, including eventually a release from the life he now leads, could curb the drugs and encourage him to function well. I assume he went off drugs in anticipation of this interview, so the nervous tics mentioned in his file did not appear. But when I switched to English and German, he struggled. He can handle short foreign trips, but long assignments abroad would require more language training. Locally he's capable of leading small teams as long as the subordinates do not threaten his position or self-image. But if left on his own too long, he will brood on his resentments and inadequacies and that could drive him to drugs."

Fourie nodded. "Your notes stay with us", the unnamed man said as she got up to leave.

"We don't have much choice for Suidwes", Viljoen said after she left. "He will have to be our point man."

"Find out why he was rejected by the Broederbond in a shithole like Keetmans", Fourie said. "And more on his family - cut off from his father for so long must have been for something extreme. You're commanding this nutcase in Suidwes, the more you know about him, the more we can anticipate problems and use him correctly."

"He's a weak link", said Basson, who was the CCB head of internal security.

"Well, prepare accordingly", Fourie replied. "Without this, Bezuidenhout could wind up in prison for robbery or drugs or buying illicit diamonds, and blab about the gas fuckup on the border. We're offering him a way out and he'll know that. This way we have more control, and we need him. If he endangers us, you'll have to deal with it."

Less than twenty kilometres away Bessie was still lying in bed in the luxury hotel Fourie's people had reserved for him. He too was thinking of diamonds. The two Valium tablets the psychologist had given him after he'd composed himself had let him sleep through the night. He knew he'd blown the interview with all the blabbing and loss of control. He'd told her of things he'd done and seen on the border that he was sworn to keep secret, including the gas attack that had spooked all the commanders on the border. A secret project of the 7th Medical Battalion (part of Special Forces) to test poison gas mortars on Angolan civilians had got the coordinates wrong and landed on South African forces. Bessie was the first on the scene and was told to "tidy it up". Revealing that would get him fired, never mind being taken on for something even more secret.

He couldn't recall the last time he had cried. The relief that followed the unburdening to a woman he might never see again left him unfamiliarly calm. He lay back in the luxurious bed, sipping coffee and preparing himself for the rejection call from Fourie. He realised that his military career was also probably going to come to an end, and he viewed that with relief too. "Moenie worrie nie, Ma", he mumbled to his mother, as he had since he was a child, comforting her and himself after his father's violence. "They worry about the gas, but they don't know about the diamonds."

There had been no call of rejection, and the next morning, he met Fourie and Viljoen in an innocuous but secure building in Pretoria's Midrand district. Delta G was one of Fourie's companies. Later Bessie learned that it was a front for a chemical warfare programme. He signed papers resigning from the army and his pension was paid out in full. As a "consultant" for Delta G reporting to Viljoen who was a "director", his army pay was doubled and there would be bonusses and success fees that could double that again. He had an expense account for cars, hotels and flights and for cash payment to associates and accomplices. In the intense weeks of training that followed, his preoccupation with the diamond cache he had found while "tidying up" the gas fiasco faded.

A mirror shows the past but not the future

Nara watches Swakopmund fade away into yellow-grey wasteland as the train rattles and sways eastwards. She's still flushed and tense – almost not sure how she had got here. When one of the maids in the guesthouse had told her that Jack was leaving and that she would be working with them, her eyes dilated with anxiety. She'd turned away and gone to fetch another load of firewood to hide her tears. Her stomach clenched – here was the terror she'd fended off so far – another abandonment. She clung to what she knew – herself – and to the young white man she'd spent the last few days with, and had begun to trust.

"|ûba te toxoba" she mumbled, part stubborn and part pleading, when Jack and the Damara stable hand came to hitch the mules. During the sleepless night she'd decided she had no choice but to challenge him with her presence. She'd waited for him by the cart. She looked at him briefly, her eyes glistening, and then dipped her head. "She says 'sorry', but she wants to stay with you", the stable hand said in broken German. Jack busied himself with the animals, ignoring her and avoiding the decision he was expected to make. But she'd made it for him. Her tears made him flush. Telling her to go took a degree of cruelty beyond him. He sensed she knew this too.

At the station she had stood to the side as they coaxed the animals up into a khaki cattle cart and then lashed the cart onto a flatbed.

Without a word or a glance between them she clambered up and into the cart.

Jack fussed in his case in the carriage where he sat to calm his nerves. Anxious, he walked back to the flatbed, pretending to check the cart and mules again. He hopped up, pulled aside the canvas flap, and gave her a water bag and one of the bread rolls the guesthouse had prepared for him before he left. On a whim, he rummaged in one of the cases and pulled out a flat cardboard box which he pushed at her. Neither said anything.

As the coast receded, the haze solidified into a bank of fog which had cooled the coastal plain. But now, despite the slight breeze from the moving train, the heat began to bake the carriages where Jack sat amongst Bruns's newly arrived troops. There had been some predictable excitement and joshing as they boarded, but quite soon the flat, grey monotony of the terrain subdued them. Some dozed, while others chatted quietly or stared glumly at the wasteland outside the carriage.

Disconsolate too, he struggled with the dilemma she posed. At least there had been no trouble about getting the girl onto the train. After all, she did not have a ticket. But she was a native amongst all the whites. And a girl among all these men. He didn't need this responsibility. She was still wearing the cotton smock they had given her at the guesthouse, which helped her blend in. But deeper within he was shamed that he had abandoned her. Her forlorn stubbornness was a rebuke. She *was* his responsibility, he knew, and he was uncomfortable that she was on her own at the back of the train.

Bruns became chatty, happy to combat the monotony of the journey by telling Jack and those troopers who could be bothered to listen what he knew of the route ahead, and what he had learned in the six months he'd been in the country. The train's first stop would be at Usakos, then Karibib, Okahandja, and then Windhuk. Jack rolled the strange names round his mouth, wondering at the languages and cultures that lurked behind them. "There are a few settlers and farmers already established in these places", Bruns said. "The farms are very big – because there is so little rain, you need a lot of land for grazing. And there is so much wild game! You could spend your life hunting here!"

"Who are the Herero?" one of the older soldiers sitting alongside them asked. "They're the biggest tribe in the area you'll be stationed", Bruns said. "They are cattle herders who control most of the area where we are going. There is another black tribe to the north, the Ovambo, but I've not really had much to do with them. They come down to work, and to me seem darker skinned.

"Around Windhuk and the south, you have the Nama. They are the fiercest people in Suidwes, the best organized militarily. They're excellent horsemen and get lots of arms and ammunition from South Africa. They're led by a *kaptein* – Hendrik Witbooi – and he keeps them unified. The Herero fight between themselves. That's our luck."

"Does anyone live around here?" Jack asked, gesturing at the flat expanse around them. "There are the Damara", said Bruns. "The Herero and Ovambo speak different languages, and the Nama have a click language you'll never understand. I'm told there are also Bushmen, small yellow people who live in the desert, but I've not seen any. There is lots of variety with the natives – like the types of buck that roam the plains."

The air grew hotter and drier – searing the nostrils. Conversation slacked off as they tried to cope with the heat and the fatigue it induced. They avoided looking outside – as much to escape the harsh light as the intimidating desolation. Slowly, after several hours of rattling around in the hard carriages, the few low clumps of twigs hugging the ash-brown earth grew into slightly bigger shrubs. Small, stunted acacias began to appear, and the sand took on a yellower tinge. "See the dark green line in the middle distance", Bruns asked rhetorically, pointing out of the window. "That's where you might find water. It's a dry riverbed and you will have to dig. The native trackers we use help us, but you will also find yourselves on your own. Nothing here is more important than water."

The heat intensified relentlessly. The mucous disappeared from Jack's nostrils and he breathed shallowly to protect his throat and lungs. Those sitting beside him dozed, or stared blankly out of the swaying carriages or at their boots, digesting the bleak reality of where they found themselves. The wooden seats were hard and uncomfortable.

"Where are you from?", a trooper sitting opposite Jack asked. He seemed about Jack's age. "Lithuania", Jack answered, "and you?" "Pomerania – Stettin -- we're almost neighbours", he said, with a smile that eased them into a quiet conversation.

"The Schutztruppen pay well, much better than the factories in Stettin", the trooper explained. He had signed up for three and half years. Bismarck, the Chancellor, had promised they would get help to buy farms when they got out. Besides which, it was his patriotic duty – his father had encouraged him and there had been a band and a big parade with crowds waving when they left the city. It was time they expanded Germany in Africa like the British had done, he said.

"I left because I *didn't* want to be in the army – the Czar's army", Jack said with irony. There was an awkward lull, but his stories about Cape Town, the trooper's curiosity, and their shared dreams of adventure and of making a fortune in this new territory carried them forward. "I plan to be a trader", Jack said. "I come from a family who are cobblers and harness makers, so I start with that, but I think Suidwes offers bigger opportunities."

A purple cone began to emerge across the flat plain to the northeast. Then after another hour of more laboured chugging a few mountains appeared, with streaks of white cloud like dabs of a brush against the blue canvas of the sky. To the south, a darker range emerged, Jack sensing from their shape and the shadows that there was a canyon at their base.

Nara calms as they progress, used to the heat and desolation, relieved at having made it onto the train with Jack. He could have pulled her off the cart, banished her at the station in front of everyone or told the Damara man to get rid of her. She'd been prepared for violence for being bold and confronting him. Her aunt had slapped her on occasion until she learned to anticipate her needs and avoid her dark moods. Piet would have thrashed her too, but her aunt had always intervened to stop him. Many of the men in the shacks behind Walvis were violent with their children. She did not sense violence in Jack. She lay back on the kaross spread out between suitcases and trunks, enjoying the rocking sensation of the train, the speed of their progress, and the smell of the smoke from the engine. Without realising it, she'd learned that she could be assertive, and that Jack could be confronted. Tired from the stress and lack of sleep from the night before, she dozed.

A screech of steel wheels against the track woke her and she sat watching the desert recede through the open canvas canopy. She was on her own for the first time since she had left the village behind Walvis, and she hummed childhood songs trying to match the rhythm of the train. For the time being she was happy in her own world. The cardboard box Jack had pushed at her was at her feet and she opened it. Inside was a tin rectangle. As she lifted it out and turned it over the shiny surface seemed to move, reflecting the canopy at the top of the cart. Intrigued she turned it towards herself. She knew instantly she was looking at herself. For the first time. She traced the lines of her face, the outline of her head, studied her eyes, then stood, holding onto the boxes to see her body. The receding horizon was reflected in the mirror –

showing where she had come from. She turned it round to see if it would show her where they were going. Confused, she turned around herself but only saw a reflection of the canvas at the front of the cart.

Eventually, the magic of self-discovery wore off and she took out her collection of playthings and arranged them on the scraped back of her jackal-skin jerkin.

She laid out the black and white porcupine quills, the ostrich eggshell pieces she had seen others fashion into bangles, seashells in rich stripes and colours, a pink flamingo feather. She unwrapped the delicate lizard skeleton she kept in a strip of sage seaweed.

And there were two tortoise shells – one in which she kept the *buchu*, the herbs her mother had taught her to collect to use as medicine and makeup. In the other, she kept a collection of coloured stones. Her grandmother had said these all came down from the mountains in the east as gifts to her. Some were tiger's eyes, dark brown with fine bright ochre stripes, others were malachite in vibrant shades of light and dark green; there were pale yellow and orange topaz stones, and a few cloudy pink and purple pieces of rose quartz. Then there were a few smaller ones, almost completely transparent, that she and her friends had found on the sand south of Walvis. And now there was the larger one she had found a few days earlier in the abalone on the beach. She held it up again, watching the strange light-pink and pale-yellow strands of colour it gave off against the late afternoon sky to the west.

Jack drew the canvas flap aside quietly so as not to startle her. The train had stopped at Usakos to refuel and take on water. Everyone had got out to relieve themselves and stretch their legs, but she had not emerged – he assumed she was being careful. A hawker was offering roasted corn and he bought some to give to her. She was asleep on the kaross, the mirror and her collection of playthings spread out at her feet. He squatted carefully so as not to wake her, and looked at the stones. He picked up a large semi-transparent one and realised he'd seen smaller examples before – in the rough hands of the old prospector who had first planted the idea of going to Suidwes several months before. He was probably holding a diamond.

Early 1900s   Buitengracht Street, Cape Town

A *tryer* (striver) you must be...

Less than a year after landing in Cape Town, Jack, then still Ya'akov in his own mind, was stocktaking in the back when one of the Malay assistants called him to the front counter. *"'n ou Jood soek na meneer Sonnenberg* - an old Jew is looking for Mr. Sonnenberg", he said, gesturing with his head.

The man was dressed as a Boer farmer – rough khaki clothing and a wide-brimmed hat. His hands and face were dark from the sun. *"Mayn nomen iz Rabinovits, ikh zukh far herr Sunnbernerg."*

Sonnenberg was one of the city's established importers, wholesalers, and ship chandlers. He'd arrived twenty-odd years previously from Germany. A jeweller by profession, he'd been drawn into trading by the opportunities thrown up by the port and the rapid expansion of the Cape colony under the British. His wife had flatly objected to his plans to move to the diamond or gold mines up country. They were a childless couple and had built a comfortable home on Tamboers Kloef overlooking the bay, from where she ran a rich social life in the city.

Although by now quite Anglicised, they, like most of their social circle, remained fairly observant and frequented Katz's – a kosher restaurant on the edge of District Six where Jack had landed his first job as a waiter. Sonnenberg had been looking for an assistant, and took to Jack because of his German and, compared to the other uncouth immigrants, relatively polished manners.

Rabinowitz introduced himself as a trader from the northern Cape and a returning customer. He had a list of supplies for his store in Steinkopf and while this was being put together, he and Jack browsed the latest imported goods. When they got to a locked glass cabinet of specialist tools Rabinowitz stopped and asked for it to be opened. What had drawn his attention was a hammer with a pick on one side instead of the usual carpenter's claw. He took it out and examined it closely, weighing it in his hand.

"Herr Rabinowitz!", Sonnenberg greeted him as he walked into the store, "how nice to see you! I already have one of those for you. Come upstairs to the office."

"Come sit with us, Ya'akov", Sonnenberg instructed, a bit like a father, "you can learn from Rabinowitz – he is the King of the Richtersfeld." He'd slipped into Yiddish to talk to Rabinowitz.

Sonnenberg produced another hammer – the head still wrapped in greaseproof paper. "This is a mineralogist's hammer, made in America. A mining house in Johannesburg ordered a few and I thought you would appreciate one."

"Well, this is what I have for you", said Rabinowitz, pulling out a few small leather pouches from the canvas bag he was carrying. "These are malachite, I think", he said as he tipped out the contents of one of the pouches. Some of the greenish stones had been roughly polished to show bright dark and light green surfaces.

Each pouch contained rocks of different colours, the two older men debating their names, Rabinowitz relaying where they came from – some he'd found himself, others he'd bought from the local peoples on his trips in the veld. His large hands were rough and scarred, but he lifted and proffered the stones with a delicacy that suggested their beauty, rarity and value in his eyes.

Sonnenberg pulled out a jeweller's loupe from the drawer of the teak desk and examined the stones closely in the light streaming in from the window above Buitengracht Street. He spent a lot of time on some bright red and some pink crystals and urged Jack to look at them with the loupe as well. "*Shenkeit vert wart auf dem tish* – beauty becomes value on this table", he explained cryptically.

Jack had never encountered gems before. Diamonds and gold were synonymous with South Africa, of course, but when he arrived, the flood of destitute refugees from the Boer War he encountered in Cape Town had dampened the vague curiosity he had about making his way to Kimberley or the Rand. Mineralogy and prospecting were new concepts for him, and he was swept along with the men's fascination with the stones.

Rabinowitz leaned back in the chair and looked out at the "tablecloth" of white cloud pouring over Devils Peak and Table Mountain framed in the large window, as Sonnenberg continued to examine the stones. "*Nu?*", he asked rhetorically when he'd finished. Jack thought he was asking for a price. But Rabinowitz got up and dug out another leather pouch out of his pocket. He dropped this on the table and sat back. Jack recognized the ritual of a trade underway as Sonnenberg laid out a sheet of white paper on his desk and then pulled the drawstring open and tipped out the contents.

The handful of rough diamonds was a disappointment in Jack's eyes. Most were quite small and did not appear clear at all. Five were larger – the size of his small fingernail. Sonnenberg separated these in a clump on the white paper sheet, and then dragged it to where the full sun caught the two piles of stones. Jack, hovering between bravado, scepticism, and curiosity, leaned forward and caught his breath as the little piles danced in the sunlight.

"The Oranje?" Sonnenberg asked, as he peered through the loupe at the largest of the stones. "Some are from that area", Rabinowitz answered. "Some I found myself and some I traded. That one I got from a Nama from Suidwes."

"Suidwes", Sonnenberg mused almost to himself, "anything there?"

"I've only been in the south", said Rabinowitz. "It's dry as the Richtersfeld. They say further north is very rich."

Jack was about to reach for the loupe to examine the stones for himself but Sonnenberg abruptly leaned forward and rolled them up into the paper cone and dropped them back into the pouch. "I mean minerals. But come, you can tell me what *chochmes*[18] you're holding back over lunch."

Their good humour when they returned revealed that their deal had been struck. Sonnenberg scratched off the cost of the prospector's hammer from the itemised bill of Rabinowitz's purchases that Jack had prepared in their absence. The goods were to be sent to the railway station on Monday morning when the trader was returning to Steinkopf. "Ya'akov, Mr Rabinowitz is coming for kiddush on Shabbat. You should come too."

After the kiddush, which for the Sonnenbergs was part tradition, part charity and part social display, Jack stood beside Rabinowitz at the top of the red brick steps leading down from Sonnenberg's house through the lush Cape garden his wife had established. "Ach, young man, I hope you appreciate the beauty of this place", he said, looking out at the mountains and the bay below them. They had arranged to walk back together to District Six where they were both lodging.

"I've lived in Steinkopf for maybe 12 years. That's where my family and my business are. I've learned to love the Richtersfeld. Now, maybe with the pretty stones I buy a farm there. But every year I try to come here, and I've promised my wife we will retire here."

They strolled passed the smart and beautifully maintained houses

---

[18] Wisdom

on Camp Street, and then the newly opened and luxurious Mount Nelson hotel. The wealth and obvious ease of life was stupendous. "Why not buy a house here? Why a life so far away and in a desert?", Jack asked.

The older man gestured at the houses around. "Many of these people are British or the original Dutch who already had money. Others are doctors or educated people who make money with their brains or with other people's money. Sonnenberg is a bit like that. When I arrived, Cape Town seemed already crowded and fortunes were being made in Kimberley. So, I set out for somewhere that seemed maybe similar."

They crossed Orange Street, where Coloured washerwomen sat with their wicker baskets on the low-whitewashed walls to receive or return laundry to their white customers. The tree-canopied avenue of the Company Gardens ran down to the centre of the city ahead of them.

It was early summer and balmy. The mild humidity of the surrounding oceans softened the stark white buildings and the dramatic sharpness of the city's permanent backdrop – the massive grey of Table Mountain against the vault of the plumbago sky. They ambled down the avenue of oaks planted by the Dutch hundreds of years before, and stopped to look at the building of the new shul, the synagogue where they had met Sonnenberg earlier.

Rabinowitz picked a lime green oak leaf off the spring growth, smelt it and sat down on a bench. "Ya'akov, you are older than my boys. I will tell you different from what I tell them. I say they need an education. If I can, I will send them down to Cape Town to learn and become more English. But to you I say, life here is too easy for someone like you. At your age you must grow. Yes, you can make a good life here. There are pretty women and you can also be a Jew easily", he said gesturing at the obviously grand synagogue taking its place unapologetically alongside the mother city's administrative buildings and major churches. "But Africa is so much opportunity. When you're young you must take it. There is so much we don't even know about. You must learn to recognize luck when it shows."

Jack listened but disagreed. Cape Town was beguiling. Yes, it was established and crowded now with immigrants like him and the refugees from the Boer War. But he did not feel desperate. He'd found work quite easily and he was optimistic that he could make his way here. Life here among all this beauty would be easy, it seemed. In fact, he already felt very at home in the city and he'd taken on Sonnenberg's admiration for the English.

Conversation in Yiddish allowed him to relax. Sonnenberg was not comfortable in the language and insisted on speaking English in the business. Occasionally they would speak German to be discreet. The tone and structure of conversation was always formal, reflecting the obvious hierarchy as well as a social striving – to be perceived as English. Careful phrasing crimped emotion and spontaneity. Both of them knew that Jack was there to learn as well as work for the firm. But the mentorship was to do with the business, not about life and its choices.

Rabinowitz's directness, his manner and the ease of their native tongue swept this aside. Maybe it was because he had children of his own, unlike Sonnenberg. He spoke slowly, peppering his descriptions of the vast arid area where he lived with Afrikaans and native words and phrases. He would look at Jack with a kind smile to listen or emphasize a point. But when he spoke of the Africa he knew beyond the Cape, he would look into the middle distance with a dreaminess that, despite his resistance, drew Jack.

"But life there seems very hard. If it's as desolate as you describe, why go there?"

"It's not only the diamonds that you saw, Yankele. Maybe they are there and they can make you wealthy. There is gold and ivory and other gems too. But there is so much more to this place, Africa. The people, the animals, the space – you can't imagine it from here. Yes, I know it sounds lonely, and I went there with a wife, at least.

"It's not for everyone – I admit that. But if I were you, I would look for a new place. Suidwes is like that. The Germans are just starting there, and you have German. That's a big advantage and you are young. You should be a *tryer* (striver), Ya'akov – only then can you go a long way; only then can you know yourself."

Karibib

A company of Schutztruppe sprawled around the station as they pulled in after the slow climb up the escarpment. Soon after Jack climbed down from the carriage, the stationmaster came up and told him to unload the wagon and his mules. The troops took precedence. He would send someone to help unload. The next train to Windhuk would be in four days. Maybe.

Karibib was little more than the railway station, itself just a single long room. A few more stone buildings, some homes with untidy gardens and one that looked like a general store. Some distance off, under scraggly light-green trees, there were a few round shacks covered in grass and skins.

It was early afternoon and the heat was intense. He squinted back along the train in the bright sunlight and saw Nara squatting in the shade of the station building alongside some women in long dresses and strange pointed hats. She was opposite the flatbed with the cart. He grunted approval to himself.

Some of the waiting troops helped unload the cart and then the mules – anxious to get their horses and gear aboard and get going. Jack turned to beckon to Nara to take the reins, but a small dark man in a ragged military field jacket came forward and led them down the ramp. "Let me help you, Mein Herr," he said. He said something in Nama to Nara and together they walked the animals to a trough under the water tower.

Jack bought some fodder at the store and asked whether he could trade in the area. The storeowner seemed reluctant to give any real information, offering instead to buy Jack's goods. He was probably seen as competition, he realized.

"*Bist du Nama?*", he asked the dark-skinned man as they spread fodder for the mules. "*Nein, ich bin Damara*", the man answered. Jack hesitated, not really knowing what "Damara" meant.

He waved vaguely towards the north when Jack asked him where he lived. "Near Omaruru. There are farmers and Herero villages there. You will be able to trade. I can help you get there."

Jack pondered waiting for four days in Karibib, doing nothing and with no guarantee that the train would be able to take them, or trying his luck with this man pointing to the scrubland in the north. He had only been spending money since his arrival and wanted to get out and trade. Windhuk remained the destination but he could try his luck in the meantime.

"How long it take?"

"Three or four days. My name is Doeseb." He had decided for Jack.

Together they inspannned the mules. The man loaded his few things and then walked ahead with a long stick and a skin water pouch slung over his shoulder, carefully skirting light-green trees that clustered around the crossing of the dry riverbed below the railway. From up close, Jack saw the vicious long white thorns. He started to take in the landscape to avoid the harsh glare of the white track – scraggly tufts of grass burnt brown and yellow, gaunt low bushes with narrow leaves, and sporadic thorny trees so low they hardly cast any shade. His uncle Itchke, a timber merchant, could never make a living here, he thought to himself, recalling the tall birches and conifers, cool dark forests and green fields around the *shtetl*, which even in the height of summer smelt of damp. Here, growth seemed arrested while the land and everything on it waited for rain. The thorns made it even more hostile.

With movement and his decision taken, his spirits had lifted. He'd handed the reins to the girl on the cart and walked alongside, happy to straighten out his body after the two days in the railway carriage. But now with the desolation surrounding him in the huge landscape, dull fear began to gnaw. He had no real idea where he was going, he had thrown in his lot with a dark stranger whom he did not know if he could trust, he didn't know if there was opportunity, water, or just trouble ahead.

"*|gáro!*", the girl said, just loud enough for the Damara man ahead to hear. She pointed across the low scrub. Jack could not see anything, but the man raised his hand in acknowledgement and brought the mules to a stop. She touched Jack's arm and pointed again, and now a slight movement almost a kilometre away caught his eye. A strange bulky silhouette with a long thin neck, long legs, and a tiny head that had turned to observe them.

"*Ein Vogel* - a bird", said Doeseb as he came back to the cart. "*Essen*", he said, moving his hand to his lips. He unrolled the kaross he had placed on the cart, and extracted a long flat blade with a bound wooden handle. He said something to the girl and together they walked across the veld towards what Jack now realized was an ostrich. He'd only seen drawings in books, and had no idea how they would hunt it. He gathered the mule's reins and watched them approach the strange bird, caught up in the excitement of his first hunt but uncomfortable as a mere bystander.

The bird began to extend its short black wings as they approached, and then ran off some distance. Nara continued towards where they had first seen it, while Doeseb made for the bird itself, raising his arms and the stick as he got closer to it. He picked up stones and hurled them at the bird, driving it further away from them. It grew more agitated, running to and fro, but seemed intimidated by the man, who also began shouting.

Nara ran forward and picked up something from the ground. She called out to Doeseb and they began to walk back, both keeping an eye on the large bird. As they approached, Jack could see she was carrying a huge white egg. He smiled at them, impressed and relieved but also abashed that he was not part of the success. "*Gut gemacht* - well done", he said, his earlier anxieties suspended at the prospect of fresh food and their reassuring skill in the veld.

They stopped in an open patch between larger bushes to camp for the night, falling into their roles without discussion. Jack saw to the mules, Nara gathered firewood, and Doeseb used the panga to chop off some of the thorny branches of the trees and bushes around them. These he dragged back and piled in a rough enclosure adjacent to the largest bush. Jack assumed this was for them, but Nara was building the fire outside the enclosure. Doeseb then led the mules into the enclosure. Suddenly Jack understood – the animals needed protection probably more than them. He dropped the feed he was carrying inside the *kraal*.

Nara was fascinated when he conjured a flame from a matchstick to light the fire. He gave her one to try herself. Sonnenberg knew that matches would be in demand, and he had brought a supply of matches as well as cigarettes to sell. They busied themselves preparing pap in a 3-legged cast iron *potjie* with salt and water, and the girl chipped an opening in the top of the large ostrich egg. She then stirred the contents with a stick and poured some of it into a pan that Doeseb placed alongside the pot, on coals he'd raked aside.

The birds in the bush around them became noisier as the day cooled. Some flitted in and out of hanging nests of yellow straw in the trees around them. Others swept between the trees, some of them with startlingly bright plumage that flashed in the sunlight as the sun sank. He followed the flight of one into the depths of a tree, and saw that its colouring enabled it to almost disappear as it folded its wings. His chest relaxed and his breathing eased as the myriad details of the life around them made him aware that he was part of the veld. The birds had sharply different calls– some melodious and some harsh. The more he looked or listened, the more varied and specific they became, and yet there was harmony too. Calmed yet intrigued, he was being stimulated in ways he'd never experienced before.

Nara used a branch to sweep the area around the fire and under the cart. "Scorpion", the Damara explained, as she carefully moved some of the larger rocks away. Jack looked at him blankly. "A poison sting", he said, making a pecking gesture with his finger.

"You speak German very well", Jack said. "How did you learn?"

"Working on the railway", Doeseb explained. "I came from my *kraal* to earn money and buy in the store."

Nara was relieved that they were talking. Jack's silence on the cart irked and worried her. It was more than the language gap between them – anxiety caused him to withdraw. Maybe he didn't want contact with her. She was a burden. Until they'd brought back the egg, she also felt he was incurious and aloof. But now he was quite animated talking to the Damara.

"Where are you from?" the man had asked her. She felt he was severe and disapproving. "The Kuiseb, by Walvis Baai." "What are you doing with the white man?" "My aunt told me to go with him", she answered, getting a grunt in response. After that he'd only told her to do things.

Casting around for something to do, she went and got her kaross and Jack's blanket roll and put them down on one side of the fire.

She'd also collected her pouch and was about to spread out its contents when Jack suddenly stood up, came across, and squatted down beside her. Quietly he said, "*Nein, Nara, nee*", switching from German to Afrikaans to emphasize his point. She put the pouch aside and began smoothing eggshell chips into little flat beads on a rock.

Dusk settled as a deepening aubergine mantle across the hills. The birds quietened as darkness stole into the trees. Doeseb said something to Nara and she poured water from a pouch over their hands and then washed her own. They ate with their right hands only, scooping up small wads of pap from the *potjie* and then the egg from the pan it had cooked in. He used a spoon.

After the meal the Damara built up the fire and placed a pile of branches close to it. He rolled out his kaross on the ground opposite them, and placed the long blade and his stick on the ground beside him.

Jack leaned back on his elbows enjoying the sense of well-being from a full stomach. He watched them as they sat by the fire talking softly – almost every word it seemed punctuated by a click, a hard consonant or a sonorous vowel. Nara's smooth deep ochre skin glowed with orange and pink tints in the dancing flames. Doeseb was furrowed and much darker, but his skin also reflected the firelight with a deep brown mahogany glow. Their limbs seemed longer than his – or at least their grace in movement made it appear that way. They squatted and curled and furled themselves with far greater ease than he. Their natural rootedness in the veld charmed him. The diversity of the plants, animals, smells and sounds he was encountering was entrancing. He was so much of an outsider, but felt content.

It grew cooler despite the heat from the fire and he covered himself in a blanket, lying back with his head cradled in his interlocked fingers. He listened to the music of their language and the soft crackle of the fire. Above him, at vast distance but startlingly clear, the Milky Way and other stars emerged as his eyes adjusted from the flickering firelight. He lay still, drunk on heightened senses, his mind expanding like the sky above – Africa above – Africa below. Exhilarated, contented, awed – he fell asleep.

Several hours later he wakes. Doeseb rolls out of his kaross and places more logs on the fire. Then a deep guttural series of grunts rolls out of the dark towards them, seemingly from a long way off. "Lion", Doeseb murmurs.

At first, Jack's reassured by the Damara's apparent calm. He's gone back to his kaross, content, it seems, to lie down. Jack lies awaiting the sound of the lion again – to hear if it's getting closer. Alert, on edge, he hears that the dark bush around him is alive. Birds flutter, insects click, and a large dark shape sweeps across the edge of the clearing, outlined against the starlit sky. A rustle in the bush draws his eyes into the dark. He senses more than sees a shape and then two yellow eyes turn towards him. Now terror pounds in his chest. A mule in the *kraal* stamps, then coughs.

Jack lies trying to calm himself and cope with his sense of inadequacy. He feels ignorant like a child and impotent in the way men need to be here in the veld. "*Danken got ikh hobn di Damara do* - thank God I have the Damara here. I should've taken out the pistol I have in the trunk. But could I trust him? Anyway, I'd be no good – I've hardly shot the damn thing."

The Point Man

After several weeks of training, Bessie was assigned to minor surveillance and backup missions in South Africa. Four months after joining he was part of a hit squad that killed ANC operatives in Lusaka. This was followed by a kidnapping in Mozambique. The pace and the pressure picked up, but Fourie held him back from his main mission in South West, letting him know he was being prepared, protected and tested.

He'd encountered many of the men he worked with before in the army and the security police. From them he soon learned that Fourie's sham companies were awash with government funding, with little accounting or supervision. Fourie and his fellow "directors" lived conspicuously high on the hog, with chauffeur-driven cars, expense-account meals and entertainment, holiday homes, international travel, and so on. They hardly bothered hiding this from the field operatives like Bessie, who assuaged their resentment by scamming and fleecing.

Occasionally he would act as a courier and bodyguard for Meitje, a beautiful former South African Airways air hostess who flew to Europe every few weeks, with a document case that was attached to his body with a Kevlar security leash. Over time he learned that these cases contained funds, bonds and other financial instruments, as well as secret government documents. Sometimes she was on a diplomatic passport, leaving him to fume as she unlocked the leash, took the case, and was whisked away in an embassy or foreign intelligence agency car, while he had to go through passport control and see to himself. She never waited for him. He was too intimidated by her icy good looks and personality to say anything. She became Fourie's personal secretary, and rumours were that occasionally she would let him sleep with her, but kept him at arm's length too. She knew too much to be intimidated – or so she thought.

Bessie still seethed from the insult of his last trip with her. At short notice he had been told to pack a bag and bring his passport to a room in the Sandton Sun hotel in Johannesburg. A man he vaguely knew from Military Intelligence took down the details of his passport, his courier's authorization and gun permit, and then wrapped the security leash of a document case around his left arm, secured it to his wrist with a bracelet, and told him he would be flying overnight to Tel Aviv. Meitje met them at the airport. The MI guy gave her the bracelet key and said they would be met at the airport by "Dani" – someone she apparently already knew. They travelled SAA business class and, as usual, sat separately.

On arrival the next morning, a dark young man was waiting for them as they disembarked. This was "Dani", and his black skull cap made Bessie feel uneasy as they traipsed behind him through corridors to a special immigration and customs counter. His Glock 17 and the travel documents were checked against a telex, and then the weapon was deposited in a flat safe deposit box and he was given a receipt.

A driver took them directly to a tall building that they entered from the underground parking. A sign behind the armed guards at the desk identified the building as the Israel Diamond Exchange. Dani escorted them through more security to an elevator and then up to an internal office with a one-way mirror. Meitje unlocked the bracelet and took the case. Another door was unlocked remotely, and she went through into another office without saying a word to him. Dani took Bessie back downstairs, gave him his card "in case you have any problems", and saw him into a taxi that took him to the Hilton Hotel. Bessie fumed at being so curtly dismissed, but consoled himself with realising that Dani could be a useful contact.

Bessie checked in and crashed after the overnight flight. He woke mid-afternoon, half-hoping he could persuade Meitje to have dinner. When he called her room, he was told she'd already checked out. Later Fourie ragged him that she'd flown on to Europe that afternoon to avoid travelling with him. Bessie turned crimson but consoled himself that he still had the courier's authorization that she usually demanded on their return. He'd also filched some blank forms while he was hanging about the office, in case he travelled on another passport under another name. A real James Bond! he thought to himself with a smirk.

All his life Bessie had struggled to hide the festering resentment at the base of his personality. His ugliness and his awkwardness were like his scars – exposed and never to be erased. He'd never had a girlfriend and had no close friends. The pressure of combat on the border had been replaced by the stress of clandestine life, and while raw violence had diminished, the yearning for another life increased. He began to lay his own plans for an exit.

Surreptitiously, or so he thought, he siphoned off cash and gathered information about the mechanics of smuggling funds abroad. On one of the courier trips to Switzerland he took a train across the border to Lichtenstein, where he opened a bank account. Swiss intelligence agents photographed him there and passed this back to their liaison with the South African National Intelligence Service (NIS).

Bessie had nursed the knowledge of the hoard of rough diamonds in the strongbox he'd filched from the shot-up vehicles in the thick bush in Angola. The potential value was enough to subdue his habitual boastfulness. He confided in no one – except for his mother, when he buried the strongbox under her headstone in the Keetmans cemetery. He had no life outside the army. He realised too that he had to put time and distance between himself and the incident. Although he now could travel and was feeling more confident abroad, he still had no idea how to turn the diamonds into cash.

The young Jew Dani Leviev worked with diamantaires with offices in Jo'burg, Tel Aviv, Antwerp, and New York, and was the contact he'd been waiting for. But Bessie knew to wait – he would only move when it was right.

Like many veterans of the border and the secret wars, he kept himself going on alcohol and dope when he didn't need to be sharp. On operations it was amphetamines, and increasingly coke, which exaggerated his tics and twitches. His bosses knew, but for the time being his viciousness and gullibility were an asset. "Plausible deniability" was at the root of the creation of the CCB, and Bessie's bizarre behaviour supplied that in buckets.

As the unrest in South West Africa mounted, and international pressure began to make a South African withdrawal inevitable, the CCB was tasked with doing everything it could to disrupt the process, and especially what looked like an inevitable electoral victory for SWAPO. Bessie was the point man.

She...

... rested in a fork of a large acacia. Under the leafy canopy in the late afternoon there was slight movement in the air that cooled her as she lay with her head propped up against the rough trunk. She would also have a better view of any other predators drawn by the scent of the small buck she had killed and drawn up into the tree. It was draped over another branch, blood dripping from the gaping abdomen where she had fed on the liver and other internal organs.

She was exhausted. Her pregnancy drove up her body temperature, and the demands and weight of the unborn cubs sapped her energy. She had missed prey several times over the past two days because she was heavy and slow. She needed to feed – birth was imminent and then she would have the cubs to nurse. A few hours before, hidden in the shadows, the little buck, thinking itself protected in a thicket, made a slight movement as it nibbled young leaves. She'd leapt instinctively, but had gashed her front paw on a thorn as she went in. Wounded and tired, she knew she was no match for hyenas or even a group of jackals, let alone the large male who had mated with her three months before and who shared the territory with her. His mere appearance would be enough to drive her off as he claimed her kill. Now she lay in the crook of the tree, resting, digesting, but vigilant, her leg stretched forward so that she could lick the wound periodically.

She heard the mules and the cart coming up the track between the *koppies*[19]. She dozed, only lifting her head when Jack steered the mules off the track and towards the large shady tree where he thought they would camp for the night. She licked the wound again with her pink tongue.

Nara saw the colour and the movement and pulled at Jack's arm on the reins. *"!kharub!"* – the glottal click of her warning carried across the clearing and the cat swivelled her head in their direction. Doeseb halted the mules and then looked at the tree, shifting the long stick he carried to his right hand. "Leopard", he said. "It has a kill in the tree. It will protect it."

Jack made out the spotted coat in the shadows up in the tree. Slightly above it he could see the head of a small antelope dangling down, its tiny horns outlined against the patch of blue sky behind. Adrenalin, curiosity, and the animal's implacable beauty drew him forward, but he sensed the tension in the others and pulled the mules around. They all looked back occasionally until the clearing disappeared.

They had been skirting a large barren mountain to the west as they moved north over the past few days. The veld was now denser and greener, with only a few isolated round grass huts with impoverished people. Jack had exchanged a bag of the salt collected in Walvis what now seemed an age ago for a few skins. They had slept on the skins the night before and were much

---

[19] Afrikaans – literally "little head" – a small hill typical of the southern African savanna.

warmer and more comfortable.

They'd replenished their water from a water hole in a riverbed by one of the huts. It was cloudy and gritty, and too meagre to wash. He felt grimy but realised that like the others he must smell of smoke from their campfires.

The scarcity of water was a constant concern, but there was now more grass and the trees were greener, enabling them to outspan the team and allow them to graze until dusk when they were driven into the makeshift *kraal* they built every night.

But even if water was scarce, animals were abundant. Warthogs, similar to the wild boar he knew from the forests at home, trotted across the clearings around them, the little piglets scurrying after their mother, who would turn and stare at the cart and mules, the long, curved tusks giving her a haughty air. Meerkats rose up in alarm at their approach, staring and then scurrying into their burrows. Black baboons barked at them from the ravines or loped across the veld ahead of the cart. There were animals that he recognized, such as zebras, but it was the variety and beauty of the bucks that stunned him.

Doeseb had pointed out the first of these – "*Kudu*", a large, grey animal with stripes on its side and magnificent twirled horns. The animal was difficult to see in the deep thicket where it stood, its neck erect watching them, perfectly camouflaged against the shadows and colours of the bush.

"*Guareb*"[20] Nara had called another impressive animal – long straight horns with a distinctive vertical mark on its face. And there were scores of others, from the dainty miniature *dik diks* hiding in the undergrowth, and the "*kau'ip*"[21], with small arched horns, that grazed in herds and bounced away as they approached, their legs gathered elegantly and their white backsides flashing, to the huge Cape buffalo with heavy set horns across their brows.

With each day his perception of the veld deepened. It was as if his eyesight was improving, adjusting to the vast distances, to the brightness and to the nuances of colour, and his hearing to the insects, mammals, birds, predators and prey that surrounded them. He was becoming sensitized to movement in a way he'd never been before, experiencing this both as a thrill – as with the sudden flash of birds as they flew between trees – but also as a warning, when Nara had pointed to a brown snake slithering away from the path as they approached. Doeseb showed him the symmetrical indentations in the white sand and mimed the rhythmic transfer of its weight as it moved, opening Jack's eyes to the spoor animals, including men, left in the veld. He began to discern animal paths – little ribbons of white or yellow sand running into the undergrowth, and trails that bucks and zebras had pushed through tall bush wide enough for a man to follow.

Late one afternoon as they traversed a valley, he saw several large birds flying in a circle in the distance. "*!xani* - vultures", Doeseb called them. "There must be a big animal there – dead", he

---

[20] Guareb – Nara name for the Gemsbok (Afrikaans) or Oryx in English.
[21] Kau'ip" – Nama, Springbok in Afrikaans

explained. Jack knew he had not really understood, but left it at that.

"*Eine Waffe* - do you have a gun?", Doeseb asked him when a group of speckled grey guineafowl emerged from the grass ahead of them. He gestured with his arms as if holding a rifle to his shoulder. Jack was embarrassed that he had not taken out the revolver he'd brought from the locked chest in the cart before. He'd thought to do so when they set out from Karibib, but had not been sure if he could trust the Damara at the time. "They always want weapons", he remembered Cameron and the Germans complaining. He was also uncomfortable with the gun, having hardly fired it since he'd bought it on the Parade in Cape Town from a British soldier who'd stolen it from a dead Boer commando. It was an Austrian Gasser, which the soldier told him was suitable for Suidwes as it was in use by the Germans who supplied the Boers. The little he had tried had proved that he was a lousy shot.

Doeseb tried to hit a bird with stones a few times, but in the end, supper was some of the dried salted fish he'd brought from Walvis and more pap. Hunting for the pot was a skill he would have to learn.

Mid-morning on the fourth day Doeseb brought them to a stop where a footpath split off to the west, snaking away between boulders towards a large conical mountain. "*Meine hause*", he nodded towards the path, and then pointed at the mountain –

"Erongo". He pointed along the track they were on. "Omaruru – *zwei tage*. Herero." He lifted his two sacks off the back of the cart and walked away.

The Damara's sudden departure felt like a desertion. Jack realized how dependent he'd become on the thin, taciturn man so at ease in this environment. For a while panic fluttered at the top of his stomach, but walking ahead with the mules calmed him. When they stopped a while later, he unlocked the chest and took out the pistol, setting it out of sight behind the seat of the cart. "*Azoi, ner die zvei von ondz itzt*" - So, just the two of us now, he said, as he got up beside her. He smiled when she looked at him for an explanation. He'd regained his confidence.

Tusks

Two young boys squatting in the shade unfolded themselves smoothly as the cart approached. About the girl's age, they were wearing leather loincloths and carried the long sticks Jack had come to expect. He'd had to use the brake as they descended a hill into a valley, but now the mules, maybe sensing water, picked up the pace as the track flattened out alongside a wide, sandy riverbed. The trees along it were significantly taller, and as they'd come down Jack had seen trails of smoke indicating settlement. The youths spoke neither Nama nor German, and they walked ahead until another track branched off to run between clusters of grass *pondoks*[22] set among the trees. Jack followed them into the village.

The clusters were widely spaced from each other, and each seemed to consist of a large central hut with some satellite hovels and a *kraal* for animals. The clusters seemed to be arranged in a spiral at an elbow in the riverbed, gradually getting bigger and grander and then tapering off to more meagre dwellings in the distance. He assumed this reflected social status or a tactic of defence in case of attack[23]. Children would run up to see them and then scatter, dogs growled and barked. They passed tall women

---

[22] Pondok – round grass huts used as dwellings in Namibia and elsewhere in southern Africa

[23] See Fractal Patterns in Notes.

carrying piles of firewood or calabashes on their heads. Others, wearing skin skirts and aprons and pointed leather caps, would look at them as they passed but there was little obvious greeting. Eventually, next to the largest tree and the largest cluster, their two escorts motioned for them to wait in the shade and went to squat nearby.

Jack was nervous. He now wished he'd continued on the main path, but it was too late – he was in the middle of the village. Without Doeseb he felt vulnerable. The girl was completely withdrawn. A few old men and some women and children were moving about the *pondoks*. The *kraal*s seemed empty too and he assumed that the men must be out grazing the livestock. There was the odd call from a rooster, but the village dozed in the midday heat. Some of the houses had been covered with mud, but most were simple domes of grass, reed mats and animal skins. The cluster closest to them was surrounded by a wooden stockade that obscured what was happening inside. In front of it, under the canopy of a large tree, a ring of blackened stones defined a smouldering fireplace and few logs were set out as seats around this fire. Eventually, a young girl came with a large gourd and offered them water. Jack hopped down and took the tin bucket on the side of the cart to water the mules, but he kept them inspanned. Periodically the girl would return to feed the fire and refresh their water.

The afternoon heat sagged, the birds became active again, and Jack heard goats and lowing cattle approaching. A group of younger men arrived, carrying a large dead buck suspended by its legs from a stave. It was taken to a nearby tree and hung from a branch. Herders began to return with their animals, and one of them came across to them.

"Where have you come from", he asked in German.

"Walvis Bay."

"Ah, you're English. What are you selling?"

"Clothing, fabric, tools, beads, wire... I have rice, salt, sugar, spices and brandy – lots of things. What are you looking for?"

"You have rifles, bullets?"

"No."

The man turned away and went into the main compound opposite. Jack was confused by the absence of welcome and the apparent aloofness, but the brief conversation conveyed no threat. As they waited, he began to feel foolish and thought that if there was no movement soon they should move on, so they would not have to spend the night amongst these seemingly unwelcoming people and would have time to find an alternative camp before dark. Just then the man came back and said to Jack that he should unhitch the cart and show what he had to sell. He also said something to the two boys, who got up and moved the mules to a *kraal* nearby and brought them grass.

Nara moved off the cart where she'd been sitting to help Jack. He took the opportunity to put the pistol back into the locked chest, and for the first time set about laying out his stock on the skins they had traded for salt two days before. They were relieved to be moving. Based on his experience of hawking on the Parade in Cape Town he kept the boxes and cases closed, but displayed what they contained by placing examples set out on top.

The village was getting busier. Beautiful children with big white smiles had come to watch them and the buck that was now being butchered. Jack could see women milking cattle and goats in *kraal*s. A few older men began to gather under the tree, some of them accompanied by younger children who brought stools and benches for them to sit on.

Most were wearing just loincloths or short skirts drawn up in the front and the back. A few had shawls of cloth or animal pelts.

Two large stools were brought out of the compound, and a leopard skin was draped over one. The fire was built up as more people began to gather under the tree. Jack struggled not to stare at the women's breasts. The younger women were quite beautiful, he thought, their dark colour showing off their necklaces, bangles and anklets. No one approached the cart to see what was being offered, and Nara sat on the wagon box quite forlorn.

Finally, an older man wearing a military cap and a field jacket that had stitch marks and patches where the insignia had been removed came out and sat on the stool covered by the leopard skin. "Sit by the *ovahona* - the headman", the younger man said, pointing to a log nearby as the entire village seemed to gather now around the fire. Two other men emerged from the compound, carrying an older woman between them. She was wearing a full-length European-style dress and a matching two-pronged cap. As they placed her on the other stool, the pink- and yellow-scarred stumps of her legs emerged. Her feet had been hacked off.

Gourds were passed around. There was sour milk and then a warm, musty beer. Both were unpleasant. Conversation was difficult via the younger man's translation, the headman interested mainly if there were many "*truppe*" in Walvis Bay and in Swakopmund.

Eventually he and some of the other older men got up to see the goods. Jack's eyes were drawn to their long, intricately decorated walking sticks some of which had black etching like snakes twirled round the length. Others had knobs of dark wood on the top. He had taken out some metal tools, pots and pans but they did not show particular interest in these. On a hunch, he opened the chest and pulled out an axe that the chief immediately wanted to feel and weigh in his hand. They moved on to beads, needles, bolts of cloth, and sacks of foodstuff, and then the men moved back to their seats and logs, apparently to discuss things.

The older woman was now lifted from her chair and carried to view the goods. Jack lifted up the bolts of cloth for her to touch and examine more closely. The other older villagers then filed past, smiling and chattering amongst themselves.

One of the older men now got up and together with the translator pulled out the goods that they were interested in and placed them on the ground in front of the chief. This was the axe, two bolts of cloth, a tin of assorted beads and buttons, a roll of copper wire, and a sack of sugar. A leather pouch was produced, and some Reichsmarks counted out. Jack rejected this first offer. Although he needed the cash, he wanted to know what they had to trade. Animal pelts and skins were brought, but Jack wanted to test if there was more of value in the village, which seemed quite substantial. He pulled out a bottle of brandy and held it up. The chief motioned to add it to the pile. More internal discussion resulted in a young man being sent back into the compound to emerge with an elephant tusk. The silence that fell on the crowd when it appeared confirmed its value in their eyes too. But Jack reasoned there must be two tusks and said so to the translator. Jack went to the crate of women's clothing and held up an elaborate green-striped dress he'd bought from a hawker on the Parade. It had been cheap as part of it was burned with the mark of an iron, and this dampened the woman's enthusiasm.

Nara touched his wrist and held up the cardboard box with the mirror. He nodded, and she opened the box and held up the shiny metal surface. This did the trick and the second tusk appeared.

The atmosphere lightened and more gourds were passed around again. Jack wondered at the collective bargaining, but was busied with individuals wanting the buy things. None of them had cash, so the few items they agreed on were exchanged for animal skins and some decorated gourds. None of the men were willing to part with their decorated sticks. Jack and Nara packed everything up into the cart as the villagers began to wander back to their individual compounds.

"You will eat with us by the *Okoruwo*, the sacred fire", the translator said, pointing back to where the chief and some of the older men were sitting. The older lady was being carried back to the compound.

"The girl must also eat", Jack replied.

The man spoke to her briefly in Nama, something harsh in his tone.

Conversation was difficult because of the translation. The chief and the other men were again interested in how many Schutztruppe Jack had seen, did they have horses and many guns? What were the British planning in Walvis Baai? When Jack tried to respond via the translator they seemed to lose interest, and he was left to eat the meat and pap they'd served him.

After a while an older man came to sit by him and asked quietly – "You are English?" Jack nodded, chewing on a piece of tough boiled meat. "How come you speak German then?"

"I grew up speaking German in Europe, and then moved to England. From there I travelled to South Africa."

"Why do you have a Nama girl with you?"

"Her mother sent her with me. The girl would be safer away from where she was."

The man got up to get a sip of the brandy that was being passed round among the men. "Where did the ivory had come from", Jack asked when he sat down.

"Aaah, many days from here", he waved away off to the east "where the Mbanderu[24] are. There are not many elephants here now - white hunters have driven them away, and they are difficult to kill without guns. We went hunting there after the Rinderpest disease and the Germans killed our cattle."

Cameron had mentioned the Rinderpest, but Jack hadn't really understood what it was. "The cattle got sick", the man said. He became quieter and pensive looking into the fire. "They couldn't eat and they died. The bush animals died too. We were starving."

He sat holding his etched walking stick in one hand and stroking his cropped grey head with the other. The noise of the other men around the fire faded. The languid gestures of his long limbs, his wrinkled fingers, and the gold-pink of his palms in the firelight settled like a melancholy presence as he spoke. "We had to go and work for the Germans – on their farms and the buildings in Omaruru. But they didn't pay us, so we went hunting. While we were away the Nama came up to this place from the south and stole what we had. They chopped off the chief's wife's feet to steal her *ominhanga*[25]. She's my sister. That was a lot of the families' wealth. Then the Germans came and set a fence in the

---

[24] Mbanderu or Ovabanderu are a Herero speaking people living in eastern Namibia and western Botswana
[25] Copper bangles and iron beads worn around the ankles

land – they said to stop the sickness spreading. They shot the few cattle remaining. Now, the sickness is gone, but they keep the fence to take our land."

Nara noticed that he'd stopped talking. There was no German. … Maybe he'll come back to the cart now. He should stop asking them questions. … I've been here in the dark so long. He doesn't think about me. These Herero don't like me – I don't know why. "You'll be fed with the dogs", the man said. The Damara servant woman who brought me pap warned me to stay in the cart. "They have fought with the Nama", she said. She wasn't friendly either. The boys on the road were angry too – I could see in their eyes. The women also gave me hard looks. If they come to hurt me, he'll be no help. He's not strong. He's not from here. Doesn't even understand the threat of animals. He can't protect me. I must stay quiet inside here. If they don't see me, they'll forget about me. I want to go from this place when he comes. I want to be safe. Auntie looked after me, but she was hard. I was another child for them. She and Piet didn't want me. And Piet wanted to hurt me. Hnnnaaah – my jaw is tense like the jawbone of a skull; I can feel tears. I can't cry. I want to go away from here. I can see he doesn't want me. I'm a burden for him too. But he's not shouted or hit me. He won't want me if I cry. He could just leave me anywhere. Or sell me. I'm still a child. I don't want to be on my own. I can't be on my own. Better to keep moving, with him. Movement near the firelight now. Coming closer here. The shadow is too big to be him. That's not his walk. It's a man … coming for me…

"Nara", he murmured. She was too scared to make a sound. She shrank when he pulled back the flap of the canvas looking for her. The whites of her eyes flashed in the gloom. She'd made a narrow mattress of the animal skins laid out on top of the boxes and cases, and had been sitting with her legs up, the kaross drawn around her. She breathed out with relief, and stretched out her taut legs when she saw him. Their eyes connected deeply in the brief wash of light before he pulled the canvas flaps shut.

He gestured in the shadows to ask if she'd eaten and she nodded. The crackle of static electricity made her jump as he removed his serge jacket and trousers. He hung up his shirt on a wire hook, and leaned across her to quietly extract the revolver from the chest. He placed it above his head and lay down beside her. She had shifted to make room for him, and lifted the kaross so he too could cover himself. But he could not get comfortable on the uneven floor despite the layer of skins. In the dim light, close to each other, he gestured that he wanted to move to sleep under the cart. She shook her head, her teeth flashing white as she inhaled sharply. He nodded, acknowledging her fear. Hesitantly he touched her shoulder to reassure her and she turned away and shuddered, suppressing a whimper, holding back her tears and hugging herself. He put his arm across her, and she snuggled back against his chest. He held her gently until she calmed and fell asleep.

He lay on his side, the girl's presence against his chest warming and comforting him too, but his mind was racing. The glimpse of the scarred stumps of the chief's wife was horrifying. They had good reason to dislike the Nama and the girl had sensed their hostility. He felt stupid and naïve. The more he went over the day's events and the older Herero's story of the difficulties of their lives, of their fear and suspicion of the Germans and of the Nama, the more he felt he needed to be away from here. It all seemed so violent, so beyond what he could handle.

The pre-dawn rustling of the birds woke them. He gestured to the girl to stay inside and went to bring the mules from the *kraal* even before the goats and cattle had been milked. As soon as they were hitched, he put the gun behind the wagon box and softly urged them on.

May 1989   Keetmanshoop

The Schützenhous

Bessie returned with a smirk to the government-issue Cortina being fuelled at the pumps. As a deliberate insult he dropped a few pennies into the cupped hands of the *klonkie*[26] attendant who'd filled their tank, checked the water and oil, washed all the windows, the head and taillights, and brought them biltong and water from the store. He looked around to check that the second CCB team were hanging back outside the petrol station.

"I've found us a base", he said to his colleague in the passenger seat. "That old Boer manages a farm not far from here. Maybe an hour from the airport. He'll help us. He thinks I'm God 'cos I taught his son to shoot. He became a sniper and then joined the Recces... [27]. Fucker got himself killed in an ambush in Angola."

The two CCB teams checked in separately to the Schützenhous – a rambling array of basic rooms anchored to the original grey stone lodging and club built for the German Schutztruppe at the beginning of the century. This was where they were told the UN diplomat Martti Ahtisaari and his American minder were likely to stay when they visited the area. They needed to scout out the place before their targets arrived. Their mission was to give the two men a "good hiding" to intimidate them and the UN mission in South

---

[26] Pejorative Afrikaans term for (young) Coloured man.
[27] Reconnaissance battalions and other special forces deployed by the South West African Territorial Force (SWATF) along and across the Angolan border during the war. See Notes.

West. The CCB operatives were to appear as angry white farmers, inflicting enough trauma to halt or intimidate the UN mission and provide the SA government with an argument to delay their withdrawal from the territory. Bessie and his henchmen had to ostensibly disappear onto farms in the area. The intensity of Afrikaner opposition was a factor in the political calculations of the withdrawal process. It was vital that they were not identified, so as to provide the government with plausible deniability.

There was little other accommodation in the town. Bessie, familiar with it from his youth, had also selected it for its proximity to major roads including that to the airport, the large courtyard with shaded parking, and the fact that you could come and go without passing reception.

The men showered and rested after the long journey up from Cape Town. Later, at dusk, Bessie drove out on his own along the backstreets on the southern outskirts to his mother's grave in the old cemetery. An old Coloured gardener, sitting in the shadow of the tool shack sipping a bottle of cheap wine before he went home, noted the tall blonde man's presence.

Bessie was the "Suidwester" among the two CCB teams. The other three men had done stints up on the border as soldiers and security policemen, but he was the most familiar with the territory, and had been tasked with building up a network of agents and unwitting collaborators as quickly as possible. They were going to draw these from ex-soldiers, collaborators, and criminals in the Coloured and black townships and locations further north.

After supper, eaten separately in the hotel dining room, the men met in Bessie's room. Over brandy and Coke they reviewed their targets, how they were to be persuaded, or if necessary coerced to collaborate, and what the various cover stories would be. They had access to security police safe houses in Windhoek, but their commanders felt these might be compromised or too traceable. They had to find alternatives, as well as see to escape routes. This was where Keetmanshoop came into the picture, but they realized that regular use of the guesthouse would lead to recognition.

"The Steyn *plaas* (farm) is perfect", Bessie bragged. "The old man is an obedient Boer. His wife's too dim to know what's going on. The place is also close to another German-owned farm with an airstrip. In emergencies we can use that."

The men were used to Bessie's bluster. But so far he'd delivered, most of his missions had worked, and those that failed had not been disastrous. He seemed to have Viljoen's and Fourie's backing, and that meant lots of money. And Bessie was generous, dependent on them, and too lazy and dumb to check their expenses.

The next morning, they drove separately up to Windhoek and got to work.

Knuckle dusters for nothing

The following is from testimony before the South African Truth and Reconciliation Commission. It has been edited, redacted and adapted to suit the narrative, and refers to an attack planned for May or June of 1989 as preparations for independence were gearing up. The South African regime's desperation to thwart it spawned ever more extreme and bizarre clandestine operations. The CCB was at the forefront of these.

South African Truth and Reconciliation Commission

Special Report from the South African Broadcasting Corporation – SABC

AMNESTY HEARINGS

TYPE AMNESTY HEARINGS

STARTING DATE 28th September 2000

LOCATION CAPE TOWN

DAY 17

...

Mr ... for the Commission: Mr ... ,..., could you now tell us about the incident at the Keetmanshoop Hotel in 1989 with Mr Bezuidenhout?

Mr ...: Chairperson, one of the bosses in Section 7 of the CCB (Section 7 was the section working in South West Africa/Namibia which was the main focus at the time)

came to a hotel in Cape Town where we were chilling out. Bessie later told me that a "Red Operation" had been approved... He and I were to go to Keetmanshoop and give a UN diplomat who was in charge of the decommissioning weapons and was with UNTAG a "good hiding". Mr. Martti Ahtisaari was the ... person along with Cyril Ramaphosa visited the [weapon] stockpile locations. He wasn't to be killed but "had to be fucked up good and well." There might be a US diplomat with him, but he was to be left alone unless he interfered. We were given two registration numbers to watch for and were told that he did not travel with bodyguards but had a driver.

Bessie decided that we would use the steel handles of metal saws as these were very effective knuckle-dusters which also protected your hands. He'd seen them used in the brothels and clubs in Jo'burg and Pretoria. When he started running those kind of businesses – sometimes with CCB and later with DCC (Directorate of Covert Collection of SADF Military Intelligence) funds he issued these handles to the bouncers...

We stole a 4x4 in Clanwilliam on our way up from Cape Town and switched the number plates. When we recce'd [reconnoitred] the hotel we realised that we could not wait for him inside, so we waited in the car opposite the parking lot. We knew what he looked like from the media. But he did not show by midnight and we withdrew.

Chairperson: We will adjourn for lunch and continue hearing testimony at 230 p.m. ... [28]

---

[28] See: http://sabctrc.saha.org.za/index.htm [Accessed 11092019]

Willem heard of the impending sale of the Levin farm and also Bessie's overnight visit in the town at the weekend when he returned from the week at the De Beers facility in Lüderitz.

After completing his three-month training with De Beers Security, he'd let it be known that he would pay well for information that would help him with his job. As examples he mentioned some of the known Coloured gangsters, White car dealers in the town who could be involved with stolen property, and Portuguese traders who were always likely suspects in diamond smuggling. He'd also mentioned Bessie, whom he'd known as a delinquent youth in Keetmans. They had served up on the border at the same time, and he had heard that he was now involved in clandestine government work. In Angola, Bessie had been involved in an incident that could be relevant to Willem's new role of tracking IDB in the area. The dusk visit to a grave in the local cemetery may well have been innocuous grieving, but, maybe not. He tipped the old gardener generously.

+++

Viljoen met Fourie and Basson at the Delta G offices in Pretoria.

"Both the magistrate and the dominee in Keetmans have known Bezuidenhout and his family for a long time", he reported. "They got him into the army even though he was underage because he was facing prison for raping his Coloured half-sister. He's never been back to the farm. His father later did five years for robbery.

He's an alcoholic now living with a Coloured woman in Aroab - a dorpie (little village) on the edge of the Kalahari.

"The magistrate recalled that Bessie had attended Broederbond meetings when he was on leave from the army, but they rejected his application because he was 'poor stock' – I assume the father and the Coloured business.

"Both had heard reports that he was a ruthless soldier on the border.

"So far, he's done well. He's built up quite a wide network in Suidwes, although how reliable they are remains to be tested. He's been effective and his team don't complain. Frankly, we don't have anyone else with his local knowledge, or the time to find and build a local alternative."

"We need to keep looking", Fourie said. "There is too much riding on this to be dependent on one man of 'poor stock'."

"It's unlikely Viljoen will find anyone suitable", Basson said, once the man had left. "We need to get Bezuidenhout out straight after the operation and get him abroad. He'll break, that's certain – the question is when and where. You'll take care of him before that." Fourie nodded, understanding the implied order.

Early 1900s

Omaruru

A white man rode towards them out of a cloud of dust. He wanted them to hold back so as not to spook a herd of cattle he was driving along the track. Sometime later, the herd was coerced through a gate into a farm. The man waited as they rolled forward and invited them to spend the night.

A young Herero woman, clearly pregnant and wearing the peaked leather headdress they'd seen in the village, met them behind a simple house and pointed out a bathing stall, and a *kraal* for the mules.

Luger, the farmer, had no real interest in trade apart from a bottle of brandy and ammunition. "I'm close to the town and I don't have a woman to keep happy", he chuckled. "Omaruru is probably supplied enough because of the Eriksson store – they're a long-established Swedish trading business there. There's even a brewery, and that keeps the Schutztruppe happy. The Herero who live around here shop and trade in Omaruru too. I think you will find more opportunity in Otjiwarongo, which is 2-3 days further north and east. It is smaller and doesn't have anything like the Eriksson store."

The young woman served Jack and Luger dinner on the stoep beside the main room of the house. Nara would eat and stay with her, she said. As dusk deepened, swarms of insects drove the two men inside. The room was in semi-darkness as the lantern would attract insects, the farmer said. The dark shapes of the sparse furnishings around them were like inanimate presences that seemed to draw closer to hear the man describe his life. At first he was gay and enthusiastic, but as the night settled in and his consumption of brandy increased he grew melancholy.

"Life here is a great adventure and the prospects are stupendous", he said. "I started out as a prospector four years ago, but without success. Everyone is sure there is mineral wealth – just as there is in South Africa. Bismarck sent expert geologists to survey the land. But I found little. So, I joined the Schutztruppe under Kurt von Francois. He based himself in this area. It was the best introduction to Suidwes I could have hoped for." As tough as the military service had been, he became sentimental recalling the camaraderie. He spoke sufficient Otjiherero to get along with the local people.

"They are really primitive and lazy. They steal at the first opportunity – from us, from each other, from the Nama. If it were not for us there would be constant war. We should treat them like they treat the Damara – like slaves. Some of their leaders – like Zeraua, who lives near Omaruru, or Mahareru near Okahandja - are more impressive, but they are very resistant to our presence. Once they are dressed in western clothes, especially uniforms, they become arrogant. It's strange – I don't know what it is about uniforms that makes them become that way."

He took a sip of brandy. "In the end, the poverty caused by the

Rinderpest forced the Herero to sell land. I was able to buy this farm with support from the colonial administration. It's thirty thousand hectares and has water, although I'll have to dig and build dams. I'm stocking it with healthy cattle. I'm even bringing in stock from the northern Cape. The Herero resent this. Trouble is inevitable."

Jack remained quiet. He was tired from the tense night before in the Herero village and their early morning departure. He was also absorbing the man's monologue – the enthusiasm, the strangeness and adventure of it all, but also, as the evening wore on, the man's obvious loneliness, present but unacknowledged until Jack asked.

Luger leaned back in the armchair with a long sigh and held up the glass to capture the light in the amber liquid. "When I'm properly established, I will be able to fetch a wife from Germany." He nodded towards the kitchen – "until then, she is my companion – in bed and at table".

Jack hoped the darkness would conceal his flush of discomfort. He couldn't see the farmer's face so he might have been joking, but the young woman's pregnant belly made him doubt it. He thought of the child. The reality of sex across colour lines suddenly confronted him. He'd never really thought of the consequences before, only taking a voyeur's pleasure in seeing the semi-naked native women. Sex outside marriage was frowned upon in his milieu, but with a *shikse*[29] it was accepted, perhaps

---

[29] Yiddish – a gentile woman

almost expected. But there was real shame with a *mamzer*[30] child, and this would be with another race.

Fatigue, brandy, the farmer's pensive monotone – the mud-plastered wattle partition seemed to become a murky transparency. He imagined the girl and her round belly, and sensed Nara beside her. There was an infant too, but in the gloom, it was not clear who was holding it. Or so he convinced himself. The pressure in his chest and his dilated pupils forced him to shut off the premonition.

+++

Omaruru was laid out on the northern bank of a wide sandy riverbed. Large thorn trees obscured the town's few buildings as they approached from the west along a pale brown road that glared at them in the afternoon sun. Eventually some shacks appeared, and then they saw soldiers hitching a field gun to a span of mules outside a long, single-storey stone building attached to a tower – a fort and barracks. Others lounged in the shade of the long verandas, watching their arrival with indifference. Buildings were spaced far apart along the track, and on a slight rise to the north east there was a smooth ochre building that looked like a church.

The man running the Eriksson general store also suggested that he aim for Otjiwarongo. It was developing fast with the imminent completion of the railway line linking Swakop to Windhoek. It

---

[30] Yiddish - illegitimate child

would also link to Tsumeb in the north, where copper was being mined. It was to be the administrative centre for the area. His main business was trading with Angola, he said, apart from the settlers, the Herero and the troops. Jack exchanged some of the animal skins he'd traded for a long-bladed machete like Doeseb had used – a "panga", the man called it. The store was also the local postal bureau, and Jack decided that he would write to Sonnenberg and his family.

An elderly man with a square white beard waved at him from the stoep of a house by the church. He wore rough khaki clothing like the Boere, and as he stepped into the sun, he slapped a big canvas hat on his head. "I'm Hamm – the Rhenish missionary. Please join my wife and me for dinner. You are welcome to spend the night here."

He'd been in the area for more than 10 years, he said, as he led them round the back of the residence to unhitch the mules. Animated and enthusiastic, he showed them a small pond behind the church, fed by a spring, and gardens watered by sluices and canals laid out on the slope running down to the riverbed. The church itself was austere but cool and orderly. He spoke enough Otjiherero, he said, to preach to his congregation.

Jack opened up quickly to the reverend's friendliness, asking questions and happily relating his journey and rough plans so far. "We can definitely talk about that over dinner. There is much to do here and much to learn. It's a very exciting place." Nara too seemed relaxed, walking away to watch children playing around the *kraal* where they'd led the mules.

Hamm insisted they speak English at dinner. It was part of his daughter's curriculum. They were all neatly but simply dressed, the Reverend having changed into a dark naval-style jacket buttoned up to his neck that made him appear more severe.

The daughter's English was good despite the isolation of their lives, and Jack was aware again of his heavy Yiddish accent. Her mother seemed to follow the conversation, but did not participate. They too were keen on news from the Cape, and were curious about why he'd come to Suidwes. "People in Cape Town said that things are just starting here and there should be lots of opportunities. Also, speaking German may give me an advantage as the Cape is so controlled by the English. What do you think?"

"Where did you learn to speak German?"

"In Lithuania …"

"Ahhh, so you're a Jew then", Hamm exclaimed. "You read the Bible in Hebrew?" He hardly waited for Jack's confirmation. "Wunderbar – you can help me translate into Otjiherero. The Lutherbibel and St James sometimes are contradictory, and we like using Hebrew place names here if we can."

Jack looked at him blankly.

"Have you seen a map of Suidwes?", Hamm asked.

"Only very basic. It was mainly empty spaces, but it showed Walvis Bay, Swakopmund and Windhuk – little more. I looked in Cape Town, but couldn't find one."

"They hardly exist. I have Rehbock's book on Suidwes – it's the best there is. I will show you after dinner."

Hamm's wife spoke to him directly for the first time. "Who is the Nama girl?"

Jack repeated the story and then, on a whim, asked them what they thought he should do with her.

"She should be in a school, best where there are some of her people", Hamm said.

"Where are you going?"

"I understand that Otjiwarongo is developing. I thought to stop there on my way to Windhuk?"

"What do you plan to do?"

"I am a shoemaker, saddle maker and tailor. Eventually I want to trade."

"The Schutztruppe will have work for you tomorrow, I'm sure", Hamm said, "but you're right, Otjiwarongo is busier because the railway is being built there. There are mainly Herero there. There are Nama in Windhuk, and I will write to the mission there for the girl. I'll show you on the map."

For the first time Jack got a picture of the place he'd come to. Hamm's square finger traced his route from Cape Town to Walvis Bay, and from there to Swakopmund, Usakos, and to where they were now – Omaruru. Otjiwarongo was to the north east and Windhoek was directly south.

They sat down beside each other, the older man pulling a lantern closer and using a large magnifying glass to bring up the detail of the map.

"Here are some of the places", he said, pointing, "– Bethanien, Bersaba, Rehoboth, Gibeon … - I'm sure there are others."

Jack struggled at first with the German and English transliterations but eventually was able to help the Reverend with the Hebrew pronunciations of most of the place names. "Why are they using names from the Bible?", he asked.

"These places were started by Wesleyan and Rhenish missionaries", Hamm explained. "It helps in the work of bringing Christianity to the natives to make the Bible real. They are herders and shepherds like the Israelites. They relate to that more than the gospels."

Jack had had little exposure to Christianity, had never been into a church, and never spoken to a priest. He did not know what missionaries were or what they were doing in Africa. But he sensed that demonstrating his ignorance could be misinterpreted – and anyway, the map was fascinating.

Hamm unbuttoned his dark jacket, and his voice deepened and softened as he made the map come alive, drawing Jack in with stories, images, personalities. They spent the evening exploring the geography, the native peoples and their languages, the climate, the history reflected in the place names, rivers and water sources, animals, trade routes, conflicts – it went on and on. The reverend was not a hunter himself, but he was knowledgeable about the huge herds and how they migrated. He had seen elephants, but said that they had become wary of people because of the hunters, who were mainly English and Boer. He had met a German official in charge of mines, but got the impression that outside of Otavi in the north, where there was copper, the most pressing geological interest was for water.

Jack lay in bed, his mind flooded by Hamm's passion for the country and his animated descriptions. It was strange that a small coloured map could have such an impact. For the first time he felt engaged with where he was. Cape Town was large, beautiful, and exciting enough for him to think of making a life there. He'd felt this soon after arriving there and had already regarded it as "home". Suidwes, until this evening, was exploratory, an adventure. Sonnenberg's backing had been cautious, tentative and paternalistic. Jack had cushioned himself emotionally to go back if things did not work out or if it was too tough. Now he began to grasp the country's vastness, its emptiness, and the variety of life it supported. His imprecise plans had become more tangible and more urgent. This journey should come to an end, he thought. But at a deeper, vaguer level, a romantic engagement was forming.

Hamm's wife told him the next morning that she had sent Nara to a reading lesson a young Herero man was giving to a group of children behind the mission.

The outdoor classroom was rows of benches facing a blackboard fixed to a tree. He watched Nara following the class and tracing the letters on the palm of her hand. She sensed his gaze, looked round and started to get up. He motioned for her to sit, and then waved a bit awkwardly once he hitched the mules and drove off to the barracks to look for work.

The *Feldwebel,* the sergeant major in charge, had him set up on one of the stoeps of the fort, and he spent the morning repairing harnesses, saddles, boots, and jackets and trousers that had been ripped by the thorn bushes. Most of the troops were out on patrol and would get back the next day, the man said, encouraging him to stay.

Over lunch in the mess the Feldwebel confirmed that the military headquarters were being built in Otjiwarongo. "The railway is almost complete, and will link Swakopmund to Windhoek and Otavi. We will only keep a small post here. Also, the land there – especially to the north and the east, near a mountain called Waterberg, is ideal for settlement. I've got my eye on a well-watered area and as soon as I'm discharged, I'll apply for it."

"Is the land not taken?", Jack asked.

"The Herero don't farm; they come and go with the grass for their cattle", the Feldwebel replied. "Eventually we will get rid of them, one way or another."

Jack's hands ached from the piercing and stitching. It had been months since he'd used his tools, but he was pleased with the cash he'd been paid, and bought some supplies in the general store. A postal runner to Swakopmund was due in the next few days, he learned. The Feldwebel wrote him a letter of introduction to the district HQ at Otjiwarongo. He felt set for the next step.

That evening he wrote to Sonnenberg, in Yiddish as they'd agreed:

Dear Mr. Sonnenberg, I hope this finds you well. I am writing from a place called Omaruru. There is little here – some barracks for the German soldiers, a trading station run by a Swedish company that claims to control the trade with Angola, and a missionary church where I am now.

Suidwes is very challenging. It's hotter than anything I knew in Cape Town. Down by the coast is absolute desert – a wasteland of sand and flies. But as I've moved into the uplands it's greener and good for cattle. There are many wild animals. But it's very empty – a huge country with very few people.

The local people are very poor and primitive. They mainly trade skins and cattle, but I've managed to get two ivory tusks! They say there are more. What is the price for ivory? There are not very many Germans – soldiers, a few farmers and traders. But more are coming all the time. They seem very optimistic about their chances here. But their relationship with the natives is bad. More soldiers are bound to come.

So far, I've not heard of minerals apart from copper that they mine in the north.

The Germans ask about British plans all the time. They think the British will side with the natives when there will be war, which they see as inevitable. Maybe there is an opportunity here for military goods from the British after the war with the Boers? They seem to need everything, and most is imported via Walvis Bay and then by ox wagon. Now there is a railway to Windhuk and that will be faster. Walvis Bay is the best port.

Everyone wants guns and ammunition, but the Germans don't

allow the local tribes to get them. There is much smuggling of these goods, it seems – especially from the northern Cape.

Here is a list of what we could bring in: saddles, reins & bridles, boots, field clothing, harnesses, tents, wagons and parts for wagons, construction materials, fencing, poles, tools, pots, pans, plates, cutlery. It seems too that they need horses and mules. Basic foodstuffs like sugar, flour, rice, tea. Everyone wants brandy! The food is very bland so – spices! There are few women, but clothing and fabric are wanted. Also, water is very scarce so drilling tools. Every farm they establish will need.

The Germans will pay in Reich Marks. I know I have just got here and not yet arrived in Windhuk, but you asked for a quick report. There is definite interest – from the Schutztruppe and local merchants – for goods from Cape Town. Perhaps we should try with a small trial or samples of these type of goods? As you said – showing is better than promising. Also, if we can get guns and ammunition, I can ask for a permit. If I get a good response, I will better know quantities.

I'm told that it can take up to three months to get goods from the Cape via the ox wagon route and there is a lot of theft. Walvis is quicker and especially now there is a railway almost complete to Windhuk.

My plans are to move to a town called Otjiwarongo where the Germans are building a bigger town and a railway station. It is closer to where the ivory comes from. From there I will go to

Windhuk where you can write to me.

+++

About ten days after De Waal's visit Lenny Levin called the farm. Frederika answered brightly – she was expecting a call from their daughter in Windhoek. "Kobus, it's for you", she called out to her husband, and handed him the phone glumly. She blamed him that their lives had come to this. The call brought the rupture of their lives closer. She walked into the kitchen.

"*Meneer* Steyn", Lenny said, greeting him in Afrikaans but continuing in English. "De Waal told me about your conversation. I did not know about my grandfather's promise to you about living on the farm, but I know I told you that Jannie could be buried there in the orchard. I was at the funeral. I understand that you and your wife want to be close there. I want to discuss things with you both. I'd like to fly down next Monday. No, I can't stay, but thank you anyway. Can you fetch me at the airport – I think the plane should land at ten a.m.?"

Steyn got to the little airport nearly 30 minutes early. He sat in the empty passenger hall and went through the notes he'd made after discussing options with Frederika. Their fall-back was that if a new owner refused to let them stay, they would ask Levin to help them move to Windhoek where their daughter and grandchildren were, and have Jannie reinterred there. It was ugly and would be very upsetting, but it seemed that they were running out of options. So was the country, he thought. Who knew what was coming – perhaps a reality like Rhodesia. Maybe, if they had to move, they'd all be better off moving back to South Africa. He'd have to persuade his daughter and her husband who had a good job and pension in the police.

He flipped back in the notebook and saw Valerie's address, and wondered if the girl had received his letter. If she did not respond soon, he'd have to break open the trunk. That would upset Lena. He was thinking whether there was another way of contacting her when a small white plane landed and taxied to a stop in front of the hangar on the far side of the apron. Whoever was disembarking didn't want to be seen, he thought. Two cars and a white combi van pulled up beside the plane. He immediately recognized Bessie as the gangly man with bright straw-coloured hair who got out of one of the cars. Three blindfolded blacks in khaki overalls with their arms tied behind them were bundled off the plane and into the combi. Steyn twigged what he was seeing – there was a secret detention centre at the Hardap Dam near Mariental a few hours north. Rumours were that senior SWAPO operatives were held there. "Held" was a euphemism for brutal interrogation – especially if the likes of Bessie were involved.

The combi pulled away and Bessie drove across to the passenger hall. "*Môre meneer* – I thought it was your car parked outside", he said, as he walked in with some other men. "*Meneer* Steyn, meet my bosses – Brigadier-General Fourie and Colonel Viljoen", he said, using their rank to impress – which it did. Bessie had puffed himself up, his height exaggerating his jerky movements. Steyn, as always, became deferential, irritating himself. Fourie, dressed in civvies was curt, almost unpleasant: "Bessie tells me you have a farm nearby here? He says you know the area well and can be trusted." He took Steyn's silence as a confirmation – the tongue-tied behaviour of a *plaas japie,* a farm boy, Fourie thought. They moved to a quieter spot on the side of the hall as other people entered. "You know things are difficult for us at the moment in Suidwes. We need our people to help us do what's necessary. We may use your farm." Bessie mumbled something clumsily to Fourie about Jannie falling in Angola, and Fourie trotted out a platitude and turned back towards the waiting vehicles.

Steyn seethed – more at his own passive acquiescence than at Fourie's arrogance. The man hadn't even asked! Frederika would roast him, he knew, especially if it meant that Bessie would be around.

Lenny had landed in the meantime. "Good morning *Meneer* Steyn. Who are that lot?", he asked, nodding at Bessie and his bosses on their way across the apron. "*Regering* - government", Steyn replied. "One of them was a local man, who hasn't been around for a long time. He came across to say hello." They discussed the farm, rather than its future, on the drive back.

As soon as they rumbled across the cattle grid at the entrance, Lenny asked him to stop the car and got out. He seemed to sniff the air, and then walked a few metres down a track that ran away along the fence. Steyn watched him, sensing and hoping that any sentimentality about his father, grandfather and his youth spent here would work in their favour.

Frederika had changed while they were away. Steyn was relieved that she hadn't overdressed or gone all formal as she could to cover up her awkwardness. She made an effort to be friendly, although like Steyn she was by nature very reserved and tongue tied in English. Lenny by contrast was effusive – "How nice to see you, Mrs Steyn, the house is as lovely as ever." And then he did that thing that all the Levins did, right back to the old man – something so alien to the Boer - he walked into the kitchen to greet Lena with the affection of extended family.

After coffee and rusks on the stoep with Steyn, Lenny walked through the orchard to look down the escarpment to the vast valley below. A parched, dusty wilderness where little grew, but where they had done reasonably well from karakul. Nothing soft on the eyes. Shades of purple and orange and ochre, but all so stark. And so vast as his eyes ran out over miles of barren emptiness. "The Cape any day...", he muttered.

A dark green squiggle of tamarisks traced the dry riverbed that ran down to the road and then onto the Fish River canyon away in the distance. "A Nama woman told me to call this place Daweb, the Nama name for the tamarisk", Jack had said on this spot, trying to convey his passion for the place to his grandson. "It's unusual to have so many down here. They can extract salt from the brackish water to survive the droughts. But I wanted something of my own, so I called it Eshel, tamarisk in Hebrew. I changed the name to Daweb-Eshel after I bought it. Most people don't know or don't even ask why. The German missionaries gave Hebrew names to places and things."

Jack's enthusiasm for the place and for South West had not passed onto Lenny, but his recollection of it imposed a vague burden. For all his grandfather's passion for his business, and his love of the Cape, there was something that made Jack a man of this land. Although the heart of his business was in Windhoek, where he'd built a lovely home overlooking the city, Jack preferred to be here. That's probably what forged the relationship with Steyn. Jack came back constantly until he became too frail for the long journeys and stayed in Cape Town.

Sam, Lenny's father, was never a farmer. He'd married into the business, and since he was also a Levin was often assumed to be Jack's son – a mistake no one ever bothered to correct. Tamara, Lenny's mother, was not even considered in Jack's succession planning. She was raised in Cape Town to become a housewife and mother. For her and Sam the farms were exciting, romantic places to give their kids holidays and entertain family and friends. But never a place to live.

Sam's focus was on growing the business, preferably in South Africa proper. When he visited it was not to ride or hunt or talk about the sheep, but to look at the books. The actual running of the place bored him. Lenny was even more of a city boy – he'd gone to school and university in Cape Town, and his family lived there. He disparaged Windhoek, and commuted by plane for a few days when necessary. He relied on De Waal, as general manager, and a strong local team.

Like his father, Lenny saw the farm and businesses in South West as no more than assets. His focus was primarily on extracting the family's wealth from the increasing uncertainty of South Africa. Soon after his father's sudden death, Lenny had sold some property in Swakop to a German family who could pay partly in Europe. Long before the Afrikaner business elite and the Broederbond began their massive extraction of wealth abroad, Lenny, like other English and Jewish businessmen, quietly passed around the names of lawyers, accountants and bankers in London, Luxembourg, Geneva and the Channel Islands who specialised in wealth extraction and asset protection. He'd won their respect when, barely out of university, he came up with a scheme to build and pay for shipping containers in South Africa, lease them to the fruit packers and other exporters, and then transfer ownership to foreign shippers beyond the scrutiny of the South African authorities. The money generated was then truly "offshore". Lenny got a percentage of each such transfer. Lenny could talk about trusts, tax havens and "Export Rands" far more than the lifecycle of karakul sheep. His expertise and connections had changed the business from a South African-based trading house to a financing and investment group with significant international interests. The trust Jack and Sam had set up now held a property portfolio in London, which would ensure comfortable lives if and when they had to leave South Africa.

He walked across to the pile of stones where Jannie was buried.

Lenny was several years older, and although they were never close, they had spent a few holidays together on the farm. It was Jannie who taught him to shoot, crack a whip, and herd sheep on horseback. And while Lenny dodged conscription, Jannie had been raised to serve and volunteered for the paratroopers. He blossomed in the army and was rapidly commissioned as an officer.

At the funeral Lenny had stood out like a sore thumb among the other Afrikaans farming families, Jannie's friends and fellow soldiers. The funeral flashed before him – six soldiers and a young lieutenant, hard bodies and fragile eyes; four Bushmen trackers ostracized behind the crowd of whites, but probably closer to the boy they were burying than most. The salvo jolted through them all, Frederika withered between Steyn and her daughter. Lena, also behind the white mourners, crumpled. "Crazy", he thought recovering his studied detachment from anything to do with the army and the war on the border.

"Shall we discuss the sale then?", he said when he came back onto the stoep. Steyn was relieved that they were not dithering. Frederika sat stiffly beside him, and it was Lenny's turn for awkwardness, which he tried to cover by being formal and legalistic.

"I've spoken to the lawyers and agents. They advise that I can sell the farm with a tenant's lease that will enable you to live here for as long as you want. This could, of course, impact the price and there will probably be rent due, but we will absorb that." Lenny stopped suddenly, as Steyn remained blank faced. Maybe the English and the legal language were not getting through to him, he thought. But he could hardly be condescending to ask them or repeat things in a simpler form.

Steyn repeated what had been said to Frederika in Afrikaans as she looked down at her hands. Lenny was relieved that the translation was accurate, and she seemed to relax when it became clear that they could stay.

"The one thing we do need to discuss, unfortunately, is what happens when you pass on. If you want to be buried next to Jannie the new owners will have to agree, as the property will belong to them." The Steyns exchanged glances and remained silent. It was clear that they assumed they would be buried next to their son. "I'm sorry, but at the moment the lawyers don't have a solution for this. It would be unusual to put a future obligation like that into a sales contract for a property. They also advise against advertising it now as a pre-condition of sale. All I can say is that I will do my best when we find a buyer."

Steyn translated again. "There's no rush", Lenny said, trying to ease the shared awkwardness, "–I've asked the lawyers to think of an alternative, and none of this is happening tomorrow – …". He smiled weakly at his attempt to make a joke. "Maybe we can go for a drive round the farm after lunch?", he said, winding up.

Classic *boerekos* (Afrikaans farm food) for lunch – mutton bredie with yellow rice and raisins, curried vegetables followed by *melktert*, milk tart. The shared meal and the Windhoek lager relaxed them, and Lenny felt drowsy. He'd been up early to get the flight. Jack's room in the old farmhouse had been aired in anticipation.

Unfamiliar contemplation settles on Lenny as he enters the silent dark house. The strong familiar smell of the red floor polish brings with it pleasant associations of order and cleanliness – the odour of civilization in white South African homes. And now the old bedspread and the curtains. It smells, feels, like Jack's room, although there is nothing personal to see. He spent such long periods on his own here, Lenny thinks. Travel then was slow and expensive and *Bobbe*, his grandmother, lived in Windhoek and then later in Cape Town. No one else ever used this room even when the house was full of guests. What would he say about the sale? Jack must have found something here that I never did. But we all had good times here… sentimentality meanders and mingles with drowsiness.

Koo-kurrrr-it, – koo-kurrr-it, – koo-kurrr-it… – a dove's quavering trill breaks through his deep slumber. He lies still in the gloom, slowly registering the soft sounds of the radio in a room at the back of the house. The servant's quarters for both houses are here – probably Lena, resting like everyone else in the heat of the afternoon. A long languid path of memories is set off by the sounds and smells as he lies in the cool, comforting shadows.

Lenny isn't introspective, or at least hasn't been until now. He prides himself on his decisiveness. He's fit, if slightly overweight, thanks to regular squash, revels in his success, and is admired for his wealth, expertise, and contacts. He has lovely kids doing well at school. The flecks of silver at his temples in his otherwise thick black hair set off his healthy, youthful tan and good skin. His wife makes him miserable. Reverie splinters.

Vacantly he opens the drawers beside the bed. Nothing – spotlessly clean. Jack's old farm jacket hangs in the cupboard. Clean, with the creases at the elbows and shiny patches at the pockets that Lenny remembers. He pulls it towards himself hoping to recall the scent of the old man but there's nothing. The Australian bush hat that he wore here – on a shelf above. It's stained and soiled. Now a scent of old sweat and the Brylcreem Jack used on his thick grey hair. Something of me will pass too with this sale, he realises.

Across the corridor, Jack's office. Dad used it too, but he never made it his own. The photo on the wall is probably why – Sydney, Jack and *Bobbe* Sarah's first-born. A typical studio photo of the time – a handsome, smiling young man, Air Force cap at a jaunty angle and pilot's wings clearly visible. How proud they must have been of him. How devastated at his death somewhere near Tobruk as the allies advanced in 1942. Unlike Jannie - no grave for them to mourn by. This photo in the various family homes was the main, or as the generations passed, the only amulet of memory.

Lenny knows he shares the smile, the nose, and the eyes. Did that make his mother Tamara remember her brother Sydney? There was a big age gap between them. I never spoke to her about that. Never spoke to her about her feelings at all. Did she miss him, or maybe resent Jack's obvious preference for her older brother? He achieved everything Jack had strived for except running the business. There isn't a picture of her here. No pictures of anyone but Sydney. Tamara was never involved in anything about the business. It's the same with me, he realizes. Lynne was also never encouraged to be involved. She's never shown any interest anyway. She probably knows how Mom felt. They were close.

How strange that there are no other photos, he thinks – not even of *Bobbe* Sarah, Jack's wife. "You carry the Levin good looks", she used to say to him as a teenager. Maybe it wasn't only said with pride but also with sadness. Or maybe resentment…?

He rummages through the drawers, cabinets and cupboards, not really looking for anything but distracting himself from an unfamiliar gush of memory, sentiment, curiosity and remorse.

Lenny needs air, but on impulse he turns to the closed door in the corridor. This leads to the servant's quarters, "off-limits" in apartheid South Africa – especially to a white man.

The radio, now louder, comes from the room near the back entrance. Lena's room, he assumes. He taps softly at the door of a room adjacent to Jack's. Sparsely furnished with a springbok skin by the bed. The shutters are closed, and the room smells strongly of the floor polish, a smell of his childhood. Also, a faint smell of Sunlight soap. A kaross neatly arranged across the bottom of the bed is brittle with age when he picks it up. On the bedside table, a narrow rectangular black and white photo in a cheap frame. A Nama woman – one of the maids from the early days who lived here he thinks. Strange it has survived over all this time. He picks it up. She's looking at the camera directly, no discernible emotion. He realizes this is a section cut out of the original photo – the corner of a building to one side and a sliver of a jacket to the other. Truncated reality. A shadow of two people on the wall behind the woman, one a youth, one wearing a hat.

Strangely restless, he walks out of the house and is pulled towards the calm and the shade of the orchard. But the sun still beats down and he veers away to the Steyn's stoep. Memories of lying on a carpet on a cool concrete floor in a darkened room by his mother's feet well up as he mounts the steps and looks through the main window.

Steyn and Frederika sit opposite each other by the stone fireplace on the far side of the darkened lounge. They're like furniture – drooped silently in the dark angular farm chairs typical of these houses. The dog raises its eyes at his shadow by the window. Two colour photographs on the side table by her chair – one of Jannie in uniform, and one of their daughter, her husband and their two children. A sudden connection between Jannie's picture and Sydney in his pilot's cap on the wall of Jack's office in the house next door. He's intruded on a silent intimacy of decades of such afternoons between the couple – an intimacy etched deeper by their loss. Age, sorrow and pain – tapestries in the gloom of the room. Closeness too. Somehow, somewhere – he's envious.

Maybe it was like that for Jack too, alone in the big house only with the picture of Sydney as company. Where was *Bobbe*?

"*Kom binne, kom binne, Meneer* – come in, come in" – Steyn says, raising his hand. Frederika takes time to gather herself, but both rise. "Mrs De Souza called from your office", Steyn says, opening the screen door. "She says you should call the lawyer and call her too."

Lenny turns towards the phone in the corridor, and then turns back – "I wonder, do you mind if I stay here tonight? I'll get Bianca to change my flight to tomorrow morning."

"*Ag nee,* Lenny", Steyn says smiling. "*Dis goed, baie goed.*"

"*Meneer* Steyn, the lawyer asked if you've ever seen the original title deeds to the farm?", Lenny said, as he walked out onto the veranda where a tray of tea and rusks were waiting. Steyn shook his head. "I'll look through Jack's papers tonight, but if I can't find them maybe you could check with the local land registry."

They sat quietly side by side enjoying the end of afternoon calm. After a while, Steyn slowly reached for an air rifle propped against the wall beside him. Holding it only in his right hand, in a single motion he lifted it, pointed towards the orchard, and dropped a bird that had been feeding on the fruit. Lenny remembered this feat as a child, and how Jannie would practice doing the same. Steyn was in his mid-sixties, Lenny reminded himself.

A normal drive round the perimeter of the farm could have taken them six hours, but anticipating Lenny's visit, Steyn had the shepherds gather in a little valley between koppies where there were stock *kraal*s they used for inoculation, dipping and sorting. Cold air from the highlands to the east carried the sharp stink of the sheep as they approached in the bakkie, silhouetted against the orange sky. The sheepdogs set out for them with wild barking and howling, but were quietened by some whistles and their recognition of Steyn. Horses were tethered between troughs of fodder and water. The flocks were in separate *kraal*s.

The shepherds were Nama, dressed in farm-issued khaki overalls. Twelve, Lenny recalled from the salary roll. The farm was sub-divided into three grazing areas, each with its own flock, a senior shepherd who lived with his family in a two-room house, and assistants – usually their sons or other teenage boys if necessary. A separate crew headed by a foreman lived in better housing behind the main farmhouses, where the children of school-going age were also housed. Once or twice a week Steyn or the foreman would supply the outlying shepherds' stock posts with water and food.

Usually the sheep were brought into the *kraal*s at night to protect them from predators. But in lambing season the ewes preferred space, and it was a fraught period, with all the men scouring the veldt for the aborted foetuses or new-born lambs which had to be slaughtered within 48 hours before their curls opened too much. The lambs also brought the predators.

Lions were now extremely rare, but leopards and jackals were more persistent threats. Hyena and wild dogs usually hunted in packs, and if these appeared the farmers in the district would get together to eradicate them.

Most of the shepherds had gathered around a fire beside which three of them had squatted to slaughter an older ewe – considered part of their pay. They worked quickly, with long sharp knives, and the entire animal was butchered on the pelt – none of the carcass touching the ground. Nothing was wasted either – the intestines were cleaned out and prepared for stuffing, the liver, heart, kidneys and fatty tail and portions of meat made ready for grilling. The pelt was scraped clean and placed on the bakkie to be washed and cured back at the farmhouse. The offal the men didn't want was cut into pieces and thrown to the dogs who were lurking on the periphery, but they were deliberately kept hungry to be alert at night and protect the sheep. They'd be fed properly in the morning.

A braai had been offloaded from the bakkie and placed on top of a bed of coals they'd raked out of the fire. Steyn had brought boerewors and three-legged cast-iron *potjies* typical of veld cooking. Lena had prepared a bredie – a stew of carrots, onions potatoes and tomatoes. The men prepared a stiff mealie meal porridge they called <u>*stuiwepap.*</u>

They talked quietly amongst themselves as the meat grilled, Steyn part of their conversation in a mixture of Afrikaans and Nama with its distinctive clicks. One of the youngest boys walked around pouring water out of jug over their hands before they dipped their fingers into the pap, forming little flat cakes and using these to scoop up the bredie or eat with the meat. Prize pieces like the liver, kidneys and tail fat were sliced thinly and offered first to Lenny and Steyn, and then distributed by age. The men were supple, sitting, kneeling or squatting on the ground without discomfort. Lenny and Steyn sat on folding stools. Despite feeling so foreign he was happy to be among them – it took him back to his youth when he'd accompanied Jack on trips like this. Secretly he was relieved too that it was not lambing season – he'd never reconciled himself to the slaughter.

Coffee was set to brew in a tall, blackened koffie pot, and some musical instruments appeared: a three-string *ramkie* made from a petrol can and neckpiece of wood, a plywood tea box and broom handle as the finger board, with a piece of cord as the bass, a !*gamaklás* - a musical bow, and a steel penny whistle. As they were getting organized, one of the men got up and told a story or perhaps recited a poem – Steyn said it was about hunting – and Lenny could follow the miming of an ostrich, a springbok *spronking*, and a predator slinking along. The story was familiar, because the men called out or repeated key words, sometimes to the emphasis of the boy with the bass tapping the plywood box.

At first, the music was plaintive – Steyn explained that it was about longing for their homes and families while spending nights away like this – followed by melodies that sounded like hymns.

A flask of brandy Steyn pulled out was met with big smiles, and the beat picked up. Some of the men got up to dance, complicated shuffles and stamping with their feet, and more miming of animals and their lives as shepherds. Then came *kwela* – penny whistle street music, led by the penny whistle with which Lenny was familiar from his youth in Cape Town. Bands of young boys had earned pennies by entertaining white passers-by, but as apartheid was enforced they were banished from the street.

"You ever seen the Nama Stap, or Nama Step?", Steyn asked as they drove off later in the dark. "It's a courtship dance for couples. It is very fast and energetic, their feet are amazing – something very special. They are a happy people, these Nama, even though they have tough lives. Sometimes I think they know to be happier than us white people."

"Jannie gave these to me", he said, handing over a pair of military issue night vision glasses. It took a few minutes for Lenny's eyes to adjust as they drove along the farm track without headlights, but then, in a ghostly green glow, he saw gemsbok with their long straight horns and black elongated faces. A bit further he saw what he took to be jackals, but they were low and disappeared into the grass quickly. Then a group of kudus, instinctively hiding in the shadows of the trees and tall brush, their heads turned towards the threat posed by the bakkie. A large porcupine crossing the track raised its long quills as they approached, and then suddenly, beyond it, a flash of white with dull spots above – a long supple shape moving into the bush. Steyn had seen the movement too, and stopped. He took the night goggles and scoured the bush, and then switched on a searchlight on the roof of the truck and played the beam across the veld. There was another movement someway further off - "a leopard, a young mother", he told Lenny. "So far she hasn't gone for the sheep. The boys have found the remains of dik diks and dassies with her spoor, so I guess she's not too big, and ok with what she can deal with at the moment. But she'll have cubs and we'll have lambing. She won't move on – too much food here. I'll have to shoot her. Luckily, I have Jannie's scope. I'll have to get it fitted."

"You can fit these to a rifle?" Lenny asked, lifting the night goggles.

"*Nee man*", Steyn said, slightly irritated at the city boy's ignorance. "Jannie was a sniper. I'll show you by the house."

They drove on towards the farm buildings twinkling in the distance. Steyn stopped and pointed ahead. Silhouetted on the white scar of the track, lit only by the moonlight, a huge owl had turned its mesmerising eyes towards them. Slowly, unperturbed, it spread its massive wings, lifted off and flew directly above them with its prey dangling from its claws. "A snake", Steyn said. Lenny was awed and intimidated by the thrill and menace of the veld at night.

Lenny took the whisky Steyn had poured him back to the old farmhouse. He still needed to go through the papers in the office, but he was also tired after an emotionally intense day. He'd anticipated the uncomfortable conversation with the Steyns, and had wanted to keep the visit short for that reason. But the drive around the farm and the braai with the shepherds had been exhilarating. He would have liked to have shared that with his children, and regretted that he had not exposed them more to it. "Cyn hated the place and always dragged her heels", he reminded himself of his wife's reluctance. "But they've missed out."

The records and accounts were arranged chronologically and there was a file that seemed to cover the first ten years. But there were no records of purchase or anything that looked like a title deed. Despite his fatigue, his habitual interest in numbers kept him scanning the files.

He recognized Jack's scrawl and the occasional note in Yiddish, and then his father's neat handwriting and methodical records became dominant. Professional bookkeepers seemed to have taken over in the fifties, but notes and comments in Sam's more expansive script continued even when the accounts began being typed in the sixties. A tinge of embarrassment as he noticed that he had never made a mark on any of the recent accounts – all were those of Steyn, De Waal, and his group accountant in Windhoek or the auditors in Cape Town.

The thirties, fifties and sixties had been profitable and there were a few letters lauding "exceptional quality", and "outstanding years" from the Hudson's Bay Company when they acted as brokers. "NL" appeared as initials on the bottom of sorting and quality reports attached to shipment statements – all before

Lenny's involvement. The talk of "karakul fortunes" and "black diamonds" had never really applied to the farm, but he knew it was what Jack loved most.

In the early seventies, ownership was transferred to a holding company as part of Jack's trust settlement, which Sam had initiated as the family prepared to move wealth out of South Africa. There was a receipt from a local lawyer's office referring to "transfer of ownership of the farm Daweb-Eshel and 'subsidiary properties' in the settlement of the Levin Trust".

This was the pointer Lenny had been looking for. He had a vague recollection that Jack had acquired adjacent properties over the years and Lenny thought that perhaps, based on that, he could detach the farmhouse area to enable to the Steyns to continue to live there. The receipt was addressed to the trustees in St Helier, which gave him another avenue of inquiry.

Night sounds floated in – crickets, birds fluttering in the eaves, a kaffir dog barking in the distance, all strung together by the rhythmic creak of the windmill down by the dam. The fatigue enveloping him was now that of his youth during holidays spent here – the smell of the fire and the veld on his skin, taut from exposure to the sun. The windmill was the only unnatural sound, but it was so regular it belonged and was calming as he relived the day. "The assessor's valuation is disappointing", he acknowledged as if he was talking to Jack in the room opposite. "But selling is the right thing to do", he said, seeing him sad but resigned.

+++

Early 1900s   Omaruru to Otjiwarongo

Padloper[31]

A click of his tongue and soft words, and the mules pulled away from the mission in the early morning. The hills ahead still shaded them from the full force of the sun. Nara had clambered into the back of the cart with hardly a word and gone back to sleep wrapped in her kaross. Jack was relaxed, happy to be on his own and focused on his immediate plans.

Hamm's glum reservations after dinner about German attitudes to the native peoples hadn't really dampened Jack's enthusiasm for the adventure ahead. "I think conflict with the Herero, a war, is inevitable. The colonists want it. They see it as the quickest way to get the land. But there is also a different attitude. It used to be different – Eriksson the trader always had good relations with them, and I think I do too. Most of the (German) men are single. They treat Herero women like chattels. There are rapes – even of married women - and the authorities do nothing. There are more and more children from these relationships and that will cause trouble too.

"The trouble with the Herero is their internal squabbling. They

---

[31] Padloper (path walker in Afrikaans), a species of tortoise

have rival *ovahonas,* chiefs who make separate deals with the Germans. They drink and get into debt with the traders and then sell the land. They mistreat their own people and abuse the Damara too. So, they now work against the Herero with the Germans. The Herero are making themselves weak.

"The Nama have been Christian for a long time. They have good, unified leadership. They are excellent horsemen and soldiers, organized into commandos, and have good relationships with their kin on the other side of the Orange River. That way they get lots of arms and ammunition. But, luckily for the colonists, they have bad relations with the Herero. There have been many wars and cattle raids. If the blacks got together there would be no German settlement here."

Once the sun struck the canvas canopy, Nara came to sit next to him. He gave her a *brötchen* and the canvas water sack, stopped the mules, and hopped off the wagon to go and pee behind a tree.

He watched her stand up and stretch on the wagon, the light caramel colour of her forearms catching the sunlight, her small high breasts pressing against the fabric of the tunic. She clambered off the wagon and made for a bush nearby.

Her senses meandered about the green veld and cool air of the highlands which were still a novelty. Her anxiety about being abandoned or harmed was subsiding. He seemed to have a purpose now instead of the aimless wandering she'd felt before. So far, she'd been included.

A tuft of grass nearby trembled, and a tiny brown head pushed through as a small tortoise emerged. It lifted its head and opened its mouth, immediately smelling her. It tried to back into the grass, but she stepped forward and picked it up.

Jack had the revolver in his hand and was trying to learn to align his head to focus his right eye along his arm and the barrel, the sight, and a tree which was his pretend target. She had a slight smile as she approached and held out her fist. He stretched out his hand – and a tiny yellow-brown shell about the size of his thumb rested on his palm.

It was light and innocuous enough to quell the impulse to withdraw his hand. Brown and yellow geometric plates and openings for a head and limbs, but these were absent. Nara had similar shells in her collection he recalled.

"Gwa", she said, turning it over in his hand so he could see the hard plate protecting the underside. The lower belly was pale, and almost immediately the little legs emerged as it tried to right itself. It was too small to be of use, although she recalled that her aunt had told her that she would learn to do so when she was older. She placed it on the sand, and it poked out its beak-like head and waddled into the grass.

A few minutes into the journey she climbed into the back of the cart and emerged with the mirror he'd given her to replace the one they had traded with the Herero. Sitting close beside him she watched her reflection, and then his, and then together. This amused them both. He pointed at her eye in the reflection – *"Auge"*. She repeated the word, but not when he pointed at his own eye. *"Nase"*, he said, touching her nose and her reflection. This she understood. *"Ich bin Jack"*, pointing at himself, *"Du bist Nara"*.

They whiled away much of the morning with the language lesson. Jack took for granted she would learn German, and it didn't occur to him to ask her for Nama words. She learned quickly, mastering short sentences, and counting to ten by late morning. Talking, communicating made them happy instead of the long morose silences of the past few days.

A pool of shade under a large tree by the track and a throbbing headache drew Jack out of the scorching sun. He'd left his hat on the stoep outside the barracks, and his dark serge clothing made him overheat and dehydrate. He pulled into the shade and yanked out one of the cow skins they used to sleep on at night, laying it on the ground. He put the revolver by his side, tapped his head, took a long drink and then pointed to the mules asking her to water them. He lay down, covered his eyes with his forearm and fell asleep.

"Jeck", she whispered, touching his leg. He lay still, trying to focus on where he was, and then heard the sound of someone running. He sat up, alert, his hand reaching for the gun. She pointed down the track.

A short dark man was trotting up the track towards them. He was barefoot, seemingly indifferent to the heat of the sand. He was wearing very little, and looked incongruous with a round upright beret with a badge on his head. He carried a stick in one hand and a pole across his shoulder with bags suspended from each end.

"*Guten Tag, Mein Herr*", he said, setting down the pole and pouches. Jack could make out "*Deutsch Südwesafrika*" printed on the side of the canvas pouches. "*Bist du der Postläufer* - are you the post runner?", Jack asked.

He nodded and squatted down beside them, adjusting a panga in a sheath at his waist. Nara handed him their canvas water sack and he took a good sip and accepted a cold roast potato that they'd been given at the mission house. He munched on this slowly, asking her some questions in Nama which she answered almost mono-syllabically.

Jack, his head still throbbing, leaned across to read the label tied to the postbag: *Windhuk nach Swakopmund* in spindly Gothic script. This man, running barefoot through the country on his own, was going to carry his letter to Sonnenberg, he realised.

His journey would end at Usakos in 4 four days, where he would hand over the bag to the train. He carried some food and water in the other pouch, and was usually able to sleep in villages along the way. "Lions are the main danger", he said.

Jack felt humbled by the man's quiet resilience. He noticed that the pale soles of his feet were calloused but there were no cuts or scratches, and he breathed quite easily despite the effort of running.

After a few more minutes, he stood up. "Otjiwarongo, two days with wagon", he said pointing west. He adjusted the beret on his head, saluted, and trotted away towards Omaruru in the blasting sun.

Jack lay back, his eyes drifting about the fractal blue-green patterns of the leaves above him. The throbbing headache seemed to ease, and he slept again.

It was cooler when he awoke, and the shadows had lengthened. There was a pile of firewood, and the mules had been outspanned and hobbled and were grazing in the clearing. There was no sign of the girl.

A clutch of guinea fowl was pecking in the dust with quiet clucks on the far side of the clearing. He rose cautiously, picked up the revolver and moved quietly towards the speckled grey, black and white birds twirling about each other as if in a dance. Their constant movement and their plumage camouflaged them against the background, forcing him to draw on his senses in a way he'd never had to before. He calmed his breathing and focussed on a bird at right angles to his line of sight.

The report echoed across the veld. Birds screeched and wheeled away, the guinea fowl scattered with high-pitched shrieks into the brush, and the mules neighed in fear. His ears rang and he thought he heard a baboon bark.

The bullet had hurled the bird into the brush. He squatted beside it mesmerized by the massive wound in its side. He wasn't squeamish. At home he'd watched the *shochet*[32] slash the throats of chickens, goats, and once even a cow. But this was the first animal he had killed. He stroked its soft speckled breast with the back of his finger, wonder tinged with remorse. The colours, the details, the sheen, and the softness of the feathers, and the cleverness with which this intricate beauty helped it disappear in the underbrush elevated it to more than a chicken. To calm himself, he mumbled the prayer for *shechita* (ritual slaughtering).

Nara emerged from the bush a few steps away from him where the rest of the guinea fowl had disappeared. He caught his breath. He could have shot her. Concern turned to anger – she should not have gone anywhere without telling him.

She'd collected various tubers and onion-like vegetables, and she washed and sorted them as he gutted and cleaned the bird with his pocketknife. A wad of leaves she'd collected freshened his mouth when he chewed them.

Dusk settled around them like a dove folding its wings. They'd let the fire diminish so as not to scorch the bird, and the tubers she'd collected were in the embers. There were no dancing flames for the moment, but a soft orange glow reflected off the canvas of the wagon. The mules had had plenty of time to graze and were settled in the *kraal*. She hummed quietly as she arranged the

---

[32] Schochet – Yiddish – ritual slaughterer.

sleeping skins and the kaross and blankets, and then came to sit beside him while he turned the stick he was using as a spit.

The bird was delicious, and he was happy to have a meal without pap. "!*Nabas*", she called the tubers, which tasted like mushrooms. Content after the meal they stretched out alongside each other.

He was enjoying the massive display of stars, but could sense her becoming restless beside him. She turned towards him and pulled back on the edge of one of the skins. She busied herself but he chose to ignore her, not out of malice but because he did not know how to communicate.

She did. "Jeck", she said forcing him to turn towards her. She seemed to have created a game with various objects and squiggles she'd made and placed on a patch of sand she'd brushed smooth.

She began to name these: - a line with a large stone in the middle was "Walvisbaai", she said, using the Afrikaans pronunciation. On one side, she drew wavy lines and pointed to him. A wide line she'd drawn with her finger, running from Walvisbaai towards her, she called "Kuiseb". He'd heard the word but couldn't recall what it meant. She then placed a rock along the line near Walvisbaai and named that "Swakopmund". She drew two parallel lines from there towards herself, saying "tsu tsu tsu" – like the train! he realised.

It was a map! The wavy lines represented the sea – where he'd come from. The line running towards her was the dry riverbed where they'd met. The two parallel lines were the railway. He nodded and smiled.

Along the line for the Kuiseb close to her she placed a smaller rock that she named "*Gobabeb*". She waited for him to repeat this. When he did, she carefully broke some twigs into various lengths. She showed him one of the shorter ones and pointed to herself, then stuck it into the sand. The shortest one was smaller than her, and she stuck this alongside the other twig. Two slightly longer ones were stuck into the sand behind the other twigs, and she indicated that they were taller than her. Behind them she inserted the two other twigs. Six twigs in all, in three pairs. She drew a circle around them.

Nara then touched one of the taller twigs in the middle row and then mimed a scene where she jabbed her index finger into her side. She drooped her head and made a grimace and then removed the twig she had touched and put it behind her. She pointed to the circle and then mimed eating or food and shook her head.

She touched the smallest twig and removed it too. She pointed at the remaining group, again miming something to do with food or her belly. She removed the remaining twig in the middle row and the short one she had used to indicate herself and moved these out of the circle and along the line of the Kuiseb River. She used her fingers to indicate walking and then said to him "*vier*", holding up four fingers, and placed the two sticks by the stone she'd named "Gobabeb". She again mimed something to do with food or water, shaking her head, and started the walking movement again until she reached Walvisbaai, where she pushed the two twigs into the sand. She then took the longer twig, broke it in two and then removed it. She took a new twig, pointed it at him and showed that it came from the sea to Walvisbaai. From there, the twig "walked" to where the only remaining twig, which she indicated, was herself, was in the sand.

Before he could react, she took the two twigs and moved these from Walvisbaai to Swakopmund and then along the parallel lines of the railway, repeating the "tsu tsu tsu", then moved them away and placed them on the skin between them.

He smiled, admiring her ingenuity. She was telling him her journey. But her face was sad, her eyes damp. She looked at him and then back at the map. She retrieved the three sticks she'd removed and cradled them in her cupped hands, tears beginning to trickle down her cheeks. He thought he understood – she was mourning brothers or sisters she'd lost. She whimpered, trying to control her crying, her shoulders bent as she looked into her lap.

Jack felt his own eyes dampen. Confused and saddened by the story, he was also intimidated by a sense that it implied further responsibility. Her soft sobs and his lack of response were like a tautening dome of awkwardness around them. He got up, telling himself to build up the fire. But instead, he stepped across the little model in the sand, knelt beside her, and put his arms around her. Instead of comforting her, she turned into his shoulder and wailed. Younger than Lea, she seemed to know more of life than he did. He rocked her gently in his arms as her body was racked with sobs. Tears ran down his cheeks as his own loneliness and the longing for his distant family and lost childhood welled up. He cupped her small cropped head, holding her close, comforting himself too. He felt her tight curls in his hand and against his cheek.

Eventually she calmed and, when she lifted her head from his shoulder, her large dark eyes searched his face deeply for the first time. He wiped the tears from her cheeks and got up to stoke the fire. When he came to sit beside her again, she stretched out on the skin. He sat watching the dancing flames and glowing embers, his hand resting on her shoulder as she fell asleep. He pulled the kaross over her as the cold seeped in from the dark beyond the circle of firelight.

Cold, premonition, or a noise jerked him awake. The fire was down, the protective circle of light had shrunk to the immediate area of their sleeping skins. It was just light; he could see round the clearing, but grey mist hung in the low trees and brush. Smoke, dust, sleep, fatigue – his eyes strained to make sense of where he was. He got up to build up the fire and noticed that the grass on the far side of the clearing had been trampled flat. Two huge grey animals with massive low-hanging horns were watching him from inside a thicket opposite. He heard twigs and branches cracking and saw more movement behind them. The two bull-like animals turned slowly, pushed easily through the bush and disappeared.

May 1989 — Daweb-Eshel

Lenny wakes from intense and unfamiliar dreams. Jack and Sydney in the study opposite. Sydney is wearing the jaunty blue-grey Air Force cap, and he's suntanned, alive - not the black and white of the photograph. Jack is wearing the bush hat and his farm jacket. Lenny notices the weave of the fabric and the shiny patches where Jack always stuck his hands into the pockets. There's even a blue ink stain above the top pocket where he would keep a pen. He'd not noticed that when he looked at it earlier. Jack is old in the dream, the grandfather as Lenny remembers him. Then Sam, his father, comes into the room and Sydney disappears. His grandfather and father sit at opposite corners of the desk, not beside each other – more recognizable by their posture than by their dress or features. There is no intimacy between them. Sadness wells up as he notices that both are vague and grey. Something in him yearns for Sydney's youth and vigour. Now, an image of Steyn and Frederika sitting opposite each other in the afternoon and his envy of their intimacy. He knows it's not built only on their shared lives in this place but also on the pain of Jannie's loss.

He drifts off again, – images of the buck bathed in the pale green light of the night-vision glasses, then the flash of the leopard and the shepherds singing and prancing around the fire. And then the owl with its massive wings looking straight at him as it glided silently overhead.

Despite the disturbed sleep, he rose with first light and the soft stirrings on the farm. His last thought before falling asleep suddenly returned – he had to let his sister know that he was planning to sell the farm. She had always deferred to his role in running the business, but he had also always kept her informed. But deeper was an urge to share the emotional turmoil the past few hours had set off in him. Lynne was far more likely to listen and understand than his wife.

"Come, I'll show you the scope", Steyn reminded him as they finished breakfast, and took him into Jannie's room.

The most striking things on entering the simple room were the record sleeves of Afrikaans alternative rock bands that Lenny associated with the end conscription campaign.

This was the last place he expected to see Bernaldus Niemand's *"Hou My Vas Korporaal"* (Hold me Tight Corporal) or *"Horings op die Stoep"* (Horns on the Stoep) by Wildebeest which featured "Bossies", a song about shell-shocked soldiers returning from the Border War. [33]

Lynne, always on the fringe of the liberal left in South Africa, had played these records which were banned from the state broadcaster. She'd also cajoled him into donating to the anti-conscription campaign. They had to support the disaffection with the apartheid regime among young Afrikaners, she argued,

---

[33] See End Conscription Campaign in Notes

especially those who served up on the border. Her husband, a psychiatrist, said he was seeing increasing numbers of men who displayed what was now called Post Traumatic Stress Disorder, a term that came into use after the Vietnam War. Earlier it had been described as "shell shock". The Afrikaans version was "*bosbevok*" - bush wacked, or bush crazy.

There was a photograph of Jannie and a Bushman soldier on the bookshelf beside the record covers. Young, smiling faces but clearly exhausted. "That's !Kabbo, Jannie's tracker. They were like brothers", Steyn said. "That was taken in the field. Maybe four months before they were killed. They lived together, knew more about each other than I or Frederika know about our boy. Jannie would bring him here sometimes on holiday. They slept on the floor. Could not get used to beds."

Steyn picked up a long canvas case from the bookshelf and took out a telescopic site. "Jannie was a sniper. They say he was one of the best. This was the sight he used, it's American and also works at night. It doesn't fit my rifle. It needs special rails which I will order after I drop you at the airport."

They were on the road before seven a.m. A full trailer had jack-knifed on the road to Keetmanshoop and they waited in a small queue with the sun in their eyes until it was safe to pass. Lenny pulled out the Carrera Porsche sunglasses he'd bought when he and Cyn had been skiing in Zug the previous season. He thought to ask the Steyn about the record covers but the seven o'clock news came on: ...

The headline item was a defiant pledge from the Administrator-General, Louis Pienaar that South Africa would not abandon the Afrikaans-speaking people of South West Africa as "foreign forces" tried to take over everything they had built;

- SWAPO election rallies were the usual shambles which did not stop them tabling their unreasonable demands in the negotiations towards independence;

- SWAPO continued to smuggle arms from Angola under the noses of, if not with the connivance of the UN transition monitors – UNTAG;

- UNTAG continued to display ignorance of the ways of Africa by meeting sub-chiefs behind the backs of the traditional leaders of the various tribes;

- The preparations of the Transitional Government of National Unity (a South African dominated body set up to counter SWAPO) were progressing quietly and impressively.

This was followed by several minutes of rugby news.

Steyn broke the awkward silence after the news. "It's clear that SWAPO is going to take over. But I don't know if this is going to be like Rhodesia. I don't really know the Ovambo (the tribe behind SWAPO who lived in the north). Down here it's the Nama and the Basters in Rehoboth. They're all Afrikaans-speakers and we can get on. It depends on how aggressive the Ovambo want to be, but the Herero will also resist them if they go too far. These tribal rivalries don't just disappear with independence. It's like the Boere and the English – we still don't like each other."

Lenny's silence spurred the older man on. "I think we – the Afrikaners – made big mistakes. When the Nats (National Party) came to power, I thought South West would become the fifth province of South Africa. I was a young man then and I thought that our time had come and that our future was secure. I thought there would be a lot of development. What we mainly got was Boere working for the state and Apartheid. I must admit I thought Apartheid was the right way for this country. But in the end, all it did was turn the people and the world against us. But that was our choice. Who knows how much revenge they will want for what we've done? And the government continues to meddle – they just make things worse. It's not really about Suidwes now but about what will happen in South Africa, where the problems are bigger. We should let the transition happen now as best we can. We Boere can't ride on the blacks forever. Not here, not in South Africa."

They continued the journey largely in silence. Lenny shied away from politics and wasn't drawn to share his own opinions or press Steyn for more. He stared out at the parched scrubland, subconsciously picking at the hand stitched "LJL" monogram on the cuff of his tailored shirt. He'd been massively over-dressed for this visit, he realised. Jack's bush jacket hanging in the cupboard was now a subtle reprimand. The old Afrikaner's frankness and pessimism resonated with him and played on the sense of urgency that had been mounting since he got here. They parted well, Lenny with a large bag of biltong and an icebox of venison.

He watched the dusty little town drop away under the wing of the plane, relieved to be leaving the desert where he was not comfortable. What had captivated Jack, an immigrant from a shtetl in Europe? he wondered. The desert was so harsh and so alien, it had to be more than the sense of space and opportunity.

Lenny twiddled the gold Cross pen absent-mindedly, staring at the massive dry expanse stretched out below and all the way across to the Kalahari and Botswana. It challenged his vision. He imagined seeing the tiny white plane from below, a small, noisy speck in the vast blue sky. "The majesty of Africa", he mumbled, confused by the unfamiliar introspection that had swelled up during the visit. Steyn's unexpected monologue about the closing of the Afrikaner chapter in South West had somehow freed him. Drive and a sense of purpose that had been missing returned. "But he meant South Africa too", he mused as he opened his briefcase and began to jot down his "to do's" on a yellow legal pad.

+++

Redder earth, thicker bush as they plodded east and into the highlands. The trees were taller and in the open veld, sightings of game and wildlife became more frequent. For Jack, the variety seemed endless; for both of them, a sense of how busy the bush was. Something always twittering, moving, hunting, fleeing, resting, dying. But the pistol was useless for hunting.

Nara's tearful story had produced an intimacy and lightened their relationship. He'd tied a cloth around his head in place of the lost hat and she brought out the mirror to show him how funny he looked. He showed her how reflected sunlight startled a bird, and they laughed more easily as he continued his German lessons and she pointed out and named more birds and other things to see. He no longer ignored her, enjoying the slow rhythmic sway of their progress, drawn into the wonders of this new land as she chatted and pointed out things he did not see or know. She was less intimidated by his silences, more confident that she could get on with him. The odd herders minding their long-horned cattle and goats acknowledged them occasionally, but never approached.

Midday defeated them and they broke to eat and rest in the shade of a large tree. She woke him from his doze with a stalk of grass and pointed at a nearby bush. *"IIGâuagu"* (praying mantis), she said pointing. He couldn't see anything until she leaned across and touched a thin branch. A twig moved – the strangest creature he'd ever seen, stick-like and mottled brown like the bush. She pointed again and he saw a procession of tiny similar creatures moving down like ants towards the heart of the shrub.

"*IIGâuagu* brings rain" she tried to explain pointing at the grey clouds building up in the east. "It needs rain to release its young." He didn't understand but was lazy and remained sprawled on the cow hide they'd been resting on. Soon after there was a rumble of thunder and she pointed again at the insect, then the clouds and made a falling motion with her hands. "*Regen*", he acknowledged. The clouds were getting closer and she got up to put out the buckets and pans to collect what they could. He outspanned the mules and hobbled them under the tree.

The cracks of lightning and the thunder were more dramatic than he'd ever experienced. He was used to winter rainfall when it was cold. But this was tropical and the rain when it came was fierce.

The child-girl stripped off the tunic to play in the downpour. She beckoned for him to join her, but he couldn't overcome his shyness. He stood under the tree beside the mules watching her wash her tight curls and caramel body. Happy she wasn't shy in his presence, envious of her spontaneity, he recognised that she brought him joy. When the rain eased, he gave her a towel, inspanned the mules, and they set out through the puddles.

In the late afternoon four men on horses emerged from the bush. A German surveyor and his assistant, and two Herero escorts. The surveyor was working on the railway from Omaruru to Otjiwarongo. After a while the trail of the railway line became apparent – trees and scrub had been cleared, and culverts, embankments and bridges were being built. A gang of black labourers dressed in rags and carrying hand tools joined them and trudged along the track with them. Their foreman, a white man with a bright red face and neck, walked alongside the surveyor's assistant talking in Afrikaans until they reached the camp at the railhead.

The assistant helped them outspan the mules. He had light-coloured skin and spoke to Nara in Nama. "My mother is Nama", he explained, when Jack asked him how he knew the language. "My father was a Boer from the Cape. I'm from Rehoboth in the centre of the country," he told Jack. "We are called Basters. We speak at least those two languages and I learnt German at the mission."

The whites and the blacks in the works camp lived and ate apart. The whites were a rough crowd. The Germans were mainly young masons and railway navvies. The few Boere seemed to be foremen in charge of the black labour gangs, and were older. Jack was asked whether he had brandy, but he'd decided it would be wiser to hoard his store. Nara was the only woman in the camp, and she withdrew into the cart. The meal, a highly seasoned stew of game meat, was served with the obligatory pap. As the light faded the men gathered around fires. The surveyor and the construction manager invited him to sit with them but, as interested as he was, he was exhausted from the night before and didn't want to leave Nara on her own. He bedded down on a skin under the cart while she slept inside.

They followed the line to Otjiwarongo. Unlike the natural paths they had been using, the straight lines of the railway irrefutably carved up the countryside. Slowly it dawned on him that it wasn't only the scar of the steel tracks and cleared veld that unsettled and almost offended him. It was the power of the vision, the planning and capacity to organise cutting across the savanna. The railways were Germany's bayonet into the country. There were piles of stone dumped in places for building; crushed stone and heavy wooden sleepers for the tracks; and at one site, steel girders were in place for a water tank. He began to realize that construction materials were an immediate commercial opportunity.

Trading trinkets, clothing and small quantities of food for animal skins in the native villages was not going to produce wealth. Cattle markets were distant – at least until the railways functioned properly. Ivory intrigued him since it was coveted like the gemstones, and he would continue to search for it as the margins seemed so high. But in terms of cash, supplying the Germans seemed the best place to focus.

"Otjiwarongo" was proudly painted on the façade of an incomplete railway station with a steep roof and high windows. The fort was complete, but the Schutztruppe were housed in rows of small tents laid out behind it while the barracks were being built. Jack made for the mission building, which stood some distance from the general store and a few private homes with gardens. Behind them at some distance there were three distinct camps of round pondoks.

The missionary was blunt about Nara – the Herero would object and would bully her. For as long as Jack stayed in the town she could stay and help his Damara maid. Schooling would have to be in Windhoek, where they accepted Nama children. In the meantime, Jack could rent a room in the mission and stable the mules in their *kraal*.

The next morning Jack presented himself at the garrison. The commander, a major, was officious but the letters of introduction from Omaruru smoothed things. Soon he was set up outside the fort, and a heap of leather and clothing repairs began to build up over the day, not only from the soldiers but from farmers and the townspeople as well. He was also able to sell some dresses to the few women who lived in the town.

Mid-afternoon, a bedraggled patrol rode in and dismounted in front of the fort where he was sitting. A man was carried inside by two of his comrades. The troopers stood beside their horses, clearly exhausted. They were dirty and unshaven, and their exposed skin was pink and red from the sun. Some of their khaki trousers and jackets were torn, he assumed from the thorns of the bush. The garrison commander noticed this too as he was addressing them, and he pointed to Jack, telling them to bring their uniforms to him for repair before they gave them in to be washed. They would have a few days to rest, he said, before their next patrol.

"*Nebech* – poor fellows", Jack muttered as they waddled off, legs wide apart – he assumed from their days in the saddle. Others limped from blisters. They remained disciplined but they were shabby. Their officer broke away and walked over to Jack. It was Rolf, the young lieutenant from Swakopmund.

"It was brutal", he said of his new recruits' first patrol. "They were sent out too soon – and we did not have enough veterans with us. Me and the sergeant had to look after them like children. They fainted in the heat, did not drink properly, got the shits and would ride into the thorns almost deliberately, it seemed. A scorpion stung one. We also lost a wheel off the wagon."

He sat beside Jack in the shade, nursing a beaker of water Jack had given him. His dejection and exhaustion stilled conversation. He'd been so welcoming, informative, and enthusiastic when they'd first met. Now he seemed older. If this was the cost of one patrol, what would years be like, let alone war? Jack wondered.

Jack was setting himself up for work on the veranda the next morning when a tall young Herero sauntered across. "*Guten Morgen mein Herr*. Have you seen that wheel?", he asked in German, and pointed at a wheel on Jack's cart. Jack squatted beside him – a long split had opened in one of the spokes. "There is no one to fix it here", the young man said. "Best bind it with *riempies* (thongs). Gemsbok would be the best." Jack looked at him blankly, not understanding the term.

The young man pulled out one of the skins Jack had traded and sliced a few narrow strips of hide. then placed them in a bucket of water. "It gets tight when it dries", he explained. Together they shaped two flat splints and bound them to the spoke with the wet *riempies*. Jack offered to pay the young boy, who seemed keen to talk but was called away.

Later, at lunch in the officer's mess with Rolf, the young Herero, now wearing a white jacket was serving. He acknowledged Jack with a slight smile and nod of his head. "Pineas, one of Maharero's sons", Rolf said, "sent here to be civilised and learn German".

"The last wheelwright we had here drank himself into madness", he said, when Jack told him of the young Herero's help. "All these tradesmen are missing, and many of those that come can't take it here. Best look for a Boer trekker to fix it."

Nara was pleased when he told her that they would be leaving the next morning. The Damara maid had been reserved, spending all her spare time with a child she had with her. Seeing the classes, hearing the games of the Herero children, and the long periods on her own had frustrated her and she'd been waiting to move on.

"What's he going to do with you?", the woman asked, as they ate their evening meal.

Nara hesitated, anxiety suddenly rising with the women's question. She'd been avoiding the future, secure so far in the journey with him. There had been no one to talk to or anyone she felt she could confide in. "Maybe I'll stay with him. Work for him? I don't know."

"The lady (the missionary's wife) said that he wanted to put you in the mission school here. She said he couldn't because of the Herero. But maybe in Windhoek they will take you."

Nara associated "mission" with the classes she'd seen with the Herero children. Her worry eased with the idea of learning and spending time with other children. "He's been teaching me German on the journey", she said her voice husky with the tension in her throat.

"Why did your aunt send you with him? Did she sell you?"

"She said I would be safer with him. Piet, her husband was always angry with me."

The woman snorted – "Angry, or wanted you?"

Nara was quiet, confused by the question and also uncertain of the woman's harsh tone.

"Your aunt knew he would take you and throw her out."

They sat in silence, Nara confused by the woman's bitterness and by what she'd said. She didn't understand Piet "taking her" to replace her aunt.

"Has the white man not touched you?"

"He comforted me when I cried, when I told him about my family."

"That's all?"

Something mysterious and adult lurking behind the questions. Scared and curious, her mind played on "touch".

"Aaai", the woman part sighed, part groaned – "he will", she said flatly. "That's what men do. White men too. Even when it hurts. In the end they all need to put their seed into you. Just like a bull. When he does, and if you're ripe – that seed will fill you with child. The child will be half white and half Nama. There are some who think that is good – like the Basters, even some of the Herero. But your people, the Nama, and the Damara think there is shame in that. That's what happened to me. A Boer shamed me and left me with his child. If you have a child, a half-white child, you may not find a Nama man who will want you. Or you will have to live with the Basters."

Away in the darkness Nara could hear men singing. "Don't go out of the compound", the woman said, getting up. "It's the weekend and the men are back from work on the railway. They can hurt you."

+++

The tavern was busy. Many of the railway workers, including the surveyor and some of the Boer foremen, had come into town. There were officers and NCOs and a few townsmen. The garrison commander, sitting at the back of the room, called out across the room- "*Kommen Sie bitte her, Herr Levin.*"

Jack flushed, intimidated by the man's rank and by being singled out. He was relieved to see Rolf at another table. He approached, but stopped sharply when a large, spotted, cat-like animal by the commander's side hissed at him, baring long fangs. Black lines like dark tears ran down from its eyes to its mouth. A black servant in a light blue uniform stood behind the officer, holding the animal by a heavy chain.

Jack shared the animal's confusion and anxiety. Noise, clatter, chatter, scraping chairs, flushed pink faces and uniforms, eyes searching for domination, vulnerability and advantage.

"It's a cheetah – don't be intimidated, young Jew, we keep Oscar well fed", the officer said, pointing to a bowl of red meat on the table. Guffaws from the others at the table.

"My feldwebel says you're forsaking us?"

"I think I've finished my work here for now, yes. I need to get to Windhuk."

"There are great opportunities in Suidwes, but the Schutztruppe are going to expand here faster than anywhere else because of the Herero." Someone pulled a chair across for Jack to sit.

As before, they were all interested in news from the Cape and Walvis Baai. English intentions and possible designs on the territory were seen as a constant, imminent possibility.

"You met Pineas, I understand", the major said, referring to the young Herero who'd helped him. "You know he is the son of Maharero, the main Herero chief? He's been sent to us to become civilised. He's an impressive young man. Colonel Leutwein wants to send him to Berlin. He will see how powerful Germany is and that will have a calming influence on his kinsmen."

"He's already too arrogant", said one of the settlers. "They all are. And Leutwein is too easy-going on the Herero."

"A few years ago, his older brother went to the Berlin Colonial Show in Treptow Park and was a big hit", said the major. "Silly German women still send him love-letters, but we intercept them at the Post in Swakop or Windhuk so he does not know."[34]

The major got up and motioned to Jack to follow him outside to continue the conversation on the stoep.

"What are you looking to do here?"

"I've come to trade. I have a group of traders from Cape Town looking for new opportunities."

"We need supplies and traders, but we also need craftsmen. You saw we didn't have a wheelwright yesterday. We don't really have a carpenter either. The steelworkers are all busy with the railway. And – how shall I say it – they are not Germany's finest sons. Most of them come from the *Hinterhofe*[35] in some of the worst towns. They will not last here and for all the talk, they won't

---

[34] See The Kaiser's Holocaust – Germany's forgotten Genocide – David Olusoga and Casper W. Erichsen, Faber, London 1988, pp-92-95.
[35] Tenement slums in Germany's industrial cities built to cope with the rapid industrialization and urbanization at the end of 19th century. See Olusoga and Erichsen, P.86.

make farmers.... Do you think there are craftspeople available in Cape Town?"

"Maybe", Jack answered. "The Boer War depressed things. But now there is demand for these skills on the Reef and in Kimberley. I will ask, but it's a long way and people will look for a big inducement."

"We can pay well, and I can offer land for people who will stay", the major said. "Mining concessions are difficult but not impossible. But land can be made available through our office."

Jack joined Rolf and the surveyor, who were sharing a table with the Boere foremen. Most seemed to be struggling farmers who had come down from a northern town – Grootfontein – for work on the railway.

"I met Herero who said there was ivory to be had in the north and the east. Is that true?", Jack asked.

"A lot has been hunted out already by the British", one of the Boere replied. "The Mbanderu round the Waterberg trade with the Bayeyi people at Lake Ngami, and they have been bringing ivory to Okahandja and Windhoek. If you want to trade for that kind of thing, the Waterberg is a good area because there are also a lot of leopards there. I've heard that a leopard skin sells for more than £50 in Cape Town. The Waterberg is no more than a two-day trip east of here for you. You can usually see the red ridges from the road in the afternoon sun."

Jack pursed his lips. He wasn't ready for that journey yet. He wanted to get to Windhuk, get the girl off his hands, and get settled in the town. None of them could help him with the broken wheel spoke. "You should look for a man called Malan – he's a transport *ryer* – came through a few days ago on his way to Okahandja. Otherwise in Windhuk."

A soldier came in to report trouble with some of the Truppe at the Ovambo compound, and the men poured out of the tavern to see for themselves. There was shouting and rhythmic chanting and prancing from men with sticks and pangas outside the cluster of huts where the Ovambo lived. A handful of armed soldiers were drawn up in a line between them and the Schutztruppe tents. The other clusters, those of the Damara and the Herero, were quiet but there were men at the entrances.

The officers went up the troops and huddled for a while. They called over the rail manager, and then he and the major walked over towards the Ovambo.

"Drunk Truppe or navvies probably tried to get at the Ovambo women", Rolf muttered. "It happens all the time."

Five dishevelled Truppe were hauled out of the Ovambo enclosure and shoved towards the white ranks, and the crowd dispersed.

Ambiguity

A giant nest enveloped a tree by the roadside. The highest, almost leafless branches stuck out of the straw mass like skeletal fingers through a shroud. But it was raucously alive with scores of small yellow-brown birds flitting in and out of circular entrances. Jack stopped the cart short of the enormous colony of weaver birds, and the noise and constant activity enveloped them and broke the glumness of their journey.

He'd woken early, keen to get onto Windhuk, which was four or five days away. Nara had awoken moody and withdrawn, and had climbed inside the wagon to continue sleeping as soon as they got going. When the heat eventually drove her out, she avoided eye contact with him, looking out at the middle distance.

Nara had lain awake long after she left the Damara woman. She sensed the fatalism, bitterness and resentment she'd seen in her mother and her aunt. Her mother had been happy and energetic until her father died. Her aunt was obviously unhappy living with Piet. Memories of her grandparents were happy and seemed safe. Vaguely she sensed that she had to control her own life. And that involved a man. Unlike the Damara woman.

She had stared at the wall of the pondok. Away in the distance she could hear men singing. Irregular strips of the pale light outside silhouetted the poles of the hut above like a zebra's patterned hide her grandfather had shown her when in the Kuiseb.

"He has the thighs of a Gemsbok!", her aunt had said to a neighbour as a young man passed the hut. "And a mighty penis", the neighbour had responded jokingly. "He will make many healthy children." They spoke approvingly but Nara's mind played on the ambiguity of attraction, power, and the apparent inevitability of pain or abuse from men. She couldn't understand why. She had seen donkeys, goats and dogs mounting females, sometimes biting them to hold onto the female. She'd never really thought of her own penetration by a man. Subconsciously she squeezed her thighs together, constriction in her stomach too. She couldn't imagine her father wanting to cause her mother pain. On the other hand, she had seen and heard Piet being violent with her aunt. There were also nights when her mother would go – reluctantly– to the main hut where Piet was, and she would hear her moaning from inside. Her aunt would be in the children's hut with them. Sometimes she had a funny smile, but usually she would be angry. When her mother would return, Nara tried to curl up close – to comfort and be comforted. Her mother turned away mewling and groaning, trying to hide her sobbing.

Piet had been violent towards her too, especially when he was drunk or hung-over. She and the other children had learnt to avoid him. His face would be flushed, and he would curse and spit, and flex his legs and arms. He'd splay his fingers, and his eyes would shrink to little black holes. Then he'd suddenly explode, striking whoever was close. It would blow over and afterwards he'd sometimes cry or just disappear into the Kuiseb.

She was more often the focus of his rages than anyone else –

especially after her mother died. She realised that this was because she was not his child. But as her body began to change, the hostility of his glances changed to something confusing that she did not recognize. He'd flex his shoulders and expand his chest; he'd follow her with his eyes and his breathing became stiff and tense. It still conveyed threat, and she would drop her eyes and avoid him. Once he had grabbed her with a kind of playfulness, but her aunt had seen and stopped him with sharp words. He became sheepish, then angry, and slunk off. Her aunt turned on her – "don't provoke him. Know your place here. You're lucky I tolerate you. For your own good, don't be around him."

The men and older boys in the village also began looking at her differently, as more than a child or a curiosity orphan. The other girls would talk about this too. They'd learned to drop their eyes or at least not return the direct, almost predatory gaze of the men. There was something flattering about the attention but also a rush of confusion. Sometimes she thought that Jack too would look at her differently, as more than a child. But there was no sense of threat.

But he didn't appreciate her. He had not sold her or passed her onto people who would abuse her, as she'd feared at the beginning. He had fed her, taken her with him, and always checked on her when he'd come back at the end of the day. But he was going to get rid of her. She couldn't stop that. She ached to trust him. This made her angry as well as scared. She'd tried to be friendly, taught him things, had collected and prepared food, driven the cart, helped him load and unload goods. He didn't appreciate her, and he was useless in the veld. He would always need help because… he was white and he wasn't from here.

The dipping, swirling, chattering birds flitted about them, their high-pitched calls musical and constant. Life for them seemed all about movement. Even perched on the nest they were constantly pecking, arranging, weaving the straw into the massive collective structure. She'd seen weaverbird nests in the Kuiseb but never colonies of this size.

"*Eins, zvei, drei…*", she said, counting three birds sweeping past them, and then opening her hands at the multitude of the nest.

"*Eins, zvei, drei, … viele*", he said, with a slight pause to lift his hands from the reins and copy her gesture for many. He smiled.

"*Viele…*", she repeated. The Damara woman's bleak and embittered spell was broken.

As they moved south the land became greener, the grass higher and lusher. More herders in the bush, and more people on the track. Late afternoon, after a long gentle ascent of a hill, they could look out across the land to the south and east – a vast plain of light green trees and bushes that stretched uninterruptedly to the horizon. Odd columns of smoke suggested villages, usually beside the darker ribbons of vegetation along a river course. A long way to the east, white clouds had formed above a smudge of a ridge that marked the end of the plain. As they joggled along, the clouds climbed and darkened along the bottom. Then there were flashes of lightning, followed eventually by low, slow booms of thunder. Jack walked forward to calm the mules and watched as rain obscured the ridge like a curtain. A few minutes later the rain cloud moved south, and a double rainbow appeared above the ridge. Then a narrow band of sunlight broke through and the ridge glowed like burnished copper. The Waterberg he said to himself.

At the bottom of the hill a man was sitting by three large wagons. As Jack pulled up, he noticed one was loaded with yokes and wagon spares, including wheels. The man rose to lead the mules into the shade and then squatted by the wheel with the split spoke. "That will make the wheel skew. It won't last either."

"Meneer Malan?" Jack asked. "I should look for you, they said in Otjiwarongo." The man nodded. The supplies were for the copper mine at Tsumeb, he said, but he agreed to sell Jack a new wheel and repair his. "I have a workshop on the farm at Grootfontein."

Malan was taciturn as he worked, dismissing Jack's fumbled offers of help, and relying on the strength and experience of his black worker, who had helped them unload and then prop up the cart. While they were working, the teams of draft oxen came out of the bush where they'd been grazing, driven by two other men. Their rank smell, their size, deep lowing, and giant horns were reassuring, like a *kraal* around them.

Malan knew of the Germans' need for a wainwright in

Otjiwarongo. "I have my farm and my family, and I do two treks a year to the Cape. Each trip takes three months. That's enough", he explained as they ate later. "Maybe look in the Swellendam area in the Cape", he suggested.

Midday the next day Jack and Nara reached Okahandja. A Sunday, and numbingly quiet. Nothing moved in the fort, the barracks, or the few houses. The railway station was incomplete but wagons on a siding indicated that the line was operational.

There were four camps of pondoks around the town – for the Damara, the Herero, the Ovambo and, for the first time for Jack, a significant group of Nama. He'd begun to distinguish the racial differences between them, the Ovambo being the darkest, almost black, and the Nama with lighter and flatter features.

They camped by the railway station and pressed on to Windhuk the next morning.

Unburdening

Lenny trotted up the stairs to the offices of the glass-fronted Levin Group building off the Gobabis Road. It was his style to convey energy and drive, and after a brief conversation with Bianca he strode into his office and shut the door. She had dressed for his return, but recognised that he was preoccupied and skipped her normal banter and flirtatious teasing.

Lynne, Lenny's sister, was the one who maintained contact. On the rare occasions he did call, it was always in the evening and never at work. So she was worried when she was told he was waiting to speak to her. She took the call in the therapist's office in the clinic in Mitchells Plain on the Cape Flats, where she ran the family services.

"There's nothing wrong", he reassured her. "I've just come back from the farm and told Steyn that we're going to sell." She waited, knowing that this couldn't be the real reason for the call. They'd discussed this many time before. It was inevitable in the current circumstances in South West. She relied on him to do the best he could for them, as she always had.

He told her briefly of the Steyn's desire to remain on the farm, based on Jack's promise, and of the assessor's pessimistic valuation. Still, she sensed, this wasn't the reason for the call to her office during the day. A listener by nature, she'd trained as a psychotherapist and focussed on children and dysfunctional families. She recognized the tone of a man struggling with his emotions.

"You have a few minutes?", he asked, but continued before she could reply. "Steyn drove me round the farm, and we had this braai with the shepherds. They sang and danced and there were so many animals at night – including a leopard. I stayed the night – last night. I slept in Jack's room. They still have his jacket and hat in the cupboard. There's a picture of Sydney, the one in the air force cap, on the wall of Jack's office. There's nothing of the rest of the family, nothing at all. I had the weirdest dreams and I don't usually dream. Then this morning, Steyn took me into their son's room – you know the one who was killed in Angola. He was this super-soldier that everyone admired but he had anti-conscription record covers on the wall! The Steyns want to be buried next to him. They are very proud of him, of course, yet it seems he was opposed to the war. Very confusing…", he tapered off, suddenly aware that he'd been jabbering.

Lynne waited, sensing he was trying to make sense of an unleashing of feeling he was not used to. This was not the Lenny she knew – always rational and controlled. Always with a plan.

"Seeing the jacket and hat, and Sydney's photo, made me realise how much Jack was of the farm. Leaving will mean closing a door on all that history. Why he went there in the first place, why he loved it so much. I know it never was the main part of the business – as a business. But being there made me feel that, in a way, it made us who we are. Or maybe, who I am? All that space, all the animals and the people. At least, that's partly what I feel for myself. And once it's sold there's no one who can tell us what was."

"Steyn knew Jack for the longest time", she reminded him.

"Yes, that's true", he mused. "I don't know if Steyn can or would talk like that."

"Mom talked to me a lot", she said gently, trying to avoid offending him. "It could be useful to pool our memories before a sale happens."

"Memories are not a reason not to sell", he said with a sigh.

"Yes, but they make us think about ourselves in a different way," she said.

Normally he would've bristled at this kind of remark. She was older and he felt sometimes condescending as they had chosen to live quite different lives.

They arranged to meet with their kids on Saturday.

+++

"Cyn" was his nickname for her. Short for Cynthia obviously, but also a wry joke that she was his addiction and was bad for him. It had been a tempestuous courtship and marriage. Afterwards, he couldn't help comparing his call with her to the one he'd just had with Lynne: -

She'd been playing terrible tennis and had to take more lessons with 'Sean', the private coach; she had bickered with her sister (as usual, twice a week); her mother (daily) and some of her friends (they took it in turns). The children are 'cute', but the boy was 'adolescent' and the girl 'sulky'.

He pictured her as she babbled in their magnificent house in Constantia, probably looking in the mirror and pouting while she played with a blond curl. He'd thought the pout so cute when he met her, and it took him years to realise it was a technique to get her way in a family of narcissists. Her father was a compulsive gambler and embezzler, her mother was torn between the pretty little blond first-born and the younger sister who was partly crippled, and needed and received more attention. The mother survived by cloaking herself in guilt, which she projected onto anyone close.

He told her he'd arranged to meet Lynne on Saturday with the children.

"Good, I'm going shopping with Diane – she's such a dear friend although she can be tiresome with all her affairs. Don't be late on Saturday night, we have dinner with the Cohens – she's just redecorated their house, and 'everyone's' been invited to see it. She won't say how much they've spent. She always lets you know what good taste she has so let's see…"

She didn't ask about his trip to the farm.

The remainder of the week flashed by. His message to his managers was to accelerate their plans to train, advance and promote their "non-European" staff. Dates and arrangements were being brought forward, and the first round of training sessions was set for early October.

While Lenny was busy pushing things forward in Windhoek, Bessie was being put through two days of intense medical tests and evaluations at the Tygerberg Hospital in Belville. He'd seen blood in his stool for the past ten days and his stomach pain had grown more intense. The Security Police GP he'd seen had immediately referred him to a consultant, triggering an alert in the CCB chain of command.

The consultant had been brutally direct. "Meneer Bezuidenhout, the stomach ulcer is what is troubling you now. But you are showing signs of what is called an abdominal aortic aneurysm as well as liver disease. There are probably other problems lurking too, and you are obviously very stressed. You are a prime candidate for cancer, a breakdown, or both. You have to stop the alcohol and the drugs, and you should be looking for a less stressful life."

A while later the specialist called a Pretoria number and repeated his diagnosis. "Can he still function?", the doctor with Special Forces HQ at Speskop asked. "If he keeps clean now, yes. For a while. But he should be released soon – at this rate, stress will kill him or drive him into Valkenberg[36]. He's already *bosbevok* and it wouldn't take much to drive him over the edge."

+++

On the Friday, Lenny wakes as the plane banks to make its approach. False Bay below, flecked with white horses. Way to the south, tucked in behind the blue hump of the Constantiaberg, the kids and Cyn and that beautiful house. Now she wants to redo the garden, although it's just fine. She's always unhappy about something. Somehow, I've never felt at home there. I like the sea, maybe like Jack needed the desert.

A few days later, Bessie takes a sip from a small flask of Maalox as the plane takes off and looks across at the same view of Cape Town. Below him the sprawling, scraggly mess of the black township of Langa, and then the industrial areas surrounding the docks. As always, subconscious surprise at how harsh and brutal this part of Cape Town is, when if you lift your eyes only a little, there is the beauty of the lush green suburbs hugging the mountains and the coast. So comfortable and so alien – where the English live.

The plane banks right over the Northern Suburbs where Afrikaners like him live. Small, regular plots and standardised housing financed by the Nationalist Party government after they came to power in 1948. Below him he sees the Tygerberg

---

[36] Cape Town's main psychiatric hospital – often used as shorthand for mental illness in general.

Hospital where the consultant had told him how ill he was a few days before. His fear hurts like the ulcer.

"There's a lot of pressure", Viljoen said when they'd met in the parking lot at the airport. "No one knows what to expect from de Klerk. Seems the SADF command will remain as is – they're too strong for him to change directly anyway for now. That's good for us 'cos we come under Special Forces. But he's bringing in new people to the NIS (National Intelligence Service). That could mean a power struggle and big changes."

Bessie was unusually calm, and for the first time not intimidated by "Slang", as Viljoen was nicknamed. He'd been off drink and drugs for two weeks because of the ulcer. He had his gas under control and was shitting almost normally – no visible blood. The nervous tics had almost disappeared. But the specialist had spooked him. 'Cancer' and 'aneurysm' sounded like time bombs. He appeared to be listening, but Viljoen's jabbering gossip about the power struggles within the upper echelons of the army and nationalist party government seemed petty.

Viljoen had flown down to assess Bessie for himself. He'd agreed with Fourie that if Bessie was ok, they would hold him and his team back from the other operations in Suidwes. The gangly soldier seemed in control. He had also been meticulous in enforcing the "need to know" at the heart of clandestine practice. None of his bosses knew the identities of the accomplices he'd recruited in South West. The result was that Viljoen and the CCB were dependent on him now.

"Suidwes is still the priority. Your mission is the main thing. The preparations at Roodeplaat are not yet complete. You have to act just before the elections. You'll get the details then. You can't share any of this with the team. In the meantime, there's soft stuff to do like surveillance" but you let others take the lead. You keep your head low.

"Bessie, listen man – you have to keep off the drugs and the brandy. You look terrible and people are noticing and asking if you can still carry this off. Your mission is important. It has the attention of the top. You can't fuck it up. As soon as it's done, we'll send you abroad with a new passport. And don't forget the 'production bonus'. Fourie will reward you well."

Viljoen talked of "Roodeplaat", Bessie mused to himself as he looked out of the plane window. That means it's going to be something technical. The stuff that poisoned Jannie Steyn came from there. That will spook the team. But it means there should be a lot more cash in it for us. Slang is making a lot of money – dressed like some tarty businessman. There's a smell of panic now. Everyone has got their hand in the till and they're covering their arses. Time to contact that Jewish diamond guy - Dani. "I need to get the diamonds out of the country, Ma", he mumbled to his mother as he'd always done when he sought comfort. Better make sure it's only the *klonkies* who are exposed to whatever shit they're making.

Tsau! tsau! – the stars take your heart

The clouds built up every afternoon as they moved south. A fecund smell of damp grass persisted until mid-morning, and the air had a languid quality that reminded Jack of Cape Town. At dusk there was a cacophony of frogs and toads, and swarms of insects chased by birds and bats swept across the dying light.

Late in the afternoon of the third day out of Okahandja they crested a hill and saw an angular white building in the sunlight, set against dark green mountains to the south.

"Windhuk", Jack said pointing. She sensed, even shared his excitement and relief at the end of the journey. But anxiety and sadness gnawed inside her. She withdrew into herself, her humming and chatter suspended, her jaw tight.

Leah had gone silent too when he and his parents had told her that he was leaving. She moped and cried and followed him around for the few weeks before he left. She tried to persuade him to wait for her to be old enough to travel with him, but the imminent threat of being drafted to the Czar's army for twenty-five years stopped that. "You're leaving me to look after them as they grow old while you make a new life", she complained. In their experience in the *shtetl* that was likely to be true. He tried to avoid or ignore her sadness and reproach by keeping out of the house, prompting rebukes from his parents. She became sharp and nasty, criticising everything he did or said. She tried blackmail, threatening to tell their mother that he'd fondled her breasts while she pretended to sleep. Eventually, on the day before he left and at his mother's prompting, they went for a walk in the fields. Away from their parents they could embrace tightly, and he too could release the tears that had been building up. "You're abandoning me", she sobbed, even as he promised to send for her as soon as he could. That was almost two years ago, he recalled. Time, distance and the adventure of his new life were diminishing the ache of their absence, he admitted. He would have to find a way of explaining to Nara what was going to become of her.

They'd busied themselves with their evening routine, but where there had been companionship and even happiness before, there was now sadness. When he stole a look at her, her face was long and she seemed paler and slighter, her shoulders drooped.

He knew he had to speak to her despite the language gap.

"*Morgen in Windhuk...*", he started as they ate. She turned to look at him, her eyes large and moist and then looked away.

"*Morgen in Windhuk, wir werden eine Schule für dich finden*", he said, pointing at her. "*Schule*", she repeated, confirming, he hoped, that she understood what he meant. "*Nein morgen*", her head low - not tomorrow.

They lay beside each other that night, both sad and tense, as they were camping on their own. The night was much colder than they were used to, and darker as clouds obscured the stars and a partial moon. He'd built up the fire and stored a lot of wood nearby – partly to create the pool of light that would protect them, partly for heat, but also to cheer themselves up.

Dark shadows of drifting clouds moved across the cold stillness of the glittering sky, the chirp of invisible insects accentuating the deep background silence of the veld at night. The circle of light, the crackle of the fire, and the occasional snuffle of the mules was their tiny, shared world. Nara's loneliness, memories of Lea's loneliness and, he realised, his too, were painful and too sharp to ignore, sharp like the stars...

"Tsau", she said softly pointing at the stars.
"Tsau..."
... the stars take your heart
because the stars are saying: 'tsau! tsau!'
and the bushmen say the stars curse the eyes of the springbok
the stars say: 'tsau!' they say: 'tsau! tsau!'
they curse the eyes of the springbok
I grew up listening to the stars
The stars saying: 'tsau! and 'tsau!...[37]

Her grandfather's thin fingers slowly caressed her face and the curls on her head as he recited this to her so long ago. She lay in his lap looking at the stars. His smell, the pitch and rhythm of his

---

[37] After 'what the stars say', - /Han≠kass'o (~ 1870's) – a poet of the /Xam subgroup of Bushmen who have disappeared. From: "the stars say 'tsau', selected and adapted by Antjie Krog, Kwela Books, Cape Town 2004.

voice as he half sang, half spoke calmed her. She was missing her father. But she felt her grandfather's love. She knew his care.

She turned and lay on her side staring out at the dark bush through the spokes of the cart's wheels. Jack turned too, settled the kaross and blankets over both of them and put his arm across her shoulders.

As keen as they were to end their journey, they got going slowly the next morning. They'd been together for almost a month and the town ahead meant separation. Nara was petrified of being alone again. Jack, to his surprise, clung to his sense of responsibility for her. And to her companionship.

A skewed sign – Brakwater – pointed to a farmhouse they could see through a stand of trees and then the white building re-emerged, now much closer. Four towers and high stone walls of the fortress built by the first German commander Curt van Francois some ten years before. Small farms and vegetable plots became more numerous as they approached the small, spread-out town set among low scrubby hills.

+++

The fort was built on a low ridge that divided the town from north to south. To the east, it overlooked hot springs that fed garden plots established by the German settlers. To the west was a large round barren area – the Ausspannplatz, where the long ox wagon columns were able to turn and "outspan" at the end of their journeys from Walvis Bay, the Cape or from Angola. Wagons and carts were drawn up behind a few traders who sat under awnings, and herders were tending to animals in clusters and *kraal*s. Jack headed for a large water trough in the middle.

A cluster of small buildings and a main street of sorts ran north to where he could make out the end of the railway line from Swakopmund. Other buildings were dotted along this street, giving the place the rudimentary sense of a town. Nara saw to watering the mules and he went across to look for feed and information.

Bales of straw outside one of them drew him, and as he pushed aside a damp hessian curtain hanging over the entrance, he noticed a *mezuzah* on the door post. A large man was hacking at a carcase hanging from a hook. Strips of biltong hung from wires along the ceiling and there was a soft buzz of flies in the air. A woman with dark hair drawn into a loose bun looked up from a basin on the counter where she was rubbing salt into meat.

"*Guten Tag*", he said, cautiously.

The woman straightened up, looking at him with wide grey eyes, and wiped a strand of hair from her cheek with the back of her hand. She mumbled something to the man behind her, who turned around appraising him too.

"*Bagrissen*", he said in Yiddish, testing. "Welcome. *Bist du gerade erst angekommen* - have you just arrived?" the man continued in German, also cautious.

"*Shulem Aleichem*", Jack replied with relief and a smile. "I'm Levinsky, Ya'akov, from Taurog Guverno[38] – extending the *landsman* bridge as was customary. "Fentinovich, Ephroim", the man replied, wiping his hands on a cloth. "The goyim call me Effi. My wife, Hanna Lea", he said motioning with his head. "Good to welcome another *Litvak*."

"Have you eaten yet?" she asked.

"No, not yet. But I need to get my cart and things", he said, gesturing back towards the Ausspannplatz. Relaxed by her smile and soft grey eyes he mentioned Nara immediately. "I also have a young girl with me. She's a Nama."

"Magda, our maid is Nama too. Get your things, and let's feed you."

"Your mules and cart she's bringing by herself already", said Effi, looking through the window by the counter. Nara was leading the mules by their reins and holding the whip loosely in the other hand.

"*An shtark meidel* – a strong girl", Hanna said quietly as they walked out to meet her. Behind the butchery there was a *kraal* and a large courtyard which seemed common to all the buildings in the compound. Hanna bustled Nara into the kitchen while Jack unhitched the mules and gave them fodder.

---

[38] Touragé Governorate in Lithuania, where many South African Jewish immigrants came from.

Lunch was a taste of home – salt beef on dark sourbread with *schmaltz*. That, and the opportunity to speak Yiddish, and to a woman, for the first time in weeks had him babbling easily with Hanna, who seemed about his age. At the other end of the kitchen table Nara and the maid talked with soft clicks.

Hanna and Effi had two boys. Effi's brother lived alongside, as did the few other Jews in the town. They had rooms which they rented out, and Jack took one and agreed stabling and fodder.

"Now, what about the girl?" Hanna asked, assessing him directly. For the first time, Jack felt he could tell the story in detail, concluding with the missionary's recommendation that he find her a school in Windhuk. Hanna repeated Jack's story to Magda in Afrikaans, which Jack partially followed.

The maid shook her head. "That woman is not her mother. It's her aunt. Her parents are not alive." She turned to Nara and repeated Jack's version. Nara paled and her eyes welled up with tears.

Suddenly he understood her drawing. "I was mistaken", he said in Afrikaans, flushed with awkwardness. The maid repeated this and put out her hand to comfort Nara.

The emotion galvanised Hanna, who began to bustle in Yiddish, German and Afrikaans – "We will find her a place – Ephroim knows lots of people. In the meantime, she will stay here – Magda, maybe next to the storeroom? You will have to pay for her food."

That evening he met the other families and individuals staying in the compound, which they referred to as "the Yard". None of them were boot or saddle makers so he was not seen as competition. But there was a tailor.

+++

Early 1900s

My beloved Tatte, Mamme and dearest Leah,
I am, thank G-d, well and I pray that you are too.
I have finally arrived at my destination, a town called Windhuk in the middle of this country. And what adventures I've had along the way! I've seen a Leopard, Buffalo, so many antelope you cannot count, with names like Kudu, Gemsbok, Springbok – what variety! I met a German officer who kept a Cheetah on a chain as a pet! There are so many different peoples here too, with names like Damara, Herero and Nama. They all speak different languages but somehow seem to understand each other.
There are few whites here - mainly Germans and Afrikaners or Boers that I mentioned before in my letters from Cape Town. More settlers seem to be coming all the time and the Germans are sending lots of soldiers. They need lots of leatherwork, Tatte, so it seems, thank G-d, that I will have a living.
The country is so extensive that you can travel for days hardly meeting anyone. At night the skies are so clear, there are more stars than I've ever seen. They are sharp and bright and cover the entire sky. Down by the sea it was a barren desert – so barren you cannot imagine – just sand and rock for miles and miles. And so

hot! Most of the time the sky is so blue and bright – your eyes burn, and your skin and lips get dry and dusty. Here, in the middle of the country it is much greener and not so hot. But much hotter and drier than anything in the guverno! And when I say green – it's nothing like in Lita – the trees are short, scraggly and full of thorns. There are no dark forests here, no pines, no birches. You cannot make a living from timber here but maybe I'll import timber for building! They mainly farm cattle and goats but there is much wild life and everyone eats meat – all the time. And a porridge of corn they call pap. Water is very scarce.

I'm now in Windhuk – the main German town. It's not really a town yet although there is a fort, a railway station is being built, and maybe 30 more buildings – all spread out. There is much building and people all have plans for the future. Everyone seems to be a tryer – even the soldiers. I'm staying in a little ghetto of Jews – mainly Litvakim. They call it the Yard. Tomorrow is erev Shabbos. To be honest, I lost track of the days during the journey. Even my arrival still won't make a minyan – that's how few we are! It was a difficult journey here, but a big adventure and I now feel much better among Yidden and able to speak Yiddish.

The people I've met so far are all very optimistic about the future here – mainly it seems because it's so big. Being a ballegolle or smous is difficult, as the native peoples and even the few German farmers have no money and little to trade apart from pelts. And, if you do trade for that, you have to schlep the skins huge distances to sell them. But I've managed to trade for two tusks of ivory! So, it seems there may be wealth here like there is in South

Africa. Having said that, the native peoples are here already and control most of the land. Tension with white immigrants is talked about all the time. That's why the Germans are bringing in their soldiers, which may be good for business.

I will register with the post office so you can write to me here. They say it can take three months for a letter to arrive. I am sorry, but I have no money yet to send to you. But as soon as I'm able I will do so.

…

```
DEAR HERR SONNENBERG. WINDHUK ARRIVED. MUCH
OPPORTUNITY. ARMY NEEDS SUPPLIES, WAGON
BUILDERS. LETTER COMING. JACOB.
```

After registering at the post office and sending the letter and the telegram, Jack went to the fort and presented his letters of introduction to the quartermaster. They agreed rates, and Jack would present himself for work on Monday morning.

He found Nara amongst other children of various ages playing in the courtyard. All seemed to get on with each other in a mix of Yiddish, German, Nama and Afrikaans. Most of the kids were barefoot.

As the afternoon wore on, preparations for Shabbos began to dictate the pace and he saw her helping with washing some of the infants. He called her over and together they went through the things on the cart to get her a dress. There was nothing quite her size so he quickly had to make an alteration, which he did in his room so that the other tailor would not see his skill while she went to wash.

The men gathered in one of the larger rooms for prayers and the communal meal was arranged at long tables in the courtyard. Hanna called Nara to join the other girls as one of the women lit candles and said a prayer. Initially they sat in family groups with the maids at a separate table. The children soon skittered about.

Both of them came alive in the warmth of the gathering. He smiled and laughed a lot as he moved around the tables listening to people's stories and histories and telling his own. Nara was among the oldest of the children in the Yard and bubbled in the company.

+++

Within a few days, with Ephroim's guidance, the letters of introduction from the missionaries, and a donation, Jack was able to register Nara at a Catholic Mission in Klein Windhoek – the small fertile valley east of the fort.

The evening before she was due to go, he sat with her, Hanna and Magda in the kitchen to prepare her via their three-way translation. Jack was quite staccato: – she would be with seven to ten other children of various ages; study was from morning till lunchtime; afternoons they were expected to help in the mission. Jack would visit her on weekends.

Hanna interrupted – "can she not come here on Friday afternoon?"

"I didn't ask", he said.

"Of course, she must. You must just tell them."

Nara sat with him in his room afterwards sorting through her things. She would take the kaross, the fox shoulder cape, the slip and the dress he'd given her. She spread out the collection of playthings and together they sorted through these. He held up the various stones and said that he would keep these for her and together they dropped these into a tortoise shell, including the big pink one. She kept a small shell with *buchu* and a few of the rings and beads she'd collected in what now seem an age away when she was still in Walvis. These she kept in the small gemsbok pouch, and the rest he wrapped up in a cloth and put in his strongbox at the foot of the rough wooden bed.

They sat beside each other in silence – an acknowledgement of their intimacy and what the impending separation meant for both of them. "*Das vet zeyn gut*", he said breaking into Yiddish when he couldn't take the awkwardness any longer. "*Zayn ver di besser* - It will be good, it's for the best."

She didn't respond, and he was not sure she understood him. Spontaneously he put his arm round her and capped her small head into his shoulder. She snivelled a bit and he went with her to the room she'd been sleeping in.

As they parted the next morning outside the mission with its vineyards and neat vegetable gardens, she prompted him with "*Freitag*", reminding him to arrange to fetch her with the priest waiting to receive her. There was some initial objection, but it was resolved. He would fetch her on Friday afternoons and return her to the school on Saturday.

Beginner's Doubt

Jack's day started early at the fort, where he had been allocated a space just inside the entrance and where the truppe could drop off and collect their boots, bridles and saddles. From here he got to know many of the officers and soldiers who came and went.

Midday heat laid a heavy somnolence on the town, and he would pack up and visit the post office on his way back to the Yard. Nearly everyone dozed in the afternoon – what they called a *schlafstunde* – inside darkened rooms. When the heat had broken, he would continue with his leatherwork sitting in the courtyard, or with the clothing repairs in his room to avoid conflict with the tailor, who had a family.

Most evenings were spent in the kitchen of one of the neighbours or in the courtyard, gossiping about the politics of the territory, plans for the future, and reminiscing of the old country. Ephroim had recommended he keep his goods for an agricultural fair scheduled for later in the year. He'd traded a sack of salt with Hanna for a week's accommodation and food, and was making a living from the leather work and tailoring. He could afford to wait a while before trading.

Settled, relaxed, and now without Nara, melancholy and doubt crept in unexpectedly. For all the talk of great opportunity, the Jews in the Yard all seemed to be struggling. Windhuk already had well-established German traders whom it would be difficult to compete with. *Smousing* among the blacks and the farmers seemed very lonely, dangerous, and they had little to trade beyond cattle and pelts. He was not a wagon meister, and even if he brought in parts, he needed someone like Malan, who wasn't interested. Importing goods and building supplies as he'd suggested to Sonnenberg was a step too far. It required capital he could not get. Maybe he'd been too *chutzpedik* in his letter. His backers had only agreed to loan him goods and money for him to scout for opportunities. He'd told them that he would earn a living as a bootmaker and tailor, and *smous* as the opportunity arose. He prepared himself for a put-down. A Yiddishe *pisher* not yet twenty could not present himself as a supplier to the Kaiser's colony.

"They're big drinkers in Suidwes", Effi said when he and some of the other men took Jack around the town one night. German traders and government officials seemed to favour the hotel bars, the soldiers and farmers the various taverns and bars spread around Kaiser Strasse. Afrikaans transport riders hung out together in one bar, and there were also a few English speakers spread around. Few women ventured out at night. Blacks never entered the bars but stuck to those in their camp on the outskirts. There was no official ban, but a strict de facto separation.

+++

TO: JACK LEVIN

C/O WINDHOEK POST OFFICE, GERMAN SOUTH WEST AFRICA

JACK,LETTER RECEIVED. 1200LBS GOODS VIA

WALVISBAY. SS LOUIS ALFRED DUE 10-12 DAYS. C/O MSSRS THOMPSON & WYLEY FORWARDING AGENTS. SONNENBERG

He confirmed receipt by return telegram and alerted Cameron.

+++

Walvis Bay

Once again, he smelt it before he saw it.

Ten weeks after his arrival, Jack approached the grimy port again, this time from the north. The afternoon south-westerly had just started whipping sand along the track when the mules whinnied in discomfort and then he and the cart driver breached the invisible bubble and trotted into the balloon of stench.

They pulled scarves across their faces and hunched down into themselves. There was something very clean about the desert, he thought. Maybe because all of the rot and putrefaction was concentrated in this hooked finger of flat sand pointing into the sea.

Three tall masts emerged above the band of dust and sand they were fighting through. There were no whalers at the dock, but the smell was just as intense. The few people outside moved quickly, their shoulders hunched to protect exposed faces and eyes, and they kept to the shade. The cart pulled up outside the customs and forwarding agents and Jack paid the driver and hurried inside.

Half office, half warehouse, the place was gloomy. Little light penetrated the sand-scarred and grimy panes of glass of the tall windows facing the bay. Cameron was sitting opposite the shipping agent next to a man in naval uniform. They looked up as Jack opened the door – the wind and the bright light of the Namib lurching into the office like a drunk.

"Aah, here's our man!" Cameron called. "This is Captain Owen of HMS Sparrow, which you see in the bay." They shook hands. "The Louis Alfred, you have news?" Jack asked. "No change", the clerk said. "There's been a nor-wester off the Cape for the past few days so that might have slowed her down."

Jack sensed that he'd interrupted something, so he arranged to meet them later in a bar along the road, and went into the bunkhouse alongside the warehouse where he'd arranged to stay until his shipment had cleared.

Later, over beer, fish and potatoes in one of the hotels, Owen asked him how he found Suidwes.

"It seems they want to succeed", Jack said. "They are investing in buildings, the railway. They're not many settlers yet, but more they say will come. Do you know Suidwes?"

"Sparrow is familiar with these waters", Owen replied. "She conducted a lengthy survey of the coast around here, before the Germans got heavily involved. Now I keep an eye on developments here and in the south Atlantic." Unfamiliar with the naval habit of referring to a ship as a female, Jack tried to understand the elliptical answer, which somehow made him feel inadequate. "We leave tomorrow to take Boer prisoners to exile in St. Helena. Things seem to be happening in Suidwes then?", Owen asked, watching him from across the table.

"Many troops they are bringing", Jack replied. "I think building materials and tools they will need."

Owen leaned in towards him. "Do you know what weapons the Germans are bringing in?"

Jack twigged that he was talking to a British naval officer. As the Germans had interrogated him about British intentions, so the captain wanted to know about German preparations. He felt young, naïve and stupid, and clammed up as more crewmen and officers off the Sparrow crowded into the bar.

"Stay in touch with Cameron", Owen said later. "He's a good man and I'm sure he –and we – can be useful to each other. There is much happening here and much opportunity. Friends will be important."

The next morning there was still no sign of the Louis Alfred. The Sparrow, however, was ready to leave with a little tug standing by. Jack walked down to the dock to see her and wondered about the Boere men going out to exile on an island in the middle of the Atlantic. Then he crossed behind the flensing yard and the mountain of guano with a scarf across his face, and walked towards the estuary. Nara had said she'd found the clear stones in her collection on the far side of the finger of land that formed the bay.

It was still early, but soon grew hot and uncomfortable on the bleak sand. There were a few decimated whale carcasses in the light surf and some bones on the beach, but 15 minutes out of the port he seemed to be the only person around. Once he'd passed the whalebones the screeching birds disappeared too. Out to the west, through the haze, he could see the long sand spit that created the bay. It was much further than he'd understood from Nara's sketch. To get there he'd have to walk along the beach to the neck of the estuary, which he could not even see from where he was. To the east was a choppy sea of soft sand dunes –yellow-white and harsh on the eyes. He gave up his search.

Back in the town he turned towards the low, dark green vegetation that marked the delta. A few flamingos on their pink spindly legs and some other gangly waders picked about the mucky lagoon water as he walked towards the track that had taken him to Nara's shanty town a few weeks before. Perhaps her aunt would know where to find more stones.

A group of Nama women with reed baskets came towards him and he tried to talk to them, but they struggled with his mangled Afrikaans and were reluctant to engage. One of them picked out the clear stone from his hand and looked at it in the sunlight - "*Miskien, by die see* – maybe by the sea", she said as they walked away. Recalling Piet's violence, he gave up his exploration.

A horn sounded out to sea while he was eating lunch with Cameron in the bar. "That should be her", Cameron said, and they got up to look outside. A ship had rounded the distant point of the spit. "We won't get your goods off today", he said. "It'll be the passengers and their baggage first. Let's try and get the bill of lading and you can clear customs in the morning. With luck we can get wagoned-up by the end of tomorrow."

+++

Jack was astonished by the quantity of goods Sonnenberg had shipped. There were tents, surplus uniforms and assorted army kit and equipment, wheels and axles, tools and building hardware, horse tack, foods, spices, and brandy. He'd also included a letter (in Yiddish) listing the original prices paid for the goods.

"... The British are bringing back a lot of material to warehouses in Woodstock and Salt River. They have also ordered from local manufacturers for uniforms and other things that they now need to sell. They only want to sell in bulk, the Boere and other farmers have no money, and things have not really picked up on the Reef yet, so we got very good prices.

If you can get good prices from the Germans, we can do well from these circumstances. We have invested a lot in this first shipment to help you prove the value of your connections. Rabinowitz writes too that German agents are buying all the horses and mules near the Cape border and have also ordered goods. I am looking for water drilling equipment in England.

We will need half of this investment plus the cost of the shipping and insurance back before we fund a new shipment so you must act quickly. We also want twenty-five per cent repayment of our initial investment. You must find a way to get money back to us.

The ivory is probably worth £200. But beware that it is not too dry, yellow or cracked. Can you get more?

Have you set up a company yet? Can we be joint owners as we discussed?

Jack, remember what I taught you – see all difficulties as opportunities. Slow means - be faster, thieves –more reliable, and remember spies and jealousy – be discreet! It is good you are bold, but you must be careful. Remember, you will need to keep a good name.

Also, it would be very unwise to import arms. That draws the wrong kind of attention from the wrong kind of people."

Soon after dawn the next morning Cameron hitched his horse to the front wagon and came to sit next to Jack on the bench. Jack had added twenty bags of salt, and there were five wagons and no cattle, so there was no need to chase up the tail of their convoy. There had been little fog and the teams of oxen were settled and familiar with the journey.

"What happened to the Nama girl?", Cameron asked as they rocked in tandem with the sway of the wagon.

"In a mission school in Windhoek", Jack replied.

Cameron pulled a packet of rusks from his coat pocket, and they munched in silence. "Owen spoke to you", he said rather than asked.

Jack nodded. "Yes."

"Where do you see your future Jack? Here or back in the Cape?"

"Here there seems promise. So as long as things are good, I try. If not, I go back. Very difficult now the Cape is."

"So, will you help us?" Cameron asked, watching him. "You are a British citizen after all."

The undulating backsides of the oxen, their long backs and low-slung horns were like a corridor he sometimes saw in his dreams leading to a threshold he could not avoid but feared falling off. He sensed his reply would be significant for him. It was clear that they needed him, and not helping could cost him too.

"What it is you want me to do? I'm not sure."

"It will change over time. For now, it would be useful to know what the Germans are planning, what they need, what they import, what they think. Even rumours are important. With your German and your business, you are in a very good place to get this kind of information."

He dictated a few innocuous code words and phrases they would use to arrange to meet, which would revolve around the business.

"We must avoid meeting regularly or in the open", Cameron said. "The Germans will be suspicious. I suggest you find an agent in Swakopmund, perhaps another Jew you can trust, and I will deal with him regularly rather than with you."

Jack jotted down the phrases in Yiddish in his notebook. "Are there others like me?"

"His Majesty's government is discreet", Cameron said, with mock formality that was lost on Jack. "You must realise that this is a serious business, Jack. Part of my job is to protect you. Outside of Owen, no one will know your role."

Jack looked out across the beach and the slate swells as the night-time blackness sank away. A transaction and perhaps some leverage formed in his mind. He glanced sidewise at Cameron.

"I need to get money to Cape Town to pay for these goods", he said. "Maybe it's better I not use the banks in Windhuk for everything."

They agreed that in exchange for the occasional passage to and from Cape Town, Cameron, or Thompson, the customs agent, would courier a padlocked strongbox to which only Sonnenberg and Jack would have keys. The captain of the Louis Alfred or an alternate British-registered vessel would counter-sign receipt and delivery. Jack wrote to Sonnenberg in Yiddish from Swakopmund explaining the arrangement, and Cameron posted the letter on his return to Walvis. He also agreed with Gerson, a recent immigrant with German citizenship who had set up as a general dealer in Swakopmund and who seemed trustworthy, to act as his agent and deal with Cameron's deliveries from Walvis Bay.

Restraint and Desperation

The pace of life picked up after his return from Walvis. The quartermaster in Swakopmund would have bought everything he'd brought in on the wagons, but Jack knew that would irritate the HQ in Windhoek who controlled the purse strings. He would also be able to charge more for the transport to Windhoek. The margins were excellent.

Within days he'd cabled Sonnenberg confirming a second shipment and adding additional items requested by the German quartermasters. They accepted they would have to make a down-payment, and facilitated a local bank account for Jack and transfer of the first payment to a correspondent bank in Cape Town.

A few weeks after returning to Windhoek, Sonnenberg sent a telegram with details of the next shipment and added – "travel arrangements agreed" – the phrase Jack had suggested for letting him know if Sonnenberg approved of the courier arrangement described in the letter.

Jack kept up his leatherwork at the entrance to the fort because it kept him in touch with the officers and troops in the garrison. It was from one of these connections he learned that there had been a suggestion that some soldiers be sent to guard his shipments as the government was beginning to count on them. To avoid this, the Fentins helped recruit two Nama who had German permits for their rifles to accompany him on his trips.

Within a few weeks Jack had enough to send some money to his family via a German bank. He'd established a business in his name and set aside shares for Sonnenberg and the others without naming them. They'd agreed via letters that it was prudent at this stage not to have British citizens in the Cape as named shareholders.

In anticipation of the agricultural fair scheduled for late September he brought in a lot of civilian goods – particularly women's and children's clothing. Hanna and the other women in the Yard had prompted this by ordering things from him – especially for the Jewish holidays. Nara too was on Hanna's list. They had grown close, Hanna finding a daughter she did not have. Magda was like a mother.

Late one afternoon, as he was basking in the warmth of the deep orange sunset over the far hills, Hanna came to sit beside him in the courtyard. They watched her youngest playing with a Nama child his age, silently acknowledging a friendship and closeness that had been between them from the beginning. "Yankel, I need to talk to you." She'd turned to face him, her large, wide-set eyes looking into him as his mother's had. "During the fair, there's often problems with the single men. They get drunk and there are so few women, they go crazy. So, there are more and more *zoine* - prostitutes, some of them Jewish."

"Yes, I've seen some of them", Jack acknowledged. "In Swakop."

"They will come here for this 'Oktoberfest' as they call it. The women are *miskoine* – poor girls taken advantage of in London or

Cape Town. But the men are *drekkes*. And if they're not pimps, they're *sheisters veganoivim* - cheats and thieves. They make us all look bad."

He was uncomfortable. She never used language like this. And sex had never come up before. He looked away to the sunset, sensing an intense, challenging empathy from her. But it was also embarrassing. Almost from the beginning he felt she knew him better than he knew himself – like his mother or an older sister.

"Yankele, you are single too. There are no *yiddisher meidels* here for you to marry. We should see to that. But I don't want you to bring one of these women to this house."

His dark face flushed. He'd not overcome his distaste and the embarrassment of going to a brothel and sensed that Hanna and the other women would know when he did. She embodied the restraints his mother and sister would have placed on him, but she was more direct and worldly-wise. She knew he was preoccupied with sex.

She ignored his exaggerated denial. "You are getting settled and making a living. You will make a good *chassen* (groom). We (he assumed the other wives or Effi) have discussed this. You will need to be patient. You will need to go to Cape Town to find a girl, and we will help you. You are good looking, you know. You will want a *scheine meidel*. The problem with pretty girls is that they will need to be persuaded to come here. That means you will have to show you are wealthy and that will take time. In the meantime, restrain yourself."

+++

12th September 1989   Windhoek Airport

Anton Lebowski was easy to pick out in the crowd of passengers walking into the arrivals hall off the plane from Jo'burg. He was unusually tall, with a wild mop of dark hair, and was the most prominent and well-known of the white members of SWAPO. An advocate and skilled spokesman for the movement, his Afrikaans background incensed the government.

Bessie watched him walk to the taxi rank and then got into a waiting car to follow him to Lebowski's house on Sanderburg Street. Other CCB men were already in place on the long circular street in Klein Windhoek to continue the surveillance. Bessie drove on to the safe house on the other side of town.

Viljoen had called earlier, reiterating that Bessie and his team were not to do anything more than trail Lebowski. Now, they were happy to lounge about listening to live rugby and drinking Windhoek Lager as they braaied a seemingly endless supply of meat. The absence of hard alcohol and real pressure had calmed his stomach.

Shortly after 11 p.m. Viljoen called again. Tension constricted his throat and his voice became sibilant – hence his nickname "Slang" (snake). This got through to Bessie despite the beer, meat and stuiwepap. "*Hulle het die kaffirboetie doodgeskiet* - they've killed the kaffir lover! On his way back from SWAPO HQ. This is a complete fuckup and will cause a lot of shit. Get out – now. Drive down to Rehoboth. Someone will pick you all up at the petrol station at the entrance. I'll have a plane for you at Keetmans airport. Bessie, move now!"

Bessie's ulcer flared and his facial twitching crawled out of its lair as they raced down the dark empty road running south.

+++

TRC FINAL REPORT

PAGE NUMBER (ORIGINAL) 80

PARAGRAPH NUMBERS 137 to 146

VOLUME 2

CHAPTER 2

SUBSECTION 17

The killing of Anton Lubowski

141 On 12 September 1989, Advocate Anton Lubowski was shot dead outside his home in Windhoek. At the time, he was the secretary general of SWAPO and the highest-ranking white person in the organisation. One human rights violation submission and two amnesty applications were made to the Commission on this case. The human rights violation submission was made by Ms Molly Lubowski, the deceased's mother. She appealed to the Commission to identify her son's killers and to clear him of allegations that he was a South African MI agent.

142 Considerable attention was given to this case, including a trip to Namibia and meetings with the judicial authorities there. A vast amount of documentation was supplied to the Commission by various parties.

[...]

145 In an amnesty application [AM1909/96] not directly related to this murder, Mr Kevin Trytsman, an associate of Ferdi Barnard, claimed that Barnard had told him that the CCB had committed the murder. This is also the view of Christoffel Nel as expressed in the quote cited earlier. Elsewhere in his hearing, Nel described the Lubowski murder, along with the killings of Ms Dulcie September and Mr David Webster, as one of the CCB's "successes".

146 This was also the conclusion of Judge J Levy of the Namibian Supreme Court, who conducted a lengthy inquest into the case. In a 144-page judgement, Levy named Irish mercenary Donald Acheson as the assassin and, as accomplices, CCB members...

THE COMMISSION BELIEVES THERE ARE NO GROUNDS TO CONTRADICT JUDGE LEVY'S GENERAL FINDING PERTAINING TO THE INVOLVEMENT OF THE CCB AND ITS RESPONSIBILITY FOR THE CONSPIRACY THAT LED TO THIS KILLING.

Early 1900s

Oktoberfest

Windhuk began to bustle a few days before the Oktoberfest which was set for a weekend. The Auspannplatz was cleared of the normal market vendors, and the watering troughs had been cleaned out and whitewashed. Additional *kraal*s had been erected on the southern perimeter and these were filling up with cattle, sheep, goats and horses.

Beyond the *kraal*s, the natives attending or working at the fair had erected temporary shelters, often no more than a piece of cloth or sacking on sticks. The dry, mica-laden air, began to carry an unpleasant pong of animal and increasingly, human shit. There were only a few trench toilets.

Wagons and carts pulled in with increasing frequency, the hotels filled up and the bars overflowed at night. Civilians heavily outnumbered the Schutztruppe as farmers and traders trekked into the capital of the colony. Jack, like the others in the Yard and some of the more settled residents of the town, tended to avoid the taverns, which became raucous and jingoistic at night.

Jack sat outside the butchery with a cup of coffee watching the bustle and the latest arrivals pulling into the *platz*. A column of Schutztruppe trotted in from the south and stopped at the *kraal*s. They were leading some camels, which he'd never seen before. He'd heard that they were in use in the deserts of the south and he ambled over to see the strange beasts.

On his way back, he saw Malan riding into the Auspannplatz ahead of several loaded wagons, and waved. As the long teams of oxen made their turn, the *transportryer* rode up to greet him and they made plans to get together the next evening.

Hanna was talking to a couple on a white-tented cart outside the butchery. She took him aside as he approached. "These people are looking for a room for the next few days. All the hotels are full. Maybe you can sleep in your storeroom and we can share the rent?" He went back into the Yard to clear his things out of the room.

The couple were waiting in Hanna's kitchen. The woman had removed her bonnet. He noticed her luminous skin before anything else. She was strikingly beautiful, with honey-blond hair drawn back from a round face and hazel eyes. He sensed Hanna watching his reaction.

They introduced themselves as Bayer, a brother and sister. Hans was a baker in Lüderitzbucht – a port in the south that was the first German settlement in the territory. It had taken them more than a week to get to Windhuk. First by boat to Swakopmund, and then train to Windhuk. Susanna, the sister, had arrived in Suidwes two months earlier and did not like Lüderitzbucht or the desert that surrounded it. Her brother was keen she should stay in the territory, at least, and had persuaded her to come up to the fair "to see softer and greener landscapes" and perhaps some *"kultur"*.

Later than afternoon he saw her again as he walked through the courtyard on his way to collect Nara from the mission school. He couldn't control his blushing.

"*Zeiyer shein*", one of the other wives in the Yard said quietly with a smile as he passed her on his way out. "*Shikses zenen nisht far ir, Yankel*, non-Jewish girls are not for you."

+++

His stall was near the middle of the path through the fairground – a beer garden at the beginning and at the end, and tents and a few vendors like himself strewn out in between. The Fentins' butchery was closed, as they did not sell pork, which was what people were consuming, but both brothers were busy at the far end trading the cattle stock they'd brought in from South Africa. Their main draw was a huge brown Afrikander stud bull that they had purchased in the northern Cape a few weeks before. It had been carefully transported and tended to in its own *kraal* behind the Yard, protected by Nama guards who were still present.

The Bayers appeared by mid-morning, clearly recovered from the journey and chatting to town residents they'd met along the way, Susanna quickly becoming a draw. While she and some of the other women browsed through the better-quality dresses he'd imported from Cape Town, Hans asked Jack if he thought there was an opening for a bakery in the town. "Schaeffer is the only baker in town I know of. Apparently Leutwein, the governor can't stand him. I think he'd welcome another supplier, for the Schutztruppe at least."

"Is his bread so bad?"

"No, it's good", said the postmaster's wife. "But he caused problems a few months ago when he flogged a Herero elder in the street. The old man got very sick and the Herero were so offended that Leutwein thought there would be a riot. Only his personal intervention calmed things."

"There was more trouble when Schaeffer was forced to settle for 20 marks", added another. "High and mighty, these Herero."

"*Der Bauer aus Omaruru* - the farmer from Omaruru!", Nara whispered soon after the midday lull when the crowds disappeared into the beer gardens. Luger was approaching the stall, and she recognized the flushed face of a drunk and withdrew behind the rows of dresses.

Luger was expansive, brash and loud. By now, so were many of the men in the crowd. He had started building a dam, dug another well and his herd of cattle was growing faster than he'd hoped. "I have a good bull, – he's just like me!"

"What happened to the young Herero woman who was with you?", Jack asked, goaded by the man for some reason.

"Sent her back to her family when the baby was due." It was almost another boast but for the slight hesitation. "That's their custom. Told her not to come back - can't have a half-breed Baster about if I want a white wife."

Through a gap in the rack of dresses, Jack saw Nara following every word.

Shouting and screaming from further down the road towards the *kraal*s cut through his bragging.

Two big horses, hooves high, eyes bulging in panic were galloping towards them, their manes whipping with each stride. The teenage boys riding them had lost control of the stampeding animals. People scattered, pulling children aside and tripping over tent pegs and guy ropes. Rooted to the ground directly in front of the charging horses, her blond hair instantly recognizable in the pandemonium, was Susanna. Luger pushed passed Jack to run forward, but it was Rolf, the lieutenant who'd befriended Jack in Swakopmund, who darted in from the side. He lifted her, covering her head with his arms, and stepped in between the huge galloping animals.

+++

Malan was sitting at the back of the beer garden of the Hotel Kronprinz, the classier establishment in town favoured by the officers and colonial officials. The afternoon's events had dampened spirits. A woman and child had been trampled and badly injured by the stampeding horses. The fathers of the teenage riders had whipped their sons in public, adding another dose of shock.

The governor's careful welcoming speech, in which he praised the settlers in the name of the Chancellor but warned that "laws had to be obeyed", had not enthused the crowd. On the other hand, his announcement that the "police zone" would be extended to prevent native cattle coming into contact with the German herds and potentially infecting them with Rinderpest was loudly cheered and applauded. Everyone knew that there was no intention of removing the fence around the zone or allowing the Herero to return to graze on their traditional lands. The band performance at the end of the day had hardly lifted spirits either, and the bar was subdued.

The old Boer made no attempt to fit in. He was wearing faded veld khakis, and his broad hat was on his knees, where he could keep his hands occupied. Most of the German patrons were either in uniform or smartly dressed for what would be the height of their annual social calendar – apart from those invited to the governor's Christmas ball. Jack wore a new dark serge suit which he'd brushed carefully.

"I came from Otjiwarongo", Malan said. 'They still haven't found anyone for the wagon shop. They told me you sent them some axles and wheels, but their needs are growing. The railway from Swakopmund has already slowed business for the long transports. The past few months I've only had short runs in the north, mainly to the copper mine at Tsumeb. My wife doesn't want me to do the Cape route any longer."

He was leaning forward, speaking softly to hide his discomfort in asking this younger man for help. But Jack didn't see it this way.

He'd fretted for months that there was an opportunity he had not been able to take advantage of, and knew it rested on finding someone skilled to run things in the town. "Of course, *meneer*, of course we should do it", he said, deferential towards the older man.

The first step they agreed was for both of them to travel to Otjiwarongo and secure an agreement with the major. Jack wanted to combine this with a sweep through eastern Hereroland to look for ivory. Malan leaned back against the rimpies of the dark wooden chair and, with his awkwardness partly abated, took a sip of his beer. "I'll find a Herero to go with you", he said.

There was a discernible lull and turning of heads as Susanna and her brother came into the garden. The men's attention was drawn like moths to a paraffin lamp. She seemed to have recovered from the shock of the afternoon and was gay with relief, the mounting buzz of the hotel at sundown, and the barely restrained attention of the men in the bar. Malan, relieved at the distraction excused himself.

The surveyor had come in with a few other colonial officials, some of whom Jack recognized. They were ordering beer and sausages from a black waiter in a starched white jacket when he saw Jack and came across, greeting him. When he heard that Jack was importing military surplus from the Boer War for the Schutztruppe he insisted on introducing him to the party, one of whom was a recently arrived finance official in the colonial administration.

He seemed put out that the Schutztruppe did not go through his department for British army surplus. Short, with glinting round glasses, he drew his shoulders back and announced loudly – "We are working on regulations about the import of military materiel – apart from arms, that is, which, as you know we're very strict about – and with good reason!" He was pompous and Jack became wary when he asked what he would do "when the military surpluses disappear?"

"Opportunities will grow as the colony grows", Jack said, surprising himself with his glibness, an intuitive attempt to divert the man's hostility.

Another official in charge of granting prospecting and hydrology licenses had heard from the surveyor about Jack's American prospecting hammer. He was keen to see it, and asked about other mining and boring tools and equipment.

"We should be taking more lessons from the Americans", said another. "They completely removed the threat from the Indians and brought in black slaves. They realise that European expansion is a war of races and of civilizations. The British policy in South Africa of trying to educate these obviously inferior peoples is doomed to failure and will just cause us problems here."

"*Streng aber gerecht* - tough but just, the governor said this afternoon, and he's right", added another official. "The natives have to be made to understand that this is *Unser Afrika*. The Reich is absolutely resolute to settle the land with force if necessary. It is our right. At the same time, there is no wisdom in needlessly provoking them. If we allow hotheads to disobey our laws how can they be persuaded to obey them? It's also not clever – we don't have the numbers to take them all on at the same time – and we're not even thinking about Ovamboland yet!"

"First the Herero, then the Nama", agreed another. "Leutwein is very good at exploiting the differences between them, and also, at getting their leaders to sell us land. All this flogging and cattle theft and rape gets in the way."

Jack hovered on the outside of the conversation. Not only was he obviously younger than the men in the group and new in the country, but his sense was that this was not his business. Without discussion, he had taken the Fentins' line – not to express any real opinions. Privately, within the confines of the Yard and the 'confidentiality' provided by Yiddish, the settlers' excesses were recounted and discussed, usually with discomfort and aversion. Izzy, Effi's brother, was perhaps the only one who felt that the government had to show a consistently tough line to cow black resistance, but he was always restrained by his older brother – "it's not our business". Hanna, however, was resolute and outspoken in her abhorrence of the violence and excesses of the settlers and Schutztruppe. "Evil and stupid", she called it.

A group of older farmers joined them. They took a much tougher line – their main frustration was that Leutwein reflected and was partly responsible for the cautious backing of the government in Berlin. Not only did the government not understand the reality on the ground, they argued, but they were ideologically ambivalent about the colony. "The Social Democrats in the Reichstag have Negrophilia and are to blame for this", one said. "They lack the virility of the German volk and try to restrain it where it is best expressed – here in the colonies."

"What does our young Jew think about this", asked one of the younger officials, his face flushed with champagne.

Jack, who'd been thinking that their stridency reflected uncertainty, was taken aback and paled. "No need to be impolite", the finance official reprimanded his younger colleague. "The Jews have no commitment to land but rather to money. They've not come here to farm or to raise the black man from his backwardness. At the moment, every white man counts."

Leutwein's entrance, accompanied by his wife and aides, defused things. Rolf, the hero of the afternoon, was among them. The governor, ramrod straight in an impeccably-tailored dress uniform, made his rounds courteously but with a degree of haughtiness that curbed even the most inebriated. He focussed immediately on the older farmers and traders.

Jack used the opportunity to withdraw but Rolf caught him at the entrance. "I hear the Bayers are your guests?" he asked with a shy smile. "Not really 'guests'", Jack smiled – "just renting my room. You don't need an introduction, surely, after your dramatic intervention", he teased.

"Well, actually I do", Rolf said bashfully. "She was taken to the infirmary immediately."

Jack, now bashful too, realised he had no choice and stepped back into the bar. Susanna blushed as they approached. "Fraulein Bayer, may I present Lieutenant Bruns. I know you've met, but have not been formally introduced."

Early 1900s

Sjambok

Malan helped Jack buy a Mauser at Wocke & Voights, the main general store in the town, and taught him to shoot along the way to Otjiwarongo. The major, impressed by the wagon load of spares and tools they'd brought, allocated them land to set up the workshop and a *kraal* not far from railway station. Jack knew from the layout of towns he'd visited in Lithuania that stockyards adjacent to the railway would become another source of income, and he made sure the *kraal* had direct access.

After a few days that saw most of the Schutztruppe wagons serviceable, Malan and Jack resumed their journey north – the Boer to see his family and farm at Grootfontein, Jack to start his sweep for ivory. Philemon, a local Herero who worked for Malan, joined them.

In the early afternoon of the first day of their journey out of the town, they pulled the wagons and animals off the main road, left Philemon to set up camp, and Malan took Jack hunting.

… The bush has closed in around us. Malan treads almost silently and moves carefully around bushes and trees – twigs and branches that bounce and wave can alert the animals. That's what we should be looking for too, he says. Avoid open ground if we can – we will show up against the skyline. Animal spoor in the sand – I can't tell the difference between them. Maybe those with a sharp depression are buck? Watch the grass he says, its movement will show wind direction. That can carry our scent and warn the animals.

It's hot, sweat on my brow – ignore it. Don't swipe at the flies ... He's pointing to the trees – the afternoon breeze is beginning. The animals will start moving again and look for water. There is noise around, mainly birds I think, but otherwise it's all pretty quiet. I have to be too. I can smell something off the trees and the dry dust. If I'm slow and quiet, I'll blend into the veld – not a strange intruder. Malan has stopped moving, he's completely still. He's spotted something – I see nothing, only bush.

I'm panting, he motions. Now I can hear myself. Calm down and breath through the nose. Follow his stare. Now I see it – a twitch. There, in the shadow behind the tree, a small brown buck. It's looking directly at us. The ears are big, white inside with branched markings. Had it not twitched I would have missed it. It's turned away, disappeared into the grass behind the tree. I can relax my grip on the rifle and wipe my sweaty palms.

The birds have started chirping and flitting again. Maybe they sense that the danger has passed too? Malan is now pointing at the buck much further on, clearly out of range. A noticeable white belly. "Steenbok", he whispers. "Look for the ears. The ears move because of sound and flies. Horns are more difficult among the trees because they look like branches. But in the grassland, they stick out too. Use the sky as background – and remember they do too."

Now, round the side of a koppie, Malan points out a dark green band of vegetation – a riverbed. "The animals will be coming here at the end of the day to look for water." There – an animal spoor that leads down towards it. We enter the gloom of a thicket that overlooks a small clearing. So different from the tall, soft green forests I'm used to. No berries here, no mushrooms – it's too dry. "*Pasop vir die slange* - beware of snakes", he says, pointing at the low branches and to the ground. I know he's smiling but he's also not joking. I have to learn to see, to hear, to relax.

He's shown me how to kneel – left foot forward pointing at the path the animals might take, my right knee on the ground at right angles to the direction of my body. Now he shows me how to relieve the tension of the wait – rest on the back boot and flex the muscles slowly. I suck on the stem of some green grass he picked before we moved in here – it cures the thirst. "*Dink soos 'n dier* - think like an animal", he says softly. I cradle the rifle.

Match my breathing to his. He's so adapted to this. So relaxed but so aware too. I can hear the veld more. The birds are calling and flitting in and out of the branches above us and across the clearing. Now I see ants moving along the branches just in front of me and there, a spider repairing tears in its web. Do they make sound too? Can Malan hear them? There, out of a crack on the rocks in the sun, a grey-green lizard. If it wasn't for the twitching of the head as it searches, it is almost invisible against the rock. What a thrill, how illicit – I'm invisible too.

It's cooling down now. How much longer will we wait. I need another big shipment. That would really impress the Germans.... Malan's hand on my arm. He's pointing – a gap at the bottom of large boulders on the left. There – two tiny buck – the smaller with horns, the larger without. They're back-to-back. One is a lookout, while the other lowers its head to graze. The bigger animal has a rough, ochre-yellow neck. He nods that that's the one I should aim for. I'm going to have to swivel my body.

Now, breathe slowly, through the nose. Feel the curve of the wood of the butt on the cheek and the thumb under the eye. Line up the near site with my eye and then the front site on the target. Russet forehead, large brown eyes and a dark patch along the nose below them. Now, breathe out and let the front sight sink down the neck, back towards the bulk of the body above the front legs. That's the mark, that's where the heart and lungs are. Now inhale again, let the sight dip below the mark and slowly exhale. The sight drifts up. Stop. Squeeze.

"*Bliksem*", Malan cursed beside him, his ears still ringing from the crack of the Mauser. Jack had hit the animal in the haunches, and it was trying to drag itself up to escape. Malan broke out of the thicket, took a few paces and finished it off with a bullet to the chest.

Jack came forward and squatted beside the little buck, noticing how pretty it was. Now he realised it was a female.

"Klipspringer", Malan said, as he tied the legs together. "Animals move forward as they sense danger. You need to aim slightly forward, so they move into the bullet. But it's ok – now you should be able to feed yourself in the veld."

+++

A day outside Otavi, at the Kombat copper mine, Jack and Philemon split off towards the south while Malan continued on to his *plaas* at Grootfontein. Once out of the wasteland of the mine's tailings and the miserable workers' pondoks, they climbed up a rough rutted track, at times having to manhandle the cart over the rocks.

Jack was lost in reverie, letting his horse trudge sluggishly some distance behind the cart as they descended towards a large plain. He didn't notice that the cart had stopped but when Philemon called out, he straightened up in the saddle and trotted forward.

A man and a young boy were sprawled in the shade of some trees. The man lay on his side and seemed unconscious. The boy sat beside him completely passive – not acknowledging them. Philemon pulled up the brake of the cart, hopped off and walked across to them. "Haai...!" he called out in shock as he leaned over the man. Jack tethered the horse to the cart and joined him. The man was grey, his eyes rolled back into his head and he stank. "*Sjambok*", Philemon said, pointing to his back.

From his buttocks to his neck there were deep, raw gouges where he'd been lashed. There was little skin left on his back, mostly raw red flesh, yellow pus beginning to outline the deepest lacerations, which were dark with congealed blood. He'd pissed and shat where he lay, and flies buzzed around him and settled on the massive wounds.

The man groaned as they tried to lift his head to get him to drink, so Philemon slowly dripped water on his lips. Jack was able to get the boy to lift his head slightly to sip from his canvas water pouch.

They got a fire going to make tea, and then outspanned the mules and hobbled them and the horse to graze on the grass by the side of the track. The boy gnawed slowly on a roast mealie they'd given him but still stared blankly in front of him.

They made the tea very sweet and the boy responded to the sugar quite quickly, his eyes beginning to focus and taking the mug himself after a few minutes. The man remained unconscious, liquid dribbling out of his mouth unless they turned his head. Jack fetched a cheap cotton slip and they carefully laid this over the man's wounds. He groaned when the cloth touched him.

They sat in the shade, tending to the man every few minutes and waiting for the boy to recover. After a while they got out a tarpaulin and stretched it out between the cart and the tree to create more shade where he lay.

Philemon poured water into his hand and washed the boy's head and face. He and Jack then went to the man and slowly did the same. They cut off his ragged and soiled trousers and poured water over his haunches to wash the yellow-brown shit away. Jack picked up the bits of cloth with a stick and dropped them into the fire.

The afternoon passed slowly. The boy had fallen asleep and Jack and Philemon took turns dozing, slowly dripping tea and water into the man's slack mouth and keeping the flies off him. They had no idea how to treat him but there was no question of moving him.

As dusk approached Philemon unhooked the cast-iron pot from under the cart and cut up some meat and vegetables to make *potjiekos* – the ubiquitous stew in a pot of the veld.

Jack took the panga and set about making a *kraal* for the animals. Slashing at the branches released tension in his shoulders, his jaw and behind his eyes that he'd not been aware of. The brutality of the injury, the extent of it, the fact that it had obviously continued for some time was barbarity he'd never encountered. He'd seen explosions of rage amongst drunks in the street. There'd been fights on the ship to Cape Town, but these were always a loss of control. This was different – a methodical, deliberate and prolonged assault on a man they could see had been tied down by the red welts of thongs on his wrists and ankles.

Philemon had spooned out some of the stew into another pot and added water to make a thinner broth to feed the man. The boy was recovering, moving about the camp to stretch his muscles and then piss into the grass some way off. He still wasn't talking but followed Philemon's instructions to fetch the sack of mealie meal for the pap.

When the food was ready, he ate while Philemon and Jack fed the man the soup. He was hardly able to swallow, and they had to hold up his head. His eyes remained closed most of the time. They decided not to move him but moved the fire closer to keep him warm. He groaned when they gently laid a blanket on him but then slipped back into unconsciousness.

They sat on British army folding canvas chairs eating out of yellow enamel plates. The boy sat on a cow skin beside them. Philemon spoke to him gently and he began to respond in short sentences.

Normally, the bush was alive with the sounds of crickets and other insects at this time of the evening but to Jack things seemed almost hushed as the boy spoke and Philemon responded with grunts or expressions of shock. There was a musical quality to the language despite the flat tone of the boy's sentences. Apart from the clicks, which were softer than Nara's, he noticed long vowels that to him conveyed emotion. A drop in tone marked the end of a sentence.

Philemon turned away from the boy. "This is his father. He was working at the mine. The boy came with him a few weeks ago. He was looking for food in the rubbish dump. He found a sack that still had some mealie meal in it. He was walking back to the pondok when a white man on a horse came by and stopped him. He said he'd stolen the sack from the mine store. Because he's so young they punished his father. Ovambos tied him down on a rack then sjambokked him. Everyone had to watch – also the boy.

Seven lashes. That was two days ago. Their village is nearby."

The man groaned throughout the night, waking them and prompting them to give him water. At dawn they made tea and woke the boy, who'd recovered sufficiently to squat by his father, talking to him and feeding him spoons of tea and pap.

They re-packed the cart so that they could lay him at the back. Ignoring his screams and groans they rolled and pulled him onto a cow skin and then lifted him up onto the space at the back.

Herders encountered along the way sent one of their youngest to run onto the village with the news. By the time they arrived the circle of huts was in a hubbub. The boy had begun sobbing quietly as they entered the village and the man's wives and relatives wailed in anguish when they pulled up to his pondok. A bower had been prepared and the man groaned as he was lifted off the cart onto a low bed of a cow skin stretched between wooden poles. People set about bathing him and his wounds.

Jack and Philemon were escorted to an open area outside the *ovahona's kraal*. Older men gathered, passing calabashes of beer around as they discussed the assault. The tone was quiet, almost hushed, as the story of the assault was repeated. Philemon said the *ovahona* wanted to know why they had come to the area. There was no response to the interest in trade or ivory. Did he have white medicine to treat the man?

Towards evening, after the herders returned, the older men began to gather by the *ovahona*'s compound again. Philemon seemed to be repeating the story of how they found the man near the Kombat mine when slow singing began from the direction of the man's pondok. Deep male voices and then a female chorus responding. Then a single woman's voice rose above it all and the chorus repeated her call. Jack stood up agitated looking back at the pondok.

"Has he died?", Jack asked Philemon. "No, it's a healing song. Music heals. So does being together. Come with me."

A group of elderly men and women holding branches of green acacia were seated separately around the man. They seemed to take the lead in turns. Some of the choruses were rhythmic but mostly it was long harmonies. Younger women standing around sometimes joined in, swaying to the song and sometimes taking the chorus to higher notes.

Men from other villages arrived and meat, pap and calabashes of beer and sour milk were passed around. Passions were rising and people got up, gesticulating or thumping the ground. Younger men had gathered round the circle of elders and anger became more palpable. Jack grew bored and uncomfortable as the obvious stranger in their midst. He got up and nodded to the *ovahona* and went to the cart to sleep.

Away from the circle of firelight and the noise, he lay thinking of what had passed. The thrill of the hunt and his enjoyment of being back in the veld again had soured. The deliberate viciousness of the lashing and the raw outrage of the village had broken his spirit.

It was intimidating too. Schlepping about the veld looking for ivory and random *smousing* was not for him.

Early dusk of the next day he and Philemon stopped on the crest of a slight hill facing west. The plain below them was sinking into shadow – the earth turning dark rust and the vegetation black. Sunset struck them full on, a yellow-orange extravaganza that turned the rocks and earth around them into glowing terracotta, like the tiles he'd seen on churches. The moon had not yet appeared, and the stars advanced against the dark indigo before the black of the night. They fell into the night-time roles of the veld, Jack building a rudimentary *kraal* for the mules and the horse, and Philemon getting the fire going and preparing their *potjiekos*.

They'd hardly spoken of the sjambokking or the night in the village since they left early that morning. Jack had told Philemon he wanted to return to Otjiwarongo at dawn and they were on their way with the first herds leaving the village. Jack rode ahead, intent on getting out of the veld as soon as possible. Anxiety and stabs of fear were driving him to make for white civilisation as quickly as possible. But he knew too that the sjambokking had come from white civilisation. Where he had come from and where he was heading.

Night settled quickly, the constant buzz of the veld seemed to fade, and he relaxed after a spoonful or two of warthog stew. He'd shot the piglet earlier in the day without much thought of the

Jewish dietary rules. They were sitting facing the valley, a cool breeze blowing the smoke from the campfire away to the northeast.

Jack stretched out his legs towards the fire and looked up at the stars, easing his back from the day in the saddle and his stomach from the evening meal. Crickets and other insects filled the night with sound, and he realised again how much he'd missed being in the veld with Nara. The last night of their journey she'd been sad and anxious. She'd looked up at the stars too and recited a song or poem. Does she miss it too? Hardly, she's so young and seems happy at the school. The long tunic they make her wear makes her look older. But when she plays with the young children in the Yard she is as girlish as when they met. But now she laughs. "The girl I didn't have", Hanna says of her.

"This a big country", Jack said, staring back into the fire and to no one in particular. "And so empty."

"*Xlt ...*", Philemon clicked – "*Nee, klein baas.*". He got up and walked away from the circle of firelight to look down at the plain below them. "*Kom kyk* - come take a look."

Jack stood beside him, his eyes adjusting to the deep darkness spread out below. Philemon pointed out tiny pinpricks of light, scores of them – spread out almost like fireflies. Some were in clusters, other lonely little stars in the black veld. "Those are cooking fires, like ours. Each one from a *kraal* or a village. Only a few will be white farms. Most are Herero. We are cattle people. And cattle need space – we take them to where there's grazing.

For us, this land is shaped by the water holes and the grazing. They belong to our people. But the German farmers build fences to keep us out and to keep everything for themselves."

"What were they saying last night?" he asked when they sat down again.

"There is a lot of anger. The Germans are pushing the people too far. Every day there are more bad things. Land, water, cattle – they take all the time. They have lots of rules. But the rules are to trick the people. The traders let you buy things. Then, when you can't pay, they take cattle or land.

"Some of the worst are the chiefs – they have the most and they sell the most. And they don't ask the people. Maharero, near Okahandja – he wants to be headman of all the Herero. But he sells much of the land, leaving his people with little."

"What will happen?"

"The young men – they want to fight now. Kambazembi, our old *ovahona,* has always opposed the Germans but doesn't want war. He doesn't want the life that Maharero wants – all the white man's things. The Germans are too cruel. The sjambok – that happens a lot. There have also been hangings – and abuse of young girls and even married women. The young men think the old leaders are too soft and too close to the Germans.

"But there will be a war and then we all have to be together. All the Herero. The Germans now use the Nama against us too. They know the land and are good fighters. If the Nama and the Herero fought together, we would defeat the Germans. They are not from here. They have to bring their truppe from far away and the truppe are weak in this country.

"But there is no trust with the Nama. A long time ago the Germans protected us from the Witbooi. Now they turn on us. There is little trust between the Herero chiefs too. The Germans know this. They are clever with this."

Friday, 22ⁿᵈ September 1989

St Georges Street, Cape Town

Continuity

Lenny recalled the smell of printing ink and the rumble of the printing presses as he walked into the chambers of N. Lurie & Co, the Levin Group's long-time lawyers, on the top floor of the Argus Building. Nathan Lurie, the founding partner had been adopted by the Sonnenbergs when his parents sent him to Cape Town after the rise of the Nazis. The boy had enjoyed a thoroughly Anglo education, and had chosen to become a lawyer rather than enter Sonnenberg's now declining business. Jack was among his first clients, and no major decision had been taken without his participation.

Subconsciously, Lenny was looking for a sense of continuity. Ever since his night on the farm – in Jack's room and office with the coat, the old bush hat, and Sydney's picture - he'd been wrestling with what the sale really meant for him. It wasn't just a rational, inevitable business transaction – it was a rupture with the past, his past, with the family's history. And now he realised he knew so very little of it. For the first time he began to sense that this history defined him more than he'd known. His ignorance disturbed him, left him unprepared and with a sense that something important was slipping away. Nathan Lurie, he hoped, would know much of that history as he had been close to Jack for a long time.

"Fuddy duddy" was how Cyn dismissed the old Levin Group's offices downtown after his father's death. She cajoled him into agreeing to a complete remodelling where she would be the designer. But she had gone too far, and it was only Lynne's uncharacteristically sharp insistence that stopped her junking the old photographs that traced the establishment and early activities of the group – the wagon shop in Otjiwarongo, the general stores, the salt mines on the coast, firewood collection, rows of Raleigh bicycles waiting for Ovambo workers at the end of their contracts on the diamond mines, motor agencies and agricultural machinery, drilling rigs, the farms, chemicals and pharmaceuticals and more. These were now tastefully reframed and displayed in the otherwise ultra-ordinary boardroom.

Lurie's offices were the exact opposite. Lenny sat at the long yellowwood table and chairs which he knew were at least sixty years old. There were original oils of sailing ships in Table Bay and of wine estates and fruit farms, some of which were still among the firm's clients. On the main wall of the boardroom, incongruously small, was a black and white photograph of old man Sonnenberg standing behind the counter of his wholesale and chandlery business on Buitengracht Street. It all spelled reassuring continuity in this time of change, which why he was meeting with Lurie and the other lawyers gathered at the table.

The main item on their agenda was a call with the lawyer in Keetmanshoop. He had put together a file of the various farm documents he'd collected over the years, and added that the army had done an aerial survey of the area a few years before when they were looking for places to build landing strips. "I think I can get these maps and aerial photographs. But I don't think the land registry in South West will accept a separate property in this area for something that is non-viable as a farm. I think a carve-out of the 'Steyn *plaas*' will really depend on the goodwill of the purchaser."

The lawyers around the table nodded – this has been their original opinion. Lurie held up his hand, well used to the ways of country lawyers – "I assume you have a purchaser with such 'goodwill' in mind? If you do, please let us know now before we start an auction for an international purchaser. I am sure we will easily agree fees reflecting your long-time association with the Levins."

The lawyer hesitated briefly; he'd wanted to discuss this with Lenny privately, but he knew that wasn't going to happen now. "Of course. Mrs Bruns, the neighbour, knows the farm and knows the family. I think she might be interested."

"I know Frau Bruns", Lenny said. "I will arrange to meet her myself."

"*Plaasjapies* (farm boys) are direct and can usually do well enough on their own", Lurie interjected with humour. "We lawyers can tidy up things later".

After the call, the junior partners left Lenny and Lurie alone. "I don't think you should wait until the deal is closed before letting the partners know", Lurie said, referring to the well-connected group of Cape Town investors his stepfather had started and which he and the Levins were part of.

Lenny pursed his lips – "It's not as if we're getting out of South West", he said. "The farm's always been a purely family asset and it's a family decision."

"I don't think they would see it otherwise", Lurie responded. "But remember, some of them knew Jack, and all of them invested with your father. You're the one that's developed this as an investment group on the basis of trust and discretion between the families. That's what they would expect. They see you as their man on the ground. You've built up the connections with SWAPO. No one likes surprises. While it's less critical for the fishing investments, remember – you're the bondholder for old man Kahan and the investment at Rosh Pinah. That's huge, we're in bed with a gorilla in Iscor and the whole thing is riskier. That's close to the farm, as I recall?"

Lenny nodded. "I'll go there when I meet Mrs Bruns at the farm and then we can have a meeting with the group."

Lurie leaned back in his chair and looked at Lenny pensively for a moment. "Selling the farm is significant, Lenny. It's the right thing to do, of course." He leaned forward abruptly, steepling his fingers. "Jack anticipated this, and the farm is part of his original trust settlement. There may be documents and other things relating to this on the farm. I know you've looked but we need to be certain. It may be in a separate envelope or box and addressed to your father or perhaps to the trustees. Anyway, once there's a contract we'll need to inform them and have a conversation."

+++

Early 1900s   Windhuk

"I only receive private patients in the afternoon", the middle-aged officer said when Jack entered his office. "And, only at my home – not here in the hospital."

"I'm here to talk about medical supplies, Herr Stabsarzt."

"Aah, that we need", the staff surgeon said, motioning him to a chair. "The Prussians up on the hill worry more about horses and bullets than they do about men. You're the young trader bringing in supplies from Cape Town, aren't you? What are you offering?"

"British army surpluses from the war with the Boers. We also have taken over some of their unfulfilled contracts with the local manufacturers and importers in Cape Town. What do you need?"

"Whisky, – and books", the man said with a chuckle. "I spent time in Edinburgh studying surgery and developed a taste for that culture. That's not popular in this shit hole where the Deutschlandlied is considered the greatest piece of music ever written!"

After more cynical banter the surgeon continued – "At the moment we are less than one thousand Truppen and maybe two hundred administration officials", he said. "We have four hospitals – here, Swakopmund, Keetmanshoop and Gobabis. There are some 20 medical officers to serve them, as well as those who choose to remain as settlers once they are discharged. They are entitled to medical care with their families.

"More settlers are coming all the time and war is inevitable - so it would be correct to have sufficient medical supplies here already. Leutwein and his advisors fear they may have to ask for thousands of troops if there is a general uprising. He is very good at keeping the natives apart but that will only work for a while if you ask me.

"We could benefit from the British war experience. And the goods are close by. An army can never have enough field dressings, splints and morphine. Other drugs and surgical supplies are also critical," he said.

"I'll need your help to note the drugs and special stuff", Jack said.

He hesitated and then asked – "What about civilians?"

"There are a few private doctors and missionaries. No hospital – but there are plans."

"And the natives?"

The man looked at him with wry amusement. He nodded up towards the Feste. "They don't think about them like that, young man. If the blacks can't work, they are of no value so why treat them? And if they're sick, they may have to sell their land and cattle. The wealthy ones like Maharero can afford care and come into town for it."

Together they drew up a list of drugs and equipment and agreed that Jack would come back with a quote.

"Next time you come, bring some whisky. That is the best cure for the social illnesses of this place. Also, I know who to share it with to make sure we get a deal", he said with a wink.

Jack added the list to the letter he'd already written to Sonnenberg and dropped it off at the post office. "Whisky (and some English books) will smooth business here", he scrawled at the bottom in Yiddish. A few days later he found someone travelling to Swakopmund and sent a letter to Cameron via Gerson, his agent in the town. The letter set out the surgeon-general's information on the numbers of troops in the innocuous business code he and Cameron had devised.

+++

Catholic Mission, Klein Windhuk

She pushed open the pine door of the mission building and, seeing him - caught her breath. He'd come early. Usually she waited for him at the gates at the bottom of the drive – keen to get away for the weekend and keen to meet him away from the mission. She skipped out, smiling.

The Friday afternoon to Saturday excursion was the highlight of her week. Sundays were dreary and boring, and the rest of the week was busy – between classes in the morning and labour in the gardens, vineyard, laundry or kitchen in the afternoon. And always, the strict supervision of the brothers at the mission.

He was sitting on the cart – flicking the whip lazily at sticks and leaves on the ground. He smiled furtively when she pushed open the door and her eyes widened with surprise at finding him there. He was happy to see her too.

She chatted happily as they trotted out of the Klein Windhoek valley back towards the town, filling him in on her week and the new Damara girl who had arrived at the mission. "I speak better German than she does. We share a room and have become friends. Most of the boys are Nama or Damara too, so we talk a lot to them. I've been teaching her how to do the laundry. The brothers say some Catholic sisters are coming for a separate school for girls."

"I have something to show you", he said, cutting north across the Ausspannplatz towards the railway station instead of making for the Yard. They passed the abandoned prison camp opposite the Feste and he turned west at the Post Office and stopped besides a small white building that was on the edge of the town overlooking a dry riverbed. The pondoks and hovels of the black workers' *Werften* (worker's settlement or 'location'[39]) were sprawled along the opposite bank. There were hardly any trees or bushes and the

---

[39] "Location" was the term for the migrant labour camps in South Africa. As black urbanization accelerated, they became sprawling slums on the outskirts of the white towns and cities.

few neighbouring buildings were quite distant.

"I'm going to live here."

"You're leaving Frau Fentin? Why?" she asked, a quaver in her voice.

"They need the space. There are more children, and I need space too."

Pigeons fluttered in alarm in the bare rafters under the corrugated iron roof as he unlocked the door and pushed his way into an entrance hall. Their shit was thick on the floor of the two adjoining rooms, and the place was baking hot and airless. There was a kitchen shed and an outside bathing enclosure behind. At the backend of the bare yard there was an outhouse and a broken-down pondok. "This is where I'll be able to store things", pointing to a partially complete shed alongside the house.

She sensed his excitement and pride. But she was surprised and confused, intimidated by the change. Somehow, she felt she should have been consulted. She stopped looking around, resentful. "*Viele schlangen*" (lots of snakes), she muttered, waving vaguely at the pigeons and the baking riverbed.

He heard her but chose to ignore her sullenness. "Don't worry, Nara, I will still fetch you every Friday and we will still go to the Yard. If you want, you can stay there with Magda…or, you can come back here. But it's time for me to have my own place."

It was a short trot to the Yard, and she sat with her knees pressed together, fiddling tightly with the hem of her grey mission smock. She could see it was very close, but she didn't want to persuade herself. She didn't want change, she wanted reassurance.

The months that had passed had been happy and stable. Food was regular and nourishing. Hunger, cruelty and the threat of abandonment that were a constant part of her earliest memories had diminished. She knew she'd grown – the mission smocks had grown tight across her chest and had to be changed. That gave her a sense of pride and confidence. Everyone remarked how tall she'd become – and she'd made friends with the other mission children. Writing, reading, counting was wondrous and gave her self-confidence. There was very little to read outside the bible in the mission school but what she could find there and in the Yard she devoured.

The discipline of school life was irksome, especially when it was enforced with severity and even the odd slap, but it was also a reassuring routine. When Jack had been away on trips, Herr Fentin had come to fetch her on Fridays. Motherly affection came naturally to both Magda and Hanna, and colour discrimination hardly affected her for the time being. Jewish customs were no less strange than the rituals she followed in the Mission and the ways of her people diminished with time.

Swaying from side to side with the trotting of the mules she processed the change and realized that it was not too severe and even exciting. Besides, there was nothing she could do about it.

She fell back into telling him about her studies and work, and skipped off to tell Magda the news.

My dearest family,...

Windhuk

I hope this finds you well.

I am well – thank G-d – and have lots of news. That's my excuse for a long time not writing. I have been very busy.

I have just moved into my own house. This is the first letter I am writing on this table. I already wrote that I was staying with the small number of Yidden who live here – they are in a place nearby called 'the Yard', a bit like our shtetl houses where we live close to each other. In Suidwes there is so much space it's unusual to live close by your neighbours. But they and I needed more space. The business is growing – and I need a storeroom for the goods I'm importing. This house has two rooms and an entrance hall as well as the storeroom. There is also a big shady veranda – they call a 'stoep' – which is important in the summer. There are also places for servants – a woman who cooks and a guard. Everyone has servants here. I also have a stable – I have now two mules and a horse.

A few weeks ago, I came back from a journey in the country, which took me past a big, copper mine. It seems there is wealth in the ground here like in South Africa. But there is much cruelty too – I came across a black man who'd been so badly whipped by the Germans that he had no skin on his back.

There are more and more German settlers arriving all the time. That is causing tension with the natives because they are losing their land and their cattle. The natives are not united and that is the luck of the whites. The government policy is to keep the natives divided and bribe their leaders. So far it is working but everyone fears an uprising – they talk about it all the time.

That does cause tension and worry in life here. But it is good for business. My partners in Cape Town are able to get military and general goods from the British, which I can supply to the German troops and administration. They seem to need everything and so far, take it from me at very good prices.

I've also started a wagon repair business in a town a day's train journey from here and will soon open a storeroom there too to supply the northern district.

There are other traders here, some of them have been here a long time and are well established. I have better connections in Cape Town, as most of them are German and import from Germany. That takes longer.

Many of the soldiers who are here also choose to stay on when their term of duty ends. They are given land on very good terms. Some of these Germans are very low-class - and they are the worst with the blacks. The local magistrate told me that there are many cases of Germans assaulting blacks and abusing their women. He says he dismisses most of these cases because the settlers would be upset, and the governor doesn't want trouble with them. He prosecutes only the worst cases.

The governor and the major officers and officials are a better class – like the Germans you admire, Immale! ...

I am well, thank G-d although I miss you all of course. I will try and send some more money once I'm paid for my latest shipment. Please write me to say how much you actually receive so I can check the bank commission.

———

Dearest Tatte and Ima,

<u>*Please keep this page from Leah!*</u>

I know I promised you and her that I would send a ticket for her as soon as I was able. The problem is that it is a very long and dangerous journey for a young girl. Not even two girls travelling on their own would be safe. The journey from our little shtetl via Hamburg - London - Southampton to Cape Town is full of sheisters and ganovim as I'm sure you've heard.

And now, here in Suidwes there are lots of newcomers too. The problem is that amongst them – there are also the worst of Jewish riff raff – escaping the depression (and the police) in Cape Town. The worst seem to be the pimps living off Jewish zoine. I have seen some of these young girls preyed on by men whose cruelty shines from their eyes. Some could be Leah's age! I saw this happening on the boat from Southampton.

Even if we could find a safe way for her to come here it would be difficult to find a chassen (groom). There are so few of us and those arriving now are not worthy. The political situation here too is unstable. Life in Cape Town, on her own, would also be too dangerous.

So, I write with a heavy heart that now is not the time. Better you find a chassen in Lita – I can help provide a dowry – and then they can travel here together. Best such a chassen hobn i handel (have a trade – no one needs a yeshiva bocher (yeshiva student) here.

+++

"!Nara is not well", the young Damara said when Jack opened the door.

"Who told you to come?"

"She did."

She had complained of a headache and fever the day before, the boy explained as they trotted across to the mission in the cart. She'd eaten but then thrown up, and had been told to go to bed. During the night she'd got worse and asked him to fetch Jack.

The mission father was pleased to have Jack take care of her. She was pale and shivering but boiling to the touch. Some of the older children helped him arrange the pile of skins and a blanket he'd brought for her in the back of the wagon, and he drove back to the house as gently as he could.

"She'll be on my bed", Jack said to the maid when he carried her into the house. The woman stripped back the bedding and then knelt beside Nara, talking to her softly in Nama.

Jack prepared some sweetened tea, not knowing really what else to do. The maid held Nara's head up to get her to sip some of the tea and then laid her back gently. "She needs medicinal plants - |*Ganab* and *gamagu*. I'll send the boy to Magda - she should have some."

Hanna and Magda bustled in a while later and shooed Jack out of the room where he'd been sitting watching the girl slumber. "She needs a wash to cool her", Hanna said, drawing back the curtains in his room to let in air. "And for that she needs privacy."

The maid crushed some camelthorn leaves and flowers into tepid water to wash her off. Hanna, like his mother, confronted health challenges with chicken soup, and that was put on to simmer. The girl's smock, drenched in sweat, was taken to be washed and they dressed her in one of Jack's shirts.

"I think she's cooler and she's kept down the tea. See if she'll have some of the soup later when she wakes. I'll come tomorrow morning. If she gets worse – send for me."

Jack sat in the main room, doing his bookkeeping and periodically going into the bedroom to check her. She seemed cooler to the touch and slept deeply most of the day.

Late afternoon her fever climbed again, and Jack washed her face and neck with the camelthorn water. Her skin, normally a deep umber colour like cinnamon, had lost its natural sheen – he noticed by its absence – and her eyes had shrunk back into her face, making her seem tiny.

The fever broke in the early evening and she woke hungry for the first time. Jack brought her some of the soup and fed it to her slowly. There was a sharp sour smell from her mouth, and he brought a bowl for her to swill with the cool herb tea they'd made. She fell asleep again and he went back into the main room where the maid had laid out a bed on top of some animal skins for him.

… Her retching wakes him.

She's sitting on the edge of the bed holding his shirt out in front of her. She'd been sick into it. The room smells of vomit. He lights a candle on the dresser and brings the chamber pot so she can empty the vomit into it. He undoes the sleeves of the shirt and lifts it up over her head. Her skin is clammy. He helps her stand and wraps the sheet off the bed around her. He leads her to sit on a chair in the shadowy corner of the room.

He makes up the bed again with a fresh bedding and brings her back to lie down. "I'm going to get some warm water and some fresh tea."

He places the candle on a stool by the bed. The yellow pool of light cups them like hands in the dark room and silent house.…her skin like tiger's eye in the candlelight. Cool scented water on his fingers as he gently washes her face, neck and arms with a flannel. Smell of the sun in the towel to dry her off. Strange strength in the tight peppercorn curls as he cradles her small head. Pleasant flush of tenderness around his diaphragm, and his heart swells as he tends to her. Large, dark, languid eyes follow his care. Trust. Sheet now down to her hips as he washes her shoulders, chest and tummy where the vomit had soaked through the shirt. Cool air, smell receding. He focuses on what he's doing avoiding her eyes. Breasts have grown, now quite round and high on her chest. Would almost fill the palm of his hand if cupped. Nipples have grown larger and darker. Flat against her skin. Flushed by pleasure and mouth dry from embarrassment he avoids her eyes. Thrill in the groin. Rinses the flannel and then carefully swabs her breasts. Careful not to touch her with his fingers.

Sheet now rolled down towards the knees. The hair between her legs, wisps as fine as a line a few months before, now a tiny neat triangle. Her hand slips down to cover her herself as he sponges off her abdomen and legs. He helps her sit up and washes her back, dries her off and fetches a fresh shirt. Her breasts lift as she raises her arms.

He sits beside her and helps her sip some of the tea. Their eyes meet. Both find something new reflected there.

Early 1903   Buitengracht Street, Cape Town

Debt

Dear Jack,

This letter is being written for delivery in person via Cameron. I do this because it seems your success in Windhuk is raising curiosity and perhaps jealously too.

Some of your competitors amongst the German dealers have recently been in Cape Town or have made enquiries via contacts to get goods from our suppliers and more British army surpluses. None of them have the contacts Axelsonn, the old Swede, had — and I think we have managed to block them for the time being.

But it won't stay that way. Even though you repaid the syndicate's first loan promptly and generously I'm not confident that one or two may not be open to being offered a higher percentage or price. I am least confident of Shochet because he has gambling debts. I am looking for another whisky importer just in case. I know how important whisky is in developing your business in such a forlorn place! But I also think we should be prepared to pay a higher price or commission or something else if competition increases. Also, there is increasing demand from the gold fields and from Kimberley.

Some of the criminal yidden are moving to Suidwes from here. You probably know and have met them. I don't think it would take much for the Germans or a competitor to persuade one of these people to translate your letters written in Yiddish. That's why I've drawn up a code on a separate page that we should use to refer to sensitive things. I have tried to make these so that they can be referred to in telegrams as well which are always inspected. Also, if there is any danger, I suggest we use the word 'bandages' in a telegram.

Enclosed a receipt from the bank for the deposit of the money you sent into your account. Please see to the payment of the remainder of what is owed to the syndicate for the previous shipment. I've also sent the safe (I'm sure you've seen it!) and some books and magazines as you requested.

Sophia sends her regards. She knows that you are doing well and asks when you plan to visit Cape Town. There are more eligible women here than in Suidwes, I'm sure! She has a number in mind. I hope this finds you well…

P.S. – you should destroy this letter after you read it.

+++

Jack and Cameron walked down to the Swakopmund mole and watched settlers, Schutztruppe and their horses disembark from the SS *Gertrude Woermann*. The mole had silted up quickly and unloading was still via lighters and long boats rowed by Liberian oarsmen.

"Every few weeks they publish more regulations", Jack said as they looked down at the churning water. "Most of these meant for the blacks – things like work permits, where they can live, how they may be disciplined. There is a lot of surveying work going on – for mines, roads and now a new railway to Otavi."

Once all the people were off-loaded the lighters came in with five pieces of field artillery. Crates of what appeared to be shells followed.

"Seems that they are really preparing for war", Cameron said when Jack told him he'd seen rows of cannon drawn up at the armoury in Klein Windhuk. "The key for them will be keeping the tribes separate."

+++

An advertisement for Raleigh Bicycles in The Strand magazine caught Jack's eye. He was sitting on his own at the back of the railway carriage on the slow journey up from the coast, paging through the small stack of papers and magazines Cameron had brought back with him from Cape Town. There was demand for news and culture from the Cape, the UK and elsewhere – a thirst in fact – but no margin, he'd concluded. He sensed too that the Germans who visited his home viewed English publications with disapproval. The surgeon general was always happy to receive them, but he too was discreet about his interest.

Bicycles may be a way to expand beyond building materials and military supplies, he thought. He was restless and ambitious, and also exposed if the Germans decided to rely only on German suppliers. War, if and when it came, would not last forever. Like the British at the end of the Boer War, he could be caught with surplus supplies. Maybe the blacks, as poor as they were, could afford bicycles, he thought. They certainly needed them as they schlepped the long distances from the *werften* where they lived to their work in the towns, or from their villages to the white farms. They would always be the biggest population, never mind what the Germans did.

+++

The train stopped in Karibib for the night and Jack stayed with a Jewish butcher who had arrived there a year earlier. The man was rough and ready – most butchers seemed to be – but he was savvy and had quickly established himself in the little railstop to deal in cattle and horses and supply the rail gangs.

After supper they went to the local bar. The surveyor Jack had met before was there to survey the new spur to Otavi to connect the copper mine directly to Swakopmund. SWACO, the concession company, seemed increasingly confident, he said.

"Leutwein has persuaded Maharero to sell off a strip of land several kilometres wide for the line to cover his debts. He lives it up, Maharero does. You should see his house, and he dresses like a German baron! He loves champagne and women. He's constantly in debt and his people are beginning to resent it. He hasn't told his people yet, but when they find out there will be a lot of anger. Leutwein is pushing for the Hereros to be in reserves, because of tension with the settlers and because the line will carve up their traditional grazing areas and make controlling them easier."

Windhoek was in an uproar when Jack got back. A German settler named Dietrich had hitched a ride from Omaruru to Karibib with Barmenias, the son of the Herero chief Zacharias Zeraua, who was taking his heavily pregnant wife by ox-wagon to her mother for the birth of their first child as was their custom. After dinner when all had gone to sleep Barmenias was awakened by a revolver shot and saw Dietrich running away. His wife had been shot dead.

Dietrich was eventually charged with manslaughter rather than murder, and initially acquitted. After much protest he was finally sentenced to three years in prison, but was later released and recruited as an NCO in the Schutztruppe.

In late July, Leutwein issued a decree that any African debts not collected within a year would lapse. Instead of curbing the indebtedness and the resulting instability, the decree spurred traders to collect what they claimed was owed to them, sometimes with violence. The German justice system was not applied fairly – even in cases of murder, rape and extreme violence – a drumbeat of incidents fuelling further resentment.

Desert winters were bitter, dry and dusty, and Jack found the evenings on his own irksome. He didn't frequent the taverns and couldn't overdo time in the Yard. He worked instead. Solitude opened space for the buzz of discontent like a wasp trapped in a room. In the town there was little opportunity to hear from the blacks directly, and deference and avoidance were built into the master-servant relationship at home. But it was there, persistent and mounting. And it was internal too – it came from the white settler's discomfort and guilt. And their fear.

+++

Monday, August 28th, 1989   Okahandja

The heavy padlock and chains securing the Levin Motors compound were still wet with night dew when Tjandero unlocked the gate to let his father enter. They set out with the night-watchmen to verify that the other gates and doors were still locked, checked the cars, trucks, tractors and other machinery parked in the compound, and then signed the men's timesheets to release them.

Tjandi was exhausted after the three days of tribal and family celebration that marked Herero Day. But his father, the foreman for the business, was pedantic about being the first in to work, as he had been for some forty years. As proud as he was of his son's leading role in this year's celebrations, his loyalty to his employer was a foundation of his identity – as was being a Herero.

Every year, thousands of Herero from across the country gathered in Okahandja, where their legendary chief Samuel Maharero was reinterred in 1923, nineteen years after *Otjitiro Otjndjandja* ('many people died in one place'), their defeat by the Germans. Maharero and several other Herero chiefs are buried at the Bantu Kirche.

Tjandero was one of the young men selected by the organising committee to lead the solemn commemorative march from the Kirche to a large open space on the other side of the town for a huge tribal parade and banquet. Here the mood lightened, and with the festivities, Tjandero made his mark too, prancing on his horse, dancing, and singing both traditional and current Herero songs. There were young Herero from all across Hereroland, and three days of flirting and socialising.

Herero Day was always fraught with tensions and rivalries between the sub-tribes and clans. This year's events were also impacted by the impending elections. Along with a much greater crowd, the Herero-affiliated party (the DTA) was much in evidence, its volunteers so active that they were expelled from the traditional procession. Behind the smartly uniformed mounted *oturupa* (troops) like Tjandero, columns of Herero women in their traditional multi-layered dresses and *otjikaiva* (horned hats) paraded slowly, recalling the Herero people's relationship with cattle. Then cadets and older men marched – part imitating, part parodying the practices of the German Schutztruppe and the South African army that replaced them.

The crimson colour of the Maharero clan was dominant in the dresses and hats of the women, sashes, epaulettes, gaiters and ribbons of the men, and the flags carried by the horsemen. Too much offended the other sub-tribes and clans. The DTA's intense campaigning upset the balance that had evolved over generations.

Tjandero had mixed feelings about his khaki uniform. His father had paid a lot for the tunic, jodhpur-style breeches, and Sam Browne belt he wore for the festival. He knew and understood its origins – from Herero warriors stealing the uniforms of German soldiers believing it gave them the powers of the fallen in battle, it had evolved to a subtle parody of the German and later the South African colonialist powers. But for his generation, the uniforms were unavoidably those of the South African army and police, to be derided rather than emulated. He thought the ranks, medals, campaign ribbons and other paraphernalia the older men wore were laughable, although he was too respectful to say this.

His father beamed as other co-workers, even Ovambo who'd not attended but had heard of Tjandero's role, came to congratulate them. But he was visibly perturbed when he and Tjandero were summoned to meet the depot manager.

"I hear Tjandi was a great success at Herero Day", the Afrikaans manager said, with a big smile. "Now, I have more good news – you've been selected for management training in Windhoek. There's no date yet but in the meantime, you will have to get to know the other parts of the business."

Within a few days Tjandero was moved from his job as a driver delivering spare parts and tools, and sent to familiarise himself with the heavy Caterpillar earth-moving machinery and other agricultural equipment Levin Motors sold and serviced. For the first time he attended sales meetings.

"You can stay with your aunt, Sewa", his father said. "She returned not long ago from Botswana and lives in Katatura. She will have strong things to say about these changes."

Saturday, 23rd September 1989   Constantia, Cape Town

Cyn…

… looked ravishing when she came downstairs to leave for their dinner party. An ice teal dress clung to her full figure. Expensive jewellery sparkled on her lovely neck and ears, her blond hair was drawn up in a lavish pile. Slim silver shoes matched the small clutch, and a silver–threaded pashmina draped across the bare suntanned shoulders, open enough to reveal her deep cleavage. He cupped her bum to feel if she was wearing underwear as they moved to the door – she wasn't. Too late, he noticed his daughter watching. He winked but she cloaked herself in her habitual teenage sulk and looked away at the TV.

They swished along the dark avenues between the luxury homes of Constantia, cocooned in the purring reassurance of his Mercedes coupe on their way to Bishopscourt. Her perfume whispered at him, the knowledge of her nakedness beneath the dress teased. This private knowledge of her availability thrilled like a women's fingers on his cock.

"You still get horny for me when you're away", she mused, breaking the silence in the car. A statement rather than a question hung like mist above the dashboard. He didn't know if it was a playful come-on, a plea for reassurance from a woman approaching middle age, a statement that she knew what he was thinking, or a prelude to one of "those conversations". He was hoping for the first.

She looked out at the leafy darkness along the manicured lawns and hedges of the estates of their neighbours. "I don't", she said. The mist above the dashboard turned to frost.

She threaded her arm through his as they walked towards the entrance, over the red brick courtyard. She pressed her full breast against his arm and leaned in towards him to whisper – "maybe I'll change my mind later if they serve enough champagne".

He knew she was playing with him. He resented it and had tired of the endless ups and downs of their relationship that she seemed to need as validation. But he couldn't wean himself into indifference. She always wanted them to be seen as one of the Cape's "golden couples", and as the door opened and their hostess welcomed them into the tinkling excitement of the dinner party – so did he.

Over dinner he was seated next to a woman who was conservatively but expensively dressed. Cyn had mentioned her before as the only daughter of a wealthy Johannesburg diamond dealer who'd gone on to make even more money in property. They had recently acquired a Cape Dutch house nearby. She introduced her husband, Dani, who was sitting opposite. Lenny smiled when he said he was also in the diamond business. There was an old Cape Town joke that was particularly appropriate in these circumstances: "IDB" generally referred to the classic South African offence of Illicit Diamond Buying, and also, in this case – "Into Daddy's Business". When he mentioned that he'd just come back from South West, Dani leaned forward – "We can talk after dinner, perhaps?"

Dani, by complexion and accent clearly Israeli, mentioned the Lubowski assassination. Would South Africa really give up? Lenny thought they now had no choice. Dani said he had investors who were looking for contacts with SWAPO. He and his father-in-law had extensive international contacts, and could sell directly on the bourses of Tel Aviv and Antwerp. They exchanged cards and arranged to meet the next week.

Lenny mulled over this conversation over as he drove home over Rhodes Drive. There had always been rumours about Jack and diamonds. The gossip was that Jack had smuggled diamonds in the salt he moved from the coast, in the truckloads of firewood, under the animal pelts he traded, in the frames of the bicycles he sold to the Ovambo workers on the mine, and the tyres he sold to the farmers and truckers. Nothing had ever been found and Sam, his father, had always become irate when this came up in conversations. The diamonds were put down as "non-existent", and the "smuggling" was rather Jack's hard work, skill at barter, and generosity in trading on credit.

Dani's interest and his connections could be useful, Lenny thought. The De Beers' hold on the local diamond industry would not be pried loose. At least not initially. They would co-opt people from the new government to ensure a smooth transition and continued control. But, like his insight that shipping containers could be used to transfer funds out of South Africa, Dani's connections could be useful.

Cyn dozed beside him – pouting. She'd had too much champagne and he had to help her to bed. He stripped off her dress, frustration like bile in his mouth as he rolled her heavy thighs under the duvet.

Images of the sway of her heavy breasts, the triangle of shadow between her legs swirled round with the glass of single malt he'd poured for himself in his study. The drink began to placate his frustration and resentment, and his mind went back to the conversation about diamonds, and from there to Jack. Better check Dani out with Lurie, he said to himself. Old man Sonnenberg was connected to the diamond business. Tomorrow he was due to see Lynne. Should he say anything?

October 1903   Windhuk

"Ein Glücksfall" (a stroke of luck)

The Kalahari starts its daily bake by mid-morning. Temperatures over the vast area climb rapidly and the air soars upwards, forming towering ramparts of white cumulus. Below them, the air pressure drops, and cooler denser air is drawn in off the Atlantic. As this massive front sweeps eastward across the desiccated Namib and over the arid Khomas Hochland, it whips up dust, heavy in mica. Many of the European settlers developed allergies to this – eye irritations, breathing difficulties, headaches. Coping with allergies was a favourite topic in the evenings as they sat out on their stoeps.

Jack had learned that the cool and relative damp nights settled the dust, so he started his days early. Tramping up the incline towards the fort, his enjoyment of the still cool air, the bright blue sky, and the twittering birds was interrupted by the sudden appearance of mounted Truppen trotting in from the depot at Klein Windhoek. By now, keenly attuned to the stirrings of the army and the administration, the grim set of the soldier's faces indicated that this was not an ordinary patrol. "There's trouble somewhere."

There's been a rebellion by the Bondelswarts near Warmbad in the south, the quartermaster's clerk confirmed. Lieutenant Jobst and two others were killed. There will have to be a big response.

Jack had hardly heard of the Bondelswarts – yet another group of Nama in the arid south of the country, probably less than a thousand people. Warmbad, a trading and mission post near the border of the Cape Colony was of no real significance, as far as he knew. "Why there?" he asked.

"It doesn't matter. These clashes are inevitable and it's better that there's a real war where we can teach them a lesson sooner rather than later."

"Good it's down there – so far away", said another official. "There are not many settlers there, but it proves to Berlin that without more help and backing we are really vulnerable." Leutwein, it seemed, was planning to lead the expedition himself.

The *Deutsch-Südwestafrikanisische Zeitung* reported the incident in hysterical terms, and this was the more sedate and controlled voice of the settler elite. It made no difference that by the time the paper hit the streets it was clear that Jobst had been at fault. He'd ignored the terms of the protection treaty with the Bondelswarts, which barred him from intervening in their disputes with other Africans (in this case a Herero woman and a goat!). It was by his orders that the first shots were fired, killing the Bondelswart kaptein – Jan Christian. Privately, Leutwein was critical of Jobst's actions but he could not hold off the pressure in the territory and in Berlin.

The Kaiser demanded that military forces be dispatched at once, not only to Suidwes but to all the German territories "lest we lose all of our colonial possessions".

"*Ein Glücksfall*", the Surgeon-General said of the attack. He was sipping Jack's whisky on the back stoep of the house, on his way home to his wife and daughter in Klein Windhuk. Jack enjoyed his company – he had a great sense of humour despite his default cynicism, and wide-ranging interests. He was a thinker who, although he could grow pensive with the whisky, would open up to Jack and challenge him in new ways. He'd also concocted some drops that eased Jack's irritated eyes.

"Lucky for all involved unless you're the Bondelswarts", the officer chuckled. "Leutwein can now be seen to be tough, and the Kaiser can keep the settler lobby happy and feed the generals some war. For the settlers this is a vindication. It answers a deep need that many brought with them."

"How so?" Jack asked, not following.

"I've been treating these people now for six years. This new wave of settlers, I've got to know them. Unhappy there, unhappy here – they see themselves as Germany's unloved children.

"They're not like us soldiers, who are 'ordered here' and can go home if we want after some adventure. The older settlers too, those who have succeeded, do not have the same attitude. They are more self-motivated. But for the new ones – those coming from the industrial towns and poor farms – many come here with a certain sense of – ... waving his hand as he searched for the word with – *missgunst* (resentment). And then of course, alone on remote farms and little towns they feel vulnerable and even more forgotten. A little war makes Papa Kaiser pay attention. It's self-fulfilling. You'll see, the more troops and supplies arrive – and the more money the Chancellor supplies – the more they will demand."

The pace of preparation for Leutwein's expedition increased. As the stores emptied of supplies, so new orders came in. "I'm sure things will be over quickly", the quartermaster said, "but perhaps you could look into delivering directly to Lüderitzbucht? That would be more efficient."

A few days later Rolf rode into town with his company. The Ausspannplatz was now filling up with wagons, and the mustering troops were camping in tents where the *kraal*s for the Oktoberfest had been. Officers were being billeted in private houses and Jack was quick to invite the young Lieutenant, who had visibly matured, to stay with him.

"You're doing well", Rolf said that evening as they ate together on the stoep. "I keep hearing of the *'junger Jude'* when we talk about supplies. And this is comfortable, no?" he said, waving at the house. Jack nodded, non-committal, slightly irked by the dismissive term. It was not new, and it wasn't inaccurate, but it offended nonetheless.

"Leutwein's pulled back many of the truppe and most of the experienced officers for a quick campaign. It leaves us exposed in Hereroland, but we have to make an example of the Bondelswarts, otherwise we will lose all deterrence. It will be quick, I'm sure."

"It can't be quick", Jack said. "It's 500 hundred miles from here, and it will be summer in the desert. Supplies will be really difficult - I know because they've asked me to arrange shipments via Lüderitzbucht."

"Ahh, well that's another thing", Rolf smiled. "I'm hoping that afterwards I can go and see Susanna."

"So, you volunteered", Jack smiled back. "Have you been in touch?"

"I write regularly. I imagine so do half the men in Suidwes."

+++

Transport, storage, and managing his own time were now Jack's most immediate issues. To overcome the logistical obstacles and the pilfering plaguing his business, Jack got permits to build storage areas adjacent to the railway sidings or the garrisons. Local partners provided guards, and some of them became satellite wagon repair sites.

In exchange for funding and building the warehouses, his leases with the administration included an option to purchase at a steep discount. Where he could, he set about building immediately – sometimes diverting consignments of corrugated iron and other construction materials he'd already sold to the army. In the rush to get supplies in and distributed, the quartermaster's pedantic bookkeeping buckled under the pressure. In all the confusion Jack's records were sometimes the only documents the quartermaster had to rely on. The Germans, relying on his goodwill, paid promptly.

Sonnenberg recruited Cape Coloured builders and wainwrights in Cape Town and sent them north. Almost every ship from Cape Town to Walvis Bay was now carrying goods for J Levin & Co. Within three months he'd imported nearly 30 long trek wagons. Izzy took on the transport opportunities using Boer, Baster and Nama crews, and ran Jack's warehouse in his frequent absences.

It was Jack's drive that set him apart in this period. The established trading firms often had better relationships with the German administration – the wealthier families moving in the same social circle as Leutwein and his senior officers. He suspected that it was these connections that enabled them to know the contents of his telegrams and letters.

Although they had good supply sources in Germany, Jack's connections and sources in Cape Town were better, and responded faster to his orders and proposals for trade. He was careful to communicate in the telex code he'd developed with Sonnenberg or via the letters sent through Cameron. Sonnenberg had expanded the financial resources of their syndicate too.

Jack was constantly on the road, travelling to Swakopmund almost every second week and stopping off at the trading posts in between. Where he could he relied on Jewish traders in these towns. Sometimes he was gone for more than a week, and he'd return exhausted to face a mound of paperwork and accounting.

His business was growing and sprawling, and he knew he needed help.

+++

The inflow of troops and money brought with it the flotsam of fortune seekers and rogues that always follows strife. The bars and hotels now began to buzz with English, Irish, American and Yiddish accents. Yiddish-speaking pimps brought in women from as far away as Rio de Janeiro and Paris, Galicia and Warsaw. Their activities and often raucous squabbling embarrassed the local community. The Windhuk magistrate and prosecutor described these new arrivals as the "Internationals", some of whom had impressive criminal records from as far as New York, acquired via the SA authorities.[40]

Early one evening Jack and Nara were returning from the Bahnhof, the cart loaded with crates and bags of foodstuffs that had arrived on the train a few hours earlier. As they passed Casino Sylvester, one of the nastier taverns on Kaiser Strasse, they heard a woman cry out from the shadows down the lane between the buildings.

"*Zal im zeyn* – leave him alone."

The shriek in Yiddish made him pull up the mules.

---

[40] See particularly The Fox and the Flies by Charles van Onselen which lays out the unproven case that the notorious Jewish pimp and criminal Joseph Silver was in fact, Jack the Ripper, the Whitechapel Murderer.

"*Ir arbet far mir ir narish pirge*" – you work for me, you stupid cunt, a man in a Homburg hat shouted out. He had his arm raised to strike a slight woman, who was trying to protect her face. Another man was on his knees beside them, holding his nose.

Shocked at the language and shocked at the scene, Jack thrust the reins at Nara and leaped off the still moving cart, the whip in his hand. With a few strides into the lane he slashed at the man's raised hand with the whip. "*Tzurik avek* - back off", he shouted, raising the whip again.

The man retreated down the lane, cursing and nursing his hand. The woman turned to face him, still holding her hands up to her face.

She went to the man, still on his knees nursing a heavily bleeding nose. "You'd better come with me", Jack said.

"Where do you live?"

"We were in the house he had", she replied, nodding in the direction that the man he'd struck had taken. He helped them onto the cart and sat beside Nara, whose eyes were large with shock and alarm.

"Take us home", he muttered to her. "They'll stay in the spare room."

In the house Jack gave them a field dressing and some water to clean up the man's face. His lips were also badly split and his attempts at speech were incoherent.

"I'm Gittel Sore Gurevitz", the woman said. "This is my husband, Solomon. Here they call me Gertie."

Jack acknowledged them with a nod. "I'm Ya'akov, Jack Levin."

By her dress and makeup, it seemed clear that she was a prostitute. She was attractive in a way that he knew could draw him, but he sensed a worldliness that made him uncomfortable. He judged she was in her mid-twenties. Her husband was several years older, and seemed muddled by the blow or blows to his face.

The couple rose quite late the next morning. She'd tried to cover a bruise on her cheek with powder and rouge, but it made her look gaudy. The man was a mess – his nose and lips swollen and distorted, and dark bruises around his eye and on the side of his head.

They sat at the table quite dejected, picking at the breakfast Nara had laid out for them. All their possessions were in the house rented by the man who'd attacked them. They refused to name him, but were persuaded to describe the house where they were staying. Jack knew immediately who owned it – the stationmaster. "By now he's sold our possessions, or burnt them", she said. "He'll have stolen my jewellery too."

"*Drekkes* like this live by the fear they exert", Effi said when he heard the story. "I'll come with you to see the magistrate. We'll try and convince him that this type of person is bad for the community. The stationmaster will also not want the trouble that comes with that kind of tenant."

They dropped Hanna off at the house on their way. They had little difficulty in persuading the magistrate and the stationmaster that the pimp was undesirable. But there was the law, and the house had been leased by contract. A policeman was sent to bring the man in for questioning.

"I don't need this trouble now, with so much going on", Jack muttered irritably as they trotted back to the house.

"Yes, I know", said Effi. "You've made an enemy, but you did the right thing."

Hanna had secluded herself with the younger woman and heard their story, which she repeated as they rode back to the Yard.

Solomon was not really her husband, but they lived as a couple off her earnings. He was devoted to her and looked after her. This was not the first time he'd been beaten protecting her.

Their plan had been to find a house and open a hotel. The pimp had met them at the station when they arrived. They knew what he was, but needed a place to stay. They did not know he would try to force her to take customers so quickly, or turn so violent.

"You'll have to put them up for a few days", Hanna said. "Perhaps they can help you with the business until they can find a place to live."

"I know they're unfortunate, but these kind of yidden are not good for us. Women like her attract trouble like flies", Effi grunted.

"You have no heart", Hanna said in a huff. "Yankele, you must be a mensch."

+++

The woman was looking at magazines on the stoep at the back when he trotted in. Solomon, her partner, was in the shed helping Nara and Petrus, the house boy and guard, sort and stack the goods that had arrived the night before.

Jack greeted them and went into the central reception room to sort through the mail and telegrams he'd picked up. He wasn't yet reconciled to having them stay with him. The room darkened and he looked up to see her standing silhouetted in the door. He noticed the shape of her body, her dress tight across her breasts and drawn above her hips unlike the looser dresses most women in the town wore. He flushed because he sensed she'd noticed the sweep of his eyes.

"I wanted to thank you," she said as she came in. "We have a little money. We will look for our own place, but Solomon can't go out yet. And we are scared of that man. There are probably others like him. I know we are a burden, but can we stay here for a day or two until we're able to find a place? We can pay a little but perhaps we can also help you?"

The awkwardness he felt in her presence lifted and he looked at her directly. Her frankness and her apparent absence of shame in talking to him enabled him to relax. But he blushed when he realised that his silence and slowness in responding was because they were appraising each other.

"Yes, you can stay here. Hanna and the little community we have here will look to see how we can help you. I don't know what we can do about the pimp. The magistrate was informed this morning, but they have bigger problems than that to deal with. But, frankly, I can't afford trouble like that. You don't have to pay me. I see Solomon is already helping in the shed and that is useful. What can you do?"

Once again, the frank look. "I can read – English, Yiddish and a little German. My writing is not so good. Perhaps I can sort through your correspondence", she said, pointing at the piles of letters, telegrams, bills, manifests, shipping schedules and so on piled on the table. "I see you have much more in your office too. Oh, I can count well too", she said with a slight smile.

Alone in his room after they had gone to bed, Jack took the holster with the Gasser pistol out of the steel trunk and hung it on the back of the chair by his bed. He snuffed out the light and then, when his eyes had adjusted, went to the window facing the street. He waited but saw no movement. Restless and anxious, he lay down. The house had quieted, and he could hear Solomon snoring through his swollen nose. From the yard he could hear the occasional snuffle and stamp of a horse or a mule.

"Youve made an enemy", Effi's first remark that morning came back to him. He realised that down here away from the Yard he was more vulnerable. He'd kept a lot of cash in his safe, uncomfortable with disclosing too much to the German bank in town. He could also not send too much through Cameron to Cape Town as that would also attract attention.

And what to do with Gertie? "...attract trouble like flies", Effi had said. He got up quietly, draped the holster over his shoulder, and went into the main room. A shipping schedule had slipped onto the floor. He picked it up and went outside.

Petrus was sitting in the shadows by the barn wrapped in a blanket. He raised his arm, acknowledging that he'd seen Jack. After a few minutes Jack stepped off the veranda and walked around the yard, checking the gate and the storeroom locks again.

Jack went to sit by the man and noticed how the shiny dark skin of his cheekbones reflected the starlight.

"*Alles goed*?", he said, more as a greeting than as a question. He knew so little of this man, he realised, but put so much trust in him. As far as he knew Petrus wasn't married. He'd said that it had taken him more than two weeks to walk from his village in Ovamboland to reach Windhuk.

"Ovambos don't mind working", he recalled Malan saying. "Hereros are smarter, but they don't like having a boss."

"Do the right thing" – both Hanna and Effi had said. "The right thing is to get them away from here", he thought to himself.

He looked down at the piece of paper in his hand. It was the latest shipping schedules from Cape Town to the ports along the northern Cape and Suidwes. He'd circled the column of dates for arrivals in Lüderitzbucht.

+++

"I have a proposal", he said to them the next morning after he'd been to see the Quartermaster. "I need to open an office in Lüderitzbucht. The Germans want to ship lots of goods through there, and I've not had a solution. It should be a good business because it's the best way to get goods into the south of the country, and they are building up troops there and bringing in settlers.

"I will pay your fare there and give you enough to get started, find a storeroom and enough to live on for a month. After that, I will pay you a fee for every successful delivery. You can repay the loan over time from these fees."

They looked at each other and accepted immediately. "You have been very kind", Solomon said. "And this is very generous." Gertie looked at him, her eyes glistening. Briefly he saw the girl she had been.

There was a ship from Walvis Bay to Lüderitzbucht in 5 days, and they set about learning how he ran the business.

Two days later, they boarded the train to Swakopmund. Now they had a lot of luggage – three of their trunks actually contained Jack's locked steel cases, which in Walvis would be assigned to Cameron or the custom's clerk, who would take them on to Sonnenberg in Cape Town. Jack and one of Izzy's Basters carrying a .45 in his haversack accompanied them.

+++

Jack waved at the couple as the ship drifted away from the dock. He'd spent quite a lot on new clothing for them, the luggage, and on the transport and the first month's allowance. They were an immediate option to start something in Lüderitz. Whomever he might have found would have been an unknown quantity, and this couple were at least *ondzeren*, our people, and had a reason to be loyal. If it didn't work out, he'd at least done a charitable deed, as Hanna had said. And now they were no longer his responsibility.

Thompson, the customs clerk, touched his cap as a gang of coloured crewmen on the aft deck of the coaster hauled in the hawser. Sonnenberg had been alerted that he and a shipment of cash were due.

Jack turned away and walked away from the docks and through the few sandy streets of warehouses and taverns behind it. Although there had been some noticeable development, particularly to the north of the town where businesspeople and

British officials had built prouder houses, the town came to an end abruptly. Human and animal feet rather than wagon wheels shaped the path down towards the estuary and away into the Kuiseb. It had been almost two years since he last walked down here.

It was worse than he remembered it. Shacks and hovels of rubbish salvaged from Walvis and the ships that visited. He recognised one of the huts close to the track from the whalebones that shaped the entrance. Now he read the layout – clusters of shacks and *kraal*s indicating extended family, solitary hovels of the even more destitute. Idle people watched him apathetically as he strode into their world.

Eventually he found Nara's aunt's shack. A toddler holding onto the canvas flap that covered the entrance watched him approach in silence. He hesitated and then called out – "Hello?" The flap was pulled back, and an older child looked out and turned back into the gloom.

The woman came out carrying an infant. Her skin was much darker than he remembered. "Are you Nara's aunt?" he asked in Afrikaans. "I came here a few years ago. Nara left with me."

The woman padded barefoot across the sandy yard where Piet had tried to club her and get at Nara. She'd aged, her face lined and grey patches in her short hair. She didn't acknowledge him or answer his question but thrust the infant into the arms of the older child who trailed after her.

"What's happened to !Nara?", she asked, looking away from him.

"She's good. She lives in Windhuk."

She looked at him directly for the first time. "What do you want?"

"Nara told me you looked after her when her mother brought her here. And then, when her mother died?"

There was no acknowledgement and she looked away again.

"I wanted to thank you:, he said awkwardly. "Perhaps I can give you something…"

"You'd better sit", she said after an awkward pause, and pointed to a low stool in the shade by a lean-to round the side where they seemed to cook. She swilled out a chipped cup with her fingers and then poured him some water.

What can you give? He realised that she probably didn't want her neighbours seeing her receiving anything from him.

Where is Piet?

Gone. She looked away again.

He gave her £5 he had in his pocket. It was a lot of money, he thought. She counted the notes, folded them and put them into the pocket of her soiled skirt.

Where did Nara's mother come from? he asked.

Up the Kuiseb, she said, nodding east with her head.

Do you ever go back there?

No. It's a long way – maybe five days. More…

He pulled out the little skin pouch he'd brought with him and poured out the stones into his hand.

Do you ever find these?

She pointed to the collection of brown, black, ochre, green and red pebbles and rough stones. There were some shimmering reds and purples embedded in rougher rocks. "These come from the Kuiseb – far up."

He picked up the clear quartz-like stone from the palm of his hand and held it up to her. "These we sometimes find by the sea. Not often", she said.

If you find any would you collect them for me? I'll pay you or other women who find.

She picked them over in his hand. "When will you come?"

Every few weeks ...

He gulped down the water and stood up.

Thank you, he said.

As he turned to go, she looked at him directly – "Does !Nara have a child?"

"No", he said, flushing, as he turned to leave.

+++

Cameron's house was on the northern approaches to the town, set back from the road to Swakopmund on a slight rise. Jack turned after he'd climbed the few steps to the stoep and looked back at the docks and the sweep of the bay to the south. Below him he could see the phosphorous white surf of the breakers as they crashed on the beach in the deepening dusk. The wind had turned and was now in his face, carrying the strong iodine tang of the kelp churned up by the breakers. No stench of whale butchery or guano.

A Nama woman opened the door after his knock. Her loveliness struck him immediately.

"You must be Jack Levin," she said. "Ian has mentioned you a lot."

Jack was slightly taken aback by her familiarity, but smiled and stepped across the threshold. She wore a smart, full-length dress and a small, neat, white lace bonnet. Incongruously, though, she was barefoot.

Cameron stepped into the hall from an adjacent room. "Welcome Jack. This is Margaret, my wife."

Jack knew they were both watching him to see his reaction. The woman's eyes were slightly suspicious or concerned he thought.

But Cameron, predictably, had a hint of cynical amusement round his mouth and in his blue eyes.

Jack thrust out his hand to cover his awkwardness, and mumbled something as they went into the parlour, which had the same view he'd been watching from outside. A telescope on a tripod stood before the window and Jack realised that nothing approached or departed from Walvis without Cameron being able to see it. A reminder that Cameron was more than a *transportryer*. Jack was drawn to the telescope, but it was already too dark to see anything.

Cameron poured Jack and himself a whiskey from a cut glass decanter, and poured his wife a sherry. Like the homes of the wealthier German traders and officials he'd visited – especially those of whom who were married, considerable effort and expense had gone into the trappings of a civilised English or German style home.

"Perhaps I should have told you I'm married to a Nama", Cameron said with a teasing smile when Margaret left. "I like to test people that way. Especially those I think are friends." That might be true, Jack thought, but it was also to avoid awkwardness that Cameron had not told him over so many years.

"Yes, I can see it is a good test because it's so unusual here. The Germans have a phrase for it – he's 'gone kaffir' or 'gone Boer'. There's talk of passing a law against such marriages."

"So, I've heard. But it's not different in the Cape. The Boere don't approve either, although they've had these relationships ever since they've arrived. By now they should have got over it."

Margaret appeared at the door with two young children. They were beautiful – pale caramel skin, and the little girl with Cameron's pale blue eyes and ginger-blond hints in her curly hair. They came in to be introduced and to say goodnight to Cameron, who obviously doted on them.

Dinner was a local fish – cob, Cameron called it, and they were left to talk quickly. It was the first time in months that they had been able to meet face to face to avoid arousing German suspicions. Their contact had been irregular and superficial, via telegram and the odd letter which both suspected were being examined.

"I think they are planning for ten thousand Schutztruppe, maybe, based on the orders I see", Jack said. "I've seen about 30 canons drawn up outside the armoury. The officers are enthusiastic about something they refer to as a 'Maxim' – a 'machine gun' but I'm not sure what that is. Leutwein may be negotiating with Maharero but the intention on the ground seems to be to defeat the Herero utterly and take most of their land."

"They will move onto the Nama next", Cameron said grimly. "And then the Ovambo. The white man will have Africa."

They talked long into the night, Jack describing the drumbeat of incidents, petty and serious abuses, the arbitrary justice "which the natives want to believe in", the debt of the Herero leaders and the loss of their land, and the pressures on Leutwein from the new wave of settlers. They covered their business, the German demand for ammunition, and the wisdom and profit they could make from supplying this, restrictions of the Cape government, German communications, and their own personal plans.

Cameron intended to move to England rather than the Cape because of his wife and mixed-race children. "South Africa is still too raw for them to be comfortable", he said. "With our business and other transport from Walvis I'm able to build up nice reserves", he said. His commitment to the British navy – his oblique and only reference to his other career – would end in about two years.

"Where did you meet your wife?" Jack asked, as they were finishing off the bottle of South African wine.

"There is a mission station up the Kuiseb delta. Scheppmannskirche it's called, after the missionary who established it. It is the first station on the bai weg (bay way) – the trek route from Walvis to Rehoboth built by the Nama. There's a small school there, and Margaret would go every day if she could. After I met her, I would go there every trek if I could", he said with a smile.

"By the way, what happened to the young Topnaar girl you collected when you arrived here?" Cameron asked as Jack walked down the outside steps.

Jack turned, feeling refreshingly confident in the Englishman's presence for the first time. "She too was at a mission school in Windhuk. I paid. She now works for me and other Jewish families in Windhuk."

+++

27th September 1989   Mount Nelson Hotel, Cape Town

Leviev had suggested they meet in the lounge of the famous hotel. The hotel was popular with foreign tourists and diplomats, so it provided a degree of anonymity Capetonians couldn't count on in the popular commercial hotels in the city. Lenny, who'd arrived early, was impressed at the young diamond dealer's caution and apparent sophistication in choosing the "Nellie", as it was nicknamed, so he was taken aback to see him sitting at the back of the lounge with a tall blond man who stuck out like a sore thumb. Lenny recalled seeing him in Keetmanshoop airport. Steyn had said he was *'regering'*. Lenny had had a sadistic instructor in basic training who looked similar. He withdrew sharply and went for an amble around the old hotel's beautifully landscaped gardens. If he was 'government' as Steyn described him, Lenny did not want to be seen with Leviev.

"You know the guy who was here?", Leviev asked, revealing that he had seen Lenny step into the lounge. "From South West",

Lenny confirmed, now wary of the situation. "He says he wants to start a courier business", Leviev said. "That could be useful in South West?"

Lenny nodded – '*Regering*' could cover Illicit Diamond Buying, so their conversation was stilted relating only to Lenny's potential contacts in the new regime in South West. There was little that was concrete or immediate to explore, so they parted as soon as it was polite. Lenny would have Lurie vet him first before they discussed anything of substance.

Sunday, January 10th, 1904 — South-east of Okahandja

"…You must teach me…"

The leaves of the trees were still damp and cool when the bull led his two cows and a calf into the small valley. Their long, prehensile tongues avoided the sharp white thorns to pluck the young leaves at the top of the acacia trees. In response, the trees released ethylene into the air.

Within minutes, acacias downwind from the browsing giraffes responded to the chemical and began to pump tannin into their leaves. Tannin was not only unpleasant to the taste but also degraded an animal's ability to metabolise the food. When the giraffes encountered the tannin, they moved on a few hundred metres to trees that had not yet been alerted.

Across the valley five Bushman hunters saw the tall animals move. This was a setback. Grazing animals would trigger the tannin response in the trees and other vegetation, they knew, and this would deter smaller game too.

The hunters carefully finished applying the poison they had prepared from crushed leaf beetle pupae to the points of their arrows, and with little discussion moved on to the next valley where the acacias and other vegetation were still sweet, and smaller buck might come to graze. They squatted in the shadows of some bushes below the ridge, and settled down to watch and read the veld again.

Twenty kilometres to the north a Boer trader rode up to the Schutztruppe garrison in Okahandja. "I've just seen a column of Herero riding north to Maharero's compound", the trader told the young lieutenant commanding the garrison. "Two, maybe three hundred men. They said they were going to pay their respects to Samuel Maharero following the death of one of the elders of the royal clan. They were all armed."

Ralph Zürn was in his twenties and was in charge of one of the largest and most sensitive areas in the heart of Hereroland. His appointment coincided with negotiations to establish a second Herero reserve in the area, which had exacerbated the festering resentment among the various clans and further weakened Maharero's influence on his people. Zürn had been high-handed with the sub-chiefs, dismissing them curtly when they would not accept his terms and informing them that Maharero would agree anyway. A local missionary had fed back their outrage at his treatment of them, but Zürn had not reported this to his superiors.

Zürn misread the veld. He was convinced an uprising was imminent. He ordered all the whites in the town to abandon their homes and businesses and gather in the fortress, and telegrammed the Schutztruppe Headquarters in Windhuk.

The news from Okahandja whipped around the town. The few soldiers and officers left behind from Leutwein's expedition against the Bondelswarts in the south returned to barracks. Primitive communications prevented them getting Zürn's information to the governor on his way south, and they waited, unsure of the Hereros' intentions.

Mid-summer heat and the stillness of a Lutheran Sunday lay heavy on the town. The streets were empty, but anxiety moved like a restless presence from house to house, husband to wife and master to servant. It became visible as soldiers left the fort to guard the Post Office and further along Kaiser Strasse to the Bahnhof.

Petrus, the Ovambo Jack employed, usually visited friends in the township on Sundays. He came back early looking grave. "People are very worried."

Together they loaded sacks of flour, sugar, and other foodstuffs onto the cart. Jack added a box of ammunition and another of field dressings to the load he was taking to the Yard. In the house he collected his rifle and his pistol.

"I'll be back before dark", Jack reassured him as he drove off. Petrus was clearly unhappy to be left alone and had now armed himself with his knobkerrie and a panga.

The next day, children were kept at home. The stores were busy in the morning as people stocked up on food and ammunition.

"Zürn is partly to blame for this mess", one of the veteran merchants said when Jack met him midday. "Some time ago he ordered the exhumation of Herero skulls and had them shipped Germany."

"Skulls! What for?"

"Scientific research", the man said. "It may be good for German science, but for the Herero, their ancestors are sacred. Zürn and those like him are too young, too ignorant, and too arrogant to learn the local ways. A *dummkopf!*"

There was no real news from Okahandja – just that the standoff continued. In the early afternoon, several wagons with women and children from some of the nearby farms arrived, spooking people further. In the Yard the atmosphere was subdued. Mendel, who was the oldest resident, had lived through a pogrom in Poland and was ashen and withdrawn. Rather than contributing to the preparations to defend themselves he'd withdrawn into prayer, depressing the others and exasperating Effi.

Towards dusk a Baster patrol that had been sent out earlier towards Okahandja returned. They seemed nonchalant as they trotted up to the fort, and the news soon spread that they had not encountered any armed Herero on their sweep of the country north of Windhuk. The town seemed to relax – almost audibly. Nara asked to sleep at his house, where she could browse the papers and magazines he had.

Although the tone of the odd acquaintances he met was mostly loud and belligerent, he knew they felt as vulnerable as he did. Without the Schutztruppe their talk was all bluster. Should the Herero move on them, they were vastly outnumbered.

The garrison commander and the police chief ordered the taverns and bars to close early and Windhuk quietened and withdrew inside. Even the black township of pondoks across the dry riverbed was quieter and darker than usual.

+++

The oil lamp cast barely enough light for him to read his mail, so he raised it on a brick for Nara to page through the magazines as she sat at the table beside him. It was baking and they had closed and locked the doors for security. Petrus was by his room in the yard and Jack had told the maid to go to her family in the Damara section of the township. They both knew she would be safer there. The window onto the stoep at the back was open but there was hardly a breeze to move the air in the stifling room under the corrugated iron roof. He'd stripped to his singlet and she was in a cotton slip, the white cloth stark against her skin. His suntanned neck and forearms were odd swarthy bands on his otherwise pale, grey-white skin.

Periodically she would point to a picture or illustration that she was interested in and he would translate the caption into German. He showed her a picture of Table Bay in the *Cape Argus* with the mountain in the background and explained that that was where he'd come from when they met in Walvisbaai.

"How far is it?" she asked.

"Five-six days by sea. By horse from here will take a month, maybe longer."

Her fingers traced the outline of the mountain as she processed this.

"They speak English there?", she said. He nodded.

"So, you must teach me English, before you take me there."

He smiled – she was so guileless. She'd slipped into life in the Yard easily, Hanna and Magda treated her as a daughter, and she seemed content so far with her life as a maid. She lacked friends her own age, but Hanna had told him that Magda was planning for her to join other Nama girls in an initiation ceremony that was some months away. Eventually he tired of the paperwork and he said he wanted to read on his bed.

A while later she came into the room, unhappy to be left on her own. Without asking, she sat beside him, her back to the wall, leafing through more magazines. After a while she began to doze off and he made space beside him for her to lie down.

She woke when he got up carefully to remove his trousers and fold them over a chair as he always did. He blew out the lamp and lay down beside her. The stillness of the night settled around them as their eyes adjusted to the dark and to each other's closeness. They had not been like this since their arrival in the town.

+++

… Soon I will be a *hokmeisie*. There will be other girls my age. I'll be able to make friends. Magda said we will be in a separate *kraal* outside the Nama township. The *taras* will prepare us for the 'water snake' ceremony and womanhood. Magda is not a *tara* and wouldn't tell me if she knew. She said it's 'women's secrets'. The girls in the school also knew nothing. One of them said it makes us powerful, but she couldn't explain how. It's to do with boys and men. Hanna and Magda say now I must be sure to be home before dark. Men in the town are not safe, they say. Like the Damara woman. Magda keeps on asking me if I have pain or bleeding in my tummy or between my legs. She calls it my 'tortoise'. Why is becoming a woman such a secret?"

She turned on her side to face Jack, half expecting him to be asleep. Maybe by watching him up close she could learn something of men and this mystery that seemed to await her. She could see his eyes were open, perhaps he was listening to her. I'll just ask him...

Jeck…?

But she didn't know what to ask.

He turned to face her.

They looked intently at each other, her eyes large and dark and deep, his irises – blue-grey even in the gloom from the lamp in the other room, and for her, so mysterious. The stillness between them became a touch. His finger traced a line from her eyebrow to her jaw. The back of his fingers brushed across her cheek and her lips, which seemed to swell in the shadows.

There was fluttering tension in their breath. His fingers traced the line from her shoulder to her wrist and then circled it like a bracelet. They watched each other intently and slowly he moved his hand up the side of her body to cup her breast. A soft mewl as she exhaled – half pleasure, half fear. They stayed still like that until he drew his fingers together on her nipple. A sharp intake of her breath as a tremor ran through and down her body.

He drew himself up on his elbow, looking down at her from close above, and gently pushed her onto her back. Then he lowered his head and gently brushed the nipple with his lips. He raised his head and leaned in close above her. She froze, not expecting his mouth on hers. He waited for her to relax, his dry lips moving gently across her cheeks and eyes. She sensed him tremble with tension and then let her lips respond slightly when he kissed her again.

He drew himself up again and eased the slip off her shoulder, exposing her shoulders and then her breast. Again, he cupped her breast and teased the nipple with his lips. She felt herself swell, her nipple tight and almost painful. Sharp thrills ran down into her belly. Pleasure, fear and curiosity buffeted her. Desire was a feeling she could not yet recognize or name. She held onto his head with one arm, her fingers gripping his thick hair almost for reassurance, the other arm flung back against the pillow as she surrendered to the surge of pleasure.

He moved his head to the other breast, teasing the nipple erect too. Her breathing was heavy, almost hoarse. He'd not expected her pleasure, had not known how she would respond. The urge to please her churned through him, along with his long-repressed curiosity about women and his own surging lust.

Her groin tightened as the pulses of his stimulation throbbed down to her pelvis. She felt warmth and then dampness she'd never experienced. She was petrified she would pee and clenched her thighs, giving herself more pleasure.

Slowly he moved his hand down off her breast, exploring the flatness of her belly. He raised the hem of the slip and she squeezed her eyes shut, as his fingers followed the line of hair above her vagina. He traced a line on her inner thigh, waiting for her to relax her legs. She tried, but couldn't. He touched her at the top of her vulva, which made her spasm again, so intense it was painful. Both sighed deeply – pent up tension overwhelming them. He shuddered.

He moved his hand up to cup her head and then kissed her forehead and lay down again beside her. She lay on her back, feeling the sensations still pulsing through her. The tautness of her nipples and her groin subsided slowly, pleasantly. She wanted to explore the dampness between her legs but couldn't with him so close and still awake. She looked down the length of his body beside her and saw his swollen shape in his linen undershorts.

She turned away to face the wall, he put his arm across her shoulder, and after long minutes and deeper sighs they fell asleep.

+++

Lenny entered his grandfather's study hesitantly. He remembered hurtling down the corridor on his pedal tricycle, knowing that even if he gave the sombre and sometimes irritable old man a shock by crashing into the closed door he would be greeted with love and affection and a ruffle of his curls.

He walked to the large window with the panoramic view of the south Atlantic. The northwester had strengthened and changed tack. The colossal swells now marched from due west and reared up massively to crash on the rocks of Bantry Bay and Saunders Rocks below. Too windy and wet for a beachfront walk with the kids.

... I used to fall asleep to that thud-crash, wake up to it too. Violent, powerful but reassuring. The beat of the earth. Don't have that now living on the other side of the mountain....

He bent his head to the eyepiece of Jack's old telescope on the tripod where it always stood. He swept north across the flecked artichoke-coloured ocean to focus on a large tanker pitching up and down in the huge seas. Magnified through the lens he could see white spume and spray whipped away by the wind from the bow as it ploughed through the combers. It was unlikely to put into Duncan Dock, he knew. Those days had passed. The ships were big enough to complete the journeys to and from the Middle East without stopping. Mail, medicines, videos were flown out to them by helicopter. As a child, though, he remembered the Roadsteads, the stretch of relatively protected water in Table Bay, crowded with rows of freighters waiting to enter the port for replenishment. That was why the Dutch first put into Table Bay. The compact commercial centre of the city between the Gardens and the Docks had teemed with sailors and passengers from all over the world. As a child he remembered visiting ship chandlers and importers with Jack and his father. Their storerooms smelt of rope, tar and spices, their shelves packed with rows of glinting bottles and cans of exotic foods like Rose's Lime Marmalade from England, Tabasco Sauce from America, Smyrna figs and green-gold tins of Kalamata olive oil, Portuguese anchovies, hessian bags of nuts, all from far off places. All that had gone. "Maybe my fascination with trade is like Jack's was – a fascination really with food!"

He traversed further, over Robben Island and the squat outline of its notorious prison. Blouberg Strand was too far and too obscured by the storm to see, so he moved the telescope back down towards the white and red block of Green Point lighthouse, where the Seafarer had run aground in 1966 in this kind of storm. Then down through Sea Point, and along the coast to Saunders Rocks and Bantry Bay almost directly below. In the summer, he'd lie on the massive granite boulders embalming himself in the warmth from the rock below and the sun above, and wonder if anyone was watching him from the house. He smiled recalling himself as a teenager, using the telescope to see if any of the girls he liked were on the beach or the beachfront promenade.

As he straightened up, he had a sense that he'd traversed across his life. The nub of his being seemed to be before him – in the heaving dark green water and golden granite rocks of the bay at his feet. Jack must have stood here and done the same. Could he have felt the same? And what of the farm?

Lenny turned away and looked round the room. Jack's desk was now piled with his sister's case files and papers: - books on therapy for childhood trauma, addiction in infants, a paper she seemed to be editing on the cumulative and long-term effects of domestic abuse on the Cape Flats. There were family pictures, Jack's old leather chair with the white and red chess set out beside it, and the large stinkwood dinner table where he would do his massive jigsaw puzzles. An oil painting of the farm painted by a South West artist hung on the wall behind the leather couch where he would rest. And where Sam, Lenny's father, had had his stroke and died.

Lenny walked over to the photos – his parents, smiling and arm in arm; Jack with Rae, Lenny's grandmother – formal with no obvious sign of affection between them, and the same picture of Sydney in uniform as he'd seen in Jack's study on the farm. "He was their first born", he mused to himself. "That must have been a terrible blow, but it did not seem to make them closer." More photos of himself and Lynne as children, Lynne and her husband, he and Cyn and the grandchildren. "Our lives are so normal."

"Find what you're looking for?" Lynne half asked, half teased as she put down the tray of coffee on the low table by the window.

October 1989   Windhoek

Katatura

"You must be Tjandero", the woman in the courtyard said as he pushed at the gate. She straightened up from the zinc basin in front of her and said something inaudible into the interior of the house.

This was his cousin, Sewa, he realised. Impending independence had enabled her return from long exile in Botswana. She was far older than he remembered, and looked at him flatly, fatigue rather than a welcome in her face.

Two small children gawped at him from the entrance to the house and then a teenage girl emerged and said he could enter. His aunt, the oldest surviving person in his family, sat on a straight-backed chair in the simple room. She wore a full-length billowing green dress and the traditional *otjikaiva* – a horizontal horned hat in the same material with a pale brown, heavily-patterned shawl around her shoulders. A copper bangle glinted at her wrist and a single gold band set off her long dark fingers.

After traditional greetings and the exchange of family news the children were ushered off to bed – some in a neighbouring house where another daughter lived. Tjandero would be sleeping in another neighbour's house, but in the meantime, he ate pap and meat with his aunt and cousin.

His aunt and Sewa lived in a standard block house built by the municipality years before to accommodate the thousands of black migrant workers who streamed to Windhoek for work. Thousands of identical houses laid out in a uniform grid of dusty and rubbish-strewn streets formed the sprawling township of Katatura, eight kilometres north of Windhoek. On this late September afternoon, the sun was low in the north and cold moved in over the sandy plots, sending people inside early when they could no longer warm themselves in the sun.

A young man arrived and was introduced as Godfrey, yet another cousin. Tjandero would be sleeping in his house nearby for the few weeks of management training. "Before you disappear", Sewa said, severe as she'd been throughout the afternoon, "you are expected at the elders gathering on Sunday. You will accompany your aunt to meet our people." Turning to the Godfrey she admonished him too – "you keep him out of the shebeens and away from the gangsters. He has important things to achieve."

Barely out of the house, they turned into an alley with raw sewage running between the piles of rubbish that led onto a larger road bisecting the township. It was Friday afternoon and thousands of people, men and women, were streaming back from the white city and its suburbs, where most worked as gardeners, labourers and domestic servants. The whole area was floodlit by glaring orange lights mounted on high steel pylons further up the hill.

"Come, you need to be introduced", his cousin Godfrey said, pushing into a shebeen, "otherwise they might think you're a spy." It was a mixed crowd in terms of age, mainly men slowly sloughing off the fatigue of the week's labour, the long commute, and the grinding frustrations of poverty and apartheid. The shebeen queen who ran the place chatted to him briefly and when she was satisfied, confirmed his acceptance by offering him a beer.

They moved on to the house where he would be sleeping and he was introduced to yet more members of the extended family. Tjandi was fading, looking forward to bed after his early start and long journey, but Godfrey and his friends were not letting him off. "Friday night is for jolling, man", and after a quick wash and change he was bundled out into the streets. In the house they spoke Herero but the crowd of young people he was with used a lot of Afrikaans slang.

Loud "Bubblegum" music and the smell of grilling meat marked their next destination. The mood had lifted, people had dressed up, and the shebeen was heaving. Here there was far more Ovambo spoken and Godfrey passed his cousin round like a trophy.

An hour later they joined the throng outside Club Thriller - Katatura's main night spot. Gaudy neon lights, splashing fountains and tall shrubs set in the squalor of the township. "This is called the SWAPO Club", Godfrey said, "but it's popular with everyone. But be careful, off-duty policemen and soldiers also come here, so you never know."

They paid, passed through the body-search, and were propelled into the multi-storey club. DJ Thabo, in a white suit and Panama hat, was a legend and he was not restrained: – "Dance for freedom", he urged, and chanted – "dance for independence" as he spun MaBrrrr on the turntables. "Power to the students", he continued, to loud cheers recalling the recent strike by school students. Tjandero was stunned by the throbbing music, pulsating strobes, and scantily dressed girls. The red, blue and green SWAPO colours were everywhere.

The girls stayed in clutches – their large dark eyes flashing and tracking the boys, and then cast down in shyness when a look was returned. Those that knew each other took to the dance floor easily, legs, breasts and bums undulating in sexual provocation he'd only seen in the few movies he'd seen in Otjiwarongo. Old Spice and Aramis mingled with 4711, Avon soap, sweat, hormones and the sharp tang of cigarettes.

They had taken a break on the balcony of the upper floor looking down at the packed dance floor when a party of men in uniform were ushered in. All had blue berets drawn through the epaulettes. "UNTAG soldiers", Godfrey explained. "Here to supervise the election and independence. These look like Kenyans."

"The girls go with them because they have lots of money to spend", a friend joked. They call them 'sugar daddies'. If they get drunk, there will be fights."

As if on cue the DJ switched to a pulsing, swaying Mbaganga track and the blue berets were dragged onto the dance floor. "UNTAG are pro-SWAPO", said another of Godfrey's friends.

"But that doesn't matter now – the main thing is to get independence."

"Don't be drawn by this excitement", Sewa said the next afternoon when he visited and told her of his impressions. He enthused about the political energy but they both knew it was sex that was coursing through him. "You can't trust the Afrikaners", she said. "They will do anything to hold onto power here. Losing here will mean losing in South Africa eventually. You can't have one without the other." She was bitter about SWAPO too – "They have secret prison camps in Angola where they kill people too. They are planning to keep everything for themselves."

+++

He dressed smartly the next day to accompany Sewa and his aunt to the elders meeting. Blue, white and red flags and banners of the Herero-dominated DTA had been draped round the courtyard of a wealthier resident, and rows of plastic chairs brought in from a shebeen and other houses. The women were dressed in their traditional billowing dresses and large twin horned hats — many in the green of the Mbanderu clan. The older men wore suits or smart military uniforms, often with medals and insignia, and most carried long sticks, often elaborately etched. Even the very elderly and frail seemed to have come.

Sewa introduced him to the women first. Everything took time as they worked out his genealogy and his connections to them. He knew that he was being evaluated as a potential groom for granddaughters. Sewa then took him across to their host, the local *ovahona* of the Hereros in Katatura. His circle round the elderly men was interrupted when the women started the proceedings with a hymn.

The *ovahona* welcomed them - mentioning and praising many of the elderly by name. He also mentioned those who had died recently, each mention being echoed with calls and murmurs of praise. He then reviewed plans for the next Herero Day, which was almost a year away but was always mentioned at any Herero gathering.

A man in an open-necked white shirt and a DTA armband was introduced. "Showing upon at DTA events and rallies is vital", he harangued. "The country is filling up with foreign journalists. They have only heard of SWAPO. The same goes for UNTAG. We have to show them how powerful we are."

Turning to the elders he said: "You know our history, our suffering. The young people do not. They are tempted by fashion and silly trends. But power now depends on the election. Insist they participate. Demand that they support us."

As the meeting broke and they streamed out onto the street, young people handed out T-shirts and flags. "Careful where you wear that", Sewa said when he took one.

"Why did you go to Botswana?", he asked later when they were sitting alone after the evening meal. "Life became impossible here under apartheid. I was trained as a teacher at the Rhenish Mission, but I clashed with the church. They supported the government in the syllabus. My husband and I were active in SWANU. We were intimidated all the time by the police. We left in 1977. I came back last year."

Tjandero knew she'd come back without her husband but waited. After a lull she said: "He stayed with his other wife. We disagreed about SWANU. They have made lots of bad decisions over time. That's the curse of the Hereros."

Empty Streets and Gust of Wind

Jack was up early and woke Nara. The maid could not find her in his bed.

But the maid did not show up. "Very few people are coming out of the township", Petrus said when Jack asked him what he'd heard. Jack's anxiety lurked – inside him, inside the house with Nara, in the courtyard with only Petrus to protect them, and outside in the streets empty of the early-morning workers.

It was still cool when he walked Nara to the Yard. Both of them were subdued and she seemed relieved to be away from him when he went into the kitchen to get a mug of tea.

"My maid did not show up this morning", he said quickly as he sat down at the table. "Petrus says no one is leaving the township." He flushed when Hanna looked up at him from nursing her new-born in the corner of the room.

"The Herero have been pushed too far", said Effi. "Even their chiefs, who benefit from the Germans, have had enough. If there's an attack, you'd be better off with us here rather than alone at your house."

Hanna looked up at him, her grey eyes seeing into him as always – "Nara must stay here. We'd be safer with another man here too."

"We'll see. I can't leave Petrus on his own. I'll find another guard."

He walked back to the post office, joining a gaggle of men speculating why the telegraph was not working. Some of them were carrying rifles. They milled about, pestering the manager and the clerks for news they knew they did not have.

Jack continued to the Bahnhof, as he was anticipating goods from Swakopmund later in the day. No trains were moving in either direction. A detachment of soldiers lounged around flatbed wagons that had been protected with rows of sandbags but there was a hesitation about sending more troops out of the town.

"This is the capital", muttered one of the traders also waiting for news from Swakopmund. "It's crazy to have left us here unprotected. Leutwein should have sent someone else to handle the Bondelswarts. The Herero are the main enemy – that's obvious."

News of the attack in Okahandja broke later in the day. Hundreds of Herero had apparently attacked the fort. The telegraph line to Swakopmund via Okahandja had been cut and there was still no movement on the railway line. Leutwein's force was days away in the south and could only be contacted by heliograph.

To bolster his depleted guard, the Windhuk garrison commander had assembled a volunteer force and these men were now gathering up at the fort. Jack walked up there to register and was told to report in the evening.

Baster patrols sent north and to the east returned grim-faced towards dusk. Outlying farms all around the town had been attacked and there were casualties, they reported. The Hereros were well armed and moving around the town. A few wagons arrived with women and children and they were put up in the hotels or private homes. The bars and taverns were ordered to close again.

The Schutztruppe were concentrated in the fort and at the magazine in Klein Windhoek. A few were sent to the military hospital on the other side of the riverbed, but it was clear to all that it would be abandoned at the first sign of trouble. The volunteers were deployed at the station, the post office and the two banks.

Petrus had recruited another Ovambo as a guard, and they were sitting in the yard armed with knobkerries. Jack gave the man a set of overalls so he would be identified as employed, since the whites were suspicious of any black person. He had them fill buckets with water and place them around the yard and the house in case of fire. Then he rode out to join the volunteers.

He found himself partnered with a teacher at the local school - a man he knew to greet but had never really had any conversation with. The Stabsarzt had described him as "well read". They were assigned to patrol up and down Kaiser Strasse, but as the evening turned into night, they tethered their horses and sat on the stoep of Wecke & Voigts, one of the main traders who also sold weapons and ammunition and was a potential target for the Hereros.

"The Hereros are unlikely to attack at night", the teacher said. "They are scared of the dark."

"Some of the farmers who came into town today said they had been attacked in their beds", Jack noted.

"Precisely. They are cowardly and have uncivilised ideas of bravery and honour. This has been the American experience with the Indians. Have you met Dr Rohrbach?" he asked, referring to an official sent from the Colonial Department in Berlin the year before to develop plans to accelerate German settlement in the colony. "He is very good in describing our mission in its widest historical context. These kaffirs are sitting on huge reserves of land that they don't know how to farm or develop. Can you imagine what a few hundred vigorous and talented young Germans could develop here. It would be a paradise to rival the American west. And that is exactly that Germany needs - *lebensraum*, that will lead to the development of an even more vital German race. Some of the new settlers coming here now are not of the right class. A war and the challenges of settlement will weed out the weak. Migration is vital for a race to survive. If we don't, other races will overtake us. Rohrbach sees Suidwes and the colonial experience as a crucible for a new kind of *volk* that will enrich the Reich."

Jack's lack of response didn't slow the teacher down.

"Leutwein was right to see the rapid development of the railway as the vital link to conquer and settle the territory. But it's Rohrbach who persuaded him to adopt the other American idea - force the natives into reserves. That's how you weaken and control them if they resist. Everywhere you look you see that the white man's destiny is to conquer these lands and subjugate the natives. And, if necessary, eradicate them. Even if they have economic value to us, the Herero need to be utterly defeated as an example to others. The Ovambo will be cowed, and they will provide labour."

Rumours skittered about the empty town like gusts of wind. Without the telegraph line or any movement on the railway the only news came from the patrols, fleeing farmers and traders, and the odd Schutztruppe who managed to get through. Some were clearly traumatised and brought reports of murders, rapes, mutilation, arson and cattle being driven off. It seemed that every town and most farms had been attacked. Despite all the rumbles of Herero discontent over the previous months, widespread tribal meetings, purchases of horses, and smuggling of arms and ammunition, the attacks had come as a total surprise to the white colony.

Every day, more white farmers and traders retreated into the town. Every night, Herero and other blacks slipped away. Those that remained were careful not to move around after dark, accosted sometimes violently by whites who found encountering black people in the dark startling. Nama scouts got through from

Otjiwarongo, reporting that the railway line had been cut there too. Troops sent out on an armoured train to Karibib had been ambushed. Four were killed and four seriously injured. There were more stories of Herero atrocities, often unproven, and some stories of individual kindness shown to German women and their children.

Sightings and rumours of Herero patrols around the town came and went with every arrival. One of Maharero's sons was reportedly seen nearby signalling that an attack was imminent. But nothing happened. The absence of any real evidence that a concerted attack was being prepared and the sporadic news from the other towns and from Leutwein away in the south amplified the fears of the thousand or so settlers in the town.

"I'm sure that Maharero has concluded a pact with Hendrik Witbooi", the hydrologist said to Jack one evening as they patrolled along the road to the magazine in Klein Windhoek. "It makes perfect sense to combine forces against us."

"Has there been any trouble from the Nama serving the Schutztruppe?", Jack asked. "Not so far, although they seem wary of us as we are of them. We are very reliant on them and they know this. Witbooi is very astute. He will be gathering his forces to cut off Leutwein. It takes days to communicate with him down near the Orange River. The Nama will move on Windhoek. Witbooi's people will have told him where we store the arms and ammunition. They know us better than we know them. When Witbooi gives the signal, the Nama serving with us and maybe the Basters too will turn on us. This could all be over in a few weeks, and with those supplies he could dominate the Herero too."

Firewood normally collected outside the town was scarce, Farmers had abandoned their lots and food was in short supply. Fear, boredom and the summer heat made people cranky. Men got drunk earlier in the day.

The dramatic arrival of a relief column from the south under Captain Franke in the third week of January gave everyone a boost. He had driven his Fourth Company over 200 miles in 100 hours in the belief that the situation in the capital was dire. When he understood that Windhuk was relatively safe but Okahandja still occupied, he pressed on. Soon after, crews set out to repair the railway line and telegraph link.

Jack was on the first train out of Windhuk. It wasn't only that he had supplies backed up in Walvis Bay and in Swakopmund, or that he needed to pay his nervous suppliers in Cape Town. The weeks of uncertainly and inaction cooped up in the town had been claustrophobic. He was desperate to get away from it, from the mid-summer heat and the fervid jingoism he seemed to encounter everywhere. He wanted to be by the sea.

He'd become pensive. The long nights sleeping alone in the house had him brooding on his loneliness. Hanna was preoccupied with her new-born baby, and Effi distracted by the other children and the pressures of his own business. The German officers and traders he occasionally spent time with were either in the field or huddled at home with their nervous families.

The train could only get as far as Osona, where the bridge over the Swakop river had been cut. The river was in flood and they had to walk several kilometres upstream to a ford. Otjiwarongo, when they got there, showed signs of the battle, with stores looted and burned and bullet marks on the walls of the fort and the railway station. The wagon shop and stores had been looted and torched. Malan had burnt his arms trying to rescue goods and tools, and had sheltered in the fort. He was now joining a patrol to reach his family in Grootfontein. Jack insisted he make a list of what was lost before he left so that they could claim compensation.

The line down to Swakopmund had also been cut in several places – some because of Herero action and some because of bad maintenance. German marines, still in their white uniforms, had been rushed in by sea and were repairing the line with gangs of Herero prisoners. Jack's depots in Karibib and Usakos had been attacked too but the damage was not severe. In most cases what had been stolen or burnt was being stored for the administration and had already been paid for. It took him more than a week to reach Swakopmund.

Cameron arrived the day after him with a caravan of loaded wagons and four cannon protected by Schutztruppe. "The British have given the Germans permission to land weapons and ammunition in Walvis Bay", he said later as they talked discreetly in the lounge of the boarding house. "There are ships arriving every few days, with supplies apparently including a locomotive and steel rails. I'm returning tonight already, there is so much demand. We need more wagons – the Germans are willing to spend a lot to hold on here."

"It says here that the German parliament has voted for another 500 hundred troops, artillery and machine guns", Jack said holding up the *Deutsch-Südwestafrikanische Zeitung*, the local paper. "It seems that Leutwein has lost the confidence of his own people. They think there must be an alliance between Hendrik Witbooi and Maharero. The Nama will trap the Schutztruppe in the south and then attack Windhuk together with the Herero. That's why there has not been a big attack yet."

Cameron pursed his lips. "That makes military sense, but there is too little trust between the Nama and the Herero. Witbooi's people are disciplined but the Hereros' will to fight disappears as soon as they've taken the farmers' cattle and clothes."

Cameron took a letter to Sonnenberg explaining the losses, listing new goods to be supplied, and arguing again for them to get involved in the financing and shipment of ammunition, which the Germans were desperate for.

Another company of German marines was on the train from Swakopmund when he returned. They too were still in their white naval uniforms, having been rushed to Suidwes from a port visit in Cape Town before they could be properly kitted out.

Jack, who was their age, kept to himself. He felt much older. Before he would have been happy to share his knowledge with them as they struggled with the heat, the harsh light, and the visual challenge of the desert as Rolf had on his first journey. But something in him had changed.

He flipped through the magazines Cameron had brought. The pictures and illustrations of life in London and Cape Town would be a welcome antidote to the tedium and depression that had settled on Windhuk. He dosed fitfully in the heat and when his mind emptied, recalled images of Nara's body. Discreetly, his hand hidden under the magazine, he pressed his swollen cock, enjoying the throb of pleasure it gave him.

There was a hushed hubbub from the young marines as they pulled into Usakos. Manacled Hereros packed in rows were sitting in the boiling sun on flatbed trucks on a siding. The men had been separated from the women and children, and Schutztruppe with riding crops patrolled on each side.

Everyone got off the train as it refuelled. This was as much to stretch and refresh themselves as it was to avoid the grim scene adjacent to their closed carriages.

The young Marines were subdued and pensive when they re-boarded, as was Jack.

"*Konzentrationslager*", the station master called the prison camp being built at Karibib, which they reached the next morning. All along the track it seemed gangs of black men and women and even children, all seemingly Herero, were being put to work supervised by red-faced men with riding crops and sjamboks.

Jack's agent in the town said he'd seen eight flatbed wagons with prisoners come down the track from Hereroland in the last week. "It's like Bnei Yisrael with Pharoah", he said referring to the story of the slaves used to build the Pyramids. "The Schutztruppe around here now seem to carry a whip before a Mauser."

The mood in Windhuk had improved when he got back, and his own bleakness lifted when he collected mail and telegrams from the Post Office:

- Sonnenberg confirmed receipt and deposit of the cash, as well as the recruitment of two additional Coloured wainwrights who'd signed on for a year. They would be arriving in Walvis Bay in a few weeks.

- The Gurevitz couple had settled in in Lüderitz and were ready to receive shipments.

- Cameron confirmed receipt of another shipment including three new wagons plus assorted goods.

He suppressed the urge to embrace Nara when he walked into the house. She was wearing one of the dresses he'd given her. He assumed the Damara maid was about and was subdued in his greeting, feigning fatigue. She'd heard he was due back and had brought food from the Yard. She followed him about the house telling him all that he'd missed while he was away.

As he put the mail on the desk, he noticed a new pile of papers on the table.

"Did you do this?" he asked her, flipping through and noticing they were arranged by date and correspondent.

She nodded, blushing slightly. "I saw frau Gertie do it", not sure if he would be pleased or irritated. She wanted to show she could do more than housework. He was impressed and pleased, and wanted to show her. He nodded, remaining slightly aloof and formal and hoping he could control the display of emotions for both of them. She was so young and inexperienced she would embarrass him. But he sensed too that his attitude confused and hurt her.

"Thank you. It's very good", he said, flashing a smile to reassure her.

"I went to see your aunt in Walvis." He'd not told her before, not really sure why but now it seemed to make sense.

She remained blank. "Why?"

"I thought she might help me find some of these stones you collected", he said, pouring out the contents of the little bag. "I also paid her something for looking after you as a little girl."

"She's not a good *sa'as*. I found these. She always said I was the best gatherer."

"Yes, but you're not there now. I thought maybe you would come there with me next time I need to go to Walvis Bay."

Her eyes glistened – rather than pleasing her, she saw the spectre of being rejected and returned there. He stepped round the desk and put his arms around her stiffly, completely unaware of her fear. Part of her calmed in his embrace, but a tight groan of uncertainty came from her belly. She stepped back from him, avoiding his eyes.

"Come," he said leading her to the entrance room and seating her at the table. He'd bought some chocolate at a store on his way from the station, but she remained unsettled as she flipped through some magazines he took out of his grip. Her mood lifted when with a flourish he held up a new dress that Hanna had chosen from a catalogue. She tried it on immediately in front of the mirror in the entrance. He watched her, enjoying their intimacy and her girlishness.

Mid-February 1904   Otjiwarongo

Signals

Within a week of their arrival in Suidwes, the company of recruits were on the parade ground. Their training at the Karlsruhe camp – chosen because its humid climate was the closest the German army could find to approximate conditions in Suidwes – had been curtailed with the outbreak of hostilities. An overnight rail journey to Hamburg, a band and enthusiastic crowds waving them on to restore German pride and ensure Aryan living space, and then they climbed the gangplank and boarded the Lucy Wormann. It was so rushed they'd hardly had time to write to their families. Most of them had never been out of the tenement suburbs of the industrial cities, where overcrowding and lack of opportunity drove young men to search for adventure and opportunity ten thousand kilometres away.

In Otjiwarongo they faced sergeants and corporals who were regular army or colonial veterans. The officers were Prussian, thirsting for battle after decades of peace. Others were often disgraced individuals evicted from the army and dumped on the colonial protection force. The officers and NCOs relished the disdain they could display for these fresh-faced youths, pink from the African sun and wide-eyed in fear. The need to "prepare them for war" excused their barely restrained cruelty.

There was little information provided – it was marching and discipline, marching and obedience, marching and the need to be ruthless. A medic was given an hour to warn of snakes and scorpions and polluted water. For local knowledge they were told to rely on the Damara, Basters and the Witbooi scouts who would accompany them. The names meant nothing to them. After a few days of marching and getting used to the horses, they rode out into the bush for target practice.

They dismounted in a shallow valley with curious mounds rising out of the red sand. Some were taller than a man. It was not yet eight and the dark patches of earth and saliva deposited overnight by the worker termites on the outside of the columns had not yet dried.

The men lined up in squads of ten and were issued five rounds each. On the far end of the firing line, a squad of gunners, also recent arrivals, set up a Maxim machine gun. Once they'd loaded a belt into the weapon, they withdrew while the other recruits stepped forward.

"Imagine a target about one metre up from the ground – belly or chest height."

"*Feur!*"

The report of the volley reverberated across the veld; the bullets pierced the mounds of regurgitated red earth with deep thuds. Below the surface, the termites paused in their industry. Some turned towards the sound and vibration. Others stretched their mandibles issuing a high-pitched noise. Those in the immediate vicinity of the bullet's impact struck the surface of the tunnel with their heads, propagating a signal down the tunnels and chambers indicating where the breach had occurred. Worker termites withdrew deeper into the mound, soldiers scurried towards the source of the threat and began drumming against the walls with their heads amplifying the intensity of the original signal. Their goal, encoded in their genes – to defend and repair the assault on their community. The signal carried through the earth in milliseconds over several metres to neighbouring colonies, where soldier termites rushed to the entrances of their mounds.

Once the riflemen had finished firing, the machine gunners came forward and aimed for the tallest mound. In a few minutes, the three belts of ammunition they'd fed into the jabbering gun had cut the mound in half.

Two young herders who'd been watching from a distance clapped their hands over their ears when the Maxim opened up. They'd never heard or seen anything as intense. The whole area now smelled of cordite. The truppe mounted their horses and rode back to Otjiwarongo.

The chattering metallic clatter and explosive bursts of gunfire drew others too. Herero men gathered around the destroyed mound watching the blind termites in a purposeless scramble to "understand" what had befallen them. Ants and birds chased and pecked at the scurrying bits of protein now exposed to the sun and to predators.

"This is finished", said an older man leaning on his long herding stick by the destruction. The younger boys picked through the torn-up earth for the still warm bullets and empty cartridges.

It took four days for news of the new weapon to reach Samuel Maharero at his camp east of Okahandja where he'd moved in anticipation of German retaliation.

+++

Since Jack had touched her, Nara had begun to explore her body nearly every night. She lay awake in the room she shared with Magda, waiting for the older women's snores behind the cloth partition to confirm that she had the privacy she now craved. Even thinking of the pleasure from her body would produce a warm softness and strange anticipation in her groin. She'd discovered that the dampness she felt was not pee but a silky liquid like her spit. It had a strange, almost spicy odour, like buchu, and exploring where it came from gave her even more intense pleasure. Squeezing her thighs together did the same. Slowly experimenting, she indulged the warm melting pleasure in her pelvis that made her want to open her legs and spread her knees, and then the sudden thrill which had her clench her thighs together. She relived and replayed the touch of fingers and lips on her nipples, the tingling inside her from caressing the hair in the groin. Then one night she found the shocking intensity of a single point hidden between her vulva that caused such a sharp intake of her breath that Magda stopped snoring. The next night she had her first orgasm.

+++

After an unsatisfactory agreement with the Bondelwarts in the south, Leutwein returned by ship via Lüderitz and Swakopmund. It was the third week in February when he finally arrived in Otjiwarongo to get to grips with the Herero.

The same week, Herero from the Zeraua clan began to traipse east from their traditional grazing areas around Omaruru. News of the fighting with the Germans in Okahandja had reached them a few days before. Most of the men had ridden off to join Maharero. It took the remaining villagers, mainly the women and the elderly, several days to pack up, collect food and set out for the hills east of Okahandja where Maharero had decided to concentrate his people. They moved at the pace of the animals and the elderly. There were no wagons – what they had, they had strapped to oxen and donkeys or carried on their heads.

Kaera, a young mother, trudged through the red dust thrown up by the straggling column of people and animals. Her 6-month-old was tied to her back with an animal hide, and her little boy trotted alongside her trying to keep up. Behind her, her mother carried a large pile of their possessions on her head while her elderly father led the two oxen carrying the poles, reed mats and hides they would use as shelter. A cousin was herding their cattle and goats. She'd given up on trying to keep track of their possessions, and focussed on the children.

She had no direct experience of the Germans and accepted the men's assurances that the Hereros' superior numbers would deter and prevail. What scared her most was the abruptness and confusion of their journey and the absence of the men. She'd experienced violence before – in clashes with Nama cattle raiders and conflicts among the clans – but the men had always been present. Like the others, she withdrew into the dogged rhythm of the march.

Her spirits lifted when some of the men returned towards evening. They were pumped up from raids against German farms and trading posts in the area, and had come back with food, livestock and goods they had pillaged. They spoke of battles where they had killed and maimed – usually only the German men. Her husband, they told her, was on a raid at the mission station at Otjikango further south.

Their stories of Herero victories were greeted with the satisfaction of deserved retribution and the pent-up frustration of years of mistreatment. The murder of the pregnant wife of Barmenias Zeraua, son of their chief, by a settler and his initial acquittal was fresh in their memories. Luger, the farmer from Omaruru, had reportedly been castrated and killed by the family of his rejected wife. Herero grudges were justified.

When her husband returned, he was wearing a jacket stolen from the mission trading store and had brought her a dress. He had escorted the trader's wife and her two daughters to safety close to Okahandja as Maharero had ordered, and had seen more German troops arriving. They had to move faster, he urged, although pillaged livestock slowed them down even more. Two days later he and some of the other men were called away again to coordinate with other bands of fighters. The Germans were preparing retaliatory attacks.

+++

Dieter was one of the four signalmen in the company of new recruits. They'd been at a technical school in Darmstadt for a year and had another year to go to qualify as postal engineers destined for secure careers with the Deutsche Post. But with the wave of nationalism following the Herero uprising and the encouragement of their teachers, parents and friends, they had volunteered for the Kaiser's expeditionary force.

The absence of decent communications hampered the German response and preparations. Telegraph lines were often cut, and roaming bands of Herero fighters captured, intimidated and delayed dispatch riders.

The young signalmen were given rushed training in the use of heliographs on board the ship to Swakopmund, and dispatched to outlying units soon after arrival. Dieter was equipped with a brand-new Carl Zeiss device and sent to join a detachment of some two hundred men under Major Glassenapp at Otjiwarongo.

As the summer waned, Windhuk and Suidwes moved more tangibly onto a war footing. The fear of imminent Herero attack that had hung like the curtains in homes to keep the mid-summer heat at bay had lifted. But instead of relief came grimness, a tight set of the jaw, and persistent tension in the neck and the shoulders. People smiled less and griped more. The alcohol-fuelled gaiety than had been the norm of settler social life was replaced by resignation to the brutality of suppressing the blacks and the violence of their resistance.

"*Es muss sein* - it has to be" was a common muttered response to the discomfort as public hangings on the gallows outside the fort became frequent. The bodies – black men with their arms bound behind their backs and often dripping blood from beatings and sjambokking – were left hanging for days as a deterrent to the black population. Mutters that this was "unchristian" were uttered quietly and from a minority.

The prison camp on the slope running down from the Fort to the town expanded. Columns of abject Hereros, men and women, would arrive every few days and be forced into miserable pondoks – arranged in rigidly strict lines – constructed of bent branches and scraps of canvas and hide. Gangs of obviously starving people appeared in the town on forced labour supervised by soldiers. Beatings were common and public. Two larger pondoks were erected outside the women's stockade. Here the guards operated a bordello where Herero women were forced to service the troops and other men in the town. In the late afternoon, as the east wind blew, the smell of excrement wafted across the town.

The black population in the work camps across the riverbed were cowed but surprisingly, many remained. Hereros had fled or been arrested – even if they had not participated in the violence. But Damara, Ovambo and Nama maids and labourers would stream out early in the morning to build and maintain the white colony. By mid-afternoon they streamed back hurriedly, and never ventured out after dark as they had done previously. Most whites could not or did not want to distinguish between the various native peoples. All blacks were at least potential spies.

Leutwein's absence in the south and the inconclusive outcome of the battle with the Bondelswarts had damaged him and his backers in the Colonial Department in Berlin. In the eyes of the incensed settlers and in Germany, it was obvious that the Herero were a far more formidable threat, and now it was clear that they had long been preparing for war. In February the Kaiser appointed his Chief of Staff, General Alfred von Schlieffen, to take charge directly of the military campaign.

Von Schlieffen was a respected strategist and planner, and set about immediately building Germany's biggest peacetime military force. Woermann Line ships were now arriving in Swakopmund and Walvis Bay every two weeks as reinforcements and supplies were rushed to bolster what had become the nub of German pride.

Many of the officers and NCOs arriving were veterans of the Boxer rebellion in China and the war in German East Africa. They brought a strident toughness and ruthlessness to the conversations in the taverns. Their tales of hangings and mass executions, expulsions and expropriations played well with the settlers. Social Darwinism, American policies against native Americans and the import of African slaves, Germany's destiny, and white supremacy ordained by God provided the ideological underpinnings. Popular commentary in Germany and Suidwes moved from "defeat" of the Herero to the need for their "utter annihilation".

By early March there were two thousand troops in the country. Every train arriving in Windhuk carried military supplies. The military depot in Klein Windhoek now had rows of light artillery drawn up on the parade ground, and Herero prisoners were building additional ammunition dumps.

German commanders toughened up their young recruits by putting them in charge of the slave labour and of carrying out the beatings and executions outside the Fort. Boisterousness and naivety shrivelled as they were forced to cope with the heat, the flies, and the subjugation of strange black people. Innate prejudice and a sense of superiority concealed acute discomfort and fear. Cruelty became a cloak.

"Why don't they attack", one of the traders complained one evening, sitting on Jack's stoep. "The waiting is what makes me really nervous."

"They say there are maybe 80,000 Herero with almost 8,000 armed men - many with German rifles. Their hesitation does not make sense", agreed a supply officer, "but it enables us to bring more troops and supplies".

"The soldiers coming in are inexperienced and don't know the territory", replied the trader. Turning to the Stabsarzt he continued – "I hear that truppe are killed or injured from heatstroke, snakes and scorpions. That doesn't happen to the blacks!"

The surgeon, the oldest among them, leaned back in his chair swirling his whiskey. "In the past, there was always a negotiation with the Herero. Maybe that's what Maharero is waiting for. But he misreads the situation today. That's not the mood in Berlin and Leutwein is no longer in charge."

The Herero had withdrawn into an inaccessible hilly area scored with deep ravines south east of Okahandja. Pessimists said that that was where they were preparing an all-out offensive, and were waiting for arms and horses from Bechuanaland further east and for the Nama in the south to get organized to rise up with them. Others said they were hampered by their herds and families, and were cowards unwilling to face a professional army and its advanced weapons.

Von Schlieffen gave orders early on in his preparations to focus on supplies and dispatched an experienced transport officer. At first imperious, threatening everyone with requisitioning orders, he learned quickly to change his approach as the complexities and interdependencies became apparent. Jack was given guarantees to justify recruiting more wainwrights in the Cape. Spare parts were ordered to be pre-positioned all across Hereroland, and Boer transporters were encouraged to come in from South Africa with their wagons and oxen. Malan in the north and Jack and Izzy in Windhuk networked with these men as the demands for transport and supplies mounted.

After a month of acclimatising, training and equipping the troops, Leutwein marched on Maharero in early April, guided by Witbooi scouts. On the afternoon of Sunday April 10th casualties began to arrive in Windhuk. The town was somnolent, but by evening the previous evening's claims of a "resounding success" in a battle at a waterhole known as Okonjira emerged as completely false. It was only German artillery that had forced Maharero to retreat. Leutwein's forces were running out of ammunition when they did so. "We can't fight in the *gramadoelas*", one of the officers admitted in a bar that evening, using the Afrikaans term for wild, remote country. "We have no choice but to use artillery against their women and children and the elderly."

The next day Jack heard that Rolf was among the wounded. He'd been shot in the shoulder and had broken ribs, injured his hip and cracked his head when he fell off his horse. As soon as he was weaned off the sedation in the hospital, Jack brought him to the house to recuperate.

More wounded arrived. Leutwein had chased the Herero further north and had clashed with them at Oviumbo. His men exhausted and supply lines stretched, he was forced to withdraw overnight. In the bars and in Berlin, what colonial warfare technique described as "tactical withdrawal" was condemned as "shameful".

But lessons had been learned in the army headquarters – improved transport and pre-positioning supplies closer to the fighting had become an imperative. Boere, Nama and Baster transport drivers were scrambling to meet the German demand. One of them told Jack that 600 wagons and carts were crossing the Orange River at Upington every month, and a similar number at Vioolsdrif, where the British couldn't control the smuggling. Jack was bringing in new wagons from Cape Town and getting priority for their delivery on the trains. The Fentins saw to the oxen, which came from Bechuanaland.

Life in the town became unpleasant. The tense atmosphere, the presence of so many single men, and the inflow of a barely concealed criminal class drove many of the more established settlers to stay indoors. Bars and brothels appeared everywhere – the biggest owned by the Postmaster. The bordello outside the concentration camp had grown into a camp on its own.

Rolf recovered slowly. The Damara housemaid was wary of him and did not speak German, so Nara spent more time with him, changing the dressings on the wounds and easing the bandages round his ribs. She read magazines to him, and would pause to ask questions or the meaning of words. Three weeks after he was injured Susanna arrived from Lüderitzbucht via Swakopmund and took over caring for him. Her presence hastened his recovery, which neither really wanted as they knew he would be reassigned to a field unit as soon as he could ride a horse. In the meantime, they socialised, and he began to spend time up at the fort on staff work.

When they were absent, often on a Sunday afternoon, Jack and Nara would have time together. They savoured their stolen time, discovery of each other, of giving and receiving pleasure. Their intimacy deepened as an antidote to the unpleasantness of life outside. But it was fraught. Jack was anxious all the time that Nara's behaviour would betray them. He worked long hours and kept her at a distance most of the time. She was hurt and confused, and bounced between tears, anger and infatuation. But he too was fixated – he just disguised it better. Every vacant moment his mind dwelt on exploring her. The intensity of his own orgasms and the wonder of pleasuring her were a drug driving him to touch her, embrace her, at any private moment. But when there were people about, he ignored her, coldly.

+++

May 9th, 1904   Swakopmund

Jack and Cameron were sitting in one of the quieter bars in the town. They'd settled the Coloured wainwrights and builders that Sonnenberg had recruited in the Cape in a boarding house that would take non-whites. A cheer went up from the men at the counter – Leutwein was to be replaced with a no-nonsense general by the name of von Trotha. The news had leaked from the post office, which had received the telegram an hour earlier.

At Usakos he nearly lost all of the Coloured artisans when they saw the gangs of Herero prisoners working on the railway. Club and sjambok-wielding soldiers shouting at Herero women – some near naked and the older women in their traditional Victorian-type dresses and hats – outraged them. Nothing in their experience in the Cape had prepared them for this. Jack had to up their salaries by a third and promise a double bonus at the end to get them to continue.

The workload just increased in his absences. Lüderitz was now operating, and he had a backlog of orders, invoices and receipts to issue. The sums he was billing for raised eyebrows in the administration, and newly-arrived accountants and quartermasters held up payments until their bookkeeping instincts were satisfied or they were overruled by their bosses under pressure to get stuff into the country. Like the other merchants, compensation for the goods lost in the Herero attacks was trimmed but paid promptly. Their goodwill was necessary.

+++

"She has started to bleed", Magda said to Hanna one morning when the kitchen had emptied.

"You can't wait now for the *hokmeisie* ceremony", Hanna replied. "You must talk to her."

"No, *merrem*, that's not our way. She won't find a husband if she's not been a *hokmeisie* and she can only learn these things there from the *taras*."

Hanna sighed. It wasn't the first time she'd worried about Nara's puberty. She'd even discussed it with Effi, who was gruff and unhelpful. "These things are best left to them", he said, referring to Magda and the Nama ways. She'd thought to talk frankly to Jack too but was embarrassed. He'd grown older and more distant with his workload and they did not meet as often. She sensed that he'd resented her pregnancy and the birth of the little girl. She felt he still followed her with his eyes, and watched her as she nursed the child. To avoid awkwardness, she'd begun to avoid him at these times.

"Well, we must make sure that she does not sleep outside the house any longer", she said, deliberately not mentioning Jack.

+++

Lothar von Trotha arrived in Swakopmund on June 11th. By this time the profile of general, a veteran of previous German colonial wars in Africa, had been breathlessly covered in the local press. His reputation for ruthlessness in suppressing the Wahehe uprising a few years before in East Africa had been spelled out – mass executions, burnings of entire villages – sometimes with their inhabitants inside, and a policy of taking no prisoners. This was just what was needed in the eyes of many. He clashed with Leutwein at their first meeting and within a few days, declared martial law.

Most of the Schutztruppe officer's ranks were drawn from the German, and particularly the Prussian military class. They brought with them the regimentation and discipline of their training and their belief system. They were a generation frustrated by the absence of any real war for many years. The surprise of the Herero uprising and the setbacks in the early clashes embarrassed and irritated them. Von Trotha's reputation and the obvious backing he enjoyed from the Kaiser, the military and political leadership in Berlin, and popular sentiment lifted spirits. They also feared his discipline.

+++

Dieter's detachment followed the Herero as they traipsed slowly east. Their orders were to gather intelligence as von Trotha built up his forces. Unnecessary provocations were to be avoided but the troops had to be toughened up. By June some 5,000 German troops had arrived and "the Shark" as he was called by his troops began to draw up his plans for the inevitable battle.

The Herero fighters were often mounted and highly mobile, and they would set ambushes and occasionally skirmish with German patrols. But they had families to protect and cattle to graze even as they moved. Maharero and his fellow leaders seemed content to harass the German forces, waiting or hoping for negotiations to commence. This had been the pattern of conflict in the past and, ignorant of the mood in Germany and of von Trotha's reputation, they were confident that their superior numbers and knowledge of the territory were a sufficient deterrent.

Kaera's clan, having moved from the western edges of Hereroland, were among the stragglers at the end of the stream of people gathering at the Ohamakari plateau. Here there was better grazing, reliable sources of water, and the reassuring presence of Maharero and his many fighters. It was also a redoubt – the red cliffs rising steeply from the thick green savannah to a narrow plateau which would also provide protection.

Her extended family – around a hundred people – were in a makeshift camp to the south. They were letting the cattle and the people feed and rest before they moved up onto the plateau. It was mid-morning and most of the men were out with the herds when the Witbooi scouts spotted them from a small koppie. Kaera was gathering firewood in a dry riverbed together with some other women, her infant strapped to her back. Her son was back at the camp with his grandmother who, like the other elders and children, was completely unaware of the scouts observing them or the proximity of a German patrol.

The scouts descended the koppie quietly and reported to the young second lieutenant. "It seems to be all women and children, some young boys. The men must be with the cattle. We saw no fighters."

The lieutenant, like most of the men in his platoon, had been in Suidwes for less than two months. They had not yet seen any real action and he and the sergeant who was a colonial veteran, were anxious to bloody the recruits before the major battles all knew were coming. A mounted charge into the unprotected settlement would be a good exercise.

A few men and young boys inside the camp rushed to confront the patrol as they came galloping into the camp. People scattered as the Germans galloped though, their shrieks scaring horses and men. The lieutenant wheeled to charge again and saw several black bodies on the ground. Further away one of his men had been knocked off his horse and was struggling with a youth wielding a knopkierie. A soldier nearby fired a shot, hitting the downed soldier and then another, felling the club-wielding youth.

Men and horses were wide-eyed and panting with adrenalin. They milled around as the Herero fled screaming. The sergeant shouted out instructions to round up the fleeing people. The Witbooi rode out to waylay Herero men who might have heard the shots and be returning. Hastily they pushed and shoved the villagers into a group, and then strung up the wounded boy and an elderly man from a tree. The women were screaming and wailing with anguish as the bodies jerked and twisted. Troops threw embers from the central fire onto the temporary shelters, the smoke and flames adding to the panic. As they rode of out the camp through the dry riverbed, the sergeant grabbed a young woman and threw her across his horse. He shouted to Dieter behind him to grab another young woman hiding under scrub. Dieter locked eyes with Kaera, hesitated and continued.

A few hours later, as their detachment set up camp, Dieter, his assistant, and two riflemen rode up to the slopes of a koppie south of the main plateau. From here he could signal Colonel Deimling of the 2nd Field Regiment, their commander, at his headquarters in the south east.

The assistant read out the dispatch from a form as Dieter operated the device:

Deutsch-Südwest- Afrika. Heliografie d. Schutztruppe (German South West Africa. Heliograph of the Protection Force)

"calling…" he flashed in Morse code
"receiving…" Deimling's signaller responded.
"incident report. attacked by herero band south west of waterberg while on patrol. five native fighters killed. one trooper wounded. herero moving north east. witbooi expect counterattack."
The assistant who'd been monitoring his morse as he signalled confirmed that it had been accurate.

As backup Dieter also signalled Captain Von Fielder's unit who were camped closer at the base of a mountain to the west.

He received almost immediate acknowledgement from both units. Von Vielder's signalman told him to wait for a further message. Twenty minutes later it followed:

"detachment commanded by hauptmann brüns sent to you".

The mood was sombre when Rolf and six men trotted into the encampment as they were eating the evening meal the *bamboesen*[41] had prepared. Rolf took the lieutenant aside to debrief him and then came back to address the men:

---

[41] Bamboesen - native servants (often young boys) recruited or coerced to serve the army

"I know that for most of you this was the first experience of combat. I realise the speed of the encounter and the violence involved is a shock. But this is war – this is what we've come here for. This is not Europe – it is Africa. They will show you no mercy if you hesitate or show weakness. The only way we will force the Kaiser's will on these primitive people is if we are resolute. They must fear us. It is vital. Fear is the ultimate deterrent. So, you should look on today as a positive experience. It will strengthen and forearm you and your comrades."

There was little of the camaraderie round the fire they usually enjoyed. Dieter rolled himself in his blanket, re-living the day. The image of the Herero woman cowering under the bush clutching her baby came back to him – she was looking directly at him as he galloped past. Did she see him as he was or as he'd become?

In the firelight he saw the sergeant get up and with two of the other troopers, grab the girl who'd been tied to a wagon. They disappeared with her into the bush and he heard her shriek in pain and then groan. More soldiers joined them. He rolled away and looked up at the vast canopy of sharp stars above them.

Rolf lay in a small tent the *bamboesen* had erected for him. He'd hardly recovered from his injury but von Trotha was driving all the officers hard. He'd curtailed Rolf's recovery period and dispatched him to coordinate the intelligence for von Fielder. His shoulder throbbed, his ribs and hip still ached, and he limped. Too many hours in a saddle brought extreme pain, which was why he'd been assigned to a staff position. He'd not joined the junior officer for the meal, and as soon as he could, lay down and took a sip of morphine from the dark brown bottle the surgeon had given him to manage the pain. He'd seen the girl tied to a wagon when he trotted into the camp, suspected why she was there and then heard her cry out in the dark. He knew it was rape. But this was war and she was black. He turned on his pain-free side and waited for the morphine's embrace ...

Logistics

Von Trotha exploited Herero hesitation to build up supplies and a transport network for the six detachments he was deploying around the Waterberg. He counted on his superior weapons, the professionalism of his officers, the local knowledge of the Witbooi and Baster scouts, Herero spies, and logistical prowess to give him the edge.

Weapons, ammunition and other supplies were offloaded from every Woermann ship arriving in Swakopmund and Walvis. The private trader network was tapping every source of supply it knew in Europe, South Africa and as far as Argentina (for horses and mules). Prices were high and the Germans, knowing that they needed the goodwill of the suppliers and traders, paid promptly.

Getting the supplies from the ports into the country and to his units was Von Trotha's responsibility. Martial law was one of his tools. Wagons and carts were often requisitioned but Jack was spared because of the urgency of getting his imports distributed.

Sonnenberg's syndicate had placed orders with most of the wagon manufacturers in the Cape Boland, effectively tying up much of the supply and enabling them to get higher prices. Importing wagons from Germany or the UK was not really an option, as centuries of Cape and Boer expertise in building wagons for the veldt was widely acknowledged. Most of the wagons were either sold or leased to the army. But the army also needed experienced *transportryers* to move the supplies from the railheads and depots out to the units in the field.

Pay was high and crews were drawn from as far afield as the northern Cape. The army had to issue the non-white transport crews with written permits or "passes" enabling them to move about the country, copying the technique of control of the native population from the British in South Africa.

+++

Koo-kurrrr-it, koo-kurrr -it, koo-kurrr-it... the high-pitched melodic trill of the Cape turtle dove outside trellised their languor.

"Animals know of water before we do", her father had explained by a water hole that had filled up with the rain that had fallen in the uplands. "The dove's call is rare in the Kuiseb. It will lead to water because they will fly great distances to drink." Bubbles in the water showed that there were also fish, swept down from rock pools upstream. He speared a carp in the muddy water with his bow and arrow.

The dove's call carried Jack back to quiet Sunday afternoons lying on the cool grass under the old oaks in the Cape Town Gardens. That's when he most missed his family.

Beyond the drawn beige curtains, it was utterly quiet. A Windhuk Sunday.

She lay with her head in the crook of his arm, he on his back, his eyes closed, drifting along on the bliss that followed ejaculation. She was on her side watching him. He was completely naked for the first time and her eyes ran down his white body to his penis, now limp and flopped against his leg. She'd never seen and didn't understand the strange ring and knob at the end of it. She wanted to touch it and ask him about it but sensed that this wasn't the right time.

This was the first time in weeks that they'd had a chance to be together. Magda and Hanna had become nosier and more controlling, and allowed her less time to be down at his house. Rolf's presence in the house until he'd been sent north and the Damara maid had constrained her movements when she did visit. He was frustrated too but also relieved, as he felt she followed him around with her eyes and he was sure that others would see this too. She was moody, irritable and sometimes teary like Leah in her adolescence. He kept his eyes closed – resting but also keeping her at bay.

Koo-kurrrr-it, Koo-kurrrr-it …. He doesn't want to talk. His seed on her thighs is sticky and uncomfortable. Rather than drowsy, she's energised. Frustrated, she sits up on the side of the bed and touches the stickiness. She recalls the smell from the shirt he'd given her to launder years before in Swakopmund. How did it get there? She turns to look at him – suspicion that he'd been with a girl then dawning for the first time.

He turns to look at her too. Her breasts are full. He rises and leans forward on his elbow to kiss her and cups her firmly as he does so. She winces slightly and gets up to wash herself at the basin. Separateness stirs inside her.

Later, after she'd returned to the Yard, a zygote of dread begins to unfurl inside him.

On the Monday morning Jack obtained new passes for his *transportryers,* the Coloured builders and wainwrights, and his Nama and Baster guards from the magistrate. He also received general passes for three *bamboesen* as well as for a domestic servant. Von Trotha's martial law edict had invalidated what he'd used before. Everything was in duplicate – one for Jack and one for each of the non-white workers he employed. The magistrate came by that evening to collect a crate of Scotch – the price of moving Jack's requests to the top of the pile.

"This is yours", he said, showing her the stiff form in the Gothic script of the German bureaucracy and adorned with the crest and stamp of the DSW administration.

"What's it for?"

"The army is restricting travel because of the trouble. This allows you to travel with me. You must keep it with you all the time. Soldiers and policemen may ask you for it. I'm planning to go to Swakopmund in a few days and you can come with me. Remember, I told you we could visit your aunt?"

She looked at the other documents on his desk. "Why do they have names and I have a number only?" she asked, pointing at the passes for the Cape Coloured artisans. "Because they come from outside the country – they came with passes from Walvis Bay."

A few days later Jack watched a long column of ox wagons loaded with military supplies move out from the Ausspannplatz in the early morning. Izzy was riding ahead, and they had a Boer and few Basters as *touleirs*. Although they'd done this route many times before Jack was particularly nervous – he had a lot of money invested in the wagons and in the goods for which he'd only been partially paid. His final payment – and his profit – would only come on delivery in Okahandja.

On his way back he stopped at the building site south of the Yard. He'd outgrown the shed on Post Street and had acquired a larger plot where the Coloured builders were completing the outside walls of much larger storerooms. The area had been fenced off with thorn bushes dragged in from the surrounding veldt, and the foundations of the Cape-Dutch style house he intended to build had also been laid. But the storerooms were the most urgent and he wanted the roof on as soon as possible. Although rains were not due until November, the sun would damage the goods. He'd been on site the previous afternoon, but still walked about irritably complaining about the lack of progress.

Nara was waiting on the back stoep, wearing a light blue dress and white pinafore and a small close-fitting hat. "How pretty and how excited", he thought. Then – "she's over-dressed". She looked down, demure, he thought. But she'd seen his pursed lips and read his irritation. He disapproves.

By the time he was ready to leave she'd changed into a plain dress and removed the hat. Her excitement suppressed, she trailed behind him when they walked to the railway station. Initially he was more comfortable separated from her in public, distracted anyway by his work concerns and his half-formed plans about her. But this too was awkward and when he turned around to her, he saw her tears. He felt even worse, but she perked up once on the train, with the chuff of the steam engine, the rhythmic sway of the carriages and the yellow-green veldt whizzing by. His mood lifted with hers.

Okahandja stopped that. Von Trotha had requisitioned all wagons and carts in the area for his impending assault. All transport was to be accompanied and operated by its owners. That included Jack, the local quartermaster insisted. Malan was already in the field. He could not continue on to Swakopmund.

His plans thwarted, Jack was frustrated by the pace of an ox-wagon trek, and bad-tempered all of the journey north from Okahandja. His agitation shut off the stimulus of the veld, and he was indifferent to sleeping and eating under the stars – something that had given him great pleasure before. Nara avoided him, spending time with a Baster *touleier* who spoke Nama.

Jack tried to cut away from the column several times, arguing that his mule-drawn carts were faster, but the lieutenant accompanying them insisted that it was not safe. They were carrying ammunition, and thus were a constant target for Herero raiders.

At the Omboroko Mountains they turned east and made for the Waterberg. The military presence and more wagon columns increased the air of tension. Nara travelled inside the covered wagon most of the time, intimidated by the concentration of men.

+++

24 September 1989   Bantry Bay

Lynne fussed with the cups and they settled into armchairs facing the large window – the wind buffeting the glass pane.

There's sadness in his eyes and he's tired, she thought. He's gone older and thicker round the middle. God, I wonder what he makes of me – older than him and after three kids! This is weighing on him. He – maybe we – are leaving the life we had behind. South West – and the farms – was always his life. Not mine. I wonder if he understands that he has to change.

She smiled gently as she realised that her baby brother, always in control and self-confident to the point of arrogance, was maybe having his first mid-life crisis. The sale of the farm was a pretext or a trigger for something deeper and more personal. Doubt he can talk to Cynthia about this. You can only really talk to Cynthia about Cynthia.

"You always enjoyed the storms", she said, acknowledging his introspection.

"Yes. I did. I still do."

"Remember how we used to lie on the beds on the stoep at the farm and fall asleep to the squeak of the windmill? When I slept over there last week it sounded exactly the same although I know we've changed that windmill. Those were such happy holidays – I remember mom and dad so happy on the farm too. They used to whisper and giggle while we lay on the stoep in the dark. I used to think they were laughing at things we'd done or said, but I could never really remember what was so funny."

"They were having sex, you dumbo!", she chuckled. He blushed. "They were a happy couple."

Intuition and concern overcoming reserve, she half blurted – "How're things with Cynthia?"

A half-beat skip in the rhythm of their conversation, then – "Aaagh, you know – tennis, shopping, fighting with her family, bickering with her friends. Now with the kids too …"

He changed the subject. "I had this dream when I was there on the farm – rare for me as I don't dream or remember my dreams – that I was in the room with Jack and Sydney. It was so intense that I could see the fabric of their clothing. I won't repeat the whole thing but it made me feel, or realise, that there were huge chapters in Jack's life that I'm not aware of. I guess that's not a surprise. Our lives were here, together, Mom and Dad with us. Bobbe too. I don't sense anything's missing. But with Jack it seems much more complicated."

Tension, discomfort made him get up and walk to the photo of their grandparents on the back wall. "They don't seem close in the picture."

"They weren't. I asked her once if they were happy. 'We respected each other', she said. I think that was typical for their generation. Rae said he had a sense of humour which sustained her in Windhoek when they were building the business. When Sydney died, she said he turned in on himself. He spent more and more time on the farm without her. They grew apart, and she wanted to be here anyway to educate mom and be near her family. They grew apart. She said things got worse when they heard and understood about the Shoah. He blamed himself for not getting his family out."

He'd moved to look at the bronze head of a man on a side table. "Doeseb", he chuckled, patting the head. "Jack used to tell us that it was a Damara named Doeseb who introduced him to the veldt, in the stories of his first journey into South West."

"You cried the first time he told you", Lynne laughed. "You thought it was the head of a real man! But it does give me an idea. The Marcuses gave that statue to Jack. You remember? – she was the sculptress? Dr. Marcus was the family doctor in Windhoek and knew Jack well. They live here now. He's probably worth speaking to. I'll find them and I'll come with you. You've made me interested now too."

"The strange thing is I feel guilty about selling the farm", he said. "I know it's the right thing to do, but after that dream of Jack in his bedroom I feel I'm betraying Jack in some way. Jack and Sydney."

"Jack knew the farm would go", she said flatly.

"How would you know that?", he challenged.

"It's time I told you."

The Waterberg

Some hours after sunrise, the heat of the Kalahari drew air currents across the red floor of the valley. As the air flowed east it came up against the red cliffs of two massifs formed some 130 million years before the single continent of Gondwana ruptured into Africa and South America. The initial crust of the earth had been elevated hundreds of metres, and then eroded over time exposing petrified red sand dunes now known by geologists as the Etjo formation. Erosion continued through the ages, leaving a few table-shaped mountains marking the boundary between the Kalahari basin and the central plateau. The largest of these is the Waterberg (water mountain) running northeast from Otjiwarongo. To the south, separated by a narrow gap is the Klein (little) Waterberg.

High on their nesting ledge, two Cape vultures sensed the air flow. When it became steady enough to generate lift, they spread their massive wings and launched themselves over the plain below. They flew north slowly for a few kilometres until they encountered the first of the day's thermals. These rising columns of warm air would keep them aloft for hours and enable them to glide over the vast distances they covered in their search for carrion.

Other vultures of various species took to the air too. Some from the Waterberg itself and others from nests on the tallest trees in the plain. As the day got hotter the thermals grew stronger and rose higher with tell-tale puff of cumulus at their apex. The stacks of circling raptors signalled the availability of food, and every day more birds and terrestrial scavengers moved into the area.

From where they soared, sometimes as much as a kilometre above the hot earth, the vultures could see scores of human encampments in the veld. They scanned laterally, with a wide field of vision under prominent feathered ridges that protected their eyes from the sun. There were no aerial predators to threaten them, and they were not interested in anything above the horizon. Their search was for the vulnerable, the dead and the slaughtered, and these were on the red earth below. This was their diet and there was more every day.

The Herero camps were scattered in the thick savanna around the two red-faced ridges that dominated the landscape. The narrow passage between them slowed the haphazard drift of the people and their cattle who, following Maharero's instructions, were drawing themselves in around the main mountain and the water it provided.

In the rainy season, the water-bearing winds from the coast would be forced upwards and deposit rain on the Waterberg and the surrounding plains. The Etjo sandstone was porous, and the water that did not run down the fissures and gullies would be absorbed and soak down until it encountered a compact, more impermeable substrate sloping to the south east. Here it emerged as springs and shallow pans, which supplied the thousands of people and their cattle. The Herero leaders' logic was that the Waterberg would provide a redoubt for the battle they knew was coming, as well as water to sustain their people and their wealth – the long-horned cattle.

For the past few days the vultures had been drawn to newer arrivals – men on horses, often with large ox wagons, mules, and small herds of cattle that they milked and slaughtered to feed themselves. Most of these encampments were arranging themselves in a semi-circle to the west. One closed off the route to the north behind the ridge.

South east of the gap and the springs fed from the mountain, a larger force was being drawn up to close the encirclement. Due east, beyond the Schutztruppe encampment was the Omaheke – the western desert reaches of the Kalahari.

+++

September 1989   Keetmanshoop

Frederika found herself sitting next to Frau Bruns at the hairdresser. She always found the formal, erect woman from the neighbouring farm intimidating. Although Anna Bruns understood Afrikaans, and no doubt spoke it with her staff, she always spoke English or German in the town, which immediately hobbled conversation. There was also the woman's beauty and poise and an unavoidable class distinction which never eased off enough to allow a friendship between the two women who lived lonely lives less than an hour apart and shared similar tragedies.

It was her directness that Frederika feared. "It's always your boys that get killed", she had said during a condolence visit following Jannie's death, airing a resentment many of the Suidwes Afrikaners felt but never expressed. No one could say anything – the Bruns were cursed with a litany of misfortune of their own.

Now, she leaned forward, uncharacteristically confidential – "Herr Levin wants to sell the farm?"

"My husband is fetching me from here", Frederika mumbled. "You should ask him..."

The Bruns were local aristocracy, projected in their bearing, culture, and everything they did. They had farmed here longer than most, their farm management was meticulous, and their tragic family history was a barrier to easy friendship or flippant conversation. Three generations of Bruns men had died young. Susanna's husband couldn't take Suidwes, and had left her with a son, somewhat older than Jannie. He had crashed near Mt Etjo two years before, on his way home from flying for the army up on the border, in an accident that was never satisfactorily explained. None of this had diminished the Bruns women's fierce commitment to their vast holding on the road to Aus, on the edge of the Namib and the Fish River Canyon.

Susanna, named after her grandmother, managed the farm herself. She drove out before dawn most mornings, visiting the shepherds and the flocks in their *kraal*s and, if necessary, would kill and skin a karakul lamb herself before the curls of its pelt began to open. She shot her own game, but called on Steyn or other neighbours when it came to stalking a leopard or repairing a generator or truck. She was also the first in the area to begin building up a stock of game, and had submitted plans for guest *rondawels* to cater for German tourists.

Like the Levins, the Bruns kept out of politics of any kind. Susanna was active in the local farm bodies like SWAKARA. Her social life was focussed on the German community in the area, visits to Germany, and the odd trip to Cape Town. Sam had hosted her and her daughter in the city several times, but that had stopped after his death.

Steyn lifted his farm hat in greeting when the women emerged. "I'd like to speak to Herr Levin", Susanna said. "I understand he wants to sell the farm."

+++

Godfrey was waiting for him when Tjandi got back to the house after the first week's training. He felt he'd been in Katatura for a month, already used to the early morning commute in the rickety taxis, the press of bodies, the police checkpoints and the *skollies* on the prowl everywhere ready to rob. He'd not got back to the house before eight in the evenings, and then had homework – technical English, manuals, cataloguing and store methods.

This Friday night would be another bender, he knew. They

skipped the night clubs but there was no absence of fun and music as they traipsed around the township from shebeen to private braais to parties in homes that seemed open to everyone.

A younger, more urbanised generation and intermarriage had eroded the old tribal differences reinforced by the white authorities when Katatura was first settled. Godfrey's circle of friends was mixed, and they spoke a jumble of languages, often spiked with English terms learned from work, pop culture, and from the news and the imminent transition of power. Tjandi's "management training" lead to conversations about "independence" and the sense that white-owned businesses and bosses were becoming more pleasant, considerate, and talking, at least, of new opportunities for their "non-white" staff. There were cynics too, but most seemed very optimistic and upbeat.

"You've not yet seen the 'white city'", one of the girls drawn to his innate shyness teased when he revealed that his entire week had been at the Levin compound in the northern industrial zone. "These are exciting times. And it's all happening there - in a small area that we can walk in a few hours."

The next morning, she and friend sauntered up Kaiser Strasse with Tjandi. The wealth on display in the department store windows, in the cars and the white people's clothing was stupendous. "It's already changing", one the girls said, nodding at a well-dressed black woman coming out of a boutique with shopping bags.

They stood opposite the Kalahari Sands hotel watching black-tinted Mercedes and BMWs dropping off and collecting SWAPO, DTA and other politicians they recognised from TV and the papers. The multinational UNTAG forces with their blue berets came and went in their sparkling white vehicles, and the international journalists lounged about the lobby in their uniforms of luxury safari kit.

There was a buzz around the hotel with the international flags draped outside, the self-important bearing of those prominent enough to warrant a visit to Windhoek's premier hotel, and the constant flow of expensive German limousines. It was as if independence had started, was tangible, could be seen and smelt, at least in this place. Others felt this too and they stood in a throng of mainly black and coloured onlookers corralled behind barriers across the street.

But it was only a ten-minute walk up the hill to the Tintenpalast for things to be what they'd always been. The South African flag in front of the neo-classical building, khaki-uniformed white and coloured policemen with automatic weapons, an armoured car parked on the gravel driveway and the long neat gardens tended by black workers.

"It doesn't look like it will ever end", Godfrey said as they sauntered up the hill towards the massive Lutheran Christuskirche, which dominated the Windhoek skyline.

"When I was growing up, I never even thought this change was possible or how it could affect me", said one of the girls. "Now, my fifteen-year-old sister is talking of going to university and travelling abroad. Now we can look at the horizon instead of at that stupid zebra", she said nodding at the R*eiterdenkmal*, the statue of a mounted German Schutztrup with a rifle, which faced them across the roundabout in front of the church.

Lynne…

… stood up, uncomfortable with the tone of resentment or disparagement in her brother's voice. She stood at the window, looking down at the houses and flats tumbling down to the churning sea, suddenly reliving the fear and even the guilt of her brush with real trouble some forty years earlier. It was winter then too and stormy.

She lay in an unfamiliar bed, trying to hear beyond the soft breathing of the man beside her. Something more than a guilty conscience about lying to her mother had woken her. Anxiety heightened her senses, and she probed the night for what had woken her.

There, again – in the gap between the crash of the waves – men's voices, close by. Afrikaans or heavy Afrikaans accents – unusual in this English-speaking suburb – coming from the adjacent flat. By the luminous hands of her wristwatch it was three twenty in the morning. Carefully she slipped out of bed and tiptoed to the corner by the window to try and hear what was being said. The bedroom was cold.

She recognised the neighbour's voice – Mr. Haddon. Bruce, the man in the bed, had speculated, only half-jokingly, that Haddon was a police spy. "It seems they are all there – they come and go – but in this weather I think they've all came back", she heard him murmur.

Maybe Bruce was right – why else would Haddon be with Afrikaans–speaking men here so early in the morning? They're standing by the window of Haddon's flat right next to me she realised.

"*Die manne is in posisie* - the men are in position", another voice in Afrikaans. Acknowledged with a grunt and then heavy Afrikaans-accented English: "We have the road blocked off at the top and at the bottom. There are men behind the house now too. We have to be quiet. You must be out of sight – you can't be seen to be involved. Stay away from the window."

She was naked. Instead of feeling sexy as she had a few hours before when she'd let Bruce undress her, vulnerability stirred between her legs. She tiptoed back to the bed searching for her panties where he'd dropped them. Her blouse and bra were in the lounge where Bruce had pulled them off. The curtains there had not been drawn and she gingerly tiptoed across to get them. Half-dressed, she stood back from the window to look down onto the road below. Moonlit clouds scudded across Signal Hill and the waves continued to pound. Streetlights shimmered on the tar, wet from earlier rain, and a line of seagulls faced into the wind on the peaked tiled roof of the house opposite - a house she shared with other students on Quendon Road.

The top of the garden gate was pushed open and a group of large men in raincoats moved up to the front door. Two others walked along the adjacent red concrete path to the maid's quarters. Lights went on, cars arrived, and the raid by the Security Police was underway. They would come looking for her, she knew.

Bruce called her name from the bedroom and she went back, quickly putting her finger to her lips and pointing to the party wall with the Haddons. "They're raiding the house", she whispered into his ear. "I have to go." It took time for his brain to engage – "They'll be watching for movement. Best stay put for now. Don't go near the window."

A few weeks before, Adrian Leftwich, one of their associates at the University of Cape Town, had broken under interrogation at the Caledon Square police station in the city. He'd divulged the names of the members of the African Resistance Movement, ARM – a group of liberal white South Africans who had opted for violent opposition to apartheid. Several of the people he named stayed in the house.

Haddon, an English immigrant with strong anti-Semitic views that festered in the predominantly Jewish suburb where he'd inexplicably chosen to live after fleeing Rhodesia, had become a security police informant while looking for work. He resented the gaiety of the students and had been happy to keep the house under observation from his flat. The Security Police raid was triggered by an ARM bomb in the Johannesburg railway station the day before – July 24th, 1964. One woman was killed and 23 injured. This provided the government with the excuse it needed for further crackdowns on the "kaffir boeties" – the white, mainly English-speaking, liberal opposition to apartheid.

By nine o'clock the raid was over, and the news was beginning to spread around the city.

Mustering

Osondjache, a small hill west of the Waterberg plain, was the mustering and resupply point for the divisions in the field. Escorts from the forward units met the supply columns, and from here they were ushered onward again. Jack's attempt to offload and return was refused, so he stayed with his mule-drawn carts so that he could return quickly. He was assigned to deliver to Colonel Deimling's 2nd Field Regiment west of the Klein Waterberg, hopefully only about a day's journey away.

They were camped on a hill that sloped eastwards towards the plain surrounding the Waterberg. From where he stood Jack could see the smoke of multiple fires rising from the vast green plain below. The sergeant who was to escort them pointed out the track they would follow – moving south and then skirting along low foothills to approach the Klein Waterberg. "You can see from the fires and the smoke", he said. "That is the Herero – they are all camped in there. Maybe 60,000 they say."

Jack turned when his name was called to see Rolf tramping up the slight incline. He still limped, but seemed much fitter. When the sergeant left Jack pulled out a bottle of whiskey from the wagon box, and he and Rolf sat watching the last of the sun's glow on the burnt orange ridges of the Waterberg.

"Von Trotha is a brilliant soldier, and outstanding at logistics as you can see. The Herero have numbers and local knowledge, but we have the Witbooi and Herero spies and very modern weapons. We are all quite confident, I think."

"Von Trotha's big advantage is that he is utterly ruthless. He is set on destroying the Herero and after them the Nama. He's let it be known already – we are not to take any prisoners – not even women or children."

"What does he want to achieve?" Jack asked, not really accepting what Rolf was describing. "You need the Herero for work, don't you?"

"You think like an economist! That's like Leutwein, and that's the big difference. Some of the officers are not comfortable with this order, but he has the backing of the Kaiser and he is a ruthless disciplinarian. He wants to empty this land of the natives. Germans will come as settlers like they have in America. They brought slaves from Africa for labour. Labour will come from Ovamboland and from outside Suidwes. That's the model."

Jack ate with Nara inside the canopy of the cart after Rolf left. He knew she'd heard him. There were Witbooi and Bamboesen in the camp, but it seemed that few of the German soldiers saw any need to keep their thoughts and plans quiet. They declared them almost enthusiastically – maybe hoping to intimidate the natives, or perhaps to reassure themselves. Or, they were just confident and arrogant.

"He said they will destroy the Nama too?", Nara asked quietly.

Jack played with the stew in the enamel plate. "Yes, he did. I think they will too. I think we have to get you to Walvis Bay as soon as possible. I will ask Cameron to look after you. He has a Nama wife, you know?"

But Deimling had other plans for Jack when they arrived. The Colonel told him brusquely that he would be taking a Maxim machine gun unit and his heliograph operator and their supplies further east along the small mountain the next morning. A Witbooi scout who was to accompany them came across and spoke to Nara.

"He told me I should stay here", she said later. "He said there may be fighting."

"It's ok for you to stay. I'll be back in a day."

"No, I don't want to." He recognised the set of her jaw. They'd grown testier with each other with each day and each setback. After a pause she looked at him, her eyes hot and glistening – "Do you want me to stay?"

"No. You won't be safe here on your own either."

They set out early the next morning, accompanied by a mounted patrol. Tension became palpable as soon as they left the camp. There was little talking. The Witbooi scouts rode on ahead probing, waited for their advance and then rode on ahead again. They used signs to gesture to the lieutenant leading the patrol. Jack watched as the scouts would break off from the path and ride in arcs on either side looking for tracks in the hot reddish sand.

Whenever they approached an area of thick vegetation or a riverbed, some troopers would dismount to scout on either side by foot. The Maxim crew rode alongside the cart, ready to grab it in the event of an attack.

Nara huddled inside, scared of the men and scared of the place.

Slowly the craggy details of the mountain began to emerge above the dense vegetation. Even from a distance it was possible to see how thick and thorny it was. The birds were hushed too. Vultures circled high above them.

The lieutenant halted the column and dismounted. Obscured behind a tree, he scanned the red cliffs with a telescope. They knew that as they were observing the Herero, they were likely being observed too. He waved the sergeant in charge of the Maxim and the heliograph operator forward, and pointed out where they were to position themselves. Then he and the rest of the patrol broke away, following the Witbooi in a slow decent through the scrub towards the plain, probing for outlying Herero positions.

Dieter and his junior signaller rode beside the wagon, with two of the gunners riding ahead as scouts. They positioned the Maxim gun with its 4-man crew first further east to enable the maximum arc of fire. Dieter and his assistant then rode back with the cart to a thick, overgrown gorge that ran up through the cliff above them.

It was only when Dieter told Jack to stop and took out the

heliograph that Jack realised they were being left on their own. It was mid-afternoon and Dieter had to get into position to meet the signalling schedules.

"I don't know when they will fetch you", he told Jack. "I'll signal them as soon as I get into position. In the meantime, look after our horses. We can't take them up the gorge."

Jack was livid. Mainly with himself for being such a *putz* and being suckered into this ludicrous situation. He'd been too busy nursing his frustrations to pay attention to what had been developing around him. He'd just wanted the mission over, and had assumed that he would ride back with the patrol the same day and then be on his way back to Otjiwarongo and onto Swakopmund. He wanted to be away from here and back in charge of his own life. And now he was stuck with Nara in a forest of thorn bushes with a war about to break out. Frustrated, angry at himself, he realised he was frightened too.

He watched the two young truppe climb up through the bush, the heliograph and tripod on their shoulders. They were only carrying small rucksacks so he assumed the patrol would be back to supply them. But they had their blanket rolls and that meant they could spend the night up on the mountain. He and Nara would be alone in the heart of this madness.

He turned and opened the front canvas flap into the cart. Nara was looking out the back at the two soldiers climbing away from them. He didn't need to tell her they were on their own.

He pulled the cart into a small clearing, from where he could see down to the plain where the patrol had disappeared. He kept the mules yoked, and Nara dumped fodder at their feet. The trooper's horses were hobbled and allowed to graze.

By five o'clock, as the red cliffs behind and opposite them began to glow like copper, Jack and Nara realised they had to prepare for the night on their own. They had minimal supplies, having assumed they would be supported as part of the German column. He had his pistol but no rifle. There wasn't even a panga to chop wood or branches to build a *kraal*.

They collected firewood and out-spanned the mules, tethering them in the space between the cart and the thicket behind, hoping that would be enough protection from predators. He remembered the stories of the leopards of the Waterberg, but he realised that a big fire could draw Herero fighters too. They chewed on biltong and some rusks for supper, and sat on a log by their tiny fire as the sun began to dip and outline the upper rim of the Waterberg opposite with a thin glowing line like heated wire.

Above them, Dieter was using the last rays to receive and transmit messages. Across the valley on top of the southern face of the Waterberg another heliograph position had been established in great secrecy with the help of Herero spies. It was set back from the rim so that Herero spotters would not see the flashes. It was this station that relayed von Trotha's order to all of the forces that the advance and encirclement of the Herero positions was to commence at 0630. It was August 10th, 1904.

Cold settled quickly on the exposed ledge. Dieter and the other signalman were not allowed to light a fire in case they gave away their position. They rolled themselves in their blankets and slept under the overhang of a large boulder that had tumbled down from the cliff above them thousands of years before.

Near the top of the cliff, the two vultures puffed up their feathers and settled on their ledge to see the night through. They were sated from the day's feeding on the carrion found on the plane below. Ample food had triggered ovulation and they had mated. They had built an untidy nest for the single egg she would lay.

A few kilometres north, in the dense thickets on the plain where Kaera and her clan were camped, she fed the children and the elderly with pap and *omaere*[42]. They were exhausted from the constant trekking and the discomfort of their temporary dwellings. There were constant rumours of clashes, and although they were aware of the German troop movements around them, they had no sense of imminent encirclement or attack. Her husband was away again but had reassured her that the Herero vastly outnumbered the Germans. Her mother slept beside her to help with the children and keep them quiet.

Jack and Nara lay on the hard, wooden surface of the cart rather than sleeping beside the fire, which they had allowed to burn

---

[42] The traditional sour milk prepared by Herero women in calabashes and part of their staple diet.

down to avoid drawing attention during the night. They lay huddled together under the blankets – no joy of intimacy now, rather an anguished, shared need for comfort, reassurance and warmth. Hesitantly, Jack cupped her belly with the palm of his hand.

Suikerbossie

"Bruce walked up here towards midday", Lynne continued. "Mom was shopping and had not heard yet, and, of course, did not know Bruce. Dad was in Europe on business, so Bruce spoke to Jack alone, which was what I had hoped for. You were away at winter camp.

"Jack drove down and collected me from the garage under the flats. Bruce, I think, was glad to see me go. I was terrified – I thought I was going to Caledon Square! Jack calmed me down. He seemed to already have a plan and know what to do. He just took charge…

"We came back here – he knew not to use the telephone – and he told Mom that he was taking me out for brunch. He didn't give her a chance to come with. He was suddenly energetic, decisive – I'd say even exited. I remember how I noticed that his voice was stronger.

"We went to the Suikerbossie, and from there he made a few phone calls and then we went for a walk on Llandudno Beach. It's that walk I want to tell you about – not this whole long story about my nonsense with the ARM. But the context is important. Remember, I don't think you were even 14 then.

"I told him about Bruce – he was my lecturer at UCT – much older and not Jewish. Mom and Dad would've *platzed*. Somehow, I managed to keep it from them. I told him that I knew about ARM, that I had not been involved in any of their activities but that I was planning to get involved. He asked if I'd told you, and I said not.

"It was July, cold and windy like now, and this was Llandudno – there was nobody out and the sand was blowing off the beach. But he insisted we get out of the car and go for a walk. Eventually we sat down behind some of the large boulders at the end of the beach.

"He told me that soon after the war a man from his village in Lithuania arrived in Cape Town. This man, Koppel, felt guilty that he had survived the camps and Jack helped him settle while they tried to find out what had happened to their families. No one knew yet what had really happened – that only really emerged with the Eichmann trial. Jack, like most, I think, thought that he would still be able to find his family once things had settled after the war and refugees had returned.

"He said that one day in the summer they went walking and sat down on a bench on the beach front. It was hot so he rolled up his sleeves. Reluctantly, Koppel did too, and Jack saw his camp number tattooed on his arm. It was the first time he'd seen anything 'from there'.

"'Just like the Nama, just like Leah', he said. He was crying. I'd never seen Jack cry. It was very upsetting – I thought I'd caused it. But he said not. He said that during the war in Southwest, the Germans tagged the prisoners of war like cattle. They caught a

Nama girl who worked for him. 'The Germans had put a collar on her with a number – just like on Koppel's arm. That's when I really realised that that's what they did to Leah, to all my family. Koppel then told me about the *Einsatzgruppen* and the camps, and I realised that they had not survived.'

Jack said that his guilt about not bringing his family to South Africa – especially his sister - had never left him. Remember, he used to call me 'Leah-Lynne' after her? It wasn't for lack of money he said, it was selfish and muddled thinking. He knew that South West would be difficult, so he kept on putting it off. 'Arrogant, I was', he said. 'I was paying, and I knew more than them. So, I thought. But I knew here – not what was going on *there*. So, they had to do it when and how I said... They trusted me. But they paid the price.'

"On the way back on the beach we stopped to look at the surf and the breakers. He was an old man then, already bent and short. I noticed that he seemed to have gone back to thinking in Yiddish. It crept into his syntax. He drew himself up and breathed in deeply. You could smell the iodine from the kelp. 'Cape Town always smells so clean. When I arrived in Suidwes there was a terrible smell – from the whaling and the guano. I still remember it. Now I could say a warning it was – the Germans did terrible things in Suidwes. All before the Shoah. They tried to exterminate the Herero and the Nama. They did medical experiments like Mengele. I saw it, heard about it, smelt it. But I did nothing.'

"'I should have let Leah take care of herself – she'd be alive today with children if I hadn't been so stubborn. But I also know I should not have kept quiet in Suidwes. The native people must make their own future. It's not for us to make it for them. Bobbe Rae tried to help the blacks, but the security police threatened her, us, and the business. I brought her and your mother down here and they never went back to Windhoek. Perhaps I could have done more. Bobbe said I should have done more. But now is not a time to be heroes. In the end the farm must go back to the local people. Maybe, it was for us to build. But it's their land, their future'. That's why I'm telling you this long story. He knew the farm would go.

"I asked him how it was living with the Germans all these years in South West. 'Complicated' was all he said. Dad later told me that his name was on a hit list of the Jews in South West that was discovered in the Nazi party offices in Windhoek when war broke out. And yet he was friendly with many Germans there too…

"We went back to the Suikerbossie. He insisted on ordering me a Pepsi-float like I was a kid. And it was winter! He went to make another call – I remember it like in slow motion – and when he came back, he said he and I would be flying to Jo'burg the next morning. I would be continuing to Israel that afternoon. The family there would look after me. Dad would come from Europe. There was no return ticket and no return date.

"Mom almost fainted when we got home and told her about the raid, and that I was leaving the next day. He left her no room to argue and said Dad had already been told and that she should not call. She was so panicked and confused by it all she did not ask where I'd spent the night. I never told either of them. Dad made me swear not to tell you anything either.

"That night, after I'd packed, he brought me here and gave me a lot of cash – dollars and pounds – that he kept in that safe. He took out a chocolate box which had old photos of his family in Lithuania and some letters. He said there were more in a box on the farm and that had a lot of the history of the family, Southwest and the farm. It was too difficult for him to deal with. 'It's difficult but it should not be hidden.' He felt that you were too young and that if he was no longer alive, I should tell you. As always, he did not really relate to Mom.

"He also showed me a book, it's somewhere on the shelves here – he called it the 'Blue Book' and said it was about the German actions against the Nama and the Herero. I'll try to find it for you. Maybe it'll help you too.

"At Jan Smuts there was a rabbi who'd brought clothes and a passport for me. I wore a *sheitl* and a long skirt and heavy black glasses. I looked like a complete *frummer*! I was supposed to be his daughter, or his niece and it worked – it got me out. By the time I got back, when Dad thought it safe to return, Jack had died."

August 11th, 1904   Klein Waterberg

Witbooi Commando

At first light Dieter was receiving and transmitting messages. By 0630 von Trotha and the forces directly under his command had reached the Hamakari riverbed east of the Waterberg. Their objective was to capture the water holes and *vleis* vital to the Herero and their cattle. As they advanced up the dry riverbed, Herero fighters attacked them in thick bush. Dieter could hear rifle fire all across the plain below, but he could see nothing. Frustrated in their attempts to find the Herero fighters in the scrub, the Germans used their artillery and fired into the encampments behind. Pondoks began to burn and panic and confusion spread as people and animals fled – some north towards the Waterberg, but most east where the jaws of the German trap were being held open.

Below him, Dieter could see Deimling's forces advancing east across the valley. His observations, and those of the spotters on the Waterberg proper and the Nama Witbooi guides in the field enabled the troops to advance steadily and soon rifle fire intensified as they came into contact with the Herero. Hordes of panicked people and animals began to stream eastward, raising clouds of red dust.

At first Kaera's clan were able to drive their cattle with them. But the clouds of dust and the noise enabled the spotters on the cliffs above and the Nama scouts behind them to track them. Cannon could now range in and the crashing shells drove them in a dash for the east towards the gap between the two mountains.

Shrapnel severed the artery above Kaera's mother's knee. She lay in the sand, still clutching her grandson whom she'd been carrying as she ran. Kaera grabbed the boy, hesitated by her mother's side and saw the patch of blood spread rapidly in the sand under her. Kaera touched her face and continued to run.

Jack and Nara had withdrawn uphill some distance from the wagon so as not to be an obvious target. From where they sat, they could hear the rifle fire and the panicked lowing of the cattle. Climbing higher they could see the smoke rising from the burning shacks, and the occasional galloping horses or bands of fleeing people and cattle streaming through gaps in the bush. Then came the boom and crash of artillery.

Nara sat beside Jack, clutching her knees drawn up to her chest. Her eyes were large and her breathing shallow. The horror of the battle and the fleeing people gripped her throat and tremors of panic ran through her body. She huddled close to him.

Jack sat strangely detached. He'd folded his jacket carefully on the rock beside him and made sure that they were sitting in the shade. There was an element of spectacle as he watched the battle from above and at a distance. The display of overwhelming German force made him feel safe. Perhaps also because he was white and spoke German, and because he was a man. He'd never experienced any real violence himself, and certainly not from the Herero. He didn't question why but sat watching, curiously impassive, indifferent. She sensed this.

And then they heard the Maxim gun. There was a sudden metallic cough. Then another. They couldn't see it, but they knew where it was – on a slight ridge that gave the gunners visibility over much of the plain below. Then a sustained maniacal chatter. The Herero had come into range.

Up above, Dieter and the young trooper with him also heard the mechanical rattle of the machine gun. They crawled to the lip of the ledge and looked down to where the sound was coming from. They too could not see the gun emplacement itself, hidden in undergrowth, but they could see cattle and people veering away from it in gaps in the bush on the plane. The dust cloud swirled, masking the panicked confusion, and then moved north as the stream of fleeing black people and animals swerved away from the chattering gun. Dieter knew, from the orders he'd transmitted, that von Trotha's orders were to "annihilate" the Herero. No one was to be spared – not even women and children. And he knew there was another Maxim on the lower ridges of the mountain opposite waiting for them.

Cordite now wafted up the cliffs to where Jack and Nara were sitting. She was pale, exasperated by his passivity and silence, but scared of provoking his nastiness. She was frightened and held on to his arm. Finally, she used his name to get through to him: "Jack, I want to go from here. Please. Now."

His name, her tone, hauled him out of his distraction and

introspection. He'd been wanting to move since the morning too, but knew they had nowhere to go. The track they used to get here would take them either past the Herero or into the advancing Germans. East was towards the machine gun, and down into the valley was a killing field. "I know, my little Mädchen", he said, putting his arm round her. "I want to be away from here too. But we're safest here."

The artillery in the west stopped and the troops closed in. As soon as they saw people, they raked the bush with rifle fire. Other Herero bands were fleeing Deimling's advance on the Waterberg proper. Thousands of people and cattle were being funnelled into the narrow gap between the two red sandstone mountains.

The crash of artillery in the east continued all afternoon as the battle to capture the Hamakari water holes raged. From his vantage point Dieter could see – and report –that the encirclement was almost complete but for a narrow gap in the south east.

Away from the tightening ring of skirmishes the vultures began to glide down, having spotted corpses. There was little of the usual squabbling.

Kaera, her infant strapped to her back and her son in her arms, straggled behind. She could no longer see any of her extended family as they scattered through the bush. She too heard the rattle of the German gun and could hear people veering north away from it. Fallen bodies just ahead showed the gun's range. A gap on her right revealed a *donga* and instinctively she veered for it, scrambling up the dry gulley covered in thick thorny bushes.

Above her, the cliffs of the mountain began to glow orange as the winter sun sank.

Dieter was frantically transmitting and receiving situation reports and orders as he and the other operators around the battlefield made the most of the last light they could capture in their heliographs. The main objective of capturing the Hamakari water holes had been achieved late in the day after fierce fighting, but the rest of the picture was confused, as far as he could make out. The tone of many of the messages was that Herero resistance had been very fierce, and that their concentration now around Maharero in the east would give them significant numerical advantage over the Germans.

Assuming things would be relatively safer as the sounds of battle faded at the end of the day, he sent the young signaller down to the cart to get fresh water and food and more of the message forms he needed for communication.

The soldier, who'd arrived in Suidwes less than a month before, was happy to have something different to do. He strode away jauntily, the tremors of his energetic strides across the boulders vibrating through the rocks. He hopped off the ledge onto the earth in front of a narrow crevice he wasn't even aware of.

Hidden in the dark crack, the khaki and brown puff adder had sensed the vibrations of his approach. Its triangular head and neck were drawn back in a taut "S". As the trooper's boot hit the ground, it propelled the front third of its body forward at a rate of some 2.5 metres per second. Parallel with the acceleration, the snake's jaws gaped open, triggering the withdrawal of a protective sheath on its upper mouth. Two stiletto-like fangs swung down and forward, and at the precise moment of contact penetrated the trooper's cotton trousers and pumped about 200 milligrams of cytotoxic venom into his calf.

Nara thought she heard a scream from the cliffs above, but couldn't be sure. She was preparing some pap while Jack was securing the animals back in the rudimentary *kraal* they'd built behind the cart. They had very little water left.

As dusk deepened, they sat eating from the pot with their hands. It was cold and they huddled by the small fire, hardly talking.

Kaera's son whimpered when he smelt the food and Nara suddenly straightened up.

"There's someone out there", she whispered.

Jack, who'd learnt to trust her hearing, pulled the pistol out of the holster.

Then the baby whimpered. Kaera and her children had crawled up the overgrown gully in the dusk and she'd seen the cart too late to move elsewhere. She'd noticed the gun on his hip.

Nara got up and moved away from the circle of firelight to peer into the thicket running down the gulley opposite their makeshift camp. First she saw the little boy's eyes, and then his mother beside him, her head down covered by her leather headdress. Nara could see the head of a baby she was clutching under her.

She motioned to Jack to come to her and they both squatted to coax the Herero woman and her children out of the thicket. "*Kommen sie, kommen...*", she said. "*Hā*", resorting to Nama.

Kaera groaned as she gave up the drive to flee. She raised her head and looked at the Nama girl, reassured by a woman's voice and her tone. Carefully, to avoid the thorns in the dark, she lifted the bush covering her son and told him to go to Nara.

Once the boy was out, Jack stepped forward and lifted the bush off Kaera and helped her crawl out.

Later, after they'd fed them and put them into the cart, Jack and Nara rolled up together on the ground by the fire. It was bitterly cold, and they were very uncomfortable but exhausted and fell asleep quickly.

By the time they heard and felt the galloping it was too late. Horsemen swirled around them in the dark, the mules whinnying in panic. The broad bush hats and white armbands identified them as Witbooi. They were surrounded and flat on the ground. The scout who'd escorted them the day before was among them and called Nara forward quietly. Others quickly discovered Kaera cowering in the back of the cart.

"The Germans will kill them, and you too for hiding them", one of the Witbooi said.

Jack sensed that they were very agitated. "Where are you going?" he asked the man who appeared to be their leader.

The man ignored him and interrogated Nara in Nama. He then dismounted and gave some orders to the others. He came to sit by Jack while one of the men prepared coffee on the fire.

Jack started to explain who he was, but the man cut him short. "You're the Jewish *smous* in Windhuk. We know who you are – you supply the Germans. Some of our people worked as guards for you and the other Jew – Izzy. The girl told me you have looked after her, but that now you're taking her back to her people in Walvis – the Topnaar. Why?"

"I am taking her to visit her aunt while I do business there. But seeing this today", he said, waving at the valley below them. "She may be safer with the English in Walvis."

The man grunted. "We are Witbooi Nama. Cornelius Fredericks is our kaptein. We have been fighting with the Germans for many years. We have never seen anything like this. The Germans want to drive the Herero into the desert and destroy them."

He nodded his head in the direction of his men – "We cannot be part of this – killing women and children. We have now realised that the Germans will then make war on the Nama too. The same way. They want all of the land. Without the people."

They sat in silence for a while as a man poured them coffee in enamel cups and empty tins they carried with them. Nara sat beside him, but they ignored her, and Jack offered her sips from his cup. She noticed there was a strong smell from these men, – of the horses, of sweat and smoke and cordite too. And the smell of men - but she thought there was fear as well, like she'd smelt from Jack. But these Nama seemed confident, competent and she was drawn to this. They were leaving this place.

"We are riding to Rietmont to warn Hendrik Witbooi", the man said.

"I want to travel with you", Jack said. "I can't wait here any longer. Can you take us to Okahandja?"

The man shook his head and clicked in disagreement. "We are riding hard and direct, not by track. We can't take a wagon. Anyway, you have to wait for the soldiers up on the mountain. The Germans will insist on that."

"I'll leave them the wagon and the mules. We'll take the horses."

The man shook his head. "What are you going to do with the Herero woman and her children? You need passes to move around."

"Jack, you can use this for them", Nara blurted, holding up her duplicate pass. She turned to the Witbooi leader and spoke to him rapidly in Nama, and then stood up and went to the wagon. "I'm going with them."

The man flung the dregs of his coffee into the fire and stood up. The rest of the Witbooi mounted quickly, and Nara came back leading one of the German soldier's horses. She crouched by the fire to roll up her kaross stepped towards him. "I will be safer with them", she said. He stepped forward to embrace her but then hesitated, the Witbooi watching. She touched his hand briefly, turned away and mounted the horse.

The Witbooi commando wheeled round and rode away down the track. Jack watched her slight figure disappear into the dark among the horsemen.

Tidy Departures

Anna Bruns was waiting on the stoep of the farmhouse when Lenny and Steyn arrived from the airport. Steyn's wife was doing her best to make conversation as they sipped tea and ate rusks.

They set out in the farm's newest bakkie. Anna sat up front with Steyn, who was doing most of the explaining. She was familiar with the property and the assessor's report but was keen to visit all the bore holes, windmills, and potential water sources, the common boundary between the farms, as well as the north-eastern corner where game migrated.

Lenny had a chance to assess her from the back seat of the double-cabin Ford. She was a few years older than he, and he remembered standing beside her in the back of a bakkie, the wind blowing her hair back and her T shirt tight against her breasts as his father drove them around the farms. He'd been intimidated then by her obvious beauty and, for him as a young teenager, her daunting maturity. As adults their paths had hardly crossed. But his pulse had quickened when he heard she was interested in buying the farm. She was still very striking, with lush skin and an erect posture emphasising her delicate neck. Smartly dressed in a white and blue striped silk shirt over khaki trousers and a short navy scarf at her throat, she wore no jewellery and no makeup. Her once honey-blond hair had not been coloured as Cyn did every two weeks – the natural grey of middle age allowed to fleck through. She was direct and intelligent and obviously very skilled as a farmer in this challenging environment.

"We will meet, yes, for dinner?", she said when they'd finished the tour, confirming their earlier arrangement. "Come at six to enjoy the sunset."

The family's deep roots in the place were obvious as he walked in. A sepia photo of her grandparents outside the farmhouse while it was being built; her mother and father alongside a 1950s era Ford bakkie that Jack must have sold them; her mother beside a prize-winning ram with massive horns. Pictures, skins, carpets and furniture from Germany, South Africa and South West spoke of years of tasteful accumulation.

There was a photo of her son on a table beside the large armchairs in the bay window that looked out over the veld softened with the blush of sunset. A black ribbon pinned across the corner. Beside it, a separate photo of a girl several years younger. "That's Caroline. She's studying in Germany." She pointed to a large aerial photograph of the farm on the raw rock wall nearby – the same rock of the chimney breast in Jack's study in Bantry Bay. "Rolf took that soon after he got his license." His eyes searched hers for sadness, but her frank gaze showed strength, not even resignation. Perhaps in the lines around her mouth, he thought. "He was named after his grandfather." She lifted the bottle she was holding to offer him some champagne.

"I need to discuss the Steyns", he said. She waved the issue away as she set her glass down on the occasional table. "They can stay of course, and my mother told me that Jack had promised them they could be buried there – obviously, even before their son was killed. It will not be an issue."

She pointed at a stack of photograph albums on the rectangular coffee table in the bay window. "I thought after dinner you might want to see some of the pictures of the families together?" He nodded, slight suspicion stirring that she might be employing emotion and nostalgia to negotiate the price down. But she pre-empted again – "I don't think we should discuss price now. If you agree, we can leave that to the lawyers?"

They talked easily over a dinner she served - fresh kabeljou delivered that morning from Lüderitz and a Cape Malay mutton stew with a Pinotage. Their conversation ranged easily over the ongoing collapse of communism in eastern Europe, Tiananmen Square, travel, their children, life on a farm, his other business interests, and the local political situation. "Paradoxically, while these changes ultimately make Pretoria more exposed and have weakened UNITA in Angola, SWAPO and the ANC still want to model themselves on eastern Europe", she said. "Politicians are always playing catch-up."

They went to sit back in the bay window.

"I want to say that I am sad that you – the Levins – are leaving. Even though we did not grow up together I've always known that you were here, next door. It's not feeling alone - life on a farm is lonely, I'm used to it and the Steyns have always looked after me and they are staying. But to me it means the end of an era – not the political changes which are long overdue – but on a personal level." She hesitated and pointed at the albums – "I think your leaving has to mean something – to me at least. This a conversation our families should have had a long time ago – perhaps not our generation even – but now that you are leaving, we should do so. 'We should be tidy about departures' my grandmother would say. I know, we Germans are tidy about everything", she giggled slightly. She'd coloured and stood up – "You will have a brandy, whiskey…?

"I may be wrong", she said, handing him a tumbler – "but I think you were quite young when Jack died, and you did not spend much time here as a teenager. Nor did your father really so I don't know if you know how" – she knitted the fingers of her hands together – "close the families were in the early years?"

She leaned forward to lift the top album off the pile. He noticed the outline of her white bra through the shirt and had the sense and pleasure of a still taut and attractive woman's body.

"This is the oldest photo we have of Susanna and Rolf. Susanna said it was taken during the war and that Rolf had already been wounded by then – she would point to a line on his face and said it showed pain. You know it was Jack who introduced them – at an agricultural festival in Windhoek. Rolf recuperated in Jack's house and Susanna would visit him there. That's how it started."

She skipped a few pages, wary not to bore him. "This is of Jack and Susanna on an early visit to your farm. You can see there's nothing there except that big acacia which Rolf said was the reason to buy it – it showed there was water. It was Rolf who found it for Jack and persuaded him to buy it. So, you can see how far back the families go, yes?

"When Rolf was interned outside Aus as a German soldier during WWI – Jack would come down from Windhoek to check on Susanna and visit Rolf. This was taken soon after Rolf was released, I think" – she was pointing to a picture of Jack and Rolf both holding wide-brimmed bush hats. "It's taken in Lüderitz by the lighthouse." Lenny leaned closer – he recalled having seen something similar in Jack's room on the farm. It was a tiny photo, probably taken with one of the original box cameras. Standing slightly apart from the two men was a small Nama woman. She was holding something with both hands.

Anna leaned forward too – he smelt the cognac on her breath and noticed the swell of her breast through the open v of her shirt. Her skin was a soft honey colour where it had been exposed to the sun. "That's Nara", she said. He lifted his eyes because she seemed to be telling him something more than a name. He knew too that she had followed his gaze down her shirt. Her blue eyes held his – "You knew Nara?"

"I've seen something similar. On the farm", avoiding her question despite himself. "What is she holding?"

"I think they called them 'Blue Boxes' – they were for tree planting in Israel. I think it was your grandmother who introduced them. I think there was a time when there was a blue box in Nama churches down here in the south. Jack and Nara would drive around once or twice a year and collect the money. He would contribute to the local community in exchange."

Lenny sensed that a moment had passed. She was intent on going over what she saw as their shared past. He was curious, but on edge too.

She flipped on until one of Rolf on his own standing by a fence post. "This is the last picture we have of him. He died a few months later." She straightened and looked at him directly again. "He'd been missing for two days. Jack came from the farm with some of his shepherds. They found him by the Fish River with an empty bottle of morphine. Muti, – that's what we called my grandmother – said Rolf had been depressed since the Herero war. He had nightmares about it and would drink heavily. It got worse after he was released from the POW camp."

They lent back in the armchairs, swirling the remains of the alcohol in the glasses. "Even if you don't sell the farm to me, I think we should acknowledge things that happened. And there is more – some may be quite difficult for you. It is difficult for me too.

"Grandma said that Rolf and Jack fought. Rolf said Jack had collaborated with the British about the 'Blue Book'. You know what that is? … Later, when Rolf had read it, Grandma said his depression got worse. But she also said that Rolf would get angry with Jack for not bringing him enough medicine for his pain.

Today I understand that was morphine. Jack was the importer for Suidwes."

Anna had coloured, and got up to open the window and then pour them each another drink.

"I don't know really... and Muti would never allow any questions. But my mother said that Jack and Muti were more than friends. She said he would comfort mother in her loneliness out here after Rolf took his life. He would sometimes stay over, and she would hear their voices together from Muti's room or the guest bedroom.

"And then there were more difficult times. My father joined the Nazi party in the 1930s. Mother told me that he would go to meetings in Lüderitzbucht, where they would listen to speeches about restoring German dignity and making Suidwes German again." She'd flipped to pages in the album with pictures of young boys and men marching past the Lüderitz railway station, which had been draped with Swastika banners, and men saluting with their arms outstretched. She pointed to one of them. "That's my father."

"This caused a lot of tension at home. Muti did not like my father from the beginning – he was not from a family of her class. We are "*alte* Afrikaners", Muti would say. And his views caused her a lot of embarrassment – especially I think with your grandfather and the other English-speaking families here. In 1938 he travelled to Germany to see his family and was conscripted. He was captured during a battle in Poland and was sent to a POW camp in Russia. He would never speak of what he did in the war. We would also never ask. In the meantime, your uncle was killed in North Africa. Muti went to see Jack for condolence visit but things were never the same, of course. After the war my father came back here but there was a lot of tension. He would drink. One night Muti told him to leave – I think he was violent to my mother – and he drove off in a rage. He was driving to Aus – probably too fast. There was a gemsbok on the road – you know, they are grey and brown, difficult to see during the day, never mind at night. The horns came through the windscreen and one penetrated his chest.

"News of what happened to the Jews started coming out and then there was the Eichmann trial. It was a very difficult time for Germans – even here. Sometimes things happened that made Muti very angry about politics here, even though we grew up knowing not to get involved. She'd say that the Germans cursed this country - that the racism and Nazism and concentration camps all started here. Mother would have to calm her."

A lull, more a reverie at the end of her story. She'd changed for dinner, he registered – off-white blouse and a dark linen skirt. No makeup, no jewellery, He watched her – legs crossed, poised and quite beautiful. Her eyes were large, moist but she was looking inward by looking at the moonlit veld outside.

The single malt had buffered his emotions – "She's tidied up for herself by telling me that Jack had an affair with her grandmother.

And that her father was a Nazi!" Her beauty, her loneliness, and the tragedy of her own life muted his distress and confusion.

"And what of your husband?" he asked quietly. She'd answered this many time before obviously: "My son's father was not for Suidwes. We met at university in Heidelberg. He hated life here. Maybe he was too young. Muti liked him but said he would not be happy here. She was right. He went back two years after Rolf was born. He re-married. He's never been back – not even to see the grave." There was a pause and she looked at him directly – "Caroline has a different father. There is another generation – we've always kept the Bruns name. This is our home."

They talked practicalities – price and mechanics would be delegated to the lawyers and broker, subject to the land surveys. She wanted him to complete the installation of solar panels for all the worker's houses and proper toilets for the remote shepherds' huts. Levin Enterprises was to continue to contribute funding to the school on the farm for a further three years.

He stood to leave. Her offer of another drink was an invitation to stay, and lingered between them. "I have to be in Aus by nine o'clock tomorrow", he said, "and I think I've drunk enough before driving." At the door she said "I hope what you've learned has not upset you. I think the truth makes for a richer life."

"I'm pleased you did. I'm sorry we did not get to know each other better." He leaned forward and kissed her on the cheek, her perfume and cognac whispering round his nostrils. She blushed.

"If all goes well there will be a Nama Stap", she said. "You will come, yes?"

How lonely, he thought as he drove away. How lovely, how capable. She never told me about Nara. And I didn't ask.

De Beers...

... maintained sizeable facilities in Lüderitz. The diamond conglomerate used dredgers and barges to slurp up and transport sediment from the floor of the Atlantic up to ten miles out from the coast. Sophisticated machinery and other technologies were used to extract thousands of high-quality diamonds from the ocean slurry. The rough diamonds were stored in a massive safe in the onshore supply and maintenance complex until they were transported to the sorters and graders elsewhere in South Africa, and from there to the major markets and polishing centres in London, Tel Aviv, Antwerp, and the state of Gujarat in India.

Security was a major part of the extensive support operation. De Beers deployed armed guards, patrols, surveillance, onsite inspectors, x-ray detectors, and couriers to exert its control over its marine concessions and the Sperregebeit – the Restricted Area that ran from the mouth of the Orange River to well north of Lüderitz. There was also an intelligence organization.

Recruited as a young detective from the Cape Town IDB section almost twenty-five years before, Conradie now ran a string of agents and informers from Henties Bay in the north to Port Nolloth in the south. In his view all the people along the Namib coast, himself included, shared two passions – fishing and diamonds. "Why else be here?", he would ask rhetorically, referring to the windswept desert and frigid ocean. But the truth was that he loved the characters and romance of the business – half-drunk Boere fishermen along the coast, endlessly devious Portuguese in Port Nolloth who would use any legitimate business they could as a front for illicit dealing, and the tough marine divers and engineers from the Cape and elsewhere in South Africa who always thought they were smarter than they appeared. There were others occasionally too, but these were the bread and butter in his bailiwick. The Greeks, English, Jews, Indians, Lebanese, Brazilians, Belgians – they were all handled from the De Beers offices in Cape Town and Jo'burg. The Ovambo workers on whose labour the whole industry rested were policed by a different unit, and the Topnaar who were here long before any white man did not count in his world view. They were marginal, desperate, and pathetic, and not really interesting in terms of smuggling.

That had changed six weeks earlier when Willem, one of his Coloured team leaders in Lüderitz, had mentioned in passing that the Levin farm in the Keetmanshoop area was up for sale. Conradie recalled rumours shared years before among his De Beers colleagues that old man Levin, who had established the farm, had traded in diamonds and that there was still a stash hidden somewhere.

He'd spent weeks going through the intelligence archives in Oranjemund but there was little concrete intelligence – just persistent rumours that diamonds would show up with Topnaar women visiting other Nama settlements outside the Kuiseb gorge and delta where they lived.

The week before he'd flown down to Cape Town and spent two days in the archive there, with no success. But Conradie knew that the rumours had to be run to ground. Besides which, he enjoyed the chase. On his last day in Cape Town, he drove out to see the man who'd recruited him. Walsh was now in his late seventies, comfortably retired in the hills above Gordon's Bay with a fat De Beers pension and a wonderful view of False Bay. Conradie wanted that too.

"I knew Jack", Walsh recalled. "He was a good host and threw really good parties in their home in Windhoek. That changed when his son was killed in the war. His wife moved down to Cape Town and Jack spent a lot of time on his own. I once went to have lunch with him on the farm and asked him about IDB in a general way – he was trading in South West long before the South Africans took over. He waved the question away – the rumours were jealousy, he said, how denigrators and competitors explained his success. There may be truth in that too. We know that he had a share in a hotel and brothel in Lüderitz in the crazy days of the diamond rush. People used to pay their debts with diamonds in the beginning. The couple who ran it used to hide the diamonds from the Germans under the kennel of their guard dog! He also had a salt pan near Walvis and that's a perfect cover for smuggling. And there was firewood and charcoal too – all good covers. We used to catch the Ovambos smuggling stones in the bicycles they bought from him. But the bottom line is, he was very hard working. He was always travelling, selling his cars and trading and building the business – that was his true passion.

Sorry to say this, Conradie, but he knew how to work the administration. After the Nats came to power, he had a box at Newlands and the senior people would be flown down for a weekend of rugby. He won nearly every tender for vehicles and earth-moving equipment. You never saw anything but Ford or Caterpillar. Also, he hardly drank himself – and you know how much of an advantage that is in South West!

"Also, early on, we were told by security people not to dig too deeply with Jack. I suspect that he was helpful to the British in the campaign against the Germans in South West.

"Jack had secrets, no question. It was said that he had a long-time affair with a German widow on a neighbouring farm. There was a Nama woman – she would travel with him round the south. They would exchange the blue collection boxes the Jews had for Israel. Every Jewish family had one, but there were rumours that they were in Nama churches as well. The stories were that the Topnaar – mainly women – would find and smuggle the diamonds out in the tortoise shells they used for *buchu* to Nama towns along the Hochland. They would store them in these boxes in the churches. Jack and the Nama woman would come every few months and collect them. Jack would then contribute something to the church or the community. The Topnaar would be paid in Walvis on his next trip there. We got hold of some of these boxes, but they only had tickies and pennies. We suspected that Jack laundered the stones through old Mo Kahan in Lüderitz who had a diamond license, but we could never prove it. You don't see those boxes any longer. The Nama woman lived out her years on the farm.

Maybe that's worth checking."

Conradie had flown in from Oranjemund and pulled Willem aside before the weekly foremen's meeting in the security offices in the De Beers compound. They walked along the dock where a bright orange supply barge was being loaded with supplies for the dredgers offshore. At this time in the morning there was still no wind and the cold ocean kept the temperature pleasant.

"There have been rumours for many years that Ouman Levin used a Nama woman to smuggle diamonds", Conradie said. "It was said that they used collection boxes in Nama churches. The woman lived on the Levin's farm, which you said is going to be sold. We need to know if there are any of these boxes on the farm or anywhere there may be a stash of diamonds. Willem – remember how it works at De Beers. We'll get a massive bonus if we make a recovery."

Willem did. The conglomerate was wealthy enough to wave a hefty carrot at its employees to keep them honest – up to seventy per cent of the wholesale value of recovered stones. The state wielded the stick – up to twenty years imprisonment.

But he was uncomfortable with this assignment. He knew Lena, knew of Nara, and knew workers on the farm who could be helpful. But it was Steyn who worried him. He'd served with the man's son on the border and they'd been close, often sharing transport to and from Keetmanshoop. He'd come to respect Jannie as a superb officer who rapidly and easily waved away the petty barriers of apartheid to lead his small team on some of the most challenging deep penetration missions of the war. Jannie had always put his men first irrespective of colour, and had been quick to challenge other whites – soldiers and civilians – in the face of the constant prejudice.

He also knew the circumstances of Jannie's death. Eventually the old couple would learn the truth. They would realise that Willem probably knew. But he didn't want to be the one who told them.

Willem had been responsible for the Nama and Bushmen trackers who worked with the troops on the border. The best of them had been selected to join the elite recce units that went deep behind the lines in Angola. Small bands – usually a white team leader and San or Nama soldiers – could spend weeks in the bush, often as the precursor to some bigger SADF operation or on sabotage missions. Often there was no helicopter infiltration or exfiltration – they tramped in and tramped – or sometimes – ran out – for kilometres as Angolan and Cuban troops hunted them.

The bonds formed between these men removed all barriers. Everyone understood that their lives depended on absolute and instinctive trust. Even the bigoted Boere townspeople and police in Grootfontein in the north where the recces would sometimes come on R&R after a mission, learned quickly that the rules of petty apartheid did not apply to these mixed-race teams of young soldiers.

Jannie once told him how difficult it had been for his parents when he brought home Kabo, his Bushman partner, on a leave. Jannie insisted that he sleep in the house – something his parents would never have even considered. Willem knew there was a picture of both men taken in the field in Jannie's room on the farm.

12 August 1904   Klein Waterberg

Via Eros

The signalman was in terrible pain, his leg horribly swollen, and mucous streaming out of his nostrils constricting his breathing. Dieter had no idea how to treat snakebite and had nothing for pain. In desperation he applied a field dressing and dripped the little water they had left into the boy's parched mouth. He screamed and groaned and whimpered until he slipped into a coma. In the early morning light Dieter could see that the entire lower leg was deeply discoloured and around the bite had turned purple black. He knew enough to recognise necrosis. He couldn't carry the boy down on his own, so he began to climb down to the track to get the trader to come up and help him.

Jack was reviving the fire when he heard someone scrambling down the slope above him. He straightened up and saw Dieter coming down. He didn't know how he was going to explain the Herero woman and her children, and stepped across to the cart and put his fingers to his lips. She'd heard the noise too and was hushing the boy.

Dieter stopped on a large boulder to catch his breath and saw Jack looking up at him. He waved and then turned to descend backwards. As he did so his boot slipped on the morning dew and he tumbled away, cracking his head on rocks and then rolling down further.

When Jack got to him, he was unconscious and bleeding badly

from a gash to his head. The rifle on his back had caught on rocks, stopping his fall, but the strap was across his throat restricting his breathing. His left arm hung limply from his shoulder.

Jack used the trooper's bayonet to cut the rifle strap and lowered his body to the ground. He was so deeply unconscious that he hardly groaned. The head wound seemed the most urgent thing and Jack realised that he could not move the man on his own on the steep slope. He went back to the cart, got a field dressing and motioned to the Herero woman to come with him. She handed the baby to the boy and they climbed up to the unconscious trooper. She put her hand to her mouth in shock when she recognized the soldier from the raid on her village. He'd spared her, she recalled, and she knelt to help Jack dress the head wound. Together they lifted the trooper's body onto Jack's shoulders and brought him down to the cart. He motioned to her to lower the back flap and placed Dieter on it.

He'd now made up his mind that he was going back, but he knew that there was the other trooper still on the mountain. He climbed up rapidly, collecting Dieter's rifle on the way. It took him almost 30 minutes to reach the ledge. As he scrambled up over the lip of the ledge two huge vultures spread their wings in threat. One had been feeding at the trooper's face – having ripped away the eye and cheek. Unperturbed by him it dipped its awful head and neck and plunged the hooked beak into the mouth cavity ripping at the tongue. The other was slashing at the belly – hell's treasure chest of glistening guts and blood. The trooper's leg jerked – he was still alive.

Jack spat out the vomit that had hurled up into his mouth. He thought to try and drive the vultures off with Dieter's rifle and collect the soldier's service papers, his rifle and the heliograph and any supplies. But he was too scared and disgusted. He could get going immediately and would not have to explain the Herero woman and her children.

The woman was inside the cart with the children. They were clearly shocked, but he needed to get her cooperation if they were going to get out of this. He opened Nara's suitcase and pointed to some dresses and motioned to her that she should wear one of these. He also took out one of the close-fitting cotton bonnets that Nara wore and handed it to her.

As he turned away to step out of the cart he stopped and looked back at her.

"I am Jack", he said pointing to himself.

She nodded but didn't respond.

"Your name?", he asked pointing to her.

"Kaera."

Having changed while Jack hitched up the mules, she came to help fix the dislocated arm to the soldier's body. Together, they dragged Dieter into the closed part of the cart and closed the back flap. She'd used items of Nara's clothing to wrap the baby and dress the boy. They no longer looked as tribal. He drove off west down the track, the Herero woman and her children hiding in the back with Dieter. He kept looking for the tracks of horse's hooves and wondering which might be Nara's.

It took them almost five days to reach the military hospital in Okahandja. The presence of a wounded German soldier who was clearly being taken care of by the trader and his domestic servant was like a pass. Passing carts and horsemen provided them with food and water, and no one questioned the presence of a native maid.

Dieter drifted in and out of consciousness for the first few days, but even when awake was not really able to remember what had happened to him. When Jack delivered him to the hospital, he just said that he'd found him by the roadside near the Waterberg.

He skirted his store and the wagon-repair yard and continued on to Windhuk. At Brakwater he waited until it was late afternoon before making for the town, which he approached from the east through the Eros hills. Petrus opened the gates and led the mules into the yard. "*Haai baas*!", he called out when he saw Kaera and the children. Herero meant trouble. "I have a pass for them", Jack muttered.

Not a joyful time

"I worry what's happened to her", Hanna said.

They were sitting on a makeshift bench in the yard behind his partially-built new house. The storerooms, however, were already stocked, and guards and the builders occupied what would be the servant's quarters. Sparse scrubland ran away down the hill to the dry Gammams riverbed and then, way beyond that, to the blue-grey Naukluft range, now in shadow as the day began to fade.

They'd walked to his plot from the Yard when the heat broke. Effi's decline over the past few months had been steady, no longer a passing illness but now an inevitability they all saw. The doctor had settled on heart disease. Windhuk had nothing to offer, he said, especially in wartime. Direct as she usually was, she'd told him she wanted to speak to him.

"I've decided we have to move back to Cape Town", she said as they walked across to the building site. "He cannot work a full day any longer, and I cannot run the butchery and the family on my own. The children are too young. In Cape Town there are hospitals and doctors – maybe they can treat him."

He sensed what was coming. "When do you want to do this?"

"Soon. We will need your help."

He agreed to buy their share of the Yard property and pay them in Cape Town. Izzy, she said, would take over the butchery and pay them over time, transferring money through Jack's accounts.

"*Gut glik mit vos* - good luck with that", he said, and they chuckled together.

"It is good to laugh", he said looking at her and noticing more streaks of grey in her hair.

"Yes. It is not a joyful time. The children are not happy either. They laugh less and fight more. They will have better schools there too and be safer."

They sat quietly beside each other, silently acknowledging the comfort, and now, the sadness of the relationship they shared.

"I'll pay for your tickets and I'll travel with you", he said. "It's time I visited Cape Town too and I want a break from here."

She took his hand and squeezed it. She continued to hold it and looked out at the kudu-grey mountains.

"I worry what's happened to her."

He sighed deeply. As always, the beat of their private conversations slowed, opening up the inevitability of disclosing himself that he'd always felt with her. He'd never expressed his attraction or perhaps even love for her. He couldn't and didn't need to. She knew him better than anyone. And she, although his age, was married and a mother. Only once, when she'd caught him looking at her forlornly as she nursed her baby, she'd said softly – "*dos ken nisht zeyn* - it cannot be."

"Yes, I do too. The war is moving down there. I don't even know where she is."

More silence – between them, drawing them together.

"You miss her, Yankele, don't you? Maybe you shouldn't have let her go. She's a *kinder meidl* but you loved her."

+++

The news of the Witbooi desertion and the reasons for it was soon reinforced by accounts of von Trotha's ruthless pursuit of the Herero into the desert. Newspaper reports and private accounts from soldiers and missionaries made it quite clear that his objective was the annihilation of the Herero as a people. They were being shot on sight, or forced to flee further east through the desert towards Bechuanaland, where they were dying in their thousands from thirst. The Schutztruppe were camped at all the watering holes east of the Waterberg and would shoot desperate people who approached and begged for water – even children.

In October, von Trotha published a proclamation in the newspapers, which was also tacked to the notice boards in every government building:

I, the Great General of the German soldiers, address this letter to the Herero people...The Herero people will have to leave the country. Otherwise I shall force them to do so by means of guns. Within the German boundaries, every Herero, whether found armed or unarmed, with or without cattle, will be shot. I shall not accept any more women and children. I shall drive them back to their people – otherwise I shall order them to be shot at.

These are my words to the Herero people.

The great General of the mighty German Kaiser

A few days later Rolf returned to Windhuk. He still limped but his physical health seemed improved, and he'd been assigned to command a unit in the south. He stayed with Jack for the few day's leave he had, hoping to see Susanna. Late one evening, after dinner with her at one of the hotels, he sat on the stoep of the house on Post Street.

"I leave tomorrow", he said gloomily.

Jack nodded, acknowledging his obvious dejection.

"I wanted to propose marriage to Susanna during this time, but I thought to do so just after getting my orders would seem stupid or childish."

Jack sighed and leaned back in the chair, looking up into the rafters. He too yearned for something to haul himself above the pessimism that had settled on him since the outbreak of the war. Pigeon shit on the beams – like Nara said there would be. Her absence and the imminent departure of Hanna and her family had added to his despondency. By comparison he wished he had a Susanna to focus on, he thought.

"I don't know. A proposal is a hopeful thing. It would give you both something to look forward to. And, there's the risk – if you don't, someone else will – she's so pretty and there are so few women."

Rolf swilled the whisky in his glass. "Maybe you're right." But his mood did not lighten.

"Has it been bad"? Jack asked after a while, sensing a larger burden on the man beside him.

"Aghh, Jack – worse than you can imagine. Maybe von Trotha's policy is right, but for those of us who have to enforce it it's terrible."

He unbuttoned one of the top pockets of his field jacket and pulled out a soiled piece of paper.

"You've seen this?", he asked, handing it over. It was the proclamation.

Jack nodded.

"In the beginning we chased them all into the desert, but they kept on coming back. They had nothing, – no food, no water. They had abandoned their cattle. They were just looking for each other – for children, for their husbands... We rode up and down the edge of the desert shooting those who tried to get back. But we were running out of ammunition. So many people. We pushed corpses into the wells to poison them.

"I removed this from the neck of an old woman in the Omaheke. She'd been sent back to get others to flee into the desert. There were too few of us to round them all up. We wanted them to die in the desert."

He leaned forward, cradling the glass between both hands, his voice dry, half an octave higher. Every so often he sighed deeply to rid himself of the stress.

"There were corpses all around. Mainly old men, women and children who were too weak to make it. You cannot imagine - thousands. You couldn't get away from them. We spared the goats and cattle! Early in the day we would see stacks of vultures in the sky, but they landed quickly, there was so much food. I'd grown used to vultures but now there were so many – it seems they are coming from everywhere in Africa! There were dogs and jackals and hyenas - they howl all about you at night. I saw corpses that had their bellies torn open by scavengers. Everywhere, the bush was scattered with clothing and pathetic possessions. Farmers came to take the livestock - like the vultures."

He gulped the whisky and then set it down on the carved stool with exaggerated care, controlling his agitation. He straightened back in the chair, rhythmically flexing his leg as he talked to release his tension. Jack watched the lantern light slide up and down the polished leather boot, searching for his own distraction from what he was hearing.

"We became so brutal. We got orders to start burning the corpses to stop the flies and disease. We used prisoners to collect the corpses and sometimes the barely living and the wounded too. Then we piled firewood on top and around and set it alight. The screaming was terrible. I had a platoon of young Marines, – they would raise a toast of rum when we'd hear bodies exploding. They said it sounded like sea mines. I didn't know we could be like this."

"She was with a young boy – maybe 12 years old", he said, returning to the old woman. "They were sitting by a bush – it was midday – there was no shade and it was so hot. So hot, it was difficult to breathe. And the smell of rot was everywhere. Death smells different in the heat – no less evil, just different. When I came up to them, she tried to straighten the leather pointed hat the Herero women wear. Her dignity I suppose. She held up her hands for water. The boy didn't even look at me – he seemed completely insane."

Jack listened the soft buzz of the moths flitting around them. He waited.

"I took this off her neck", Rolf said. "Then I shot them. Those were the orders, and they were dying there anyway."

Jack followed the lamplight sliding up and down the leather boot.

Rolf shuddered. "Now you understand why I can't propose. She's so pure. I have this in me now. That smell, that evil is on me, in me. I know I will never get it out. And eventually I would have to tell her."

+++

Jack and the Fentins travelled in November. He planned to stay on for the Christmas holidays and return via Lüderitzbucht. He'd be gone for six weeks – his first time away from Suidwes and his business in more than three years.

He'd moved Kaera and her children to the new house to be safer. It was closer to the Yard and he hoped he could trust the Baster guards and the Cape Coloured builders on the site to protect them.

From the moment she changed her clothing in the cart and ditched her traditional headdress, Kaera had understood that her and the children's survival depended on hiding the fact that they were Herero. Her boy hardly spoke out loud and learned to be content playing in the warehouse and the courtyard. He never ventured into the street. The baby was always wrapped up on her back to be easily comforted at her breast.

She spoke some Ovambo and communicated with Jack through Petrus or his girlfriend, who now shared his room near the stable at the back of the yard. She practiced German with Jack as often as they could, and by the time they moved to the new house near the Yard before his trip she could get by. When he left, he emphasised again that she should carry Nara's duplicate pass all the time.

The trip down to the coast with the Fentins was shocking. Gangs of emaciated Herero – men, women and children – were working on the tracks, supervised by crop-wielding troops. In Swakopmund, women in their long dresses and hats were being used as labourers to offload cargo and drag wagons through the sand as if they were mules. The outskirts of every rail stop, it seemed, had rows of neatly arranged but miserable pondoks behind thorn bush *kraal*s where the Herero were kept.

His time in Cape Town was almost too brief to enjoy. His days were full of meetings with lawyers, bankers, importers. He visited manufacturers, stores of remaining British military surpluses, and building supply yards. He secured the agencies for English borehole drilling machines, pipes, agricultural machines, and even bicycles. There was potential for almost everything, he told Sonnenberg. He loved being back in the city, but somehow remained quite glum,

He had a discreet meeting in the Castle with Cameron's new commander – also a naval officer. "We have to walk a fine line", the man said. "The German treatment of the natives, especially the Nama, is upsetting the Coloured population here. We can't afford to have the slightest suspicion arise that we are helping the Germans in the war – after all, they are basically the same people. On the other hand, we don't want to provoke the Germans. Their demand for goods has boosted the Cape economy significantly. But the Germans have become very aggressive – they have agents down here, all along the Orange River, and Cameron says in Walvis too. Do you think they have designs on the port?"

Sonnenberg arranged two dinners – one with the syndicate members, who feted his success in Suidwes as he'd made them significant profits, and a smaller, more intimate affair where Mrs Sonnenberg introduced some of the unattached women she thought he should meet. But Jack was clearly distracted. They hadn't realised how intimately the war had affected the lives of those in Suidwes. By contrast, the Boer War had been relatively remote for those in Cape Town.

"It's not the right time", she said to Sonnenberg afterwards. "He's grown older, more impressive but he's distracted and seems sad. Anyway, we can't send any of these young women to a place where there is war. But he needs a woman – it's a pity, he's so good looking."

"He *is* a very good catch", Sonnenberg agreed. "The boy has a nose for business opportunities. He thinks ahead. But the most important thing is, he is lucky, very lucky. And he knows what to do with that."

She looked at him quizzically. "Anyway, he has to fix his terrible Yiddish accent!"

Sonnenberg was referring to the stones Jack had brought back. The small clear ones were definitely diamonds, and there were also stones that looked like garnet, malachite, and so on. "I don't trust the Germans on this", Jack said. "The war is costing them so much, they would seize everything. They will also not let a Jew be involved. Everything has to be very discreet."

"How can you mine discreetly?"

"That is my problem. You must sell the stones, but protect the source. No mention of Suidwes otherwise we will lose. Now, explain to me how you price them."

He knew... before I did

They let her rest for a day before bringing her to meet the Witbooi elders. She hobbled bandy-legged, her bruised crotch and inner thighs aching from the five days of brutal riding. The men had made no allowances for her as they rode almost 200 miles from the Waterberg to the Witbooi camp near Gibeon. They rode mostly at night, stopping only when the horses were exhausted and needed to graze and drink. During the day they walked. They were constantly on the lookout for Schutztruppe patrols, and were particularly wary of the Basters around Rehoboth because of their close alliance with the Germans.

She told the elders what she'd seen and what she'd heard Rolf tell Jack of the German's plans. The old man, whom she assumed was Hendrik Witbooi, the Witbooi kaptein, asked her questions about supplies and weapons she'd seen. He'd heard of the Maxim gun from the scouts and waited for them to explain its effect to the other elders. "Better we all rise up now", he summarised. "We have no choice. The girl has told us they will come for us after they finish the Herero. I will write to the Baster and Ovambo leaders. We need to warn the other Nama. I will ask the British to help but we cannot count on it."

The next day two older women came to collect her from the *kraal* where she'd been resting, and took her into a pondok on the edge of the settlement. Had she had a *hokmeisie* ceremony? they asked.

It had been delayed by the war, she explained.

"Have you started bleeding?"

Embarrassed she nodded yes.

"When?"

"About two-three months ago."

They told her to undress and one of them squeezed her breasts firmly. Already tender, she winced and shrunk away. Then the woman squeezed her stomach.

"Whose child is it?" she asked.

Memory of his hand on her belly ten days before gushed through her... He knew then... before I did.

Unable to talk, gasping as the enormity of this reality sunk in, tears welled up and she hugged her belly. He'd been taking her to Walvis Bay to get rid of her.

"You didn't know?" The women weren't cruel, but there was no kindness either. "Has it only been one man?"

She nodded, beginning to sob.

They left her in the pondok overnight. The next day they came and explained menstruation, conception and birth. Sex and how to win and live with a man, her role and power as a woman – all the mystery that was the *hokmeisie* ceremony that she had so looked forward to – was not revealed. No *uitdans*[43] where her eyes and cheeks would be painted like a gemsbok and she would look beautiful, mysterious and powerful, no young man to lead her out and reintroduce her as a woman to the village and no party. Pregnant and unmarried she had no status. They took her to another *kraal*. "You will be with these people until you have the baby. After that, we will find you a man."

---

[43] "Stepping out dance", when a *hokmeisie* is lead out of her seclusion.

"Nein, mein Herr"

He stepped out onto the stoep at the back of the new house for cooler air and to get away from the insects that plagued him around the lamplight. He'd been trying to write a letter to his parents and sister explaining, once again, his reluctance to send for her with Suidwes still at war. Their latest letter had also suggested that he "would be less lonely" if she was with him. In trying to come up with a response to this, he realised he was just confirming their intuition of his situation. Effi and Hanna had been the heart of the little community in the Yard. Izzy and his wife could not replace them. Nara's absence and his concern for her gnawed at him. The flood of soldiers, officials, and new settlers and the general atmosphere in the town was unpleasant. He knew he'd become withdrawn, burying himself in his work and hardly socialising.

He stood smoking, his eyes following a track – ghostly and white in the moonlight, which ran from below the house away out to the mountains in the west. When it was full moon the cold light transformed the landscape into something alien. Very little seemed to move on the track that ran to the arid Naukluft. Vaguely he heard water splashing into a metal basin nearby. He blotted it out as he tried to think again of what to write to his family, and stave off the isolation that seeped into his words. It had been almost five years now and Leah would be a young woman, his parents would have aged. Echoing his own melancholy, he thought he heard soft sobbing from the behind the servant's quarters.

Stepping down quietly, he walked past Kaera's room towards the sound. She was sitting on a stool in the courtyard with her back to him, a zinc basin at her feet. She was naked, bent forward as she washed her hair. The moonlight glistened on her dark wet skin. She straightened and then he heard her sob again.

She stood up and reached up to dry her head with a cloth. Without clothing she seemed taller, her limbs slim and long. Her hips, he noticed were wider, more curved than Nara's. His voyeurism couldn't continue he knew. He coughed quietly – "Kaera?"

There was no indication that she'd been startled. She turned, her arms still up, wrapping the cloth around her head. Her nakedness did not embarrass her, and she looked at him quite directly – tears streaming down her face and her breath shuddering as she tried to control her crying. She turned away then, wiping her cheeks with the back of her hand.

"Nein, mein Herr."

He turned back. As he walked past the room she shared with her children, he noticed them sleeping on hides on the floor. He'd not brought Nara's bed from the old house, he realised.

Sometime after he'd had a new bed delivered, soon after he'd blown out the lamp, he heard the kitchen door at the back of the house creak open. He lay still in his bedroom, searching with his ears as his eyes adjusted to the dark. There was a tap and the door to his room opened.

She was barefoot and padded across the floorboards almost silently. His eyes slid to her hands in embarrassed anxiety – she didn't have a knife.

She stood by the bed and undid her cotton wrap and then removed her headdress, all the while watching him. Slowly she pulled back the sheet. He was so shocked that he remained limp despite the sight of her body. She was fuller than Nara, a woman's body rather than the barely adolescent girl he'd seduced, and he was acutely aware of how white he was in contrast with her. Suddenly, he too felt like a boy. It was only when she pulled his underwear down that he began to stiffen.

He could never discern when she might come – there was no smile or accidental touch or any other signal. She did not avoid his gaze but there was never even a hint of acknowledgement in her eyes. There was no pattern either, sometimes once a week, sometimes longer gaps. He knew she must sense his growing fascination with her.

They never talked. In the beginning she seemed almost detached as she watched him from above. She did not rush him to orgasm, but watched with knowing patience or confidence, and lifting herself off him as he was about to climax. Only after a few visits did she begin to reveal her own needs – bringing his hands up to her breasts and moving herself against him. After several times like this, one night she groaned deeply, her head thrown back and her body quaking above him. Then she leaned forward against his shoulder and sobbed into the pillow. He put his arms around her to comfort her. When he moved aside to make room for her to lie beside him, she got up and left.

This was their pattern for more than two years.

+++

26 September 1989　　　　　　　Khomasdalb, north Windhoek

Dear Mr. Steyn,

Thank you very much for the letter. I would very much like to come and get my mother's and great-grandmother's things that you say are stored with you.

I can take off work on Monday 16th of October. I can arrive in Keetmanshoop about one p.m. Thank you for saying you could fetch me. I will call on arrival at the bus terminal.

Please give my regards to Lena. I remember you and Mrs Steyn well. You were very kind when I was living with my grandmother on the farm.

Respectfully,

Valerie Pieterse

Steyn reread the neat letter while he waited for the armourer to finish with another customer. He didn't want to pull out army-issue sniper sights in front of strangers. He tried to recall her as a little girl on the farm living with the old lady but couldn't put a face to her. He did remember her mother being killed together with Lena's sister. They were thrown out the back of a *bakkie* taking workers from a nearby farm into town on a Friday night.

The gunsmith knew what rail interface was needed to fit Jannie's scope to the Ruger. "I can get it in a week, perhaps, and need a day to fit and adjust. I'll call you when it's here."

Driving back to the farm Steyn passed the spot where Valerie's mother had been killed. A pile of stones probably put there by the families. Like he and Frederika had done for Jannie. "*Haitsi Aibeb*", he muttered recalling the Nama name. They believed that spirits would reside in or visit piles of stones, and raised them in places of significance to them – water holes and grazing and hunting routes. Nara, the old lady, was buried in front of a pile she had built on the koppie above the farm when the Ouman had died. She'd planted an aloe there and, with their permission, one for Jannie too behind his grave. Lena would go there sometimes, to visit the old people, she would say. Lenny should not hear of this, he thought.

Suddenly he recalled that it was the neighbour's son, one of Bessie's teenage friends who was driving the bakkie. The police said he'd been drunk and was driving too fast. He didn't have a license and was probably looking at a lengthy jail term. But the boy's father was a Nationalist Party activist and well connected. The victims were just local Coloureds. Like Bessie, the boy disappeared into the security forces and Steyn had barely heard of him again.

Lena filled in the gaps in Steyn's and Frederika's memory. She seemed reluctant or couldn't recall all of the family history. It was "*die oubaas*" – the old boss, as she always referred to Jack, who said that Valerie should come to the farm to be with her grandmother when she was orphaned. Lena, then a young girl, helped raise her. When Valerie was about ten, she had been sent to school in town and only came back on the odd weekends and during school holidays. "When Valerie came, the old lady would send me away", Lena chuckled. "She wanted her all to herself. They were very close."

Jakob

Two months after the baby was born a man from another clan north of Gibeon came on a donkey cart. She was to join them, she was told. Her interest in the world around her had shrivelled with the shock of her pregnancy, and her diminished status as an unmarried mother and a servant in the clan that was hosting her. She had not attempted to make any friends among the women, and when the baby was born was able to focus on him as a way to withdraw. As it was, there was tension among the Witbooi. The men were constantly away, and everyone was distracted by talk of conflict, which, at the moment seemed to be far away in the south. But all sensed it would not pass them by.

The clan she joined was among the poorest of the Witbooi clans. They had very little livestock, mainly goats. Only the clan leader and his two sons had horses; others had donkeys if anything at all. The *!haru oms* and hokkies they lived in were spread out over the arid landscape, and they seemed to have little to do with each other. Depressingly similar to her childhood in the Kuiseb. She'd grown used to the green acacias and thick grasses of the veld, and to western housing and its comforts. The Germans were evil and responsible for the violent change in her circumstances. But deeper within, she blamed Jack.

An elderly woman greeted her kindly outside one of the pondoks, and happily took the baby when Nara got off the cart. After an hour or so rest and some water and food, the woman walked away to a nearby hut and brought back a man in his twenties. He limped, his neck and head twisted away spasmodically, and he was clearly a simpleton. He was her son, she said. Nara was to live with him.

There was no discussion or ceremony. For Nara it was a grim, bitter accommodation with her reality. Impoverished and marginal, it provided her and the child with shelter and food.

The man, Frans, was not unkind and enjoyed playing with the little boy, whom Nara still refused to name. She learned to satisfy him quickly, and twisted away during intercourse when he became insistent. Most of the time he sat on a bench in the shade just watching and smiling.

His mother doted on the baby and gradually Nara relaxed enough to leave him alone in her care when she went about her tasks. They lived, semi-ostracised, on the edge of the community and life was a grind of just coping. At times, when she allowed herself, she recalled her childhood outside Walvis Bay, where at least there was the excitement of being a strandloper by the sea. Here, there was little *veldkos*, and Frans could not hunt or herd their few goats. Everything fell to her and his mother, who was the clan leader's sister. Her husband had abandoned her soon after Frans was born, when his spasms and twisted posture became apparent. Her brother looked after them grudgingly and provided some food.

In the winter, skirmishes with the Germans forced them to move north and west. Without acknowledging it, it seemed that their clan wanted to avoid association with the Witbooi.

When spring came Nara was persuaded to name the baby. She'd reluctantly concluded that Jack's idea of taking her to Walvis Bay would have left her better off. She still suspected that he knew she was pregnant and did not want the embarrassment of a coloured child – if he wanted children at all – and wanted to be rid of her. Anger and resentment became her constant companions. But she missed him all the time, and reluctantly acknowledged that he'd taken her away from circumstances like these and had looked after her. Deep inside there was a hope that she would see him again. She named their son Jakob.

+++

Early 1906   Keetmanshoop

Rolf's term of service had been extended. He was tired and resentful, having already been allocated a farm nearby and, based on that, planned his marriage to Susanna. His injuries played up and the long months in the veld had taken their toll, as with so many of the troops. He'd had typhoid but was reassigned a week after being discharged from the hospital.

The war was not going well, but Rolf knew he needed to recuperate, and his spirit was broken. He made no effort to hide his reluctance to return to combat. Recognising his fatigue, and to compensate, his commanding officer assigned him one of the easier areas to control. He had an enlarged company based in

Mariental, and their main task was to ensure that the Witbooi did not move north. This involved long sweeps east towards the Kalahari or west towards the Namib – both harsh arid areas. But there was little fighting. He was able to rely on Baster soldiers who knew the area well. A policy of capturing Nama cattle and moving them well north towards the Baster town of Rehoboth stretched the Witbooi capabilities and removed some of the incentive for their raids.

+++

By October Jack had concluded that it was time to find a wife. Although the war in the south continued, the inevitability of a German victory was no longer in question. In addition to the soldiers, settlers and government officials were pouring into the country and government funds were driving spending. Herero land and stock were being allocated to settlers and discharged soldiers. Civilian demand was driving his booming importing business and his general dealership. In the south, however, the army was still his major customer, importing goods from the Cape via Lüderitz.

The Yard had filled up with new residents, but being single weighed on him. His material success and belief in his business gave him the self-confidence now that he could persuade a woman used to the comforts of life in Cape Town to build a life and family with him in this remote place. Maybe Leah could come then.

In December he travelled to Cape Town, stopping over briefly in Walvis Bay to see Cameron and see if Nara's aunt had collected any more stones. There were garnets and a few more of the "semi-precious stones", as Sonnenberg called them, but no diamonds.

After almost two months in Cape Town, Jack proposed to Sonia Sachs, the niece of one of the city's prominent doctors. She'd been educated in England and had been in the city for a year as her family searched for a suitable match. Petite with dark hair, she struck him first as overly demure, almost boring. But during walks along the traditional courting grounds at Muizenberg and the Sea Point Beach Front he realised that she was far more experienced at assessing suitors than he was. She was attentive and, if probing, was careful to keep him at ease with indirect questions or statements that were slightly open-ended, leaving him to complete the thought. She hardly ever disagreed and if she did, it was a tease. She was gay and popular with a large set of friends made in the short time she'd been in the city. This charmed him, and although she showed no interest in "life beyond the suburbs" let alone Africa, he looked forward to the time he spent with her and saw how she would fill the social void in his life.

Eva Sonnenberg had enthusiastically taken charge of finding him a wife. "She's been waiting for this ever since she met you – you're the son she never had, and Sonia the daughter", Sonnenberg said one evening as they sat on the stoep of the house in Tamboer's Kloof looking down at the city. As Eva's excitement grew to become almost overbearing Sonnenberg himself seemed to withdraw, and Jack felt at times he was no longer in charge of his own life. As the pace of the courtship intensified, he increasingly found himself "fitting in" with plans drawn up by others. On the odd occasions he tried to do otherwise he was thwarted by less than surreptitious *faits accomplis*, the deployment of guilt and other manipulations by both women.

In the end it seemed quite transactional. Sonia and he had little time on their own and when they did, she seemed quite uninterested in life in Suidwes or what it meant for him. Her focus was on the wedding, and how they would spend their summer holidays in Cape Town, where she'd already told him she wanted a house.

It was important to him that Sonia meet Hanna, who would be able to tell her more about life in Windhuk and whose judgement of her suitability he relied on. But every attempt to arrange this was pre-empted or thwarted by the tittering hive of aunts, cousins and friends who now seemed to accompany Sonia at all times.

In the end, Hanna met her only after he'd proposed, and tacked onto the end of a day visiting Garlicks and Stuttafords department stores on Adderley Street. The bill for the "things we will need" was over a thousand pounds. Sonia came with friends who wanted to know the price of every item. Hanna herself was too distracted with Effi's ill health and the children to really engage. She did ask about Nara in a quiet moment, but he had nothing to report. For a brief moment, the wide grey eyes took him in deeply and then the babble reasserted itself.

Jack left for Walvis Bay two days later. As he stood on the aft deck watching Table Bay and the mountain recede, sadness at leaving the city hovered about him like the seagulls following the coaster. But when the gulls wheeled away, he let out an audible sigh of relief as the tension of the past few weeks receded and his privacy returned like an old familiar jacket. His thoughts turned to Nara.

Die Nama kommen…

"Does he look like his father?" Frans's mother asked. Nara had taken to calling her Antis, as was customary for older Nama women.

Nara looked lovingly at the boy flexing his legs as he held onto her knees. "His hair…" she said, running her hands through his thick dark locks. His skin was slightly lighter than hers, although both of them were dark where they'd been exposed to sun. His features were more European than hers, she thought, and it was too early to see if he would have Jack's prominent nose. "… and his eyes are his father's."

"It's time for the next one", Antis said. "I know you are worried, but my family are healthy. It was my husband's family who were sick – his sister was like Frans. I need a grandchild. You must let him seed you."

Nara had anticipated this. Antis must have already spoken to Frans, because he had become more insistent and even aggressive about entering her and holding her while thrusting.

"If you don't, my brother will look for another *meisie*."

Nara knew they would, and understood the implied threat. "But what if the child is born like Frans?", she argued. "There is the fighting, we're already moving away towards the desert. I can't look after Jakob and a sick child while we flee from the Germans." She could still see the terror in the Herero woman's face as she crawled out of the thorns with her children at the Waterberg.

"We are moving towards the Topnaar, your people. My brother says the Germans will not follow us down the Kuiseb, if it comes to that. We are too few to bother them. I will be with you, and I will look after both of them. You know I love Jakob as my own."

Unhappy as she was, Nara thought that to be true. She also knew she had no real choice. Within a few months she was pregnant again as the winter brought colder, longer nights.

+++

Winter 1907   Mariental, Hardap Region

Encounters with the Witbooi were waning, as was the willingness of the combatants to really engage. Both sides were exhausted – men and horses. Supply lines were stretched. The Germans were gaining experience, but new troops and the normal shambles of war plagued them. A month before, two of Rolf's soldiers had gone insane from thirst near Aranos in the east, where the wells had been blocked with rotting carcasses by another German patrol.

Many of the men had chronic dysentery and other illnesses. Most had saddle sores and Dhobi's itch and infected scratches from the thorn bushes. Scorpion, spider and snake bite were common. Despite the threat of Prussian military discipline, they lay listless in their tents or, when these were too hot, under the small trees surrounding their camp.

When Baster scouts reported a small band of Nama moving north round Klein Aub three to four days to the north, Rolf was inclined to let them go. Better he and his men rest for a more significant engagement, he thought. The scouts said that there were only three mounted men in the band, and they were armed with old Martini rifles. It seemed clear this was only a very marginal nomadic band and no threat to the Germans. But his discipline kicked in and he wrote a telegram, which was heliographed down to Keetmanshoop.

Lethargy had apparently set in at the southern command headquarters too, as it took more than two days for them to reply to his report:

pursue nama. all armed men to be executed. all suitable for labour to be transported to nearest camp. adult detainees to be registered and identified with tags of gibeon district. elderly and unfit to be driven west.

The company, weary of war, assembled their gear and wagons reluctantly. They were under strength, but Rolf decided that the weaker men would be left to look after the seriously ill and guard the camp. Two of the younger Baster guides were sent out to find and track the band. They were to report back to Rolf, who would move up to Klein Aub.

+++

Nara's band moved slowly, their pace dictated by the few cows and goats that needed to graze across the sparse grasslands. But now there was a sense of purpose to what had been a generally passive or meandering mode of existence. They tended to break camp and move on every two days, always to the north. This gave her time to rest. As the summer waned, she became heavier and the clan became more supportive. They brought her more food, particularly eggs, and took up some of her tasks. Frans's mother spent hours with the boy, and they formed a strong bond, which reassured Nara. He too called her 'Antis'.

She rolled up the note written on the piece of paper she'd scrounged and stuffed it into a tiny tortoise shell she'd found in the veld. She threaded a *rimpie* through the shell and sealed the openings with plugs of chewed leather.

"Antis, this must always be on Jakob", she said, tying the *rimpie* round the child's neck. "If something happens to you or to me, this may help him find his father, who will look after him."

Jakob's sister was born a few days later. Her limbs were straight, and she appeared healthy in every way.

+++

The clan knew the attack was coming. For a few days they'd noticed Basters on horseback and, since they were clearly armed but kept a distance, it was clear that they were tracking them for the Germans. As fast as their animals and elderly allowed them, they aimed for the Kuiseb gorge.

Rolf had observed them through his telescope and saw that the weak and elderly straggled behind the mounted men and a smaller group who were urging the few cattle and goats ahead. Hardly worth bothering with, he thought, especially given the dire state of his troopers, some of whom were constantly shitting with dysentery. Although he didn't make the connection, their dehydration was causing them to faint and fall from their saddles. He decided to rely on the four Basters, since they, at least, were healthy and had some energy.

"We need to split them up", he told the scouts and his sergeant. "The best time to do this will be at the end of the day – the darkness will cause panic. You will ride in between them just before dusk, driving them apart."

He tasked his sergeant with targeting the men with weapons. "The weak and the elderly we can leave – later we can force them towards the Namib. The others who can work we will herd towards Windhuk."

The Basters approached the Nama on foot, leading their horses along a shallow donga that would get them closer without being detected. The front group of Nama were slowing down for the night, the stragglers maybe a kilometre behind them. The scouts split up, one pair aiming to panic the main band to break north, where the company would corral them, and the other pair to scatter the frail to fend for themselves.

The young scout had taken off his hat and watched from the lip of the gulley as the young mother with the baby on her back broke away from the stragglers. She'd hesitated briefly next to the small boy with the elderly woman, but then moved to squat in a small dip only a few metres from him. She was his sister's age and he couldn't drive her into the desert with a nursling. He mounted and rode up out of the donga in the deepening dusk, startling her. "Move up to the others now, quickly. The Germans are coming!"

"Antis, Jakob!"

Her scream galvanised the other scouts who rode into the gap between the band and the stragglers, firing into the air.

The Baster blocked her path and raised his rifle. "Move that way – I'm trying to save you and the baby. The others are finished."

Antis grabbed Jakob and tried to run towards Nara, but a soldier appeared, slashing at her with his crop. Dust swirled up around the dark shapes of the charging horses and soldiers and the fleeing, screaming people. The Baster jumped off the horse beside Nara and pushed her onwards with his hands – "Keep moving, you can't go back."

She darted sideways. Another soldier rode up and blocked her path back. "*Komm Nara, komm Mädchen.*" She stumbled, confused by the use of her name. The soldier leaned down from the horse and pulled her roughly by her arm and shoved her forward again. When she was able to turn around again Antis and Jakob had disappeared in the dust and shadows of the dusk. All she could recognise was the dystonic twist of Frans's head silhouetted high against the aubergine sky.

+++

Isabis, Hardap Region

The next day Rolf rode round the pitiful band of captives. He was hardened to this now, and knew he needed to give them time to rest if they were to endure the march across the desert highland. They'd lost their possessions; it was bitterly cold at night and mercilessly hot during the day. Anyway, they had to wait for the rest of the company with the wagons of supplies to join them before moving on.

There were less than a hundred people. Three armed men had been captured. He kept one alive as he seemed to know more about the other Witbooi bands. The other two were executed. Almost all the elderly and infants had disappeared overnight and there was no sign of them. The rest now posed no threat and were broken - they would not flee. The cattle and goats were being held separately and he would send these onto Rehoboth.

Nara was in the centre of the crowd with other women and a few older children. They seemed to have water, as far as he could see. He kept his distance, as did most of the soldiers. He didn't want her to recognize him.

The supplies arrived at midday, and they were given some sacks of pap. A sergeant began the process of registration and tagging the captives. He had a small field table and chair which he placed in front of the quartermaster's cart. The captives were lined up and one of the Basters translated their names, which were logged in a book against the number stamped on the brass tags. The tags were fixed round their necks with wire which a soldier closed off with pliers. Every time Nara approached the table the sergeant would wave her away, saying *"nacher* - later".

Rolf had ridden up on a small ridge to satisfy himself that there were no Witbooi lurking in the kloofs around them. When he pulled his horse around, he saw that Nara had been left on her own sitting on the ground near the sergeant's table. The man called her forward and he registered her name in the logbook. Then he took the tag and pliers and moved round the back of the cart. He must have said something to her because she followed him.

Rolf watched him lift her leather jerkin and grasp her breast. She was completely passive. The man lowered his head and suckled at her as she held the infant in her arms.

The hardness of war that had built up inside Rolf was already a familiar ache, but now it shrivelled into a brittle crux under his heart.

The sergeant pushed her round to face the cart and forced her to bend over. Rolf's core shattered and he kicked his horse forward viciously, galloping down the slope and slashing at the man's head and back with his crop. Nara barely registered, covering the baby's head with her arms.

+++

Jack heard a horse gallop up to the back gate of the house, which was unusual. Most visitors approached from the Ausspannplatz. He heard indistinct voices, maybe a man's voice in Afrikaans, but waited at his desk.

Kaera appeared at the door, pale and agitated, and he stood up tense. *"Ein Soldat – ein Baster"* she said gesturing towards the courtyard. All along he'd feared that the Germans might come for her and the children, and the confrontation that that would lead to. She stepped out quickly onto the back stoep and pointed west. *"Die Nama kommen"*, her mouth quivered, "the Nama are coming".

A bedraggled column escorted by mounted soldiers was approaching along the road from the Naukluft mountains. They were maybe a mile away, and indistinct in the dust and against the sun in his eyes. They'd all grown used to columns of miserable prisoners being driven in from the veld to the concentration camps. Why was Kaera upset? Magda suddenly appeared, her face ashen.

Anxiety and hope wrangled in his belly as he walked down to the Baster soldier at the gate. "Kaptein Rolf says he has your Nama girl. You must come and get her outside the town."

He found himself half-running down the track with Kaera, Magda and Petrus close behind. Anguish tore at his face, his mouth open, eyes wide, and his hairline stretched back from his skull. Suddenly he felt ridiculous and he stopped and walked the last few metres. Kaera was wailing. Rolf acknowledged him with a raised hand and then steered Nara away from the column and towards them with his horse. She collapsed when Kaera embraced her. They unwound the skin wrapping the baby and Magda took the child. As Petrus lifted Nara, a brass tag round her neck flashed in the sun.

A tag and a pass

Before the women washed her Jack removed the tag from her neck. The number 02108 and "Beck & Co; Leipzig" were neatly stamped on the back.

She was almost comatose for the first 24 hours, and someone was constantly in the room with her. She had to be woken to nurse the baby – its plaintive wailing seemed not to reach her. She was pitifully thin, her ribs sticking out and her legs and arms like sticks. Only her breasts seemed normal, although Magda said she was not producing enough milk. They fed her by spoon, and she had to be lifted from the bed by the women to use the chamber pot. She recovered slowly, seemed indifferent to the infant, and sobbed intermittently. If she talked at all it was in Nama to Magda, and then almost in monosyllables. Whenever Jack entered the room, she would look beyond him.

Kaera came to him in the office about two weeks after Nara's return. "Some of my people are back near Okahandja. It is time for me to go to them. I will need a pass and I will need money for cattle."

It cost him a couple of bottles of whiskey to get a "replacement pass" issued, noting that the bearer was "returning to Okahandja". The surgeon-general was similarly persuaded to write a note recording that Kaera had treated an injured trooper.

Two nights before Kaera and her children were to leave on a wagon Jack was sending to Malan, she came to him. She lay beside him, their silence an acknowledgement of their intimacy. For the first time she did not lead but let him explore her body slowly in the dim light that came in from outside. Finally, both of them aroused, he rolled over her as she spread and raised her dark legs. Her full breasts juddered as he thrust into her. As he climaxed, she held him and held his eyes with hers – dark, close and searching. When she got up to leave in the wee hours, she touched his eyes gently.

Callous and bud

It was Magda who got them through this time. She would take the baby after her morning feed and wander around the garden and the neighbouring slopes, cooing and talking to the child and introducing her to neighbours as her grandchild.

It was not that she ignored Nara - whom she embraced, dressed, fed and encouraged constantly – but Nara, who'd yet to emerge from behind a *kraal* of silence and lethargy. She was never left on her own but barely engaged with the old woman who'd been a surrogate mother to her, or another Nama woman who had come to help. Jack, she ignored entirely.

"You must wait, Baas", Magda said when Jack grew impatient. "She will heal."

Magda would often return from these morning walks with cuttings from plants. Most of these were various succulents that were popular with the settlers as they began to establish ornamental gardens in the arid landscape.

The most popular of these she called *Augoreb*. The Germans called it the Bergaloe, Mountain Aloe, and were fascinated by its propagation, which used the plant's ability to heal itself. Where the thick succulent leaves are broken or cut the wound seals itself off and develops a callous. Magda would lay the cuttings on their side in containers on the stoep. Behind the callous, a new plant would begin to bud, with roots, stems, leaves and, eventually, flowers.

Slowly, after weeks of persistent, patient coaxing, Nara began to engage. The rhythm of the housework, the routine of nursing, bathing and bedding the child helped her get through the days without falling asleep or into a deep stupor. But she would not acknowledge Jack.

He could see her constant and profound sadness. Magda said she would not speak of what had happened. But he knew or feared that this was to do with the first child, his child. Somehow, he was mourning too. He couldn't find the courage or a way to acknowledge this. There would be no healing without this, he knew. He could only wait for her, he told himself. And he had to tell her about Sonia.

Early on a Saturday morning, having nursed the baby, she came out to the back stoep where he was sitting in a low armchair. Part of him registered that she was no longer haggard as she was when she arrived; she was wider in the hips, her skin smoother and her breasts obviously fuller; part saw her set jaw. He tensed for the confrontation he'd been anticipating.

Abruptly, she placed the baby in his lap. He welcomed the distraction as she walked along the railing, jerking and jabbing at the tins of plant cuttings Magda had placed there to root. The baby gurgled as she clutched his finger. Nara began to sob.

"I lost him. I lost him over there", she said, nodding out towards the Nuakluft where she'd come from. "The Germans came at night and they separated us in the dark. I couldn't get to him. They stopped me. His name is Jakob and he's your son. You knew you had filled me with child when you were going to send me away."

+++

Petrus came into the store and waited for Jack to finish with a customer. "The Baster soldier is at the back gate. He is here with his father. They want to speak to you."

The boy was not in uniform. He stood by his horse with the broad Australian-type bush hat favoured by the Basters and Schutztruppe in his hands. An older man by his side stepped forward. A large sheep had been tethered to the fence.

"I am Barnardus Christiaan Beukes", the older man said. "This is my son Hendrik. We are from a good family in Rehoboth. My father and my grandfather were Boere who came here many years ago. We have always served the Germans well. We have good land and cattle and sheep", he said pointing at the animal. "I have come to ask your permission for Nara to marry my son."

"Have you spoken to her?" Jack asked, trying to control his surprise. And his panic.

"That is not our way."

"Well, I need to. I need to think about this. You know she's had a terrible experience. And there's a child..." He was babbling.

"I know this", Beukes said, far more in control than Jack was. "We will come back tomorrow." They left the sheep tied to the fence.

Where is Hanna when I need her? Magda will know what to do. I can't go through the house to the Yard – Nara will ask me.

Magda knew of course. "I told him to ask you."

"It's not for me to agree. She's not my daughter."

"Baas Jack, if Frau Hanna was here, she would say it's the right thing to do. Nara knows she cannot be your wife. That's not allowed except for the Basters. This young man will look after her. He has shown it already. And she needs a family."

"Well, he will have to court her. He can't just come and take her. She needs to want this."

Nara was nursing at the kitchen table when he came back in. "I will go with him", she said, not looking at him.

+++

1907 Lüderitzbucht

They limped into the bay five days out of Cape Town because of engine trouble. The ship wallowed on a limpid pearl-blue ocean, lulled by the slow swells from the south as they waited for a tug. The preparations, the wedding, and even the honeymoon had been hectic. An endless social whirl with people he was meeting usually for the first time. When they finally boarded the boat for Walvis Bay it was with a sense of relief. Life around his business would resume. For her, a new adventure she had spent months planning for.

Jack and Sonia strolled up and down the deck – still getting to know each other. His eyes were drawn landward – the pale-yellow sand, the faint line of breakers, and the vast expanse of the Namib behind. She focussed on him, relentlessly correcting his English and his still heavy Yiddish accent, and discussing plans for their house and events she wanted to organise to establish their social life.

He had an office here, he told her, and a share in a hotel. They should be comfortable while waiting for the boat to be repaired. This was not their destination, she knew, so she was not interested. Anyway, it was boring to look at. Even intimidating.

They stood at the rail as the tug towed them past a tiny island off the stony peninsula that formed the bay. The island was covered in scores of round pondoks – like pustules on diseased skin. Even at a distance they could see brown and black humans crawling around the island, in and out of the hovels. A wooden bridge linked the island to the peninsula and as they came past, they could see soldiers manning a barbed wire gate. Sonia's normal happy chatter evaporated.

Solomon met them on the wharf. A donkey cart collected their luggage, and as they walked out of the grim docks up the hill to the hotel the easterly wind picked up, sending stinging sand into their faces. At the railway station gangs of pitiful prisoners – men and women – were loading goods onto a flatbed carriage. They were painfully thin, dressed in hessian sacks with holes cut out for their heads and arms. Their limbs were exposed to the wind, and uniformed German overseers supervised with crops and clubs in their hands.

The shock of the encounter and the stinging wind curbed conversation. "They're being treated as slaves", Sonia mumbled as they climbed the steps to the hotel veranda overlooking the bay which had turned grey as the wind drove sand across it and churned up white horses.

"There is worse than this", Sol muttered to Jack in Yiddish. "I need you to come to the warehouse before you leave."

It was an inauspicious introduction to Suidwes for her. Gertie and Solomon seemed resigned to the treatment of the Nama and Herero. "It's war", Sol mumbled, "and what can we do? There's a minister who's tried to do something, but the garrison commander refuses to meet him, and he's been reprimanded by his mission." Things got worse when, during the course of the evening, Sonia realised that the hotel was also a brothel.

"I would not have married you had I known this", she almost shrieked later in their bedroom. "How could you not know what your partners are doing? What will my parents say? My uncle in Cape Town will disown me!"

The next morning Sol took Jack to the warehouse they had by the docks. There was an immediate powerful stench when they opened the doors. – *'Wal..vis'* – Jack murmured, remembering. As they approached the back of the warehouse the smell became distinctly chemical. Sol pried open one of five unmarked wooden packing cases. Inside there were four human skulls each packed in an individual crate. A buff label in neat Gothic script described the skull as – "male, Herero, age approx. twenty, originally from Hereroland obtained in Lüderitzbucht"; Another described the skull as "female, Nama, Shark Island, age about twelve". A letter in one of them was addressed to a dealer in Hanover explaining that they had been collected from Herero and Nama prisoners who had died or had been executed in Lüderitz, and gave approximate dates. The letter was signed by a Schutztruppe captain who listed the details of a bank account where the proceeds of sale were to be deposited.

Sol pointed at the other packing cases – "They all have skulls or body parts. That one contains skulls addressed to a doctor at a university in Berlin. They force the women to boil the heads and scrape them clean. They could be dealing with the heads of people they know. They do this on Shark Island, which you passed on your way in. They used to do it on the docks, but the pastor objected. They tell me in the bar that scientists and museums in Germany want these for research. But individuals buy them too, as curios."

"There can be no *mechila*, no forgiveness) for this", Jack muttered, shock and disgust swelling up like vomit in the back of his throat. "Send them to the Woermann warehouse. They were obviously delivered here by mistake. Nothing must show that we had them here."

"There's another thing", Sol said on their way back to the hotel. "There's a doctor here, with the Germans, but not a soldier. He experiments on the prisoners with arsenic and morphine and other chemicals."

Jack wondered if he should share this with Sonia once they were back on the boat, but she remained angry and tight-lipped, and he decided not to. She smiled for the first time when she met Cameron on the docks at Walvis. Jack had prepared her for the mixed marriage, and she was charmed by Margaret, their children, and the decidedly Anglo hospitality which put her at ease.

Cameron was not surprised by the skull story. "I've seen Herero women doing this on the road into Swakopmund. German researchers think they will discover the missing link."

Boom

The Nama War petered out during 1907. The concentration camps – including the one on Shark Island – were shut down, von Trotha was recalled, and black labour was now organised under pass laws. The Herero and Nama were defeated and exhausted, their land and most of their cattle distributed to German settlers, many of whom were Schutztruppe who had been discharged from service and encouraged to stay with generous loans. The Ovambo in the north had hardly been directly affected by the war, but they too were cowed and desperate for work.

Rolf and Susanna married soon after Jack and Sonia arrived back in Windhoek. The marriage was Sonia's introduction to the Windhuk social scene, but her inability to speak German limited the impact she had hoped to have. The new couple was only around for a few days, as Rolf was keen to establish his farm on a huge tract of land he'd been awarded west of Keetmanshoop. "I don't want to be near the Waterberg", he explained to Jack, "and Susanna is happy to be near her brother in Lüderitzbucht".

The discovery of diamonds near Lüderitz the next year accelerated the post-war boom, and Jack's business along with it. Suddenly the colony was no longer a drain on Berlin but a source of tremendous wealth. Investment and settlers poured in. German administrative control tightened.

Lüderitz became a boomtown and even Sonia condoned the push Jack made to capitalise, although she never agreed to go there again. Sol and Gertie were often paid in diamonds, and when that became illegal, became adept at hiding the treasure from the German concession company. Jack acted as their agent, sending the diamonds to Sonnenberg in Cape Town through a network of couriers that he and Cameron, now harbour master, had established. The establishment of the *Sperrgebiett* (prohibited area) by the German administration and the concession company curbed the free-for-all, but smuggling was endemic. The area was so vast and so challenging that Topnaar and Nama desert skills were an asset, although they themselves saw very little of the wealth. Jack's network of Topnaar women was never detected.

Jack and Sonia's relationship never got off the ground. Windhuk society was German, and not really welcoming of an English-speaking Jewess who could not speak German and didn't really try. The German victory validated the idea of "*Deutschstum*", 'Germanness', which rested on ideas of racial (white) and German cultural superiority.

The Jewish community was tiny and its members were almost all the "*Grobbe Yidden*", the coarse eastern European Jews she detested. She made no real friends. They remained childless and their relationship loveless. She lived for their summer holidays in Cape Town, spending a fortune on decorating and establishing the garden of a large house he'd bought in Newlands – one of the most luxurious and most Anglo suburbs of Cape Town. Her holidays got longer, returning to Windhoek more reluctantly each year, even after having spent 3-4 months in Cape Town.

In 1912 he stopped off in Lüderitz as he usually did on his way back from the summer trip to Cape Town, and rode out to visit Rolf and Susanna on their farm. They'd built a charming little house on a ridge, and had one child. Their lives were tough, and they were barely making ends meet from the small flock of Karakul they were raising in the arid landscape. But they seemed content and optimistic. Rolf told him that the adjacent farm was for sale and insisted that he see it. "There are huge herds of game. If they can survive so can we. We must just learn how to."

The next day they rode out with Jack along the old ox-wagon trail to Keetmanshoop. Rolf pointed out the giant acacia up against the bare flat-topped grey hills. "That's a clear sign there is water here", he said. "These too", as they brushed through a thicket of dark green tamarisk in a dry riverbed.

Jack was sceptical. Sparse stunted shrubs, tufts of sparse grass on parched rusty earth, ancient eroded hills, and baking heat. It would be crawling with snakes and scorpions.

Susanna had brought a picnic and they sat in the shade of the acacia. Occasionally a turtle dove cooed, floating Nara up in his heart. Rolf complained of pain and went to rest on the far side of the tree. Jack saw him take a sip from a small brown medicine bottle, and when he looked back he saw Susanna watching him. He knew it was morphine because Rolf would badger him for it.

Gently, quietly, they coaxed each other to talk of their marriages. Susanna seemed content, her main concern was Rolf, who suffered almost continuous pain in his hip. "Morphine seems to help but the doctors ration it strictly. But he gets melancholia – there are days when I struggle to get him to rise. I don't think that is from the pain, but from the war. But he won't talk of it."

Jack was matter of fact. "There is no child to bind us. She is unhappy here and each summer holiday grows longer. She will stop coming back. When she's away I do not miss her. So, it won't last." He saw that he'd shocked her.

"There is no love?", Susanna asked.

Koo-kurrrr-it, – koo-kurrr -it…. Jack looked up into the tree, as if searching for the dove but really hiding the glistening in his eyes. He shrugged when he looked back at her. The tears had welled up not for Sonia but for Nara. And for himself.

"The farm would be a challenge that could replace her in your life?", she said after a while.

That resonated with him. He'd felt bored by the business for some time, and although Rolf and Susanna's life was spartan and tough, it was outdoors in the veld, and he was envious. The disappointment of his marriage had left him lonely again, and he'd fallen back on his habit of looking for business challenges and making plans. It was also the conventional business wisdom of the time that one should own a farm. Land development was being underwritten by the government, karakul seemed to be the answer to livestock farming in the south, and the ex-Schutztruppe who'd become farmers were an influential lobby group that it would be useful to be part of.

The farmer who wanted to sell was in Keetmanshoop. He was desperate too. They met in the Schützenhous and agreed within an hour.

Within a few days of the outbreak of the First World War, Jack was placed under a dusk to dawn curfew as an "enemy alien". He'd never taken out German citizenship in Suidwes. Uncertain of the outcome of the war, he and Sonia decided that she'd be better off back in Cape Town. She never returned, and they divorced in 1916.

Late 1915

Walvis....

… was small and quiet enough for Cameron to come home for lunch. The build-up of troops and supplies that had preceded the South African invasion of the colony had abated. Like most, he was enjoying a kind of euphoria, which seemed to affect all unless you were German. Despite a particularly severe drought, it was a time of celebration as German restrictions were lifted by the new administration, and displaced people of all groups could move back to their original areas and reunite with their families.

Margaret called through to him from the back stoep as he walked in. She was talking to two elderly Nama women, while a young boy tossed horseshoes at a peg Cameron had placed in the ground for his children to play with.

Cameron now recognised the woman who had thrust the girl on Levin in the shantytown when they had first met – maybe 15 years ago. He remembered how she had tried to distract the drunk who was trying to get at the girl. "She says this lady has something from !Nara who went with Baas Levin, the Jew", Margaret translated.

The other woman, even older, called the boy. He came up to them and held up a small tortoise shell tied round his neck. "*Nara*" had been branded on it. "This is !Nara's son", the older woman said in Nama, Cameron's wife translating. "She made it when we were running from the Germans. She said if anything ever happened to her, I was to bring the boy to Meneer Levin in Windhuk or to you here in Walvis Baai. The Germans took her a long time ago. She had a baby daughter, my granddaughter. They disappeared. She put something in the shell for you."

The boy removed the little amulet from around his neck, and Cameron used a penknife to pry open the leather and gum plug that sealed the hole where the animal's head had once emerged. He straightened out the rolled-up piece of paper that emerged:

Meine Name is Jakob Levin. Ich bin der Sohn von Herrn Jack Levin von der Yard in Windhuk

+++

Five days later Jack, Nara, and her husband Hendrik Beukes met Jakob on the platform at Swakopmund station. He clung to Antis, and stayed next to Cameron whom he'd come to trust. Nara, who was pregnant, had tried to control her tears as she approached but buckled in front of him. Her smell, her touch, and the sound of her voice thawed his hesitation and caution and he melted into her embrace.

Jack was swept along in the excitement and joy – uncomfortable with the indisputable fact of his mixed-race child, but fascinated too by the blue-eyed boy with his thick, black hair and dark fawn skin. He watched Nara from across the carriage as they rattled their way up to Windhoek and saw the flashes of joy, fun and animated communication with others which was the girl-child he knew. Her perpetual sadness, despite the comfort of a settled life, a husband and new children, had evaporated and by the time they returned to Windhoek it seemed almost as if she and Jakob had never been separated. But she avoided Jack other than for essentials. Without any real discussion, Hendrik slipped into the role of father, Jack having reassured them on the way down that he would provide for the boy. Jack was relieved to see them return to Rehoboth. He'd never been to visit since the wedding, although Magda would keep him informed. Now he wondered about the boy constantly.

The Baster community in Rehoboth was recovering from its own mini rebellion against the Germans, and saw the reunion of the mother and her child after the horrors of the war as a miracle. Antis, – reunited with her granddaughter – was asked again and again to tell of their long trek through the Hochland, their years barely surviving in the canyons of the Kuiseb, and the long wait at Gobabeb until they were sure the Germans had been defeated and they could complete the journey to Walvis.

A few weeks after their return from Swakopmund, Jack travelled to the Rehoboth with Magda. Baster and Nama families from as far south as Keetmanshoop gathered for celebration incorporating several weddings, a *hokmeisie* ceremony, and also the reunion of Jakob with his mother.

People in white and gaily coloured clothes streamed from *kraal* to *kraal*, entertained with a constant supply of grilled meat, pap and sweet pastries until late at night. Old man Beukes was strictly teetotal, and he and his boys kept the drunken and rowdy at bay. After church on the second day everyone gathered in the centre of the town for the Nama Stap.

"Jakob knows you are his father", Nara said, sitting beside him in the shade of a cornstalk canopy set up for guests. She seemed content, her hand resting on her belly, but avoided looking at him directly. "These things are easier here in Rehoboth. Hendrik is good to him. I don't think he should call you 'Pa'. So far, he calls Hendrik by his name. He is learning Afrikaans, but he should know English too. School is difficult for him."

Jack watched the boy, who seemed to have made friends amongst the children his age. They were arranging themselves in groups of boys and girls, preparing for a dance they'd apparently been practicing in school. Periodically he would look across at Nara and Antis, but so far had avoided any real contact with Jack.

Banjos, guitars, a fiddle and an accordion started up and as soon as they did a few of the younger men stepped forward and began to prance with tight intricate steps, some of them blowing on whistles, clapping their thighs or stamping as they moved in a clockwise circle. Women and girls joined, moving much more sedately, and then pairs began to form, the men slowly twirling the women as the circle swept round.

"This Nama Stap is how we tell our stories as a people to the next generation", said Beukes, who was sitting next to him. "It is how we form our community. But now, after the Germans, it is also about healing. Happiness heals, and the Nama Stap makes us happy."

There was a break as the school dancers were introduced. Separate lines of boys and girls formed on opposite sides of the dance area. The girls wore white bonnets and the boys, small hats and white kerchiefs. When the music started, they danced towards each other and, to the amusement of the crowd, it now became obvious that the girls were much taller than the boys who had to stretch up to twirl their partners. The music quickened and got louder, and it was time for individual displays by the boys, who began to prance and leap in turn, and, Jack could now see, mimic animals. Jakob excelled and Jack, surprised at himself, beamed with pride. He sensed that Nara saw this too.

The school class completed its show, and the adults joined the dance again. As the circle looped past, Jakob broke away and came up to Nara holding out his white kerchief inviting her to dance. Jack felt his eyes glisten at Nara's obvious happiness as she danced sedately, led by her son. Magda and Antis made no attempt to hide their tears and when Jakob returned his mother to her seat, he invited them too.

Jack watched the twirling dancers, his mind drifting to wonder how his life had become entangled with these people.

When Jakob returned Antis to the family seating area, Nara leaned across to speak to Hendrik and then told Jakob to give the kerchief to Jack, who fumbled and faffed, not knowing what to do. She turned to him and looked into his eyes, with Hanna's and his mother's deep insight into his soul. "Come dance with me, Yankele, come dance."

+++

Late 1930s   *Rehoboth*

Nara sat at the kitchen table flipping slowly through the condolence letters and cards. For the first time in ten days since Hendrik's death the house was silent and she could focus on herself. The band of tension in her chest eased as the names of the well-wishers registered and conjured up memories of their association with him. He'd been well liked and respected in the community, and although government policy and restrictions bore down on the Basters as it did on all non-whites they'd had a relatively good and happy life together. Jakob had been a major source of anguish over the years but he'd removed himself from their lives and although not forgotten, he'd faded as an irritant. But now he'd broken the bond. He'd not come to visit Hendrik once during the months of his illness and not come to the funeral. She touched the pile of letters and cards as if to make sure – not even a card from him.

Hendrik's family had left after the last meal of the mourning period. As she'd anticipated they wanted the house. They all had growing families. Jakob's absence was one of the reasons the brothers gave for dismissing any idea she might have had of any inheritance. "Even if he was a real Beukes his behaviour disqualifies him", her most waspish sister-in-law said.

Nara reached for the last envelope in the pile. Telegrams were a rarity in Rehoboth and everyone had noticed when the postal clerk had arrived to deliver it. She'd read it then of course, but had put off considering what it meant.

Sincerest condolences on your sad loss. Hendrik was a good man and will be missed. Please contact us if you need anything.

Rae & Jack Levin

What to make of Rae's name on the telegram? They had met over the years and Jakob had even stayed with them when they tried to settle him in St Georges Anglican school in Windhoek, which at least claimed to be non-racial. But race, class, social awkwardness and the boy's constant delinquency got him expelled. Contact faded apart from an occasional meeting at the Levin depot and store on the main road. Now she was offering help. Maybe Jack was reluctant?

So she wrote to both of them, addressing the letter to the house near the Ausspannplatz she'd returned to after the war. The house she'd come to regard as her home until Hendrik had fetched her. She'd been direct but not too terse, she hoped. "The Beukeses want the house back. I need to move from here and need to work."

A few weeks later Rae was waiting for her outside the sparse office in the depot that Jack used on his visits. It smelt of tyres and motor oil. Rae's presence and chattiness put Nara at ease despite the situation and Jack's mumbled condolences as he showed her in. His blue eyes were clouded with anxiety, she thought. It was Rae who made their proposal.

"The farm near Keetmans is doing well. We've had good rains and there are a lot of Karakul. The problem is to make sure that the quality of the pelts is good so that we get the best prices. Jack says you have good eyes and are a good sorter. We also need to keep good records and the letters to the agents which are in English. The manager can't do this.

You can come and live with us in Windhoek if you prefer, but we won't have room for any children or grandchildren. That will not be a problem on the farm and we would of course pay for schooling."

Before the truck came to take their things to Daweb Eshel, she took the photograph of Jack, Jakob and herself taken so long ago outside the Lüderitz lighthouse, and cut away the image of their son.

Early September 1989   Daweb Eshel

The Hamerkop

Lena heard the bakkie pull up outside the house. Frederika had told her Lenny was going to have dinner with Frau Bruns, hopefully to agree the sale. The workers on her farm spoke of her as being fair and even generous. Lena had a pension, she knew, but at this stage of life she wanted security and continuity. For her that meant seeing out her days with the Steyns.

The Bruns had never needed a manager. She probably could manage the additional farm with one of the Nama foremen. That's what Baas Steyn said, and he'd taken her around the farm that morning. The German woman had enough of her own tragedies – why would she want this old Boere couple moping around with their son's grave in the corner? And they wanted to be buried on the farm too. Who would agree to that?

She lay listening to the squeak of the windmill and the maudlin voices and music on the little transistor radio the Steyns had given her as a Christmas present. The younger families on the farm would be needed, but she had to make plans. It was fortunate that Willem had called to offer her a lift to Keetmans on his way back from Lüderitz on Friday. He'd asked about Valerie too. She would use the time at her sister's to chase the girl to come and get her grandmother's stuff. The sale was imminent, and things could move quickly.

The *klein baas* – Lenny – came into the house softly. Frederika had warned her not to talk about the *Ouman*'s life on the farm. "He doesn't need to know, and we need his help now with the sale of the farm."

"*Julle mense,* you people", she'd muttered to herself, meaning Boere and white hypocrisy.

She heard him piss into the bowl – still a strong flow – flush and wash his hands, and then move around the rooms. Now he was in the *Ouman's* work room, next to hers, the creak of the chair at the desk, and then picking up and putting down things. There was a hollow rap – that was the blue box on the desk – she'd lifted and returned these objects so many times over the years as she dusted and cleaned, she knew their signatures. There was a scratch on the wall – he was lifting the picture of his uncle, the one who died in the war. He sat in the chair again, pulling open drawers softly and ruffling the papers and files. Then there was the click of a knob as he switched on the old Bakelite radio on the desk. She could hear the slight hum-hiss as the valves warmed up and then the melancholy woman announcer's voice – the same programme she was listening to.

The presenter started reading out a listener's letter – usually anonymous, these were one of the main draws of the programme, which had been running for years. It was from a woman in an unnamed town in the northern Cape. Her husband worked far away, and would often not come home on the weekend. Sometimes he would prefer to spend his time off fishing in Port

Nolloth, even if he hadn't been home for three weeks. Her son had come back from the border "not right". He couldn't or wouldn't find work, and drank a lot. They'd fought and his father had thrown him out of the house. They hadn't heard from him for many weeks. Her daughter lived with a man in Springbok. She had a child, but they could not afford to come and see the grandmother.

"Thank you, dear listener,", the announcer said, marking the end of the quotation. "Maybe your husband is fishing for *meerminne* (mermaids) rather than snoek (barracuda)." Lenny smirked, although the announcer's tone was not snide. The dirge continued: "… Sometimes the truth is easier to tell or to hear as a story. We Platteland people know that our loneliness lets us see what the city people have lost – the skies, the seasons, the animals, the stories of sad hearts. Your sadness and loneliness reach out to us on the Platteland like a cold *vlei* – a shallow lake – of moonlight. We may not say it, but we know what happens to the heart. It is reflected in the light of the moon on the *vlei*. We know that loneliness cannot heal a sore heart. Sharing that leaves us – and you – less alone."

+++

Lenny leaned forward to switch off the radio but now, hearing the same voice from Lena's room, listened more as he scanned the tuning panel: Moscow, Frankfurt, Paris, London, Cairo… 'Jerusalem' had been marked with a red pen. Guess this is how

Jack spent his evenings here. Jesus, it must have been lonely. It *is* lonely. How did he heal his heart? Did he feel at home here?

"We want to leave you with an old Nama lullaby", the presenter continued. "My *meisie* used to sing this to me, and to my children too:
'tsau!, say the stars, tsau!
it is summer when the stars say tsau!
they are always two [Sirius and Canopus]
they are always close but never touch
one shimmers, one winks
tsau!, tsau!
always together but they never touch
even in the dead springbok's eyes
tsau!, tsau!'

What did the anchor mean when she talked of truth told or heard in a story? he wondered, – something had touched him despite his city-slicker cynicism.

Lynne had talked of this programme as "therapy by radio", and she was not being disparaging. Empathy made the programme – that and the mournful songs and nuggets of Readers Digest wisdom. Almost an hour of induced collective depression was wound up before midnight when the dominee recited an evening prayer. Afrikaans-speaking people on the farms and in the little towns all across South Africa in the era before broadcast TV were the programme's devotees, Lena among them.

Lena heard Lenny move back the chair and then switch off the light in the *Ouman*'s study. He didn't cross into the main bedroom, but walked down the corridor softly towards the servant's quarters. Where she lived. He opened the door and then came down to Nara's room. A strip of light appeared under her door.

Lenny stood at the entrance of the neat room not sure what he was looking for. He sensed Lena was awake even though her radio was now off. He knew he'd crossed a threshold – you hardly ever entered the maid's quarters, and never at night. But he was driven by the sudden need to fill in the gaps about Jack – gaps Anna Bruns had opened up over dinner. And what must have been Jack's awful loneliness in this place. This Nama woman, Nara, seemed to be a key part of that.

He sat on the bed, next to the old kaross, the smell of the floor polish and moth balls rising around him, and picked up the photo of Nara from the bedside table. It was a bigger format than the picture Anna had shown him earlier, and he could see more details. She was slight, like all Nama, and seemed in her thirties in this picture. She was well dressed – in a suit, blouse and a dark felt hat set at an angle. A brooch on her lapel –incongruous, he thought, racial snobbery, he acknowledged. She was looking directly at the camera. The picture had been taken against the backdrop of a smooth plaster building with large windows – the dark paint of the moulding faded, cracked and peeling in the obviously bright sunlight. Behind and below the building there was the view of a bay, he now realised it was probably Lüderitz.

The woman was not in the centre of the picture but close to one of its edges. And now he noticed again the shadow of another, taller figure beside her with a hat and of a child.

The light in the corridor went on and Lena opened the door of her room. She'd dressed in the dark, he realised, her pink housecoat peeping out from under a pale green woollen gown.

"Master?"

He babbled an apology – Frau Bruns had spoken a lot of Jack and the early days on the farm. She'd also mentioned Nara, and he recalled this picture and wanted to see it again.

"Nara was my grandmother. She used to sing to us that lullaby that you heard on the radio. Tsau!, tsau! – it always makes me sad, the two stars, never touching in the dead springbok's eyes." She moved into the room and sat down on the straight-backed chair opposite him, dabbing her eyes with a tissue.

"*Sy was baie kwaai* - she was very fierce. Even with the *Oubaas*. I never heard her call him 'baas" or 'master', just 'Jack'. She seemed to remember everything. She and Baas Jack went back to the beginning of his time in Suidwes. The picture was taken in Lüderitz. There was a Jewish hotel and Baas Jack would go there to collect the blue boxes. Sometimes Nara would go with him on his trips to talk to the Nama in the area.

"We grew up with her here on the farm. On Friday nights she would light candles, like the Jews taught her, she said, and we would have dinner together with him. We were in the room I'm in now. Nara was always in this room. When Baas Jack was not here – or no one else was in the house, we would be in the lounge. In the winter we would make a fire there. And she would tell us stories. Lots of stories.

"She was a Topnaar, the people near Walvis. She said Baas Jack had rescued her from there. Sometimes she said she'd been given to him. I don't know why she changed this. She said she came from 'up the Kuiseb' and had no parents. She lived with an aunt. Baas Jack put her in a school – a mission school in Windhoek, and that's where she learned German and to read and write. On the weekends she said she spent time with Baas Jack's people – the Jews, and she came to know their customs, like lighting the candles and separating milk and meat. That was her happiest time, she said – she had two mothers who looked after her.

"When there was war with the Hereros, Baas Jack wanted to take her back to Walvis Baai. But they got caught in a battle near Otjiwarongo. Nara escaped with the Witbooi. She said she rode a horse for five days. Later, when we got older, she said that ride prepared her for childbirth!

"Here in the south there was also a war with the Germans. Nara and the people she was with tried to escape, otherwise they would have been put to work on the railways or sent to Shark Island – at Lüderitz. Many people died there. She said a German soldier helped her get back to Windhoek. After the war she married a man – a Baster from Rehoboth. We think she had five children but two died as infants. When Nara's husband died, she moved down here."

She leaned forward to take the photograph from Lenny and pointed to the shadow beside Nara. "There was a boy, Jakob, and my mother and another sister. Jakob was much older than us and went to school in Rehoboth and then in Windhoek, and we lost touch with him. But he had a child late in life, a *laat lammetjie*, with a young woman. He was a *gemors* (a mess) and he disappeared again. Nara cut him out of the picture. She said he'd survived the Germans and an escape down the Kuiseb, but was too weak to fight alcohol. She was very angry. Nara brought the mother and child down here to the farm. The mother died in an accident with my sister on their way into town. The daughter – Valerie - grew up here with Nara. Baas Steyn has contacted her about collecting Nara's things that are still stored here."

"What things?" Lenny asked recalling Lurie's vague remark that there might documents on the farm. "We don't really know. There's a steel trunk that is locked. Valerie stayed with Nara in this room. She then went back to Rehoboth or Windhoek for high school. She's a clever girl and Nara insisted she go to school. English school. She said Baas Jack had paid for it. Valerie has the key.

"When Nara got frail, she told Meneer Steyn and me to send the box to Valerie. But the truth is we moved it into the storeroom above the barn and forgot about it until now. Valerie is due to come and get it soon.

"Baas Lenny, I said Nara was fierce. She was a strong but bitter woman, and we were frightened of her. She was very strict with us. She would smile at the grandchildren, especially Valerie. She said the Germans and the Boere stole her happiness. I saw her happy or smile a lot only once – when Baas Jack took me and her to Kaapstad many years ago. She laughed and cried then – Baas Jack had promised to show it to her, she said. You were very little – we stayed in your house on the mountain and saw the sea from the window. Every day we saw the sea.

"We Nama know that when the Hamerkop flies over your house, someone you love has died. There is a Hamerkop nest by the dam. Nara said it flew over this house before they heard about your uncle Sydney. They never found him, he died so far away. Then, she said it flew over the house when Jakob died but we never really knew. It seems he died in a hospital in Katatura. She knew about Baas Jack even before your *Ouma* called to tell her and Baas Steyn. We couldn't find her, but Baas Steyn knew she would be up at the koppie where she used to sit with your *Oupa* when he'd miss Sydney. When Baas Steyn went to fetch her, she said she knew he was dead because the Hamerkop had flown over the house. She planted an aloe for him there. Next to the one they planted for Sydney. She also planted one for Jakob and Jannie. That is where she is buried too. After she died you came here with the family. Your *Ouma* Rae came too. She asked Baas Steyn to take her up the koppie. She planted an aloe there too. I think it was for Nara."

+++

Lenny sat on the stoep of the Bahnhoff Hotel in Aus sipping water, orange juice and coffee, hoping these would cure his hangover. He'd had too much to drink the night before, and was tired and confused by Anna's and Lena's disclosures. Steyn had got him up early as he was due to meet the manager of the Rosh Pinah mine at the hotel at nine o'clock. On the way down Lenny had told Steyn that, pending the surveys and agreement on the price, Anna had agreed that he and Frederika could stay on the farm and be buried there. Steyn looked away into the distance to hide the glistening in his eyes. "*Dankie* Lenny. Frederika will be easier with that news." Some ewes were dropping lambs earlier than expected, he said, and after introducing Lenny to the proprietor as "Meneer Levin's grandson" he drove back to the farm.

An elderly woman came out with the young Nama waitress who brought him breakfast. "*Ich kannte deinen Großvater*", she said. She switched to Afrikaans, realising Lenny didn't speak German. "I knew your grandfather. Come inside when you've had breakfast and I'll show you a picture of him." He was sure she spoke English but refused to. It had been a long time since he'd encountered Germans in South West with this attitude, but given her age and the remoteness of the place he was not really surprised. The waitress returned with two headache tablets, which he gulped gratefully.

Lenny enjoyed the solitude. It helped him nurse his head and confused emotions. It was cool on the stoep and he watched idly as an overalled boy tended to the succulent garden in front of the hotel.

"That was probably taken in the fifties", the woman said, pointing to a photo of Jack and some other men standing at the bottom of the steps to the stoep. "That's Kahan", she said pointing at a monocled man beside him, "and those are the Jewish brothers from Keetmans, the Luchtensteins. They would come here quite regularly – my father said they came to force old Kahan to come out of the mountains!"

She pointed to another, older picture – "that's my father at the POW camp up on the hill. Lots of young Germans died there. My father said your grandfather worked for the British during the invasion, but he served him anyway."

She's not holding back, Lenny thought to himself wryly. Nursing the hangover and preoccupied with Jack's uncomfortable past, he browsed other pictures of early Aus and German military maps of the area that decorated the bar and dining room. Bobbe, his grandmother, had been mistreated and Jack had been more selfish than he'd ever realised. He had an urge to share this with Lynne – she would accept it for what it was, but Cyn, who knew that Jack disapproved of her, would feel threatened and make a *tzimmes* of it. And how to tell the children? The sale of the farm would be more of a rupture for the family than he'd assumed. He was relieved when a young man in khaki shorts, long socks and *veldskoene*[44] bounded up the stairs – Johann, the mine manager.

"I'll be your driver this morning, and I'll be your pilot this afternoon", he said with a grin as they drove up a hill out of the Aus. "Instead of flying from Lüderitz we'll fly from the mine. That will save us a lot of time and I'll use the opportunity to get to Windhoek."

Johann was the antidote he needed to overcome the hangover and the glumness that had settled on him. Energetic and knowledgeable, he was passionate about the industry and the area. He was unconcerned about the impending change of government, he said. "ISCOR management brought some of the SWAPO people down here and they seemed reasonable. It's obvious they will need us for the time being – the geology, engineering and chemistry is so complex, especially in such a remote area, they won't be able to recruit replacements easily. And ISCOR are the main customer.

"Also, I don't have any of the Suidwester baggage – I never fought up on the border. I started off wanting to be a geologist – not stuck in one place, but able to travel around. But I come from a mining family up on the Reef, and my Dad told me I'd make better money working underground! Maybe yes, maybe no. Then I fell for a Suidwester *meisie* so I came out here. Now I want to

---

[44] Literally (veld shoes) are rawhide three-quarter boots attached to leather or rubber soles without nails or tacks and popular in South Africa, particularly with Afrikaners

be an archaeologist."

"How so?" Lenny asked, triggering a lecture on findings in the area – including a cave where a figurative rock drawing of an animal had been uncovered, estimated to be at least 25,000 years old. He had to confess that he was ignorant of the area. "I've not even been to the Fish River Canyon."

"We have the plane. I'll fly you around – I promise you, man, it's amazing!"

They drove straight to the mine entrance and walked down the main gallery to where tunnels branched out along the seam of minerals. Lenny found the dry heat brutal. He was also always uncomfortable with the obvious exploitation of the industry – black and coloured miners and white foremen doing dirty, noisy, and dangerous work underground. And so far removed from the real value of the product they produced. His headache still lurked, and provided his out.

After a quick drive around the rest of the mine they headed for Johann's office. "How far is the airstrip?" Lenny asked – he'd had enough of the desert and the mine.

"You're on it", Johann laughed, pointing to a little hangar where a plane was parked. "We close off the road when we need to use it for landing or take off."

His office was full of mineral samples and fossils. There was another picture of Mo Kahan with his monocle, and hand-drawn maps of the mine. Johann's knowledge and enthusiasm drew Lenny along again despite his pensiveness. "There is some lead and silver, even traces of gold here", he said. "We are working on qualifying an even bigger source of high-quality zinc further west. That will be easier to extract, as it will be open pit. Old man Kahan had a nose for this business and he loved these mountains – you'll see why when we fly."

The roar of the six-seater Cessna's engine and the thrill of their take-off lifted Lenny's mood. Johann had pointed out their route on a map before they took off, and now shouted above the noise as they flew south east towards the Orange River and the formal border with South Africa. At first, Lenny found the vastness and utter aridity of the land below them boring and intimidating. It seemed almost featureless as it stretched away to the horizon, where the pale blue sky just meant more infinity. But as Johann explained the shapes of the mountains and canyons and how they revealed the composition and age of the earth, and pointed out details like tiny black shadows that were caves that had probably been used by San hunters and the odd scratchings of early prospectors, Lenny's curiosity was kindled.

"That's Mt Lorelei", he said, pointing to a dark shape in the crumpled surface of the earth. "The aquamarine tinges on the slopes – that's copper. That's where Kahan first started mining. There's the access road. That was in the 1920s. I can't imagine how tough and lonely it must have been for them then. They had determination we can't even imagine. And before them, the San, who had nothing but their knowledge of the veld."

"The Nama say the Orange is like a python", Johann said as they turned off the muddy river's long meandering course, "but the Fish is a *sywind* – a sidewinder". And the image was correct – the Fish River was a canyon of convoluted twists and folds gouged through the mountains. Lenny's eyes had become sensitised and the mountains were no longer monolithic masses of brown or grey rock but dabs of purple, orange, pink, soft ochre … like an impressionist painting. Green pools of water trapped from the previous rains glistened in the sun like gems on sandy patches of the riverbed.

They climbed higher to get a better view of the upper canyon, which in places was more than twenty kilometres wide, and then swung south-west. The rocks got darker and the earth's surface even craggier, more canyons and tighter swirling twists in charcoal cliff faces.

"The Hunsberge", Johann said, wonder in his voice. "They are over 600 million years old and have been eroded like that by water. I've been in there with archaeologists who've found prehistoric animal and plant fossils. They are what makes the rock so dark."

"Those patterns and twists make it look like a human brain", Lenny mused. "Yes – fractals!", Johann said. "It's amazing. You find them in a snowflake, the patterns of a moth wing, an acacia, and now on this gigantic scale. Up close you wouldn't notice but from here you get perspective."

Lenny had a sudden sense he was flying alongside the plane, listening to the shouted conversation and seeing his own life as a repetition of patterns.

The plane banked north-west back towards Aus, and they followed the escarpment with the Namib expanse to their left. Sand – miles and miles and miles of sand. They settled into the reverie of flying, Lenny preoccupied with Jack. Flying high above the vastness of the Namib, so very different from the soft greens and cool forests Jack must have known as a boy, Lenny had a sense of observing himself. His grandfather's life, with his achievements, his selfishness and secrets, his loneliness, was forcing itself into Lenny's life. "I've lived above history", he thought to himself. "But I can't any longer."

After about an hour Johann turned left into the depths of the Namib and they came in low over the sand. Ahead of them a giant deep terracotta and pink dune rose up above pale salt pans – Sossusvlei. "That dune is over three hundred metres high", Johann said. "They get their colour from the oxidation of the iron in the sand – the older they are, the deeper the red."

By the time they reached Eros airport in Windhoek Lenny had contained his emotions about Jack. His urge to tell Lynne immediately had passed. "Better in person, and I need time to process this. Anyway, who am I to judge him in this place all those years ago. I need perspective – on my own life too."

Later, sitting on the stoep of the house Jack had built on Schweringsburg Road, Lenny looked out across Windhoek and thought of Anna Bruns – "You will come to the Nama Stap, yes?"

Beads of Memory

It was a sedate amble home after Sunday prayers. Selma, Tjandero's aunt was elderly, but it was also customary and dignified for Herero women, dressed in their multi-layered dresses, to move slowly, reminiscent of the cattle in their culture. She was the matriarch of the clan, and together with her friends in their identical sage-green outfits they were stopped, greeted and blessed on their way, and set the pace of the colourful and gracious procession through the grimy littered streets.

Tjandero, by now familiar to the neighbours, walked alongside Sewa behind the elderly women, greeting those he knew. He'd led in singing a hymn earlier, and enjoyed the attention and acceptance. The *ovahona* had invited him to visit. "You must first spend time with your aunt", Sewa said as they entered the little courtyard. "She will go with you once she's rested after lunch."

He brought out the most comfortable chair for the old lady, and placed it so that her body would be in the sun but her face in the shade cast by a rickety canopy of corn stalks. He turned away as Sewa arranged her mother's voluminous petticoats, dress and shawl. One of the granddaughters brought out tea, a bottle of Fanta and glasses, and then a jug and basin and poured water for them to wash their hands. They were left alone.

Selma took her time, meticulously arranging her clothing and her posture with slow grace. Occasionally she would look at him as she evaluated him and ordered her appearance and her thoughts. Like Sewa, she seemed sombre most of the time. Eventually, revived by the tea, she fiddled inside the sleeve of her dress and slipped off a bracelet of copper and iron beads threaded on a thong.

"Ominhanga", he said, recognizing the traditional jewellery of village women, usually worn on the ankles. "These were collected by my mother, Kaera, after the war when the Germans tried to destroy us," Selma said. "The women had to take them off because they slowed them down and cut their legs when they had to run."

Tjandero had only heard snippets of the family history from his father. The beads draped round the old lady's long fingers made it more tangible. It seemed fitting that he would hear from her.

"Where was she during the war?" he asked.

"She was running from the Germans near the Omaheke. They were killing everyone, even the children. A white man found her and took her to work in Windhoek. He had a pass for her. She had two children with her. After the war people started to come back, although the best land had been stolen by the Germans. This man gave her money for cattle so she could start our family again.

"Kaera and the other elders would tell us stories about what happened, when we got older. Terrible things were done to us, and the Germans forced the people into the Omaheke to kill us all. There are no graves, so these beads help us tell the memories."

Sewa had come out and sat beside her mother. "When she worked for this man", Selma said, "she would see lines of Herero men tied by chains at their neck being taken to work. The Germans kept ladies and girls at a camp in Windhoek. They were dishonoured all the time.

"Kaera, your grandmother, was not dishonoured in this way. The white man in Windhoek looked after her. Your grandfather was born when she returned to Okahandja. You get your eyes from him. She used to find the *ominhanga* in the bush when she was herding the cattle carrying him on her back. She was the one who re-started our family."

"Did she not re-marry?" Tjandero asked.

"Kaera re-married when the British defeated the Germans. I was born then, after your father. When he was old enough, Kaera sent him to work in the white man's place – where you now work."

She sighed several times weighing her words, weighing the beads and weighing their history. "When you marry, your wife will get this. I will tell her these stories, and she will understand and tell these stories to her children. That way memory will continue, and we will maintain our pride as Herero."

+++

Beach Road, Sea Point

"That's familiar", Lenny said, drawn to an oil painting of golden orange *tafel koppies* (table hills) at sunset behind a cluster of farmhouses. "That's Daweb-Eshel!". "Yes, it should be", said Esther Marcus, clearly pleased. "There is a very similar one in Jack's study, no?"

"Yes, it's there", Lynne said.

"I also saw a similar painting in Anna Bruns' lounge a few weeks ago", Lenny continued.

"Yes, Jack bought it for them. That was my 'koppie period'. I spent a lot of time down on the farm then. Long holidays with the kids before we could afford to come down here."

"Is she going to buy the place, then?", her husband Isaac – better known as 'Ike' – asked.

"Seems so, hope so", Lenny replied – the Bruns name now floating and waiting to be addressed.

The Marcuses had retired to one of the comfortable apartment blocks on the Beach Front popular with retirees. Lenny and Lynne had met outside, and he'd briefly told her about Anna Bruns' revelation that Jack had had a long-time affair with her grandmother. Lynne pursed her lips – "I guess they would know", she said, as they rode up in the lift.

The flat was light and airy, with a view of the stormy sea and Graafs Pool, where men could swim naked. No one was doing that now, in the late winter, with sullen cold swells crashing against the rocks. The furnishings were of an older era, but their collection of art from South West set their tasteful home apart from many others of their generation.

"It was your grandparents who got me started", Esther said. "I couldn't do much during my first pregnancy and I was miserable with boredom. Rae had seen me doodling and told Jack, who brought me my first box of watercolours from one of his trips. I had it for years. When I moved to oils, he would supply that and the canvasses too. Then later the modelling clay and tools for these", she said, gesturing at the bronze heads for which she'd become quite famous.

"They got *us* started", her husband added. "We had nothing when we arrived. I think it was 1934 – I had just got my license and only the railways in a remote place would employ such a greenhorn. The promise of furnished housing turned out to be a lie. Jack let us stay in a house on Post Street that he owned. That's where I opened my first surgery, and it was Jack who financed the fittings and equipment for that too. Without his help I don't think we would have stayed."

"It was a tiny community, 50-60 families at most. Jack and Rae were its heart and soul. But they were well-liked in the general community too – famous for their parties. Jack had a way with the Boere especially. He would go hunting with them. Rae kept a kosher home, so apart from biltong he never brought the meat back. Go understand!

He would tease Rae and tell Sydney and Tamara – your mother – that he had a special knife to keep kosher in the veld: one side for meat and the other for milk!"

"They were a happy couple – then", Esther said. "They doted on the children, he on Sydney especially. He would take him hunting on the farm, and fishing – real boy's stuff. As he grew older, Jack involved him in the business as much as there was time for. He was being groomed and seemed to want to follow his father. There was always laughter in their house when we visited. Things were going so well in the business that even the rise of the Nazi party did not seem to bother him. It should have, he was one of the first names on their assassination list!"

"Sydney's death in the war affected them deeply, of course", Ike went on. "But Jack always had a shadow in his personality – as if from before. In those days we didn't have treatments for depression – certainly not in South West. He'd always been a curious man, always looked you in the eye, interested and assessing, but he withdrew into himself. He told me that his early years were very lonely, and that he'd seen some bad things in the war with the Herero and Nama. He wouldn't open up about it. He definitely had a deep or hidden side, which I also put down to his business skill and a habit of keeping things to himself.

"Rae tried but she couldn't help him. Maybe he didn't want to be helped. She said he refused to see a psychiatrist here in Cape Town. In those days there was a big stigma about mental illness.

Still is.

"The war years were also very tough for the business. There was nothing to sell and no money to buy. Luckily for your family they had good and honest managers, because Jack would disappear for weeks on the farm. He was close to Mo Kahan and Ernst Luchtenstein – both old timers like himself who shared a passion for the country. They lived around Keetmans and I think they were his closest friends.

"I have to say that those two –and maybe Sydney's death – sort of 'corrected' Jack's ego", Ike continued. "His success had made him a bit of a *gvir*, a rich man, you know–pompous and bossy. He was chairman of this and president of that and resented the younger generation, especially those that had a university education. That dropped away after the war.

"Rae had Tamara to focus on, and got tired of waiting for him and his excuses. Anyway, after the Old Location riots it was clear that Rae had to move down here. She was the one with a social conscience. She helped me treat some of the wounded, and hid people who did not have passes when the police came looking for them. They caught one and beat him until he confessed that Rae had hidden him in her bedroom. The security branch called Jack in and threatened to harm the business. Rae and Tamara moved down here within days."

"Anna Bruns told me that her grandmother had a long-time affair with Jack", Lenny said bluntly.

The Marcuses exchanged glances. "There were rumours", Ike said. "In a small place like that there always are. Especially in those circumstances. I, we, never knew anything. And we would spend time down on the farm and meet the Brunses too. To me, it's like the stories of the diamonds. It made a good tale over beer and biltong, but there was never any evidence. Now you've confirmed it."

"What stories..."? Lenny asked. "Oh lots, – about smuggling diamonds in salt or firewood", Ike said. "All feasible but never proven. The most bizarre I heard was from Walsh, the De Beers man in Lüderitz. He said that there was a rumour that Nama women smuggled diamonds in the tortoise shells they use for *buchu* – their herb mix that is the "women's potion" in their culture. They would leave the diamonds in the Blue Boxes in the Nama churches. It was actually Rae who started those in South West. Jack would collect the boxes, and pay the Nama women. Romantic, eh? Walsh thought it was bullshit."

"Did Rae ever discuss any of this", Lynne asked looking at Esther. "Only once, indirectly. She was reluctant. She said that when Sydney died Jack forgot how to love. She said he didn't want to be happy and was never settled – she had a funny way of putting it – 'not of one place'. When he was here, he longed for the farm, when he was there, he thought of here. Never settled or at peace. It's very sad but they lived like that for the rest of their lives, even in that lovely home where you now live."

Lynne turned to Ike – "You were a doctor there – you've heard the stories about the Herero after the war, controlling their birth rate or even infanticide?"

"Nonsense", Ike said. "There was some study in the twenties to try and explain how a tribe of eighty thousand people had suddenly become so small. Their genocide had been hidden and denied. There was some theory of collective suicide because their defeat in the war made them so depressed. Of course they were – after a campaign of deliberate extermination! We of all people should know! What is true is that when you visited Herero villages and townships as I did, men were scarce. Many of the older ones had been killed, of course. But there was also a deliberate policy of taking their land to settle the poor whites and keeping the native people poor to force them to come work in the mines and cities in South Africa. Like blacks everywhere in South Africa. Having said that, the effect of the war on the Herero's psychology and their culture seems to have been more severe than the Nama. I'm not sure why."

"What do you think Jack would say about selling the farm?", Lenny asked.

"If he was sentimental about anything it would have been the farm. But he was basically a very rational businessman. He'd understand your reasons now."

"So, what drew him back all the time?"

"Rae said that he would go to a koppie above the farm – that one there in the painting with the aloe", Esther said, pointing – "that's where he said he could talk to Sydney. That's where he was less lonely."

Monday, October 16th, 1989

DF Malan Airport, Cape Town [3 weeks to the elections]

The Blue Book

Lenny looked south over Blouberg Strand towards the bay and mountains as the plane banked to the right after take-off. Ahead, he had four days in Windhoek, beginning with reviewing the management trainees and hopefully agreeing the sale of the farm by Thursday. Steyn had told him the surveys and the aerial photos were ready, and planned to send them up with Valerie, the Coloured girl, later today. She would also be bringing the trunk that might have the documents that Lurie and Lynne had mentioned. If all went well, he could fly back on Thursday evening, although Bianca had raised the idea of a dinner or party for the trainees.

He flipped open his briefcase and pulled out the battered old book Lynne had given him the day before. "I think Jack would have wanted you to read this", she'd said. "He marked what he thought was important. It's not easy but you'd better know this as you move ahead with the sale."

In January 1918, the Office of the South African Administrator in Windhoek issued a report on the treatment of the native population by the previous German administration. Entitled: "Union of South Africa -- Report On The Natives Of South-West Africa And Their Treatment By Germany" – it was published in the UK by the British government's official publisher, His Majesty's Stationery Office (HMSO) and sold at the unit price of 2s 6d. The report was presented to both Houses of Parliament in London "by command of His Majesty" in August 1918 and like all such reports to the British Parliament was referred to as a "Blue Book".

Most of the report was prepared by Major Thomas Leslie O'Reilly who had been appointed as the military magistrate for Omaruru on 22 August 1916 and drew heavily on statements from 47 different witnesses. Another section entitled "Natives and the Criminal Law" was prepared by Mr. A. J. Waters, who had served as the crown prosecutor in South West from October 1915 and dealt with German punishments of the native population.

Although there has not been any serious challenge of the veracity of the report, its motivation has been the subject of sharp academic dispute. The Blue Book, it is argued represents the climax of a concerted South African and British propaganda campaign at the time to present their administration as enlightened liberators of the native populations in order to retain control of South West Africa after the First World War.

Yet, eight years later, the British and South African administrations ordered the "total destruction" of the book. Germany was now being rehabilitated by the Allies, and the Blue Book had become an "embarrassment" as it "painted the European in too poor light". Copies of the book have survived.[45]

Note: The term "Hottentot" in the report generally refers to the Nama population.

---

[45] See "Blue Book" – in Notes.

UNION OF SOUTH AFRICA

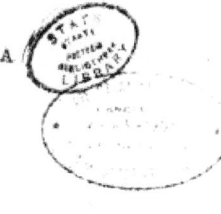

REPORT

ON THE

NATIVES OF SOUTH-WEST AFRICA

AND

THEIR TREATMENT BY GERMANY.

Prepared in the Administrator's Office, Windhuk,
South-West Africa, January 1918.

Presented to both Houses of Parliament by Command of His Majesty.
August, 1918.

LONDON:
PUBLISHED BY HIS MAJESTY'S STATIONERY OFFICE

To be purchased through any Bookseller or directly from
H.M. STATIONERY OFFICE at the following addresses:
IMPERIAL HOUSE, KINGSWAY, LONDON, W.C. 2, and 28, ABINGDON STREET, LONDON, S.W. 1.
37, PETER STREET, MANCHESTER; 1, ST. ANDREW'S CRESCENT, CARDIFF;
23, FORTH STREET, EDINBURGH;
or from E. PONSONBY, LTD., 116, GRAFTON STREET, DUBLIN.

1918.

[Cd. 9146.]   *Price 2s. 6d. Net.*

CONTENTS.

PART I.

NATIVES AND GERMAN ADMINISTRATION.

CHAPTER	PAGE
I.—How German influence was introduced into South-West Africa	12
II.—First acquisitions of land	14
III.—Germany's declared policy in regard to the native races	18
IV.—First steps after annexation	19
V.—The massacre at Hornkranz	23
VI.—Leutwein and the Protection Agreements	28
VII.—Native population statistics	34
VIII.—The Hereros of South-West Africa	35
IX.—Confiscation of Herero cattle by the German Government	42
X.—The German traders, and how they traded	46
XI.—Gradual appropriation of Hereroland and violation of Herero customs	50
XII.—The value set on native life by the Germans	52
XIII.—The outbreak of the Herero rising and the humanity of the Herero	55
XIV.—Preliminary steps and treachery of the Germans	58
XV.—How the Hereros were exterminated	61
XVI.—The Hottentots of South-West Africa	67
XVII.—Laws and customs of the Hottentots	72
XVIII.—The Hottentots under German protection	77
XIX.—The Bondelswarts rising of 1903 and the general Hottentot rising of 1904-7	90
XX.—The treatment of the Hottentots in war and of the Hereros and Hottentots after surrender	97
XXI.—The Berg Damaras of South West Africa	103
XXII.—The policy of Germany after the great rising of the natives up to the British conquest of South-West Africa in 1915	110
XXIII.—The Bastards of Rehoboth	121
XXIV.—The Ovambos of South-West-Africa	134
XXV.—The Bushmen of South West-Africa	142

PART II.

NATIVES AND THE CRIMINAL LAW.

CHAPTER	
I.—The native as an accused person	151
II.—The position of a native when complainant	162
III.—The relations between Germans and natives as evinced in criminal proceedings after our occupation	184

APPENDICES.

APPENDIX	
1.—Medical report on German methods of punishment of natives (with photographs):—	
A.—Chains	201
B.—Corporal punishment	202
C.—Hanging	203
2.—Original German text of secret letter addressed by His Excellency the German Governor to his District Officers on the subject of the treatment of natives (see Chapter XXII)	203
3.—Original German text of three letters addressed by the District Officer at Luderitzbucht to the Government at Windhuk, protesting against the ill-treatment of natives and the attitude of the German Courts (see Chapter II. of Part II.)	204

CHAPTER VII.

NATIVE POPULATION STATISTICS.

The actual Government control by Germany commenced, therefore, only in 1894, when Major Theodor Leutwein took over the command from von François, and was appointed first Governor of German South-West Africa.

The attached sketch will indicate—

(1) the boundaries of the new colony;
(2) the location and spheres of influence of the various native tribes in 1894.

It will now be advisable to deal with each native race separately, showing briefly—

(a) their origin and characteristics;
(b) their laws and customs;
(c) their relations with the Germans, and their treatment;
(d) the causes which led to the various rebellions.

Having done this it will be necessary to indicate what treatment was meted out to the natives during and after these rebellions. It will be necessary, moreover, to deal with the German judicial system as applied to the natives, and in conclusion to voice the views of the native population of South-West Africa in regard to the future destiny and government of this country.

These views are reflected in voluntary statements made on oath by surviving chiefs, headmen, and prominent leaders of the aboriginal tribes, and they represent the unanimous views of the peoples concerned.

At this stage, however, it is necessary to quote certain figures the details of which should be burnt into the memory, as they are in themselves the best indicators of the black deeds which, were it possible to record them all, would require more space than the scope of this report allows.

While there is little difficulty in fixing the areas in which the native tribes lived and exercised influence, it is not so easy to arrive at an accurate idea of the total numbers of the population.

The only guides we have are the considered estimates given by the men, who after years of residence in the country, extended travel, observation, and inquiry, were able confidently to place on record certain definite figures.

The British Commissioner, W. C. Palgrave, in his report of 1877, estimated the native population in 1876 as under:—

(1) *Ovamboland:*

Various Ovambo tribes	98,000

(2) *Hereroland (or Damaraland):*

Hereros	85,000
Berg-Damaras	30,000
Hottentots	1,500
Bastards	1,500
Bushmen	3,000
	121,000

(3) *Great Namaqualand:*

Various Hottentot tribes	16,850
Making a total for all races of	235,850

In his book, Governor Leutwein gives the following estimate of the native population at the time of his arrival (1894):—

Ovambos	100,000
Hereros	80,000
Hottentots	20,000
Bastards	4,000
Bushmen and Berg-Damaras	40,000
Total	244,000

In the second edition of "Mit Schwert und Pflug" (published in 1904), Captain K. Schwabe, of the German Army, while remarking that a correct estimate of the Berg-Damara and Bushman population is difficult, gives the following figures in regard to the other tribes, as at 1st January 1903:—

Ovambos	100,000 to 150,000
Hereros	80,000
Hottentots	20,000
Bastards	4,000

It will be seen that, in regard to the Hereros and Hottentots these authorities entirely independently, and dealing with the years 1876, 1894, and 1903 respectively, give practically the same estimate.

If Palgrave and Leutwein were at all accurate the later estimate by Schwabe of

80,000 Hereros, and
20,000 Hottentots

may reasonably be regarded as a minimum figure for the adult native population, no allowances having been made from 1876–1894, and 1894–1903 for natural increases.

The consensus of opinion and evidence goes to show that, if anything, the population of those races was in 1904 nearer 100,000 and 25,000 respectively.

Palgrave's estimate of 30,000 Berg-Damaras in 1876 was probably too low, but it is practically confirmed by Leutwein, and as it is nowhere called into question by German writers who were conversant with and quoted from his report, there is no reason why Palgrave's estimate should not be accepted and, again discarding natural increases, fixed at the same figure for the adult population in 1904, i.e., 30,000.

The minimum estimate of the adult population of the three races in 1904 is therefore fixed at—

80,000 for Hereros,
20,000 for Hottentots,
30,000 for Berg-Damaras.

In 1911, after tranquillity had been restored and all rebellions suppressed, the German Government of South-West Africa had a census taken. A comparison of the figures speaks for itself.

	Estimate, 1904.	Official Census, 1911.	Decrease.
Hereros	80,000	15,130	64,870
Hottentots	20,000	9,781	10,219
Berg Damaras	30,000	12,831	17,169
	130,000	37,742	92,258

In other words, 80 per cent. of the Herero people had disappeared, and more than half of the Hottentot and Berg-Damara races had shared the same fate.

Dr. Paul Rohrbach's dictum: "It is applicable to a nation in the same way as to the individual that the right of existence is primarily justified in the degree that such existence is useful for progress and general development" comes forcibly to mind.

These natives of South-West Africa had been weighed in the German balance and had been found wanting. Their "right of existence" was apparently not justified.

CHAPTER VIII.

THE HEREROS OF SOUTH-WEST AFRICA.

The Herero tribe is probably a branch of the Great Bantu family, which at one time occupied approximately one-third of the African Continent from 5° North to 20° South.

Monday, October 16th, 1989 — Keetmanshoop

"Ongemaklik"

Steyn had parked opposite the bus station after dropping off his rifle at the gun store. It would take a day to mount and align Jannie's telescopic sniper sights. The lawyer's office was next door, and he'd collected the buff-coloured government folder of the farm documents and the aerial survey. As he waited for the bus from Windhoek he paged through the copies of planning, zoning and title documents the lawyer had prepared. Some of the original documents were in German, and although he didn't really understand the language, it looked like Jack had acquired parts of adjacent farms over time to create Daweb-Eshel as it was now. The air force aerial surveys were easier to understand, but they only showed the situation as it was at the time – not legal title or indications of parcellation, which was what he was hoping for. Although he knew this all personally, the view from the air showed several tracks running between the farm and the Bruns ranch. On the bottom-left corner of the four reprints there was a label stating the coordinates, height and direction of the aerial photograph, the date, and the name of the pilot – "Bruns Rolf – 2nd Lt."

"Ongemaklik, awkward", he muttered and recalled the rumours that the young pilot's "accident" on his way home was perhaps deliberate sabotage by the likes of Bessie because he'd "seen too much" on the border.

The bus came in and he got out to stand beside his pale apple-coloured Mercedes. Valerie had been told to look out for it. There had been some unspoken hesitation about this back on the farm – he was a white man, she a Coloured girl. It would have been quite unremarkable at that time of the day for him to fetch her in the farm bakkie. But in apartheid times, a mixed couple in a white man's sedan would be noticed. In the end, though, Frederika, without acknowledging the awkwardness, said that the Mercedes was more clearly recognisable and that the girl would be more comfortable in it after the five-hour journey in a minibus.

The awkwardness dissipated as they left town. She had a boy and a girl, she told him (he knew from Frederika), she and her husband worked in a bank where they'd met…

She was pretty, with dark curly hair and light almond skin. He was used to Nama who worked outdoors, and their skin darkened in the sun. She had a slightly disconcerting manner of looking directly at him and outside or beyond him at the same time. It wasn't disrespectful or challenging in any way, but her eyes seemed to search for a wider picture as they spoke. Then it became clear, she was looking at the veld and landmarks as they passed. She'd grown up here, after all. Her parents had not survived. She remembered Steyn and Frederika from when she stayed on the farm, she said. She was sent to school in Keetmans and she remembered this journey from then. Her grandmother had had a great influence on her and had driven her education. She was very grateful that they had invited her back to get the things. It had prompted all sorts of memories and questions. Steyn was relieved when they pulled up at the back entrance to the house mid-afternoon and Lena and Frederika could take over.

Sorting out Nara's things was postponed until the next morning, as she was tired after a very early start. Many of her old acquaintances on the farm also wanted her to visit in the evening.

Tuesday, October 17th, 1989   Daweb-Eshel

Rotten Potatoes

The Ridgeback raised his head, alerting Steyn to the dust from cars approaching the farm entrance. He was on the stoep with coffee and a rusk after he'd taken the girl up to storeroom at the back of the barn and shown her the tin trunk and the old cases they believed to be her grandmother's. "Take your time. One of the boys will bring it all down once you've been through it", he said. "Incidentally, I'll bring you an envelope that is to be delivered to the Levin offices. It's important, so perhaps you'll keep it in the trunk too."

Two sedans and two combis rumbled over the cattle grid by the road, triggering the sudden realisation that this was Bessie and his "*staatsbesigheid*" - state business, which he had not mentioned to Frederika.

"Some people are coming", he said to her in the corridor. "I think it's government people, and Bessie might be with them." She blanched, and then flashed back in anger – "Why here? Why did you let this happen?"

"Security people said they might need the farm some time ago, but nothing happened. Now they're here. I know Bessie works with them." She stomped back into the kitchen and he went out to the stoep to wait for the cars.

They drove passed him to park at the entrance to the barn. Bessie and another man walked back towards him as he came down the stairs, letting his anger show. "This is Colonel Viljoen", said Bessie, his bright blue eyes bobbing with anxiety. "He's responsible for the South West district. "*Môre meneer*", said Viljoen. "General Fourie spoke to you. We have an operation under way and need your barn. He'll be here in a little while. We should only be an hour or so." The same curtness and arrogance.

Steyn clenched his jaw, but knew he had no choice. He was being put down for his age, and for being a farmer, and for not being part of the Afrikaner establishment. From his perspective that meant being on the government payroll. He ignored Bessie and said, unable to hide his habitual deference – "I should have been told you were coming, Colonel. Your presence here will upset people on the farm, so stay in the barn. I'll get the key and have coffee sent to you." He turned to Bessie, now letting his anger show – "Don't go wandering about. You left here a long time ago and don't belong."

He walked into the kitchen through the back door. Lena was crying and Frederika was pecking about trying to contain her anger. "How long are they going to be here for? We're not making lunch for those people." "Make them some coffee – five cups. They won't bother you", he said, re-directing his anger and resentment back at her.

He took the barn padlock key off its hook by the entrance, and one of the farm boys came with to deliver their coffee. They waited for him to leave after he'd unlocked the big double doors, and then backed the two combis into the barn and shut the doors.

Steyn climbed up the stairs at the back of the barn to tell Valerie that there were men in the barn and that it would be best for her to be quiet as she sorted out her grandmother's things.

When he came back into the kitchen Frederika and Lena had changed. "I'm taking Lena to Magriet", referring to her closest friend's farm which was an hour away. "Valerie should not be there."

"She chose to stay – she needs the time to sort through things. I'll look after her."

He paced around the house, periodically standing at the small pantry window to keep an eye on the barn, and increasingly concerned about the girl in the storeroom. He was about to go and collect her when another car pulled in and Fourie got out and went into the barn.

Valerie had read the short note from her grandmother she'd found in the trunk, and was about to start sorting things when she heard the vans come into the barn and then the men's voices. When she'd peeped through the narrow cracks of the partitions that boarded off the storeroom, she recognised them as Boere policemen. Now she was too scared to go down the stairs at the back. She could not hear what they were saying, and the barn filled with a strange unpleasant odour – something like rotten potatoes. Another man came into the barn, whom they all seemed to defer to, and then he and the tall blond man walked out. One of the men who remained was wearing strange long leather gloves and gumboots, and another had on a surgical mask and rubber gloves. Periodically, they appeared in the gap between the open doors of the minivans, shifting large rectangular briefcases and other types of containers. She was petrified. Then she heard two men murmuring by the stairs below at the back of the barn.

Fourie unlocked the brown leather briefcase his driver had brought across when they came out of the barn. "This is the cash for this operation", he said to Bessie, handing him a banker's pouch. This was deliberately done away from the others involved so that Bessie could make the allocations as he saw fit. Skimming was part of the MO for the CCB.

He pulled out another manila envelope and sat next to Bessie on the step. "Listen man, I know that you've been under a lot of stress over the past few months. It's been hell for everyone, but you've done more than most and I recognise this. Appreciation for your work has gone right up to the top. So, here is a new passport and driver's license, and a ticket to Zurich for Friday. There's five thousand Swiss francs and Vatican bank bonds for another two hundred and fifty thousand. There are also 25 Krugerrands. Once you get to Zurich, call control at the Armscor office in Paris. They will let you know the next steps, and who to go to convert the bonds. Probably one of the banks in Lichtenstein."

Bessie was teary with gratitude, both for the money and the

escape route, but also for the recognition he craved. But he also panicked – he thought he'd have more time before leaving the country. He would not be able to see Leviev as he'd planned. Luckily, he'd had enough foresight to bring the courier authorization and other travel documents he'd accumulated. They were already secured in one of the false panels of the Nissan Skyline he was using, together with some more cash.

He put the envelope under the briefcase on the step behind them to remind himself to keep it separate from the other operational documents and equipment. He had time to build a story of why he would leave his henchman straight after the operation. It was best anyway if they split up as soon as possible.

"There's one more thing I need you to do when you're in Europe", Fourie said. "You know Meitje, of course. Well, she's not just the pretty little air hostess you all wanted to fuck. She's been stealing – for a long time. Now she's bought a little nest for herself and her lover in the south of France that she thought we did not know about. It's in a town called Grasse. Her lover turns out to be CIA. Not only a thief, but a spy too. I need you to take care of that, of both of them. You'll get the details from control in Paris too. Can you do that, or do you need help?"

Help was the last thing Bessie would want in dealing with Meitje. His blue eyes bounced about his head and saliva swilled about his yellowed teeth. "Vok, no!", he barely managed to say.

Fourie had noticed and stood up. "Look, Bessie, for your own sake and for these operations you have to keep off the drugs and alcohol. You're looking fucking mad with all this jerking, so just focus on the jobs. Incidentally, Meitje's lover is a woman. Yup, she's a fucking lesbo, who would have guessed." Bessie wasn't focussing - he was already fantasizing.

Fourie had calculated that the anticipation of having Meitje would keep Bessie crazy enough not to think of any danger to himself.

Viljoen came out to join them and they went over the plans once again. "This is the last chance we really have to stop SWAPO winning the elections", Fourie summarized. "You have to make this work. You have the cash and the people, and now you have the tools you need. Remember, you must keep the cases cool so park in the shade and use the air conditioners if necessary. Keep off the fucking drugs and drink like I've told you and you'll come out on top. Three days from now you can be sipping coffee in Zurich and choosing whores to spend the night with."

The phone rang in the hall behind Steyn. It was Frederika asking about Valerie. He reassured her that he was watching all the time. As soon as he put it down it rang again. This time it was his son-in-law. Hansie Barnard was the head of the drug unit in SWAPOL - the South West African Police. He was also a famous rugby player in the province, and Steyn was enormously proud of him. Despite the notorious "stickiness" of fighting the drugs trade, Barnard had a reputation for integrity and had a quiet authority that came across in any dealings with him. Steyn's daughter had heard from her mother about Bessie's arrival on the farm, and had called her husband.

"Bessie's on the farm with government people?", Barnard asked. "What are they doing?" Steyn told him briefly. When he mentioned Fourie and Viljoen, Barnard grunted. "Can you see the car numbers?" he asked. Steyn went back to the pantry window and jotted down the numbers of the cars parked outside. "If they move or if there's trouble, call me", Barnard said to Steyn.

Barnard drummed his fingers on his desk. This one was a political pickle. He had to do something about the "invasion" of the farm and his parents-in-law being taken advantage of in such a crass way. But he knew he couldn't tangle with the likes of Fourie and Viljoen without clearing this with his commanders – especially not in the current political climate.

Drugs were his out. Bessie's name had come up before as a possible drug smuggler. Some of his former black and Coloured associates both in 32 Battalion and in the Koevoet had been picked up for dealing, and one or two had been turned and become informers. Bessie had been named as a possible key courier. The suspicion was that the vast quantities of Mandrax and Ecstasy now being consumed in South Africa were actually coming back from the Angolan front, where Barnard had heard they were being used against SWAPO and the Angolan forces by the secretive South African 7th Medical Battalion. They were leaking into the domestic market through corrupt security people like Bessie.

He called the detective in charge of the drug unit in Keetmanshoop, gave him the car numbers, and said he wanted

Bessie watched. He also made a call to a friend on the rugby team who was a farmer in the area to ask for his help if Bessie continued to intimidate the Steyns.

Steyn watched from inside the house as Fourie and Viljoen drove off.

"Do you think he can keep it together to pull this off?", Viljoen asked. "He looks crazier than ever."

"You have to be crazy to do what we've sent him to do", Fourie mused, "and yes, I think he's coming apart. But I've given him a big incentive to make it happen. None of them are coming back to the Republic after this. Theron has been put on alert and will take care of them here if need be. Bessie should be out of the country in three days. Someone will take care of him once he's in Europe and the dust settles. That's been arranged."

Bessie, addled by Fourie's appreciation and the prospect of Meitje and her partner, picked up the briefcase and put it under the passenger seat of the Nissan, and went back into the barn. A few minutes later the doors opened, and he and the others came out and drove off. As they did so, Steyn noted the numbers of the combis that had been inside and called Barnard. Meanwhile Valerie had waited a few minutes and then escaped the storeroom as quickly as she could. As she came down the stairs, she picked up the manila envelope, which was identical to the one that had been in Steyn's car when he fetched her the day before. She assumed he'd left it there for her.

Steyn went into the barn. The Ridgeback hesitated and whimpered – clearly reluctant to enter. Usually the dog was happy to be here, inevitably spoiled with a piece of the biltong that hung like bats from the rafters. But he was whining and scratching at the ground at the entrance. Steyn now picked up the unusual strong odour – part organic, like rotten potatoes, and part chemical, like disinfectant. "What the fuck are these people up to", he wondered.

Good Practice Gone Bad

Barnard's men picked up the cars as they came into town. The white Merc and a Combi were tailed as they made for the airport, where the detectives noted the tail registration of the eight-seater Cherokee that Basson and Fourie boarded.

Bessie drove into town a few minutes later in the black Nissan, and made for the Schützenhous, reversing into a parking place in the shadiest part of the lot which "Hond" (Hennie) Steenkamp, his henchman, had roped off earlier. He then checked in, carrying a large grip and Fourie's briefcase. Hond, following tradecraft, arrived twenty minutes later and reversed the white combi into the adjacent space. He stretched a cable from the van to a power source and left the a/c in the van running. Both men crashed in their rooms – they'd driven up separately from Cape Town overnight and were exhausted.

A drunk sleeping it off under some eucalyptus trees on the road opposite the hotel noted the car numbers and the men's movements, and after waiting for a few minutes cycled back to the police station to report.

It was late afternoon when Barnard got the various reports and forwarded the car numbers and the plane's identity marking to police HQ in Pretoria, stressing the urgency. He called his lead man in Keetmanshoop and said he wanted Bessie and the others watched in the hotel.

Bessie had showered and was going over the maps and aerial photographs Fourie had provided when there was a tap at the door. He was expecting Hond, but nonetheless pulled out his automatic and opened the door only slightly, blocking it with his knee. He relaxed and grinned when the man walked in with two beers.

"*Vok jong*, I need that beer", Bessie said as he closed the door. "This thing is creepy. I don't like snakes to begin with. Now we have to carry them around in a fucking briefcase like we're going to the bank!"

The two men stood by the bed where the map and aerial photos were laid out. Bessie, who had the local knowledge, pointed out the main locations and landmarks relevant to the operation. "I'm going to sort out the money after supper. I'll give you half your payment tonight and half after the operation. You pay the Koevoet klontjies you're using only *after* they've released the snakes. You must make sure they do that where there is a big crowd, so there will be real panic. You've got be up on the roof of the police station with glasses to follow them after you drop them off."

Hond nodded. "I just spoke to Shumba – you remember him from Omaune[46]? He's ready – he thinks it's a straight hit on the rally, and asked how much ammo we were bringing for the AKs. I told

---

[46] A camp near the Angolan border used by the special forces and Bushman trackers

him it wasn't like that but cleverer, and that he'd have plenty of time to get away. The problem is I can't find Gonko. He's not answering at home, and at the shebeens he goes to, they won't talk or they say he's away. He's the key, he's smarter and more *bevok* – he'd kill his mother for a hundred rand and a Mandrax. I don't think Shumba or the other one will do anything without him."

"Vok these Ovambo!" Bessie cursed. "Fucking unreliable. They never really became soldiers. They can track and kill, but that's it. We're going to have to get to Windhoek earlier to find him."

They leaned forward over the map and photos again and went over the plans once more in detail. Hond was assigned to the SWAPO rally that was planned for late afternoon the next day at the soccer pitch, which was in a narrow basin between the hills of the squalid township. The rally had been planned for 4 p.m. but SWAPO affairs were notoriously late, and they didn't expect things to start before 6 p.m. when evening was setting in. He would drop the three former Koevoet men they had used for other operations at the narrowest choke points around the pitch. Two would have the document cases. Gonko would get the guitar case. They would be told that the cases contained CX, a vicious variant of tear gas they had encountered in the border war, and that it was delayed release. The men would be provided with satchels with gas masks to reinforce the ruse. Hond would liaise with the Security Police, who always observed the rallies from a high point above the pitch – the roof of the dilapidated three-storey police station at the entrance to Katatura. When they judged the crowd to have peaked, he would fire a flare and the Koevoet were to place the cases on the roads behind the crowd and press the hidden release catches. They would then make their way to where Hond would be waiting, and make their escape. The CCB planners and technicians had tested the cases at Roodeplaat and found it took a few minutes for the snakes to sense the chink and force their way out – enough time for the operatives to get away. They had settled on a huge Black Mamba – in the guitar case– and three Rinkhals – spitting cobras – as they were the most aggressive and were relatively large. They were also the most intimidating, as they rose up off the ground when threatened and would be easily seen. The idea was that in the ensuing panic the crowd would stampede and the SWAPO pre-election rally would breakup in shambles.

Bessie's target was the Gammam Water Works, which fed Katatura. He and another ex-Koevoet accomplice would be wearing the khaki overalls and badges of municipal employees, and would use the distraction of the stampede around the soccer pitch to enter the pumping station. CCB planners had obtained plans and photos of the facility, and had shown Bessie where to close off the chlorine purification supply and then pour in the bottles of typhoid and cholera virus to get the fastest distribution.

The Windhoek municipality and the white government had washed their hands of Katatura in most respects. It was now run de facto by SWAPO. An outbreak of infectious disease would not only disrupt or even postpone the elections, but would also strengthen the South African argument that they were incompetent and were not ready for government.

After the two operations they would all meet up at the truck lot outside the Windhoek railway yards. The Koevoet accomplices and Hond would be paid off. Bessie and Hond would take different flights from the airport – Hond to Cape Town and Bessie to Jan Smuts airport.

Fourie's backup plan in case things went wrong was to detain the Koevoet accomplices when they got to the yards. CCB's head of internal security, Theron, who was hardly known outside the unit's command, had "tidied up" hundreds of embarrassments. The few men he used were drilled in sedating prisoners with spiked drinks, or, in duress, with an injection in the neck. They used a small plane to fly them out over the desert or even out over the sea, where they were disposed of. Fourie was not immediately concerned about Hond, as he was absolutely loyal and reliable. If things went wrong with Bessie, he could be taken care of at Jan Smuts where Theron would have men on standby. If all went well, Bessie would be eliminated by an Irish mercenary or one of the former Foreign Legion assassins they had used in the past once he was in France.

Although good practice dictated that they should keep separate, Bessie and Hond ate dinner together in the hotel.

A few tables away Conradie was eating with the pilot of the De Beers plane that had brought him in that afternoon. Alerted by Willem two days before about Valerie's imminent arrival, he'd flown in from Oranjemund. Willem had met them, and they'd driven out to the Steyn farm to see where and how they could track the girl once she left – presumably with the steel trunk that was the focus of their interest.

Both de Beers men twigged Bessie and Hond immediately. "Those two are not local farmers", Conradie said quietly. "There are no coincidences in this business – not in a shit hole like Keetmans. They may know what we know, and they are not IDB. These are crazies from the border or BOSS. They've gone rogue before. This is getting interesting and sticky."

Willem had seen Bessie crossing the hotel parking lot as he drove away after dropping Conradie and the pilot. Then he saw the detective in the shadows on the other side of the road. Something else was happening, and intuitively he sensed Bessie was involved. He scribbled a note telling Conradie he was waiting a few hundred metres up the road, which one of the waiters delivered.

"He's not here by accident", he said of Bessie, explaining how he knew him. "He's now supposed to be with BOSS. He's a pure psychopath. On the border, I saw him tie a SWAPO suspect to the front of a Casspir and drive him into camel thorn. The screams were terrible, and the fucker just laughed and did it again."

"Why would BOSS be involved?" Conradie mused.

"I wouldn't be surprised if this is Bessie gone *bevok*. But I don't think he can act on his own."

Willem thought to tell Conradie about Bessie's visit to the cemetery, but it now seemed peripheral to the drama that was building.

A few minutes later Conradie was talking to his boss in Cape Town. The conversation was short, with a lot of code words. Conradie's boss then had a similar coded conversation with a man living on a large estate in Upper Houghton, Johannesburg.

The information was now at the top operational echelons of the diamond syndicate. Rather than speak again on the phone, the man drove himself to the De Beers senior lawyer in nearby Saxonwold. Shortly after nine o'clock they called their long-time contact in the National Intelligence Service in Pretoria. Both knew that the NIS was in the ascendency under PW Botha, and engaged in a bitter turf war with the old security establishment in the army, Military Intelligence, and BOSS. The request to intervene wasn't subtle – "It won't do to have BOSS stealing from De Beers".

The NIS did not need prodding. Incensed at the clumsiness and the totally predictable international fallout from the Lebowski assassination a month earlier, their man in Windhoek now had additional clout. "Don't overplay your hand", his boss in Pretoria instructed. "Let them put their hand in the till before you shut the trap. Photograph everything. A surveillance and backup team is being assembled now and will arrive tomorrow morning. They'll carry IDB identity."

Bessie and Hond sat in the bar drinking Oudemeester brandy. The Coloured waiter who served them picked up disjointed snippets of their conversation about the SWAPO rally, and the names "Fourie", "Viljoen", and "Gonko". Shortly before 10 p.m. the waiter stepped outside the hotel kitchen door for a break and reported this to the detective who was keeping the hotel and the cars under surveillance. By 11 p.m. the information had been relayed to the drug unit's duty sergeant in Windhoek.

Around midnight, Gonko was picked up outside Club Thriller – the Katatura hotspot. He'd been observed from a shack on the other side of the road as he used a few youths to run cash and drugs between his car and people in the club. The detectives who nabbed him found more than a hundred tablets stashed in the car. Barnard and his bosses didn't care a toss about the drugs being supplied in Katatura. They were, however, fired up about the drugs reaching the white schools and bars in Windhoek, and Gonko was the best lead they had so far. The 20-minute ride from the club to police HQ in the caged police bakkie was brutal enough to have him bloodied and blabbing on arrival. He shouted and moaned in between blows about being with Koevoet, and about contacting "Kaptein Bessie" and "Lieutenant Hond", and about a special operation set to happen the next day.

In his room in the Schützenhous in Keetmanshoop, Bessie took a sip of the brandy that he'd brought from the bar. He snorted a line of cocaine from the glass top coffee table and opened the case Fourie had given him to sort out the money for the operation. It was then that he realised he'd forgotten the buff envelope with the passport, cash and bonds on the steps behind the barn. Panic and anger at himself rose up, his neck and face flushing almost crimson.

"Fourie left the operational plans on the steps at the barn on the farm today", he babbled at Hond's door, almost screaming and berserk with agitation. "We've got to go out there now to get them." Hond looked at him blandly. He recognised the effects of the brandy and the coke on his colleague, and had learned not to be swept up in his panics. He was already in bed in his shorts when Bessie banged on the door, and his dress, demeanour and low-key personality calmed Bessie down a bit. Unwittingly, he touched the 'calm down switch' – "The farmer's dog will alert him, and he'll probably shoot us before we even get near the barn", he said. Bessie knew only too well that Steyn could shoot. "We'll go out there first thing in the morning. Even if they found the folder and opened it, they probably wouldn't understand what they're reading."

Bessie's panic, however, was also because he had planned to go to the cemetery in the morning and recover the strongbox before setting out for the long drive to Windhoek.

ON RESUMPTION: 28TH SEPTEMBER 2000 - DAY 17[47]

CHAIRPERSON: Thank you. Good morning everybody. We will now proceed with the evidence of Mr ███.

███████████████ (s.u.o.)

CHAIRPERSON: Mr ██████?

EXAMINATION BY MR ██████: (Cont)

Thank you, Mr Chairman.

... he and his people were involved in the disruption of the elections in Namibia. Then he gave me examples of how they planned to interrupt the elections. One had to do with poisonous snakes.

He conveyed it as such, that there were projects under way. He said that the CCB had a vegetable farm in Namibia, that that was allegedly the front.

...

... said to me in a nutshell that there was a project where poisonous snakes were purchased in South Africa, in the Northern Transvaal, that they were placed in a specially manufactured cage, in a carrier bag with a mechanism which, when activated, would make the bottom of the

---

[47] https://www.justice.gov.za/trc/amntrans/2000/200928ct.htm

case drop out. An unknown agent was recruited in Namibia, who would then attend a large meeting of SWAPO members, which would be addressed by former exiles. This person would have caused a stampede among the people present, by activating this cage. If people were bitten by the snakes, then it would be as such, but the idea was to get people to trample each other to death during such a stampede.

Whether this really took place, whether the plan was ever implemented, I don't know. Furthermore he told me of the sabotage of vehicles, that a project was to be launched which would disrupt SWAPO's logistical structure, which would involve taxi's, which transported people to the major centres such as Keetmanshoop and Swakopmund.

There were mixtures of liquid which were manufactured to get the vehicles to stall. Experiments were conducted with gas cans which would be placed in the exhaust systems of the cars as well as causing an explosion in the silencer systems of the cars. Then there were also persons in SWAPO who were targeted, for their vehicles to be burnt out so as to discourage other white people from becoming members of SWAPO.

Wednesday, September 18th, 1989

0600 Daweb-Eshel/Windhoek

Steyn listened to news while he shaved. So did Barnard up in Windhoek.

Both knew that they were hearing messages dictated by the South African Administrator General for South West Africa, whose goal was to impede and delay the transition to independence as much as possible. Both were innately conservative and loyal Afrikaners. Intuitively and by upbringing they accepted the line and policies coming out of Pretoria and the spin on the news. Despite the increasing disillusionment with the war and scepticism about the army and security forces, in general they felt that the government was doing what was best for them as Afrikaners.

The last item in the bulletin before the weather was about the forthcoming rally. "SWAPO are planning a public meeting later today at the Katatura football pitch", read the announcer. "Although not many people are expected to attend, the security forces are on standby because these activities are often accompanied by hooliganism. *Ontwrigting word verwag* – disruptions - are expected." Steyn and Barnard both registered the strange use of the term '*ontwrigting*' instead of '*versteurings*' – disturbances.

0710

Bessie, groggy from the night's drinking and drugs, and stressed by his midnight realization that he'd left the document wallet at the Steyns, heard the same phrase at the end of the seven o'clock bulletin on the small transistor radio he carried. *"Ontwrigting"* was the phrase Fourie had told him would signal the green light for the operation. "Here we go, Ma", he mumbled into the mirror as he splashed cold water on his face at the basin. "We're on our way out."

Steyn and Valerie were well on their way into town when they heard the same phrase at the end of the bulletin. Twenty minutes later he helped her unload her small case and the steel trunk from his car, and the driver of the minibus stowed them in the back behind the seats. Steyn knew the man vaguely from the town, and told him that he was to wait with Valerie until she was picked up by the Levin driver, who should be waiting when they arrived in Windhoek. "*Totsiens* Valerie, it was very good to meet you. I'll call the office when I get back to the farm and let them know you're on your way."

Conradie and Willem watched from across the street, noting the green steel trunk. When the minibus pulled out, Willem followed in the grey De Beers bakkie. Conradie took a taxi to the airport.

Tjandero listened to the same 7 o'clock bulletin in Otjiherero. He was squeezed in among the other morning commuters from Katatura to Windhoek, and even at this time of the morning the combi smelt of sweat. The SWAPO rally, one of the main subjects of interest among the crowds streaming into town for the day's work, was an item almost at the end of the program. But there was no ambiguity in the message the SA administration was putting out to the black people of South West Africa – "…trouble is anticipated. Any display of violence will be met by force, and the presence of UNTAG observers will not be a deterrent."

Tjandi heard this, understood the threat, but was distracted. He and the other trainees were due for assessment later in the day, and he was running through the replies to the draft questions they'd been given on Friday. He knew he was expected to reply in English and Afrikaans – the latter a distasteful challenge for most blacks. What he'd heard from his aunt had also left lingering resentment and distress, which he was still processing. The Herero tragedy had become more personal.

0740

Barnard scanned the overnight reports on his desk. Bessie's name had been underlined in the first report about Gonko's arrest outside the club the night before. He walked down to the cells and had the man brought into an interview room. He watched him with habitual flat eyes as he came into the room dishevelled, and dismissed the Herero gaoler.

He came straight to the point: "Gonko – the tablets they found in your car are Mandrax. Because you were seen supplying them to white school kids 4 days ago, we're going to ship you to the Republic. You are looking at 15-20 years. Or, we can release you in Katatura with your Koevoet card round your neck. You better have a good reason for me not to do that…"

Their transaction was brief and comprehensive, but Gonko had no idea what the operation Bessie was planning for later in the day was to be. He was due to meet Bessie at a safe house in the early afternoon, where he was to get the details.

Searching for the source of the drugs, Barnard pressed him on Bessie and on connections with the 7th Medical Battalion. What Gonko then told him made Barnard go up to his office and phone the farm immediately.

"He's already in town" Frederika said. "He should be calling, because he's waiting to go and get farm supplies and go to the gun store. He knows that I have a shopping list. I'll tell him to call you."

A few minutes later she called Barnard again, audibly upset. Bessie had been on the phone asking about a brown envelope that been left behind at the farm. When she told him that it had been included in a trunk being sent to the Levin offices in Windhoek, he went berserk, she said. He was shrieking in rage and slammed down the phone. He then called back and asked where the Levin offices were, and who had taken the envelope. He kept screaming about "*staatsbesigheid*", so she told him that a Coloured girl was going to the office with a tin trunk.

Barnard called the Keetmanshoop station commander and got him to send someone to look for Steyn as urgently as possible. Barnard then called his friend on a neighbouring farm, and told him to go the Steyns to reassure Frederika and watch for Bessie.

0810

Bessie left the hotel on his own. He drove south and then east on the back streets. The detective watching the hotel radioed this in, and another team in a car picked up the black Nissan Skyline parked on First Avenue by the cemetery. As they pulled in behind a burnt-out car up the road, they saw him stride down the slope of the cemetery carrying something and, by his body movements, place it under the driver's seat. To them he seemed agitated, and he did not look around at all. They followed him to the entrance to town, where he stopped alongside a white combi. He talked briefly to the other driver through the windows of their cars, and then both tore out of town at high speed. The detectives followed, but Barnard emphasised that they were not to be seen. Teams along the way were alerted to take up the surveillance in tags.

0910

The SWAPOL Commissioner's meeting was set for 1000. Barnard was trying to organise his thoughts and information, for he knew now that Bessie was involved in far more than drugs. He also couldn't get Gonko's story out of his head.

The door to his office swung open and the head of the security police came in, ignoring his secretary outside. He shut the door – "*vok*, Barnard, what are you tracking government planes for?"

"What's a government plane doing in Keetmanshoop with a suspected drug smuggler?"

"Bezuidenhout's an arsehole but he works for us – this is bigger than fucking Mandrax for kids and kaffirs. That plane belongs to the Defence Ministry, and you'd better back off. This is out of your league and frankly, out of mine. Wait this out, man."

His secretary opened the door and, as politely and as firmly as possible, said to him – "Meneer Steyn's on the line". The security police chief turned and left, saying that he would have to bring it up at the meeting.

"Kobus", Barnard greeted him. "*Waar is jy* – where are you?"

"I'm at the gun store. Frederika told me to call you and she told me about Bessie's call. What's going on?"

"I've sent someone to the farm, and we've got men watching Bezuidenhout. Are you alone – can you talk?"

"I'm in the gunsmith's office."

Barnard spoke slowly. His tone was flat, but his voice caught and was hoarse with constricted emotion. "Kobus, we picked up a Koevoet klontjie last night for selling drugs. He also works for Bessie in the shit he's doing now. He told me that he was in Angola when Jannie was killed. But it was not like the army told us. Jannie and his trackers were on their way back from some mission, and saw UNITA people meeting our people – probably military intelligence. They handled contact with them. Cubans ambushed the meeting. Jannie reported what he was seeing over the radio, and then went in with his two scouts to help the MI people. For some reason the area was hit with gas mortars. It was a new chemical weapon from the 7th Medical Battalion.

"Bessie and his Koevoete were nearby and were sent in in Casspirs. Bessie was the only one with a gas mask, and he went in on his own. There were some shots and when he came out, he told them to throw grenades and shoot everyone to make sure they were dead. It had to look like they were killed in the ambush. Gonko said that some days later, Bessie got very drunk, and told him that he knew the 'Recce' from Keetmans. It was Bessie who shot Jannie."

Steyn walked out of the gunsmith's office and collected his rifle, which now had the telescope rails fitted and aligned. He added a box of heavy hunting rounds, and paid. Once in the Mercedes, he did a U-turn and drove east out of the town to the B1 – the road north to Windhoek.

0945

As Barnard entered the SWAPOL Commissioner's bureau, the secretary told him to go into the office instead of continuing into the conference room. He told her that he had an operation under way and needed to be interrupted if he was called.

Things had taken a step up, he saw as he entered. In addition to the Commissioner and the head of the security police (BOSS), there were two civilians – the Military Intelligence advisor to the Administrator General, and the National Intelligence Service man for South West. The Administrator General's involvement in regular police meetings had become commonplace with the arrival of UNTAG. But NIS involvement was new and further indication of the pressure building up in SA and in the local administration.

Barnard smiled to himself – he and the NIS officer had been at school together. Tobias Nel, was the son of the headmaster at the Okahandja High School, and was probably the cleverest of his classmates. Nel was studious but wasn't bookish – he'd been a fine rugby player and was as "outdoorsy" as the others. But his father was unique in the community in the emphasis he placed on learning and on knowing the world beyond *verkramte* (narrow) Afrikanerdom. Nel had blossomed at Stellenbosch University, rapidly becoming a junior lecturer and then completing a PhD – the first from their school. They had remained good friends despite very different career paths. Barnard put it down to Nel's innate talent and honesty that he had been recruited to the "hassies", a pejorative the security police and military intelligence used for the NIS. He had been promoted rapidly despite coming from SWA – the "backwoods" in the eyes of the entrenched Afrikaner establishment. If Barnard was going to get boxed in between a dirty op headed by a berserk drug-dealer and his loyalty to his parents-in-law, he knew he could count on Nel. They just acknowledged each other when they were introduced.

"Barnard's people have picked up a Koevoet who's involved in an operation to disrupt the SWAPO rally later this afternoon", the BOSS man said. "He has to be released."

"What's the op and who's involved?" asked the Commissioner. Before the security policeman could answer, the administrator general's advisor said "No offence, but we don't want it divulged and we certainly don't want it to come up at the weekly meeting".

"We have a lot hanging on disrupting SWAPO", the administrator general's man added. He was MI and had spent years in the General Staff. He was Nel's polar opposite. "Our only hope in persuading the kaffirs in South West and the outside observers that SWAPO is not ready for government and therefore not to be elected is if we can disrupt them and make them look incapable at every turn. We're putting a lot into this."

Barnard spoke when the Commissioner looked at him: "The Koevoet guy had more than 100 tablets outside a club last night. This is not 'Durban poison' or regular dagga – this is Mandrax – it's real *kak*. He's been seen running drugs into white schools and white clubs in town. We suspect he gets the drugs from the border, and that his supplier is a white officer – probably with access to military supplies and transport. The officer pitched up at my parents-in-law's farm yesterday together with some civvies who had come in on a plane that we traced back to the army. The same plane has been observed loading what our sources say has been drugs up in Rundu. Supplying drugs to white kids is not '*staatsbesigheid*'."

"*Vok*, you must realise just from this that this is bigger than getting some drugs to bored teenagers", the BOSS officer interrupted. "You can deal with these characters afterwards."

The Commissioner knew he was out of his depth, and was looking for a way to cover his arse. The Lebowski business was a BOSS fuckup that had made him look bad. Now there was this hassie wunderkind here watching to see he didn't do it again. "We need to know what's planned – even in a smaller forum than this, if necessary", he said to the BOSS officer.

"I don't know – it's something to do with the SWAPO rally planned for later today, but these things are only 'need to know'."

Their eyes swivelled to the MI advisor, since he would, in the normal course of their experience, 'need to know'. He shrugged his shoulders – "whatever it is, it's been ok'd at the highest levels in Pretoria".

"That needs to be verified", said Nel, who'd not yet spoken. They all knew that he was the only one in the room who could do this in the time left.

The Commissioner grabbed the safety blanket Nel had thrown him. "OK – I'm leaving this with the two of you", he said to the intelligence advisor and to Nel. "In the meantime, Barnard, hold onto the Koevoet. If he's released, he'll disappear, and we'll lose a good chance of catching the vermin supplying drugs to our kids. This is not to come up in the weekly."

Barnard's mind was on the scene he imagined was now taking place on the farm as Steyn told Frederika how Jannie had really been killed. He feared too what this would mean for his wife. She said that Jannie's death had made her parents fragile. To her surprise, they had not turned to each other for support and comfort but had withdrawn into themselves and bickered a lot. For the first time in her life she saw that her parents did not have the relationship she had taken for granted. It had shocked her and, as she told Barnard, threatened her faith in her own marriage if it was tested.

He had thought to talk to Nel after the meeting, but his concern for his in-laws was uppermost and he returned to his office immediately.

1100

"*Mevrou* Steyn called", his secretary said as he walked into his office. His gut constricted.

"Frederika, you called?" he asked hesitantly, anticipating a flood of anguish, and puzzled that it was she and not Steyn himself calling.

"Did you speak to Kobus?" she asked. "Yes, I did, at the gun shop. Why, is he not back yet?"

"No, I guess he must have decided to do something else then. Sorry to bother you."

"OK, if he does call or come in, ask him to call me." She also confirmed that the neighbour had arrived in case Bessie returned to the farm.

The gunsmith knew Barnard was a policeman, so he was cagey about telling him that he'd fitted Jannie's military sniper scope. Steyn had taken his rifle after alignment, he said, and he bought a box of high-powered ammunition. "He said he had a leopard on the farm. He did a U-turn on the street and drove east towards the B1."

That was the opposite direction to the farm. Barnard saw an image of the pale green Merc on the main road north. He knew now what was happening.

Willem followed the minibus carrying Valerie and the steel trunk at a distance. Bessie's presence and his behaviour made him uneasy. The man was crazy and would resort to violence easily. He was bound to be well armed - probably with a Kalashnikov at least. Willem was concerned, too, that he'd not told Conradie about the root of his real suspicions about Bessie. The Bushmen and Nama trackers Willem was responsible for when he was in the army had told him of the rumours that Bessie had gone in on his own to the site of the firefight with UNITA wearing a gas mask, and had shot the survivors. He had come back with a steel strongbox, which he hid in the commander's locker in the Casspir, telling his Koevoet crew that it was maps and documents from an Angolan spy. Knowing how UNITA paid for its arms, Willem suspected that the strongbox could have contained diamonds. But he could not connect that to the graveyard in Keetmanshoop. He knew that if this ever came out, he could lose his job. He touched the pistol on his hip for reassurance.

He pulled ahead of the minibus to refuel at the truck stop at Mariental. As he pulled in, he recognized two men in a car parked in the shade by the tyre shop as local detectives. Whatever was happening was big, and his unease increased.

He went to piss and when he came back pushed the seat back pretending to rest, while he waited for the minibus to come in and refuel, as he knew it would. All the time he was trying to connect Bessie and his strange visit to the cemetery to the rumours about the strongbox. He watched Valerie and the other passengers clamber out of the bus for their pit stop, and noticed the detectives were focussed on the road and not on the minibus. They were waiting for Bessie's black station wagon, he was sure.

The passengers climbed back inside the minivan, and he followed them a few minutes later. As he pulled onto the highway the sun flashed off a small plane flying parallel to the highway, which made him think of Conradie flying up to Windhoek. Then the connection hit him – Rolf! Rolf Bruns, from the neighbouring farm! He was a pilot and had a plane, and was up on the border at the time that Jannie was killed. He flew them down from the border to Keetmans for Jannie's funeral. Bessie had pulled rank to get on the plane, but didn't attend the funeral. Now Willem understood why.

A few kilometres behind, Steyn drove on autopilot. His pale eyes scanned the parched land – Suidwes in its driest season – without seeing. Images and recollections of times with his son filled the car as if they were passengers with him on the road north. He too saw the small plane and wondered about Rolf's death - the rumours that he "had seen too much". It now seemed so much more credible than just conspiracy rumours of old Boere in a bar. He reached back and touched the Ruger in its case. "This won't bring you back, son, I know. But it has to be done."

1140

Forty minutes behind Steyn, Bessie also mumbled to himself. It's what he did when he was on his own. And that had been most of the time since he'd left the army. He leaned forward and touched the flat strongbox under his seat, and also felt the rusty old blik – the tin can his mother had told him to keep as a memento of her. "I told you Ma – *alles sal regkom*, everything will be all right."

Willem sped ahead of the minibus and pulled in at the petrol station at Kalkrand, from where he called the De Beers office in Windhoek. Conradie had not come in yet, so he dictated the information to a secretary.

1210

Conradie scanned Willem's message:

There had been rumours that Bessie had removed a metal strongbox from the scene of a firefight in Angola – possibly containing diamonds;

Bessie had recently visited a grave in the local cemetery at the end of the day when it was almost dark;

Detectives were stationed along the B1 ...

...and then called the number his bosses had given him and introduced himself to Nel, the local NIS man. He confirmed that the police were shadowing Bessie on his way north. "You must understand, Conradie", Nel said, "there may be diamonds involved, but this is much bigger and involves state security. We need and appreciate your information, but you and your people cannot be involved."

Like Steyn ahead of him, Bessie's mind meandered on the long drive. Recovering the strongbox and screaming at Frederika had partly vented his anxiety. It was also better, he realised, that he did not have to go out to the farm to confront the Steyns to get the folder. A bit of aggression and his police card would be enough to recover the folder from the girl at the Levin building. There was still time to find Gonko, or if necessary, find other "unawares" – it was really just a question of money or threats in one of the shebeens where the demobilised Koevoete hung around. They had until 1700 before he needed to let Viljoen know that they were in place at the Katatura police station. He and Hond had also fixed to meet along the highway outside Windhoek, just in case. Everything now seemed under control. By midnight tonight he should be on the flight to Zurich with this shit life behind him. "I told you, Ma, I'll pull it off and we'll have no more worries."

He saw the donkey cart trotting out of the farm gate at some distance, but did not slow down as it was on the opposite side of the road. His eyes and attention were way off in the mid-distance, imagining the relief that always came with the feeling of acceleration and take off in the plane seat, leaving everything behind. "I have cash, I'll pay for an upgrade", he said.

The donkeys galloped up the verge and onto the road, the cart swinging out in a wide arc into the opposite lane as they turned south. The black station wagon hurtling towards them braked and slalomed on the tarmac, blue smoke from its locked wheels and the screeching tires sending birds aloft in panic.

Bessie cursed as he fought for control of the car. He knew that if he pulled onto the shoulder at this speed, he could flip the car. In the end, it was the donkey driver who evaded what would have been a fatal collision. The donkeys trotted by him with what seemed like indifference.

Bessie tried to change down gears but couldn't depress the clutch – one of the boxes had slid forward as he braked and was wedged under the pedal. He let the car deaccelerate, and it drifted to a shuddering stop on the shoulder. He leaned forward and pulled out the rusted can. He took a deep breath and dropped it onto the passenger seat beside him, and got out of the car to calm down.

Flat, featureless veld stretched out for miles on both sides of the black tarmac strip. Even though he'd been born and bred here, the huge blue sky still made him feel insignificant and foreign – his pale blue eyes always tightening in the brightness despite his Ray-

Bans. Anxiety and the brandy of the night before had tightened and soured his stomach, and the ulcer had begun to stab. He swilled out his mouth before taking a long gulp from a can of Coke. He was tired, he knew, after a sleepless night. The effect of the Adderall he'd popped before he went to the cemetery was wearing off.

Some way off in the veld two ostriches were watching him, alerted by the screeching brakes. Now, without a sign of threat, they dipped their heads to continue pecking at the veld. "*Onverskillig* – indifferent", – he muttered, the word reverberating as a judgement on his life.

He got back into the car, popped two more amphetamines and then a chaser of coke in each nostril from the bag hidden under the floor mat, and pulled back onto the road, feeling in charge once again. As the car settled back into its optimal speed he picked up the rectangular tin from the seat and looked at it for the first time in years. Tears poured down his cheeks.

"Ag, Ma, why did you leave?", he sobbed, as memories of her flooded back. The tin was bright blue and white then. She kept it in the drawer of the dresser in the room they shared in the hotel. That was the best time of his life, just he and she, away from the shouting, *klapping* drunk who would hit him across the head and chase him out of the house. Once, he hid behind the sofa and saw his father tear off her dress – her nakedness terrifying him more than the violence. There was always her whimpering, screaming and groaning when he came home in these rages.

1220

Nel had his driver deliver a note in person to Barnard at police HQ, and then walked on to the kudu statue on Kaiser Strasse and waited for his former school-mate. "I don't trust the phones in your place", he explained as they walked further up into the city, and he repeated Conradie's information. "I don't think diamonds are the whole story", he said. "You heard this morning that this stink starts in Speskop", he said, referring to the army's Special Forces HQ outside Pretoria. "It has more to do with the struggle for control between the security state and FW (de Klerk) than with De Beers. But they need to finance their operations, and everyone is skimming, so we need to know what was in that grave. Be careful." They agreed to meet at a tyre shop near the Levin building on the Gobabis Road just before Barnard deployed his men.

Bessie liked Lüderitz – the wind, the sea, the endless interest of the docks. The other boys at school were friendly, did not pick on him, and he enjoyed the regular schedule. His mother was happy there too, she smiled at her work at the front desk, and the people in the hotel were kind to both of them. They had a charity box like this too, on the counter at the entrance. He remembered her showing him hers in their room – "these are our savings, Bernard", she would say, always touching his hair or his face gently. She was the only one who ever used his proper name.

When she died, the old man and his wife from the hotel brought the box and showed him the space under the headstone of her grave. "She wanted you to have this, not anyone else", the woman said, before meeting his father. He was going to live with him on the farm as they were not his legal guardians. He'd never revealed it, despite his father's beatings, and over time had forgotten that it was there. It was only when he needed to hide the strongbox that he remembered the place under the headstone, and then the little rectangular box. When he looked at it then he saw it could only be cut open with a can opener. Nostalgia for his mother had stopped him doing that.

He weighed it in his hand, tears clouding his vision. It wasn't particularly heavy and when he shook it there was no sound of coins which was what you'd expect from a charity box. Just a few soft thuds. "Anyway, what could you have saved", he said to her. "We were so poor we shared a hotel room!

He wiped away the tears with his knuckles, and focused on the black strip of tarmac stretching on and on. "Just two more jobs, Ma, just two more. Then I can get healthy and we can be happy." And then it hit him. 'Indifference' – just like the ostriches. Why bother? As soon as he picked up the folder with the passport, the cash and the bonds, he could fuck off. Forget this stupid operation with snakes and poison. "They call me *bevok*, Ma. But all of this they're doing, that they've made me do, is *bevok*. They just hide in their suits and their smart language. But they're desperate because they know it's all coming apart." In the end, he knew, independence was inevitable. There was no point in delaying it except for the cash the army and the CCB people were getting for it. Now he had his pay-out plus the diamonds. There was a five o'clock flight to Jan Smuts. He had cash and could be on a flight to Europe by 2100.

Two more sniffs of coke and he pressed down on the accelerator, focussing on getting to the Coloured girl who had everything he needed.

1400

"The white combi with the dark windows is my crew", Nel said, nodding at the vehicle across the road when he met Barnard in the courtyard of the tyre shop. "They're here just to photograph what happens. They won't interfere."

"The detectives who saw Bezuidenhout at the cemetery this morning went back", Barnard reported. "Luckily one of the old gardeners who knows the place was there, because they would never have found it. The graves there are broken and abandoned. But he'd seen Bessie come there before, and knew where to take them. There was a space under the headstone, but it was empty. Who would have guessed Bessie was that smart – no one would look for a Bezuidenhout in the old Jewish cemetery!"

Some twenty kilometres outside Windhoek there is a culvert where the railway line cuts over the B1. Bessie pulled in there to wait for Hond, as they'd arranged. He had planned that they would go the Levin building together, but now that he'd changed his plans, he wanted to get rid of his partner as quickly as possible.

He was tense and scared that his behaviour might alert Hond, so he took deep breaths as he paced up and down alongside the car.

When Hond pulled in Bessie walked across to him, fighting to appear calm and focussed. "You go and find Gonko straight away. If you can't find him, get another klontjie in the shebeens. I can handle the girl on my own. It will be obvious that she has the plans by mistake. I'll take one of the snake cases now, so you don't have all of them in your car. I'll meet you at the safe house. If I'm held up, we meet at the Katatura police station at 1700." He carefully took out a case from Hond's combi and secured it to the side of the trunk of his station wagon with a bungee cord. He also double-checked the stubby AK 74 and spare clips hidden behind the quick release panel on the opposite side of the trunk. Then he gently lowered the tail gate of the station wagon.

Bessie waited for a few minutes to let a gap open up between himself and Hond in the white combi, and snorted another pinch of coke, believing it would calm him.

At the turnoff to the Leopardsvallei military base the police maintained a semi-permanent check post. Bessie drummed his fingers as he waited in the queue of cars, and saw a white man dressed in civvies in the prefab office by the roadblock pick up the phone as Hond's combi drove through. A few minutes later, a Cortina pulled out from behind the police post to follow the white combi. Something was up, he sensed. His anxiety went into overdrive.

Bessie watched the white man in the police booth in his rear-view mirror as he drove away from the check post. Again, the man picked up the phone. He increased speed and, just before the Eros airport, swung away to the east without indicating and cut through residential suburbs. The pressure mounted in his chest, his ulcer had come alive, and he could feel his face and neck were flushed.

Valerie spotted the small white delivery van with the Levin logo waiting by the Windhoek bus terminal. A young black boy in a white shirt with the same logo on his chest and dark blue pants jumped out and came across as the driver lifted out the green trunk. "Miss Valerie?", he asked, putting out his hands for the trunk. "I'm Tjandero", he said. "I will take you to the office for your meeting."

The long journey had given her time and privacy to reflect on the weekend. She was curious about meeting the young Levin and going through the contents of the trunk with him, as her grandmother had written she should. But she was also resigned to finding herself as no more than a delivery girl, if it came to that. She was also pleased to be away from the farm – not only because of the incident with the white men, but because of the sad and oppressive atmosphere in the Steyn household. She missed her husband and her children who would be waiting for her – full of life and happiness, and not dwelling on the past.

Steyn made straight for the Levin building, turning off the B1 early to avoid the downtown traffic. He parked under a pepper tree on the opposite side of the parking lot that surrounded the two-story building. He'd overtaken Valerie's minibus on the way in order to be well-positioned before she – and Bessie– arrived. He sat for a few minutes to recover from the journey, and then got out to stretch his legs and back, standing by the back door of the Merc. A few minutes later the small Levin delivery van pulled in.

Bianca saw the van pull in as well, from her office on the second floor. She got up and interrupted Lenny, who was on a call, to tell him that Valerie had arrived and ask him where he wanted the trunk delivered. "My office is best", he said covering the mouthpiece with his hand, – "the conference room is being used for the training, and that's about to start again".

Valerie came up the stairs with Tjandero, who was carrying the trunk. Bianca showed Valerie to the bathroom. "Wait a moment, Tjandi" she said, "I'll want you to take that into Lenny's office when he's off his call". She'd taken a shine to the young Herero as soon as he'd arrived. He was shy and respectful – and had none of the brash ways of the new generation raised in Katatura and on independence politics.

Steyn reached into the car and removed the Ruger from the battered case on the floor, out of sight of any observers. Keeping the rifle pointed down behind the open back door he slid the telescopic sight onto the rails and locked it into place. He filled the rifle's clip with the heavy hunting rounds and slotted it into the rifle, muffling the click with the palm of his hand. Then he quietly cocked the rifle, feeding a round into the chamber, and let it rest by his leg.

"You are Valerie, then, you've just come from the farm", Lenny said as he walked out of his office. "Meneer Steyn told me that you are Nara's granddaughter?"

"Yes" Valerie said – "she looked after me when I lived on the farm."

"I only vaguely remember her", he said.

Tjandero put the trunk on the table and stood aside as Valerie approached. There was a sudden awkward silence as they faced each other, arranged around the table. Bianca had seen how Lenny had taken in the shape of the girl's body, and now she saw the girl's face full on for the first time. She looked at Tjandero and then at Lenny. Despite a premonition, she blurted out – "you all have the same eyes!"

And they did. All starkly arresting, given their dark complexions. Bianca giggled – "Better get back to the training, Tjandi", she said, leading him out of the room.

Lenny had registered the remark and taken in the same blue-grey eyes but did not know what to make of it. Valerie flushed and focused on opening the trunk. Then she looked across at Lenny – into the same blue eyes that had drawn both compliments and insults all her life. Her father's eyes. Lenny felt his world tilt towards the desk, towards the past, and, he knew, towards a future that was being opened up as the girl's slender brown hands lifted the lid.

A black station wagon sped into the parking lot, tyres squealing, and stopped at the entrance as Bianca followed Tjandero out to the outer office. A tall, gangly man with a red face and white-blond hair leapt out and quickly stepped back to the trunk. She watched him pull out a deep document case and a short-stocked automatic rifle.

Steyn also saw Bessie arrive. Carefully he slid the rifle over the top of the car and rested his arms to form a tripod. He lowered his cheek to the stock and, through the telescopic sight, followed Bessie's race into the building and up the steps. As he inhaled the sharp smell of the pepper tree registered, tingling his senses as smell had done since he was a boy when he first started hunting. "Rotten potatoes" – he said, as he recalled the smell in the barn after Bessie had left. Now he knew what was in the document case.

Like many other businesses in South Africa, the Levins had installed security systems as public tension, crime and violence increased. Bianca rushed to her desk and pushed the red panic button.

The alarm went off and the heavy steel grid dropped down, sealing off the top floor in front of her desk. Tjandero and the other trainees rushed back into the conference room. Barnard and two of his men ran into the building after Bessie, their weapons drawn.

"*Vok*", Bessie cursed at the grid, and put down the case. He lifted the Kalashnikov, shouting at them that he had government security papers in the steel trunk.

"Bessie", Barnard shouted from behind him – "put down the gun. You're covered. You're trapped."

"*Vok, man, wat ken jy* - what do you know?", Bessie said, aiming the weapon through the gate. "This is *staatsbesigheid* ."

"Put the gun down, and get on your knees", Barnard repeated, as calmly as he could. "This is not going anywhere." Bessie turned and saw the levelled weapons. He could hear more men coming up the stairs. Barnard took in his madly dilated pupils and the sweat on his forehead. His finger tightened on the trigger, realising that the Bessie was on the edge.

Bessie crumpled, sank to his knees, and put the gun onto the floor. He pulled the document case towards him. "*Los af* – let it be", Barnard shouted. "*Vok man*", Bessie said raising his face, wretched in blotched anguish. He flipped open the lid and thrust his hand in.

"*Los af*!", screamed Barnard, suspecting a grenade.

Agitated by hours of confinement, heat and vibration, the Rinkhals propelled itself up out of the case and spat venom directly into Bessie's eyes. It drew its hooded head back as it prepared to strike.

Steyn inhaled slowly, the heel of the rifle butt sunk intimately into his shoulder, and he eased off the safety. The crosshairs of the scope sank slightly, and he saw the panic unfolding in slow motion behind Bessie and the snake. Lenny rushed forward and shut the door to his office, a young black pulled Bianca back into the conference room. As that door shut, Steyn exhaled, and the crosshairs rose and settled on his target. He held his breath and squeezed the smooth steel of the trigger.

My dearest family...

Lenny and Valerie sat at the conference table by the open trunk. She had removed a white A3 envelope and handed it to Lenny before the police had come in. Barnard had taken the sealed manila government folder that had driven the berserk Bessie into their lives, and he and his men were now outside taking statements and collecting evidence. Bianca had closed the door of Lenny's office.

"My grandmother, Nara, wrote that I should wait for you to read this", Valerie said, pointing to the envelope. Lenny got up and locked the trunk. "I think that can wait until things are calmer", he said, giving her the key, and took in the envelope:

> To: Mr Sam Levin
> Mr Leonard Levin
>
> <u>To be opened in the event of the impending sale of Daweb-Eshel</u>
>
> N Lurie & Partners
> Advocates, Notaries Public and Trustees
> St George's Street, Cape Town.

Inside was a letter in Jack's spindly handwriting, and a letter from the Trustees in St Helier. He glanced at it, noting that Lurie was copied on this.

October 1964   *Daweb-Eshel*

My dearest family,

I am writing this letter to you from my desk on the farm. I think this is the last time I will be here. The Nama say that the Hamerkop visits the house where someone is due to die. We have one down by the dam and yesterday I saw it. It didn't fly over this house, but I've taken it as a warning – time to prepare. I have lost strength and it's enough with travel.

If things are as I've planned, you are reading this because the time has come to leave Daweb-Eshel. I think you will have wanted to discuss this with me. This letter is to tell you that I knew this time would come. It is as I've intended. In time I realised it was unfair to expect you to love the farm as I did. Sydney did, but he grew up in South West, spent much more time here and it was a different time. Anyway, it is no matter now. You should be making new lives elsewhere.

Also, you should be reading this with Valerie Pieterse, who would have brought it to you with a tin trunk from the farm. If not, I want you to find her to let her read this letter too. I wanted to tell you these things myself, but the time was never right. I also never had the courage or honesty.

Valerie is your cousin. She is the daughter of my first son, Jakob. Nara, who lives on the farm, is his mother and Valerie's grandmother. How this all came about is too long to write, but you should know that Bobbe Rae knows this story. It all happened before we met and were married. I have not told you because there has been no need and it will be difficult for you in South Africa of today. It has always been too difficult for me, and that is wrong but of this time. She will tell you if she is still alive when your read this. If not, Nathan Lurie knows.

Jakob was born during the German war with the Herero and Nama. It was a terrible time. Things happened like in Europe to the Jews. He was separated from Nara for many years. She went on to marry a good man in Rehoboth and had more children. Lena and her sister are from then. When South Africa took over Southwest in 1915, Nara and Jakob – and I – met again.

Like now, although not as bad, life for the Nama and Coloured people was very difficult and very unfair. Jakob knew Sydney but they grew up separately. Their circumstances were different, and I could not fix that. Nor could Nara. Sydney, like you, had lots of opportunities. Jakob very few. He struggled with all of this and could not find his place. We had little contact. Then we lost Sydney in the war in North Africa. With both of them, we know not where they are. Jakob had Valerie late in life, but he drifted away. Valerie's mother died when she was six and so she came to live on Daweb-Eshel with Nara and Lena.

Leah-Lynne, you bear my sister's name. Since our walk on the beach, I have thought about our talk. It's easy to say the world could have or should have stopped the Nazis. But I could have, should have, rescued Leah and my family. But I didn't and now there is only our family left. I was stubborn then, but stubborn can be because you don't want to see. I didn't want to see that I –we– have responsibility for our privilege. I could have and should have done more for Nara and Jakob, but I knew it would harm us and the business. I know that none of you asked for this. But we have all benefited – so we must do the right thing.

I have changed the trust so that the money from the sale of the farm and the contents of the blue boxes in the trunk will go to a fund for the young and the elderly native people of Southwest. You, Nara, Valerie, and Lena are provided for in the original settlement.

I have arranged this with the trustees and Nathan Lurie.

I know this will come as a shock and it will be difficult – especially in these apartheid times. You will be embarrassed, maybe angry. But there was never a good time and I must put right what I started.

Lenny passed the letter to Valerie. She caught her breath where he had, and lifted her eyes to search his. "Sorry, I want to read it again", she said.

He scanned the amendment to Jack's original deed of settlement which had been notarised and accepted by the trustees. This was the letter Lurie had referred to. The old lawyer had known these secrets all these years and never let on.

Finally, she finished, and they looked closely at each other again – absorbing each other's identical eyes and the news the old man

– their grandfather – had delivered. Valerie spoke first…

"Who is Tjandero?"

Sources & Notes

Bibliography

The Kaiser's Holocaust – Germany's Forgotten Genocide; David Olusoga and Casper W. Erichsen, [2010]

A History of Namibia; Marion Wallace; [2011]

History of South West Africa, Israel Goldblatt, Juta and Company, 1971. [Israel Goldblatt was related to me]

The Revolt of the Hereros; Jon Bridgman, [1981]

The Scourge of the Kaiserbird (Translated from the original Afrikaans novel "Die Keiservoël oor Namaland"); Koos Marais; Kwarts Publishers. Kindle Edition [2018]

A German Soldier in South West Africa: Recollections of the Herero Campaign 1903-1904-Peter Moor's Journey to South West Africa by Gustav Frenssen, ... by Francis J. Reynolds [2017][48]

Namibia in Jonker Afrikaner's Time, Brigitte Lau, Windhoek Archives Publication Series No. 8, 1987

---

[48] Frenssen himself, whose description of the train journey from Swakopmund to the interior of the country is echoed in Jack and Nara's journey in Chapter 6, is an illustrative figure of the period. A former pastor he gave up his Christian beliefs because Christian morals contradicted his racialism, and he was a vocal antisemitic who supported and defended the Nazi party and favoured euthanasia.

The Glamour of Prospecting, The Wanderings of a South African Prospector in search of copper, gold, emeralds and diamonds, by Lieut. Fred C. Cornell, OBE, T Fisher Unwin Ltd; London 1920

The Sheltering Desert, Henno Martin [1957]

The Fox & the Flies; Charles van Onselen [2007]

Secret Revolution – Memoirs of a Spy Boss; Niël Barnard [2015]

Jewish Life in South West Africa-Namibia, Windhoek Hebrew Congregation [2014]

The Jews in South Africa; Richard Mendelsohn and Milton Shain [2008]

Words Cannot Be Found - German Colonial Rule in Namibia: An Annotated Reprint of the 1918 Blue Book: Jeremy Silvester and Jan-Bart Gewald [2008]

Herero Heroes: A Socio-Political History of the Herero of Namibia 1890–1923, Gewald, Jan-Bart (1999), Ohio University Press,

Namibia under German Rule, Bley, Helmut (1996)

Last Steps to Uhuru, David Lush, 1993

Building Bridges, Israel Goldblatt by Naomi Jacobson, Karen Marshall 2010, Basler Afrika Biliographen

Otjikango and Gross Barmen – The history of the first Rhenish Herero Mission in South West Africa 1844-1904, N. Mossolow, [1993]

Biographies of Namibian Personalities, Klaus Dierks, 2004

[https://www.klausdierks.com/]

See too the novels of Lawrence Green on Namaqualand and Namibia and Negly Farson

Mark Behr, The Smell of Apples, 1995

The realization that the attempted extermination of the Herero and the Nama was the first genocide of the twentieth century and was the precedent for the Nazi Holocaust, has led to a growing body of academic research, both on the genocide itself as well as on Namibia in general.

Among those I drew on are:

Urges in the Colony. Men and Women in colonial Windhoek 1890-1905, Wolfram Hartmann, Journal of Namibian Studies, 1 (2007)

Robert J. Gordon, "Hiding in Full View: The 'Forgotten' Bushman Genocides of Namibia." Genocide Studies and Prevention 4, 1 (April 2009)

'Ja, es musste sein!', German settler perceptions of violence during the Herero and Nama War (1904-1907), Asher Lubotzky, Journal of Namibian Studies, 24 (2018)

Flags, funerals and fanfares: Herero and missionary contestations of the acceptable, 1900-1940, Jan-Bart Gewald, Journal of African Cultural Studies vol. 15, 1 June 2002

Britain's Response to the Herero and Nama Genocide, 1904-07, Daniel Grimshaw, Master's Thesis submitted to Upsala University (2014)

The Nama Stap as Indigenous Identity and Cultural Knowledge, Micheal M. van Wyk, Journal of Human Ecology - October 2014

Parody and Subversion, German Colonial Culture and the Herero Oturupa in Today's Namibia, Larissa Förster, Forum Goethe-Institut, München (2005)

Remembering against the nation-state: Herero's pursuit of restorative justice; Karie L. Morgan, Time Society 2012 21:21

This research follows in a tradition of passionate research on the country and its peoples, started primarily by the early missionaries and German settlers. There are scientific and historical societies in Windhoek and Swakopmund (the latter including the Sam Cohen Library and the Ferdinand Stich collection), the Basler Afrika Bibliographen, and the Namibian National Archives. Increasing tourism and the international reach of digital media has produced further publications, much of which is available online. The pursuit of a demand for reparations from the German government and Deutsche Bank submitted by the Herero through the New York courts has also spawned numerous articles and documentaries.

Additional sources are cited in the explanatory notes below.

Notes

Afrikaner(s): - refers to the white ethnic group descended primarily from Dutch-speaking settlers in the Cape in the 17th and 18th centuries. They speak Afrikaans, developed from vernacular Dutch with influences from indigenous languages and the languages of slaves from Madagascar. They practice a reform Dutch Calvinism and their linguistic, religious cultural and economic struggles with the English around the Cape colony and with the black peoples descending from the north gave rise to a fiercely nationalistic separate identity. The Afrikaner Nationalist Party came to power in 1948 and went on to develop and enforce a strict ideology and policy of racial segregation known as Apartheid (see below). Afrikaners as a white category currently make up some 5% of the population of South Africa. Afrikaans is also spoken as a mother tongue by the Cape Coloureds (see below). For a history of South Africa from an Afrikaner's perspective see The White Tribe of Africa by David Harrison [1984], and for a more recent perspective, My Traitor's Heart by Rian Malan [1990], in addition to the works of Breytan Breytenbach, Andre Brink and J.M. Coetzee.

ANC: – African National Congress, the current governing political party in South Africa. Formed in 1912 to promote the rights of black and multi-ethnic people in South Africa, the organization was initially non-violent. In 1960, following the Sharpeville Massacre in which 69 black Africans were shot and killed by police and hundreds wounded during a peaceful protest, the ANC was banned, and then formed Umkhonto we Sizwe (Spear of the Nation) which pursued an armed struggle. Nelson Mandela was one of the founders and leaders of Umkhonto we Sizwe, and together with many other ANC leaders was imprisoned on Robben Island in Table Bay for 27 years. He was released in 1994 and elected in democratic elections as the first black president in 1994. The ANC has dominated South African politics since then.

ARM: - African Resistance Movement – a militant anti-apartheid movement active in South Africa in the early 1960s. It was an outgrowth of the South African Liberal party. Adrian Leftwich, one of its organizers, was a student leader who participated in the bombing of a signal cable on a Cape Town suburban railway. He was arrested on July 4th, 1964 and, under threat of torture, collaborated with the security police, leading to the arrest of his co-conspirators.

See: The National Committee for Liberation ("ARM") 1960-1964, Andries du Toit, MA thesis submitted to the University of Cape Town

Apartheid: - "separateness" or "apartness" – an ideology and policy of institutionalised racial segregation adopted and enforced by the Afrikaner National Party in South Africa and (then) South West Africa, designed to ensure and pursue minority white supremacy. It grew out of the racial and cultural discrimination present in the Cape colony from the outset of white settlement.

Aus: - a small village on the road from Lüderitz to Keetmanshoop. The name means "big snake" in Khoekoe, probably a reference to a rock python that lived around the spring which gave rise to the settlement [see Snake below]. In 1915 South African forces established a POW camp on the outskirts for captured German Schutztruppe. The camp was shut in 1919 after many of the guards and prisoners died in the Spanish Flu epidemic. Situated on the cusp of the great escarpment, Aus was the first source of fresh water for the early trekkers moving inland from Lüderitz and across the desert plain of the Namib. Feral horses inhabit the desert close to the escarpment. Their origins are unclear (perhaps escaped from the Schutztruppe), but they are unusual in that they barely urinate and can survive without water for some five days. The road to the zinc mines at Rosh Pinah starts in Aus.

Bismarck, Prince Otto von: - Chancellor at the time of early German settlement in South West Africa. His wariness of British reaction to German activities in Africa and mindful of Germany's naval weakness made him initially hostile to colonialism, but he eventually succumbed to popular pressure.

Blue Book: - see "Words Cannot Be Found: German Colonial Rule in Namibia: An Annotated Reprint of the 1918 Blue Book" (Sources on African History, 1) (Sources for African History) – June 1, 2003 by Jeremy Silvester and Jan-Bart Gewald.

Bondelswarts: - a Nama clan living in the Warmbad area of southern Namibia. Their uprising in October 1903 drew the German Schutztruppe away from Windhuk and Hereroland, probably partially enabling the Herero uprising a few months later. The South African administration used their air force to crush another uprising in 1922. More than one hundred people were killed in a clan numbering less than a thousand people.

Broederbond, Afrikaner: - The "Afrikaner Brotherhood" was a secret, all male Afrikaans and Calvinist organization founded in 1918, dedicated to protecting and advancing the interests of the Afrikaners. It exercised an enormous secret influence on South African politics, counting many major Afrikaans political, military, business, religious and cultural leaders amongst its membership.

Bushman poison: - See Caroline S. Chaboo et al., Beetle and plant arrow poisons of the Ju|'hoan and Hai||om San peoples of Namibia – Insecta, Coleoptera, Chrysomelidae, Coleoptera, Anacardiaceae, Apocynaceae, Burseraceae, in NCBI, Published online 2016 Feb 1

Coloureds: - South African term used to refer to the mixed-race people formed when European, Bantu and south Asian people mingled with the indigenous Khoi and San people in the Cape. They developed a distinct culture of their own and are commonly referred to as "Cape Coloureds".

Mission Life: - From Mission to Local - One Hundred Years of Mission by the Catholic Church in Namibia with special reference to the development of the archdiocese of Windhoek and the apostolic vicariate of Rundu, by Adrianus Petrus Joannes Beris, PhD thesis, University of South Africa [1996]; Otjikango or Gross Barmen, The history of the first Rhenish Herero Mission Station in South West Africa 1844-1904, N. Mossolow 1993.

CCB (Civil Cooperation Bureau): - A government-sponsored death squad and dirty tricks organization set up by the South African regime to counter African nationalism and anti-apartheid activities. It was active in attempting to thwart the UN-mandated independence of South West Africa, now Namibia. See also: Apartheid Guns and Money, 2017 | Hennie van Vuuren | Bayer.opensecrets.org.za

Damara: - an ethnic group making up some 8% of the Namibian population. Referred to as ǂNūkhoen (Black people) in Khoekhoegowab, and Bergdamara in German referring to their extended stay in hilly and mountainous sites, they are thought to be among the oldest residents of Namibia. Their origins are not clear, but current scholarship suggests that they are related to the Himba Herero and made a cultural and language switch when the Nama peoples subjugated them.

Democratic Turnhalle Alliance [DTA]: - formed in 1977 at a conference held at the Turners Hall in Windhoek as a counterbalance to the South West African People's Organization (SWAPO), as the South African regime slowly and reluctantly permitted black politics in the territory. They lost heavily to SWAPO in the elections of 1989.

End/Stop Conscription Campaign: - an anti-apartheid organization formed in 1983 to oppose the conscription of young white South African men into the SADF. It started out as an organization of conscientious objectors, but developed more political messaging, particularly against the war in Angola and the involvement of the conscripts and the army in the suppression of the black population in South Africa. Banned in 1988, many of its members were harassed and intimidated by the security police and some sent to psychiatric wards. The campaign and its political messages spawned a wave of popular music in English and Afrikaans, and is seen by some researchers as seminal in the change in direction of young Afrikaners, leading to the end of apartheid.

"Bossies" is based on the Afrikaans vernacular "*Bosbevok*" ("Bush fucked...")..

See Schalk van der Merwe, "How Afrikaans Rock Ignited South African Anti-War protests", The Wire, 20/07/2017. and Gary Baines, South Africa's 'Border War': Contested Narratives and Conflicting Memories. 2014.

Fractal Patterns - See research suggesting that natural fractal patterns – especially perhaps of the Acacia Tortilis that dominates the African savanna – are genetically imprinted in humans, induce calm, and are associated with an optimal environment, including the layout of a village. The fractal pattern of the acacia leaf is reflected in the shape of the tree itself. See: Lance Hosey, The Shape of Green - Aesthetics, Ecology, and Design, Island Press and https://www.fastcompany.com/1672318/a-design-revolution-that-could-lift-humanity;

Fractal design in Africa: See: Horace Campbell, Fractals and Benoit Mandelbrot: Lessons for Society in Pambazuka News, https://www.pambazuka.org/governance/fractals-and-benoit-mandelbrot-lessons-society, and Ron Eglash, The Fractals at the Heart of African Designs, TedGlobal 2007, https://www.ted.com/talks/ron_eglash_on_african_fractals#t-996234.

Gardens Schul (Shul): - A synagogue consecrated in 1905 and built in the Dutch Company gardens, which served originally as the home of the German and English Jewish communities in Cape Town. The eastern European immigrants built smaller, poorer synagogues in District Six, Vredehoek, and elsewhere as the community expanded.

Great Escarpment: - a major topographical feature of southern Africa where the high central plateau is surrounded by steep slopes that run down to the sea on the three sides of this part of the continent. In the west it runs through Namibia up to Angola, and forms the eastern border of the Namib desert. [Wikipedia]

Gwa – (Nama). There are seven species of tortoise in southern Africa including the world's smallest often referred to as *padlopers* (path walkers in Afrikaans) because of the tiny tracks they leave through the vegetation. They are considered a delicacy in some cultures while tortoiseshell is valued in jewelry and other arts and craft. In Nama and San cultures the women often used to keep *buchu* – their traditional perfumes and medicinal herbs in tortoiseshells suspended from their belts.

!haru oms - Nama for the traditional oval hut of woven reed mats laid over bent wooden supports that are easily transported as the people moved to find grazing. Children shared a separate hut or slept with the

grandparents. Parents slept separately in their own hut. The *!haru oms,* or *Matjieshuise* in Afrikaans, has distinct significance in Nama culture and many homes still have one in their yards.

Gondwanaland: - was a supercontinent that existed from the Neoproterozoic (about 550 million years ago) until the Jurassic (about 180 million years ago), see Wikipedia and GIC Schneider & MB Schneider, GONDWANALAND GEOPARK- A proposed Geopark for Namibia

Heliograph: – Veit Didczuneit, Flashes of Sunlight in the Desert. Light Signalling Systems in German South West Africa 1899 – 1915. https://dgpt.org/wp-content/uploads/2017/09/Flashes-of-Sunlight-in-the-Desert_with-annotations.pdf accessed 12 November 2018.

Hokmeisie: - Afrikaans word meaning "hut maiden" referring to the mat-covered hut constructed at the back of the home or on the edge of a village where young girls are separated and undergo the socialization and initiation rituals of puberty. The re-entry of the initiates into their society is often celebrated with a ritual meal and dancing of the women alone.

See: Khoisan ancestry and Coloured identity: A study of the Korana Royal House under Chief Josiah Kats by Sharon Gabie, Masters paper submitted January 2014, University of Witwatersrand, P.L. Waldman - The Griqua conundrum: political and socio-cultural identity in the Northern Cape, South Africa, and Koos Marais, The Scourge of the Kaiserbird.

Iscor - South African steel and mining conglomerate, now part of ArcelorMittal.

Kahan, Mosé ("Mo"): - was a German-born Jew who arrived in the territory in 1924. He discovered a copper deposit in an inaccessible range between the Orange River and Aus, and mined it successfully until copper prices dropped in the Great Depression. He went on to develop a diamond concession north of Lüderitz which was so difficult to reach that he modified surplus Centurion tanks to run on bulbous low pressure aircraft wheels to cope with the sand, and flew in men and supplies on Dakotas to a landing strip he built on a salt pan. He had a penchant for biblical names and named one of the concessions Ophir. In the mid-1950s he realised that there were diamonds on the seabed, and introduced the Getty Oil company to De Beers and formed Tidal Diamonds. In the mid-1960s he and an English geologist discovered zinc in the Huns Mountains south of Aus and he named the mine they developed there "Rosh Pinah" (cornerstone) as he believed it would become the cornerstone of the Namibian economy. Hours before his death in 1968 he signed a partnership with Iscor. See: Jewish Life in South West Africa – a History, pp 212-215.

Kaiser Wilhelm II: - The current academic consensus is that the Kaiser gave implicit support to von Trotha and his superiors in the army in their policy to "exterminate" the Herero.

Keetmanshoop: - "Keetmans hope"- a town in the ‖Kharas region of southern Namibia on the main road and railway lines to South Africa. Named after Johann Keetman, who was a German trader and who supported the local Rhenish missionary station established in 1866 to convert the local Nama people. It is a centre of karakul sheep farming. Often shortened to "Keetmans".

Koevoet – "Crowbar" was the counter-insurgency para-military unit of the South West African Police (SWAPOL). It was led by white South Africans, usually seconded from the security police, and Ovambo volunteers and was modelled on the Rhodesian Selous Scouts who developed the tactic of "prying" insurgents out of the civilian population – hence "Crowbar". The unit developed a reputation for brutality, human rights abuses and outright criminality and were considered extremely effective by the government in Pretoria.

Kuiseb: - an ephemeral river that runs from the Khomas highlands west of Windhoek to the Atlantic at Walvis Bay. It has carved a deep canyon that is bordered in the south by some of the tallest sand dunes in the world, and in the north by barren rock. Along the lower Kuiseb there are several small settlements of the Topnaar Nama. Rainfall in the highlands sufficient to cause the river to flow its length until the delta on the Atlantic is extremely rare. For two years following the outbreak of the Second World War, two German settlers – Henno Martin and Hermann Korn, hid in its remotest parts to evade internment. See: The Sheltering Desert, Henno Martin [1957] and a film by the same name.

Luchtenstein, Joseph, Ernst etc: - a colourful family who arrived in Lüderitzbucht in 1903 and became deeply embedded in the German and Boere communities of Keetmanshoop. Koos Marais's The Scourge of the Kaiserbird is a novel based on their early years in the area, including the Nama War with the Germans. See also Jewish Life in South West Africa – a History, pp 256-258.

Lüderitz/Lüderitzbucht: - a port on the southern coast of Namibia. The Portuguese explorer Bartolomeou Dias was the first European to visit the area, naming the bay Angra Pequena (Little Bay) in 1487. A German trader acting on behalf of the Bremen Hanseat, Alfred Lüdertiz purchased the bay and the surrounding area from the Nama leader Josef Frederiks II in Bethanie in 1883, which is regarded as the date of the establishment of the town as a trading post. By unilaterally changing the description of the borders from standard to nautical miles he extended the German holdings. Lüderitz himself drowned off the mouth of the Orange River and the town was named after him. The discovery of diamonds in the area in 1908 lead to a boom period. Many of the German residents were deported after South Africa took over the administration of the territory after WWI.

Mbanderu or Ovabanderu: - a Herero speaking people living in eastern Namibia and western Botswana

Mission Life: - From Mission to Local - One Hundred Years of Mission by the Catholic Church in Namibia with special reference to the development of the archdiocese of Windhoek and the apostolic vicariate of Rundu, by Adrianus Petrus Joannes Beris, PhD thesis, University of South Africa [1996]; Otjikango or Gross Barmen, The history of the first Rhenish Herero Mission Station in South West Africa 1844-1904, N. Mossolow 1993.

Music: - Namibian music reflects the folkloric and tribal cultures of its peoples as well as the influences of African, South African and western music. The Nama peoples play drums, penny whistles and reed flutes, and various stringed instruments, while the Bantu peoples rely more on xylophones, gourds and horns. Popular music is almost always accompanied by vigorous dancing. Hymns, laments and praise songs are also part of the tradition. The main musical traditions referred to in this book are:

- **Bubblegum** - A distinctive mix of vocals, electronic keyboards and synthesisers popular in black South African townships in the 1980s. The music sought to appeal to the younger generation of urbanised black South Africans and featured energetic beats that were easy to dance to. Bubblegum borrowed from the traditional sounds of mbaqanga, marabi and kwela. It was a fun genre of feel-good beats and progressive vocals. Brenda Fassie and the Big Dudes, Yvonne Chaka Overlander etc. were among its leading performers.

- **Kwela -** Pennywhistle based music often played by young black boys on the street corners of South African towns until the enforcement of racial segregation under apartheid, and in the townships. Kwela propelled South African music onto the world stage.
- **Boeremusiek -** Afrikaans folk music popular at social gatherings. The concertina is the main instrument, often accompanied by guitars, drums, harmonica and double base.

Nama: – the indigenous Khoikhoi pastoralist inhabitants found in Namibia, Botswana and South Africa, earlier referred to as the "Namaqua" – the "kwa" suffix meaning "people" in the Khoekhoe language. Early European settlers referred to them as Hottentots (now derogatory) based on the clicks common in their language, today called Khoekhoegowab or Nama/Damara. Afrikaans is also widely spoken. The term Khoisan includes the San or Bushmen peoples, who speak a similar language but live a nomadic life. The Nama are divided into "nasies" (nations) lead by "kapteins". See also Oorlam below. The Nama and Damara make up just over 11% of the Namibian population.

The Nama Stap: - the "Nama Step" in Afrikaans, or Ikhapara in Khoekhoegowab, is considered one the oldest cultural and educational tools of the indigenous Khoisan peoples. It is similar to the Rieldans (perhaps based on the Scottish "reel ") and has distinct Irish and Scottish musical influences as well as of "Boere musiek". It is characterised by energetic fancy footwork – sometimes described as "dancing up a dust storm" – sliding movements, animal mimicry, fancy costumes, and courtship gestures and rituals. Popular at weddings, women's puberty and initiation ceremonies, funerals and other celebrations, the Nama

Stap and the Riel dance became the dance of the working classes, and in particular of the shepherds and itinerant sheep shearers who would travel from farm to farm. It has seen a revival after the abolition of apartheid as a way of reinforcing and conveying a separate Nama culture. See: E. Jean Johnson Jones, The Nama Stap Dances: an analysis of continuity and change among Nama Women. For examples see http://pancocojams.blogspot.com /. Videos of the Nama Stap can also be found online on sites such as You Tube.

Namib – a Khoekhoegowab word meaning "vast place" or sometimes "barrier" or "shield" describing the 2,000-kilometre expanse of desert that runs from the Olifants River in the western Cape into Angola. From the Atlantic coast it extends some 200 kilometres inland until the Great Escarpment. Annual precipitation in its most arid regions is 2 mm making it one of the driest places on earth, and having been so for between 55-80 million years it is thought to be the oldest desert. The collision of the cold Benguela current with the warm air of the Hadley cell gives rise to a coastal fog belt that moderates temperatures but is notorious for causing shipwrecks – there are more than a thousand wrecks littered along the Skeleton Coast. The Namib is sparsely inhabited, with only small settlements and indigenous pastoralists such as the Ovahimba and the Obatjimba Hereros in the north, and the Topnaar Nama in the central region. [Wikipedia]

Namibian medicinal plants: - See: Medicinal Plants of Namibia, Honours Thesis submitted to University of Arizona by Brumbaugh, Michaela Amber, May 2015, and *Harpagophytum procumbens* at Namibian National Botanic Research Institute.

!Nara Melon: - fruit of *Acanthosicyos horridus* - a spiny, leafless plant endemic to the Namib coast that grows in the sandy riverbeds. The plant can survive extreme drought for more than a year due to a taproot system which can grow down to more than 50 metres to reach moisture. In the absence of leaves which would cause moisture loss, photosynthesis occurs in the stems and spikes, and water is also absorbed from precipitation from the coastal fog. A single plant can cover more than 1,500 m^2 and plants can survive up to 100 years. Before the introduction of maize (pap), nara fruit (the pulp and the seeds – sometimes called butter-nuts or butter pips) were a stable food of the Topnaar in the Kuiseb. Plants are considered the private property of the Topnaar families who tend to them, although not the ground on which they grow. There is archaeological evidence that the melon seeds and perhaps even the dried fruit pulp were traded 8,000 years ago. See: https://uses.plantnet-project.org/en/Acanthosicyos_horridus_(PROTA). Accessed 07092019. ǂAonin or !Naranin is the Khoekhoegowab expression of "people of the nara".

Okahandja: - Okahandja means the place where two rivers (Okakango and Okamita) flow into each other to form one wide river in Otjiherero. A German pastor, Heinrich Schmelen, became the first European to visit the town in 1827. In 1844, two missionaries were permanently assigned to the town. A military post was established at the initiative of Theodor Leutwein in 1894, and it is this date that is officially recognized as the town's founding. A number of important historic Namibian people are buried in Okahandja, among them Maharero, Jan Jonker Afrikaner, Hosea Kutako and Clemens Kapuuo. [Wikipedia]

Old Location: - "Location" is a South African word for township and refers to the racially segregated and usually "illegal" or "unofficial" suburbs occupied by black and coloured migrant workers who flocked to the towns for employment as South Africa industrialised. They are still notoriously crowded, crime-ridden and impoverished, and larger such settlements such as Soweto in Johannesburg have satellite squatter camps. The "old location" in Windhoek rose on the site of the former informal black labourer camps – "Werften" – on the western edge of the town. On December 12, 1959 South African police killed 11 and injured 44 while suppressing a boycott and other disturbances in protest at the move by the authorities to force the relocation of the black township (then the "Main Location") to Katatura, 8 kilometres out of town, to make way for new white Afrikaans-speaking suburb. This massacre and the Sharpeville massacre four months later led to the first "white flight" from South Africa and an ever-tightening security crackdown from the Apartheid regime.

Omaruru: - In Otjiherero the name means "bitter milk" as the local vegetation the cattle grazed on would turn their milk bitter. The town was established in 1863 by Wilhelm Zeraua, the first chief of the White Flag clan of the OvaHerero people. In 1871, Anders Ohlsson and Axel Eriksson established a brewery at Omaruru. Eriksson also established a trading post, which flourished, and by 1878 he employed about forty whites. Eriksson's business was based upon long-distance trading between southern Angola and the Cape Colony, which necessitated the establishment of regional trade routes. The descendants of Lothar von Trotha and the von Trotha family travelled to Omaruru in October 2007 by invitation of the royal Herero chiefs, and publicly apologised for his role in the Herero genocide. [Wikipedia]

Oorlam: - also Orlam, were clans of mixed-race people who descended from European (usually Dutch) men, indigenous Khoikhoi women, and slaves from Madagascar, India and Mozambique who migrated away from the Cape to escape Dutch domination and conscription, and then subsequently, English colonialist pressure. Their migratory lifestyle and organization into "commandos" of cattle raiders lead by "kapteins" resembles that of the Cape Boers with whom they often clashed. The Oorlam spoke Afrikaans and adopted the Boers' strict Calvinist Christianity. They established themselves in the northern Cape (Namaqualand), and in Namibia. They subdued and intermarried with other Khoekhoe clans, and clashed with the Herero, who were moving into the grazing areas of the central part of the country. Over time they were absorbed in the Nama culture and adopted Khoekhoegowab as their language. There is no distinction between them and the Nama today.

Orange River – separates the northern Cape Province in South Africa and southern Namibia. Following the discovery of diamonds in Kimberly many prospectors theorized that stones might also have been washed down the river.

Plant Communication: - see Peter Wohlleben, The Hidden Life of Trees; Antelope Activate the Acacia's Alarm System, New Scientist, 29 September 1990

Post Runners: - were a (mainly) Herero unit attached to the Schutztruppe. The Post Runners were recently honoured by a Namibian postal stamp. [http://Bayer.gondwana-collection.com/article/2017/09/08/postal-runner-a-postage-stamp-for-a-gravestone/].

Project Coast: - was a reformulation of South African apartheid-period death squads and covert dirty tricks programmes, including chemical and biological warfare, which went back to the 1970s. One of these was known as "Barnacle" and drew on the experience of the Seolus Scouts in Rhodesia. See: Chandré Gould and Peter Folb, Project Coast:

Apartheid's Chemical and Biological Warfare Programme, United Nations Institute for Disarmament Research and the Centre for Conflict Resolution, 2002; Stephen Burgess and Helen Purkitt, The Rollback of South Africa's Biological Warfare Program, USAF Institute for National Security Studies USAF Academy, Colorado, 2001. The SADF Special Ops, Project Coast and the Seventh Medical Regiment had a covert program to dispose of people deemed as security threats, as well as SWAPO and Angolan detainees who had been tortured and would embarrass the government, and hundreds who were deemed merely "surplus". Many were injected with toxins, heavy doses of drugs, and dumped in the Atlantic from planes. In addition, the CCB used mercenaries in Europe to conduct assassinations.

Rabinowitz, Solomon, a trader and prospector was known as "King of the Richtersfeld" – see Thunder on the Blaauwberg, Lawrence G. Green, published by Howard Timmins 1966. I've taken the license of having Rabinowitz already established in the northern Cape and the Richtersfeld when Jack met him in the early 1900s, although Rabinowitz only moved there in 1905 according to Green.

Rinderpest: – Cattle plague or "steppe murrain" killed up to 90% of the cattle in the outbreak of the mid-1890s in southern Africa, where it advanced rapidly because of the use of ox wagons for transport, and where there was a more advanced road system compared to the territories further north. It also devastated wildlife. The Herero in particular were impoverished by the disease in 1897, and saw the disease and the veterinary cordon raised by the Germans as a pretext to seize their land. International efforts enabled the United Nations Food and Agricultural Association (FAO) to declare the disease had been eradicated in 2011.

San/Bushman: - Exonyms applied to the various groups of indigenous hunter gatherers found in southern Africa. They are Khoisan-speaking with linguistic differences between the various groups, and are thought to be descended from the original hunter-gatherer peoples in Botswana, Namibia and the northern Cape. Their culture is thought to be one of the oldest in the world, and San rock drawings discovered in Botswana have been dated back over 70,000 years and are by far the oldest known art. Genetic studies have found that certain San groups are among the 14 basic "ancestral population clusters". The term "Bushmen", derived from the Afrikaans 'boes man', is today regarded by some as derogatory although there are Bushmen who use the term to define themselves. "San" is a Khoekoe word used to describe gatherers as opposed to "Khoe" – pastoralists. See further: Whose Language is 'Khoekhoegowab'? a series of lectures at the University of Cape Town Summer School 2020, by Wilfrid Haacke, a former professor at the University of Namibia available on YouTube. Haacke together with Eliphas Eiseb produced the major Khoekhoegowab dictionary with English translations in 2002.

Schutztruppe: - Colonial protection troops sent to counter native resistance to German settler activity. The name reflected Chancellor Otto von Bismarck's insistence on using the term *"Schutzgebiete"*, (protectorates) rather than colonies. Although these units were subject to German military law and discipline, they were never organizationally part of the Imperial German Army but rather under the colonial department of the German Foreign Office.

Smous: - itinerant (Jewish) peddler, often romanticised in the history of South African Jews but also a term of derision. The origin of the term is not clear. See: The Jews in South Africa, Richard Mendelsohn and Milton Shain, Jonathan Ball 2008, pp 40-41

Snake: - Snakes, particularly large snakes, are significant in Khoesan culture and folklore. They are thought to embody both male and female qualities and are associated with fecundity, rain and healing. Some researchers associate the word or association of the "large snake" (*turos*) with the African rock python, the largest snake in southern Africa which can reach 6 metres in length. They are generally found close to water sources, and there are several sources alleging that a particularly large specimen lived in the cliffs along the Orange River. See: KhoeSan shamanistic relationships with snakes and rain, Chris Low, Journal of Namibian Studies, Vol 12 (2012).

South African Defence Forces (SADF): - was South Africa's standing army, largely made up of whites, including conscripts. Non-whites could join as volunteers and in the 1970s units of black and coloured soldiers were raised, usually along tribal lines and generally in support roles only. The SADF was deployed in the conflicts with Angola and Mozambique and in support of the SA police in supressing domestic unrest. By the late 1970s more than 60,000 South African troops were deployed in South West Africa. It was renamed the South African National Defence Force in 1994 following independence.

Special Forces – The SADF special forces, colloquially referred to as the "Recces" were deployed in deep penetration sabotage missions in Angola. The brigade HQ is at Speskop outside Pretoria.

7th Medical – grew out of the requirements for combat medical support for SADF airborne ("Parabat") and Special Forces. It was formed in 1984 commanded by Wouter Basson and based too at Special Forces HQ at Speskop. It supported Project Coast.

South West African Territorial Force (SWATF): - was an auxiliary arm of the SADF. It was formed in 1977 and commanded by SADF officers. It included black battalions organised on tribal lines and commanded by white officers. Among these were:

- **31 Battalion** – a light infantry battalion mainly drawn from San (Bushmen) from the Khwe and! Xun tribes in southern Angola and north-eastern Namibia. Their origin as soldiers was with the *"Flechas"* – the Portuguese special forces in Angola and Mozambique who exploited years of enmity between the San and the Bantu-speaking people of the area.

- **32 Battalion** – a light infantry unit mainly drawn from Angolan soldiers who had served with the defeated *Nacional de Libertação de Angola* (FNLA) in the Angolan war of independence. Commissioned ranks were drawn mainly from White South Africans and ex-Rhodesians, but in the early stages included Australians, Portuguese and American individuals. As Portuguese speakers they often masqueraded as Angolan soldiers and were deployed mainly across the border. They were nicknamed the "Buffalo" battalion or "the terrible ones." Eventually disbanded and many of the members joined private military companies such as Executive Outcomes and Sandline International.

- **101 Battalion** – based on Ovambo recruits with white officers, deployed as a rapid-reaction force on the border. Many captured SWAPO insurgents were "turned" and re-deployed in the unit. The rapid-reaction or Romeo Mike concept was to have trackers and infantry troops relentlessly pursue insurgents or suspects on foot while others rested in the Casspir armoured cars until the insurgents were exhausted and surrounded. Soldiers were paid a bonus for successful contacts.

South West Africa People's Organisation (SWAPO): – was formed in 1960 as the Ovamboland People's Organization. The name was changed to support the claim that the party represented all of the people of South West Africa, but the party was always dominated by the Ovambos, who make up 50% of the population. The party conducted a guerrilla campaign against South Africa from 1966. The party has been in power since the independence elections in 1989.

South West African Police (SWAPOL): - was established after the First World War and was effectively an extension of the South African police, with up a third of its personnel and its senior command transferees drawn from South Africa proper. It had both civilian and para-military responsibilities, and these were much enhanced in the struggle with SWAPO – see Koevoet above.

South African Broadcasting Corporation (SABC) – the South African state broadcaster operated in the territory until 1979 when its services were transferred to the South West African Broadcasting Corporation. However, the SABC continued to provide technical personnel and services and a lot of the programming.

Swakopmund: – the "mouth of the Swakop" river was established in 1892 as the seaport for the German colony. The Nama word for the place is Tsoakhaub ("excrement opening") describing the Swakop River in flood carrying items in its riverbed, including dead animals, into the Atlantic Ocean. Another theory is that the name stems from the San language – xwaka (rhinoceros) and ob (river). The river rises in the Khomas highlands and descends through the Namib desert. It is also an ephemeral river, but its catchment area is north of the Kuiseb where rainfall is more common, enabling some agriculture on its banks.

Termite communication: - See Felix A. Hager, Wolfgang H. Kirchner, Vibrational long-distance communication in the termites Macrotermes natalensis and Odontotermes sp. in Journal of Experimental Biology 2013 216: 3249-3256;

Tokolosh: - A Zulu word for an evil spirit created or invoked as a curse by witchdoctors and common in South African folklore. The *tokolosh* took on a hairy dwarf-like form and in African popular culture people sometimes placed their beds on bricks to avoid the creature's tricks. The origins are more likely from the realization that people who inexplicably died in the middle of the night were sleeping on the floor – most likely from carbon dioxide and monoxide poisoning when they slept around fires in their huts or rondawels and pondoks.

Topnaar: - ǂAonin in Khoekhoegowab, a clan of the Nama people. They first settled in the area around the mouth of the Swakop river in the early 19th century, and then moved to the Kuiseb delta at Walvis Bay. They cultivate the Nara melon, and are small-scale pastoralists and gatherers.

Truth and Reconciliation Commission: - established in 1996 after the end of apartheid as a quasi-judicial body to hear testimony from victims of human rights abuses on both sides of the conflict, and hear testimony from perpetrators to whom it could offer amnesty. It was set up as a vehicle of "reconciliation" and "restorative justice" rather than the de-Nazification and "retributive" approach taken by the Nuremberg trials after the Second World War. The chairman was Archbishop Desmond Tutu. It was this Commission that revealed the existence of the CCB and the extent of South African covert operation in South West Africa prior to independence.

UNTAG - United Nations Transition Assistance Group (April 1989 - March 1990) was established to assist the Special Representative of the Secretary-General to ensure the early independence of Namibia through free and fair elections under the supervision and control of the United Nations. Independent Namibia joined the United Nations in April 1990.

Usakos: - Damara word meaning "grab the heel", is a town on the banks of Khan river, one of the tributaries of the Swakop river. It was sold to German settlers by the Herero leader Samuel Maharero. In 1903 they sold it on to the German Otavi Mining and Railway company, which built a station and railway workshop to support the line they were building to connect Swakopmund to their copper mines in Tsumeb.

Veldkos: – literally "bush food" in Afrikaans, refers to indigenous edible plants. These include leaves, tubers, shots, fruits, berries and seeds.

Windhuk, Windhoek: - established on the site of hot springs by Jonker Afrikaner, leader of the Oorlam in 1840 who ordered that a church be built. The settlement was eventually abandoned following persistent clashes and cattle raids with the Herero who were moving into the area from the north. The origin of the name is either from "Wind Corner" in Afrikaans or the name of the Winterhoek Mountains at Tulbagh where his ancestors came from.

Acknowledgements

What started off as a personal exploration and pet project has now emerged as a book. This would not have happened without the warm and persistent support of my family and close friends. They read and re-read, offered comments and insights and made corrections along the way. But mainly, they badgered and pushed for publication of a remarkable story. This is the place to acknowledge their contribution.

Many people helped and encouraged me during my research and field trip to Namibia. The following is not an exhaustive list and if there are omissions I apologise.

Margaret Courtney-Clarke of Swakopmund, the doyen of Namibia's photographers, whose picture of Nama women dancing the Nama stap is the front cover of this book, was a welcoming hostess and passionate guide to her country. Caroline Swartbooi and Johannes Swartbooi in Igubas in the Kuiseb delta, Christine Witbooi in Walvis Bay, Kape Tjiroze and her gracious mother of Katatura, Selma Kwaisa-Makono in Otjiwarongo, a Nama lady called Marta in Helmeringhausen and others I'm sure I've overlooked and forgotten were warm and open about their cultures and perspectives and deeply impacted the "flavour" of the book. Harry and Sonja Schneider at Waterberg, Eberhard Hoffman, former editor of the Windhoek Allgemeine Zeitung, Jörn and Adrienne Miller - Karakul farmers on Auburis, and others I know I've overlooked filled in the German elements and perspective as did Charles Courtney-Clarke on English-speaking

Namibians and Coral Momberg in Swakop and Schalk van der Merwe of Stellenbosch University on the Afrikaners, the Angolan war and the painful transition to independence. Zvi Gorelick, honorary life president of the now tiny Windhoek Jewish community was a vital source and contact, Sharon and Solomon Rabinowitz provided background and useful books on the early history of the area and on their grandfather and it was on their late father's farm near Karasburg that I first encountered Karakul farming; my extended family and friends, most of whom have left Namibia, have over the years provided stories, colour, contacts and context; Koos Marais has written passionately of the early period of Namibian history and he shared his knowledge and love of the veld and of hunting, Jan Nel of DebMarine helped on De Beers and the diamond industry. Dag Henrichsen of Basler Afrika Bibliographien was an early academic source and mentor and hosted me at their institute in Basel, Switzerland; Marion Wallace of The British Library in London and author of the monumental History of Namibia, Vanda Potgieter of the Sam Cohen Library in Swakopmund and Gunter von Schumann of the Namibia Scientific Society in Windhoek and Asher Lubotzky were also helpful. Jill Harish has been my patient and pedantic editor catching and correcting the numerous typos, misspellings and bad grammar.

To all of you, *ÆKhawamûgus, Gangans, Okuhepa Ndangi, Danke, Dankie, my thanks.*

David Richardson is a former journalist who wrote for the Jerusalem Post, the Irish Times, the Guardian, the Sunday Times and others. He has worked in Israel and the Palestinian Territories, Lebanon, Northern Ireland, and South Africa. He was born in Cape Town, lived in Namibia as a child, and has lived and worked in New York, London and Nice. He lives in Tel Aviv.

Printed in Great Britain
by Amazon